The Monk's Cell

Sept 22, 2019

For dear Ellen,
on the occasion of
Peter's retirement.
With thanks
+ respect,
Paula Pryce

The Monk's Cell

Ritual and Knowledge in American
Contemplative Christianity

PAULA PRYCE

OXFORD
UNIVERSITY PRESS

OXFORD

UNIVERSITY PRESS

Oxford University Press is a department of the University of Oxford. It furthers
the University's objective of excellence in research, scholarship, and education
by publishing worldwide. Oxford is a registered trade mark of Oxford University
Press in the UK and certain other countries.

Published in the United States of America by Oxford University Press
198 Madison Avenue, New York, NY 10016, United States of America.

CIP data is on file at the Library of Congress
ISBN 978-0-19-068058-9

3 5 7 9 8 6 4 2

Printed by Sheridan Books, Inc., United States of America

For Rosemary, Olivia, and Thomas

~

Speak through
the earthquake, the wind, and the fire
Still, small voice of love.

and in celebration of the lives of

Dirk Rinehart Pidcock
(1939–2014)

Br. Tom Shaw, SSJE
(1945–2014)

Br. Eldridge Pendleton, SSJE
(1940–2015)

Contents

viii   Contents

Acknowledgments

ONE OF THE reasons I love cultural anthropology is that our sources draw from the wisdom of living people. Ordinary and extraordinary, people experiment with knowledge and practices in creative, unexpected ways. In the ethnographic research I did, experimentation was exceptionally dynamic. People were unafraid to engage in debates and alternative positions, and were on the move with ideas and innovations that rose from their knowledge of the past and present. I am indebted to the people from whom I learned during fieldwork and have tried my best to convey the beauty and meaning of the worlds in which they lived, practiced, taught, worked, and contemplated. My interpretations are part of the wrangle of those pluralistic worlds and are not likely to please or convince all who read them. Some may feel I got it wrong, and for this I am sorry, but consider me a part of the animated landscape of discussion and meaning. I ask your patience for my views, welcome any corrections or contestations, and take responsibility for misrepresentations or any errors of fact.

Many thanks to all of you who participated in the research of this project. I am especially grateful to the religious leaders who allowed me to work with them and their communities, especially Fr. Thomas Keating, OCSO, Rev. Dr. Cynthia Bourgeault, Br. Curtis Almquist, SSJE, Br. Geoffrey Tristam, SSJE, and Rev. Ward Bauman. All were extraordinarily kind, patient, and generous with their time and knowledge. Other teachers to whom I am indebted include Dr. Darlene Franz, Dr. Lynn Bauman, Fr. Carl Arico, Julia Slayton, Fr. William Meninger, OCSO, and Rev. David Stringer, plus a number of others whose anonymity I here preserve.

Heartfelt thanks to all the Brothers at the Society of Saint John the Evangelist at Cambridge, Massachusetts. Br. David Vryhof, SSJE, was an especially thoughtful, caring guide and a good friend. As bishop of the Episcopal Diocese of Massachusetts, Br. Tom Shaw, SSJE, was a quiet support. I am grateful to the staff at SSJE who offered help and friendship, particularly Jamie Coats, Conor Byrne, and Alice Reed. Thanks also go to the abbot and community of St. Benedict's Monastery, OCSO, at Snowmass, Colorado, and five other monasteries and convents that shall remain nameless to preserve their anonymity. The people at the

Episcopal House of Prayer at Collegeville, Minnesota, offered me exemplary hospitality, as did other unnamed retreat houses where I worked.

Helen Eberle Daly gave kind encouragement and permission to include her insights and an account of her journey to death. Special acknowledgment goes to her husband, John Daly, as well as to her brother- and sister-in-law, Roger and Sandy Daly, for trusting me with Helen's story.

Many thanks go to the women and men who committed to a six-month exercise of writing ejournals about their personal experiences of living as non-monastic Christian contemplatives. This work would have had far less depth without their perspectives about contemplative life in the solitude of their homes. Many people in my research greeted me with hospitality, candor, and enthusiasm. Though you are here nameless for the sake of your privacy, you know who you are. I offer my sincerest gratitude for all you have taught me.

This book derives directly from the original version of my doctoral dissertation, *The Porous Cell: Monastic Ritual, Intentional Living, and Varieties of Knowledge in American Contemplative Christianity* (Pryce 2015). I owe an unpayable debt of gratitude to my trinity of dissertation committee advisors, Charles Lindholm, Robert P. Weller, and Nancy T. Ammerman, whose individual talents and expertise complimented each other perfectly. Together they pushed me to intellectual and creative places I could not have imagined. I certainly could not have written this book in the same way without the close and careful guidance of such an inspiring, demanding, and knowledgeable team of senior scholars. Their combination of rigor, wonder, and trust was just the kind of mentorship that encouraged me to blossom.

I give thanks to the other professors and mentors, past and present, who have guided and supported me, particularly Kimberly Arkin, John Barker, Fredrik Barth, Michael Blake, Alan Cairns, Doug Carter, Matt Cartmill, Sarah Coakley, Christian Cross, Julie Cruikshank, Peter Elliott, Gastón Gordillo, Cheryl Knott, Frank Korom, Adam Kuper, Michael Lambek, Rupert Lang, Harry O. Maier, Bruce G. Miller, Eva Orr, Robin Ridington, Dana Robert, Richard Schechner, Parker Shipton, Krystyna Sieciechowicz, and Nancy Smith-Hefner. Special thanks go to Deeana Klepper and Thomas J. Barfield, who were readers for my dissertation defense, and to Robert Hefner for his guidance and support in my early years at Boston University.

Three institutions provided generous financial support, without which I could not have completed this work. I am most grateful to the Louisville Institute for a Doctoral Dissertation Writing Fellowship, the Social Sciences and Humanities Research Council of Canada for a Doctoral Fellowship and a Postdoctoral Fellowship, and Boston University for the Presidential Fellowship, as well as yearly Graduate Scholarships. Many thanks to Terry Muck and Don Richter at the Louisville Institute for their kindness and hospitality.

A number of people gave me much needed technical assistance, for which I am thankful. Franziska Witz designed the diagrams and Dr. Agniezska

Budzińska-Bennett drafted musical notation of plainsong chant from aural sam-
ples. John O'Brien generously allowed me to reprint his illustrations of Trappist
monks, and Cynthia Bourgeault, Darlene Franz, and Charles Rus gave kind permission to include their chant compositions. Robbin Brent Whittington, The Society
of Saint John the Evangelist, Diane Downs, Regina Roman, Christian Korab, Jill
Sabella, Michael Blachly, Eileen Scully, Maria Arabbo, The Episcopal House of
Prayer, St. Benedict's Monastery, and Contemplative Outreach generously provided photographs. Conor Byrne, Jamie Coats, Robbin Brent Whittington, Kristin
LeMay, Ward Bauman, Susan Sink, Patricia Benson, Bob Sabbath, Deborah Rose
Longo, and Regina Roman did photo searches on my behalf. Vika Zafrin, Thomas
J. Casserly, and Brendan McDermott of Boston University Libraries helped me
negotiate concerns about the online doctoral dissertation repository. My gratitude
also goes to three anonymous reviewers and to Oxford University Press editors
Theo Calderara and Drew Anderla, who showed a great deal of trust in this project.
Special thanks go to Thomas Digby, who faithfully read and commented on each
version of the manuscript.

Friends and neighbors from two continents have stood beside me, far
more than I can name. Some of those special people include Dirk and Karen
Pidcock, Anne and Jim McCullum, Pamela Dalziel, Liz and Tony Hodgson,
Susan Anderson, Andrew McCracken, Catherine Walsh, Mary Ross, Sergia Hay,
Renée Steinbrecher, Cathlyn Robinson, Irit Tamir, Julie Hannon, Philip Abrams,
Angela Schwartz, Shepherd Mead, Angela Ehrenzeller, Felicia Birkenmeier,
Rachel Eggenberger-Holl, Claudia Jahn, Rose Schultz-Rehberg, Rose Kovacs,
Ann Bradbury, Daryl Jahnke, Kit Pearson, Kath Farris, Amy Durlach, Elizabeth
Oehlkers Wright, Wendy Johnston, Mary Anderson, Lisa Persons, Kent Morton,
Beth O'Brien, Gail Wiggin, Rachel Nelson, Polly Chatfield, Amber Ridington,
Mark Mealing, Lori Barkley, Alicia Hawkins, Chris Annear, Lucia Huwy-Min Liu,
Chelsea Shields, Susan Emanuel, Tricia and John DeBeer, Kate Ekrem, and the
community at the Waldorf School of Lexington, especially my daughters' teach-
ers, Lauren Smith, Leslie Svilokos, and Leah Palumbo. My thanks to them and
so many others whose interest, insights, and practical help kept me walking on
the long journey.

My extended family has been extraordinarily patient and supportive. My
thanks go to all of them, but special acknowledgment goes to Susan Watson, who
understood my limits and found ways to help, to Barb Pryce, who knitted a meditation shawl for long hours of research in drafty places, to my brother, Conrad
Pryce, for his encouragement, and especially to my sisters, Teresa and Judy Pryce.
Without Teresa and Judy's dedication and commitment to caring for my aging
mother, I would not have been as free to do this work so far from home. As it
happened, my mother, Margaret Pryce, died within days of my submission of the
final version of this manuscript to Oxford University Press. I salute my mother

and my father, Colin Pryce, for all the extraordinary ways they loved, guided, and shaped me.

Most of all I give my deepest gratitude to my husband, Thomas Digby, and my daughters, Olivia and Rosemary Pryce-Digby, who for years sacrificed a great deal and steadied the ladder. Without their willingness, trust, hard work, and enthusiasm, I could never have undertaken this project, let alone completed it. This I do for you.

Photograph courtesy of SSJE.

I

Portico

FINDING A WAY TO THE DOOR OF AMERICAN CONTEMPLATIVE CHRISTIANITY

I am the rose of Sharon,
I am the lily of the valley . . .
Let him kiss me with the kisses of his mouth;
truly more pleasing is he than wine.
I am my beloved's, and my beloved is mine.

—SONG OF SONGS[1]

My inner heart was yearning desperately for something
I could not name, a space for falling in love . . . I simply
knew that the God of my heart was calling me deeper and
deeper into silence and solitude. My Beloved was yearning
for me . . . and so I sat and listened. As St. Benedict names it,
I listened "with the ear of my heart." . . . I knew I had to go.

—BRIGID'S EJOURNAL

Eros and the Call for Intimacy with the Divine

The call to contemplative Christianity is not an easy one. Those who answer set themselves to the arduous task of self-reformation through rigorous study and practice. They learn through the teachings of monks and nuns and the writings of ancient Christian mystics, often in isolation from the parish-centered religious life of family and friends. Those who are dedicated can spend hours every day in meditation, prayer, liturgy, and study. Why do they come? Indeed, how do they find their way to the door at all?

Brigid's ejournal[2] entry tells us of their motivation: they yearn for the divine. Theirs is a strong compulsion to strengthen an experiential union with the divine that they have already tasted, a form of eros in the classic sense, a longing to make whole what was broken, to bring together what has been separated. Contemporary expressions of contemplative Christianity in America, augmented frequently by the contemplative branches of other world religions, is primarily a way of seeking to live in union with the divine and with all beings, to open oneself to what has been variously called *unio mystica*, "divine indwelling," "incarnation," or more recently, "unitive being" and "non-dualism."

Though its aesthetic expressions favor silence, stillness, and interiority, this is a strongly relational and intersubjective Christianity. Practitioners intentionally work toward what anthropologists have called "effervescence," "solidarity," and "communitas" (Durkheim 2001; Turner 1969). Unlike many forms of Christianity that primarily look to a future union with a transcendent God, their Christianity is oriented toward immanence, the divine here and now. Their task is to work toward the reformation of ideas and behaviors that create a separation from God and others through a life of disciplined practice, prayer, and study. Contemplative Christians believe that practice, including communal liturgies, solitary contemplative rites like meditation and *lectio divina*, and intentional or ritualized action in everyday life (Bell 1992; Mahmood 2005), could effect an awakening to the divine, which is ideally expressed through compassion, humility, gratitude, hospitality, and service to others. They believed that a dedication to practice, regardless of emotional states, could assist one in working toward *unio mystica* and "transformation"—a deepening awareness of one's integral intersubjectivity with all others.

Unio mystica is tricky ground, both for contemplative Christians and for anthropologists trying to understand it. "Divine indwelling" and "incarnation" are the province of the great Christian mystics like Symeon the New Theologian, Meister Eckhart, Angela of Foligno, and John of the Cross, some of whom had ambivalent, even fraught, relationships with the institutional churches. Theirs were prophetic voices that have not always played well in the conservative ranks of institutionalized religions, yet have nevertheless had an enduring (if uneasy) place. Christian mystics have frequently skirted what the institutional churches have called heresy because of their expressions about experiences of unification with the divine. The wall between self and God can become extraordinarily permeable for contemplative Christian practitioners as they work toward an experiential, non-objectified understanding of the divine arising from the "mutuality of desire" between themselves and God (Fanning 2001: 87–90; Petroff 1994: 62).

Consider the experiences of Hadewijch of Brabant, a Beguine mystic in thirteenth-century Flanders, whose desire to "taste [Christ] to the full" caused her to be "wholly melted away in him and nothing any longer remained to me of myself." Writing in third-person Middle Dutch, she wrote that neither she nor her

Beloved could "perceive difference between them. But they possess one another in mutual possession, their mouths one mouth, their hearts one heart, their bodies one body, their souls one soul, and sometimes one sweet divine nature transfuses them both, and they are one, each wholly in the other, and yet each one remains and will always remain himself" (quoted in Petroff 1986: 196; 1994: 61). A similar sentiment comes six hundred years later, from nineteenth-century English mystic William Blake, who said of Jesus, "He is the only God!" which he immediately qualified with, "And so am I and so are you" (quoted in Fanning 2001: 189).

Does "I am God" indicate anything other than spiritual narcissism and megalomaniacal psychosis, or could the paradox of distinction and indistinction from God—their "I am God's beloved / I am God"—be pointing to something else? The official line between saint and heretic, between reverence and trial by fire, has historically been a shifty one. Mystical expressions have received varied degrees of religious tolerance over time; so too contemporary manifestations of contemplative Christianity have not gone unopposed. While American contemplative Christianity is gaining popularity among both laypeople and those in positions of religious authority, the Vatican has published recent documents warning against the errors of certain manifestations of Christian contemplative practices and ideas (Ratzinger 1989; Vatican 2003); more colloquial critiques appear in blogs, newsletters, and magazines (e.g., Dreher 1997; Peth 2012). Contemporary followers of contemplative Christianity have wrestled with the phenomenological boundary between divine and human through their lifeways, thoughtways, and practices in an attempt to enter the world of the mystic, alternately revered and abhorred by those who are unsure of the porous line.

Regardless of doctrinal hesitancy, this yearning for a merging of other and self is sanctioned by the institutional churches. We find especially colorful illustrations in the Hebrew Bible's Psalms and the Song of Songs, whence comes the motif of Christian Bridal or Love Mysticism, but also in the historical writings of Christian mystics, many of whom have been canonized as saints. We see yearning in St. Anthony, the fourth-century Egyptian desert hermit who lived in extreme asceticism, staving off all desire except a passion for God, in the monk St. John Climacus's seventh-century depiction of divine love as "an abyss of illumination, a fountain of fire, bubbling up to inflame the thirsty soul," in St. Hildegard von Bingen's twelfth-century experience of "a fiery light of the greatest brilliancy coming from the opened heavens . . . [which] kindled in my heart and my breast a flame" and in her contemporary, St. Bernard of Clairvaux's eager search for the "spiritual kiss of Christ's mouth," in St. Catherine of Siena's fourteenth-century visions of her mystical marriage to Jesus, and in the Jesuit priest Teilhard de Chardin's twentieth-century confession that in his pursuit of the physical sciences and evolutionary theory, including the discovery of Peking Man, he sought Christ and "saw, as though in an ecstasy, that through all nature I was immersed in God."[3]

So, too, this yearning for intimacy with God arose in Brigid's ejournal, written in the American Midwest in the twenty-first century especially for this research. While I give no attention here to the personal intricacies and cultural distinctions of the ideas and experiences of these diverse historical figures, together they nevertheless reveal how eros for the divine has had an enduring place in the history of Christianity. Such desire continues to work through the impulses and actions of contemplative Christians today.[4]

Mysticism, Wisdom, Knowledge: Understanding the Terms of Engagement

Eros has compelled people throughout history to seek intimacy with the divine, to intentionally pursue an engagement of self with other. My research asked what people actually do to effect that sense of union, which anthropology has most often called *communitas*, after Victor Turner's (1969) classic ritual studies, or *communal effervescence* and *solidarity*, after Durkheim's (2001 [1912]) earlier theories. A considerable amount of cultural anthropology has been devoted to understanding communitas. Thomas Csordas (1990), for example, added to our understanding of communitas with his theory of embodiment. Csordas developed the idea of embodiment partly to account for synchronous ritual behavior that he encountered in fieldwork. He said that *habitus*—unacknowledged cultural ways of being and thinking—was the underlying source of a process of perception that created phenomenological experiences of unification or "embodiment."[5]

However, in reading through theoretical contributions like that of Csordas, I felt that key elements were missing. The instances of communitas I have observed did not seem quite so passive as Csordas described. In addition, neither he, Turner, nor Durkheim showed the intricacies of how experiences of unification actually occurred. I wanted to learn the fine details of cultural practice that prompted unification between self and other, and whether people intentionally engaged in the process of their changing perception. In other words, did *agency* have a role in shifting perception from phenomenological experiences of separateness to ones of unification, and what role did habitus have, if any? Pursuing these questions, I found myself also asking where the boundary lay between self and other, and whether experiences of communitas were entirely distinctive from feelings of separateness—that is, were feelings of unification a wholly different category of perception from feelings of being a distinct individual, or could there be intersubjective degrees of unification and separateness? My questions about unification in ritual thus sought to understand the boundaries of personhood in a given cultural context.

I chose a field site that emphasized desire for union with the divine, American contemplative Christianity as it was enacted in both monasteries and everyday society.

This variety of immanence-oriented Christianity has been classically described as Christian mysticism. In the introduction to a volume of essays devoted to understanding Christian mysticism, Amy Hollywood (2012: 7) emphasized the ambiguous character of mysticism. She wrote, "The complex interplay between transcendence and immanence, time and eternity, nameability and unnameability, and community and individuality can best be articulated when due attention is given to the vital role of practice in Christian life." My research focused very much on how contemplative Christians practiced various aspects of their chosen way of life. However, observing the action of ritual and everyday life was not enough to uncover the processes that brought people to communitas, the phenomenological aspects of mysticism. I found that both external forms and inner processes were crucial to what Christian contemplatives called "transformation," a kind of intentional, ongoing conversion of perception that practitioners sought as a way to become aware of the divine they believed was everywhere around them (whether or not they could perceive it).

To better describe this process of mystical conversion, I adopted the terms *cataphasis* and *apophasis* from some of the contemplative Christian teachers with whom I worked. These concepts may be a useful addition to the anthropological study of ritual, especially in contemplative environments that emphasize interiority and silence. Cataphasis describes the physical action, the intentional "doing" of ritual, while apophasis describes practitioners' "not doing," their reliance on the ambiguous inner aspects of transformation over which they had little control, what contemplative Christians called "unknowing." (Perhaps Thomas Csordas's embodiment is a form of apophatic unknowing.)[6]

Mysticism is a slippery term. While it has the advantage of being recognizable, mysticism also strongly connotes a focus on private experiences that are exclusively within the well-bounded domains of "religion" and "spirituality." Hollywood (2012) discussed the history of the development of the term, noting that the specific category called "mysticism" did not emerge in the literature until well after its prominence in medieval western European Christendom had waned. Hollywood pointed out that the original idea of mysticism is inseparable from the holistic framework associated with Roman Catholic religious institutions in which medieval practitioners' lives were embedded. The term emerged in the Protestant Reformation as a vehicle for scholars to understand the fervent desire for union with the divine that was not uncommon in the Middle Ages.[7] Writers wanted to mark it out specifically as a "religious" phenomenon, which they opposed to the experiences of exuberance and connectedness they associated with newly distinctive modernist categories like philosophy, politics, and literature. After the work of Niklaus Largier (2009), Amy Hollywood suggested the term *enthusiasm* to replace the problematic term mysticism.

In the context of American contemplative Christianity, in which many practitioners do not closely distinguish between categories of the religious and the secular, the term enthusiasm does not quite fit, however. The contemplatives with whom I did research used many different words for feelings of connectedness. Not unlike their medieval exemplars, their understanding of unification with the divine and others extended well beyond the bounded notions of religion or spirituality that arise out of an oppositional understanding of religious/sacred and secular/profane. Occasionally they used the terms mysticism and *unio mystica*, but they more often used terms like divine indwelling, non-dual consciousness, and unitive being.

Wisdom, a term for experiential knowledge that arose repeatedly in my fieldwork, deserves special attention. One of the teachers in my fieldwork, Cynthia Bourgeault (nd), described wisdom as a strong part of the history of Judeo-Christianity, which is exemplified in the Bible's "Wisdom Books," especially Psalms, Song of Songs, Proverbs, and Ecclesiastes. She said, "Wisdom is not a curriculum, a philosophy, or a set of esoteric ideas," but is rather a way of knowing that

> shows up in all the great spiritual traditions . . . a higher level of human consciousness characterized by a supple and alert awareness, compassionate intelligence, a substantial reduction in the "internal dialogue," and the capacity to engage reality directly, without the superimposition of mental constructs and categories . . . . Wisdom is not about knowing more, but about knowing deeper, with more of you participating.[8]

Unlike the term mysticism, this definition of wisdom does not depict an exclusive association with religiosity. Used both in monastic and non-monastic venues, the term wisdom better incorporates the diverse, pluralistic social spheres in which contemplative Christians dwelled.[9]

Along with wisdom, I use the simple and purposely indistinct term *knowledge* to describe contemplative Christians' various ways of knowing. Using the term knowledge places so-called "spiritual experience" into the mix of other epistemological forms (and perhaps de-stigmatizes it), rather than opposing spirituality with Enlightenment categories like rationality. Calling all ways of knowing by the same term is my attempt at recognizing that hierarchies of knowledge vary in different cultural settings. In the world of American contemplative Christians, many varieties of knowledge were of equal worth, including intellectual, performative, embodied, unitive, and apophatic.

Like perception, these forms of knowledge are diverse and ever shifting. AJ, a woman who wrote ejournal entries for my research, described the moving ground of personal awareness and knowing as "working toward." Her understanding that human knowledge was always in flux, never complete, and sometimes fragile revealed a core principle, humility—contemplative Christianity's safety check against narcissism and hubris. AJ's idea of practitioners continually working toward Christian ideals and perception of an immanent divine showed knowledge not as a static object, but rather as embedded in an ever-moving process. "Working toward" also showed how the idea of "transformation" or conversion was a combination of ongoing individual effort and a learned ability to let things be.[10]

The immense variability of American contemplative Christian worlds—their knowledge, experience, and social forms—demands a theoretical framework that can incorporate diversity in a substantial way. I came up with the idea of *clines*, or degrees of knowledge, experience, and phenomenological intersubjectivity, as a way to depict the complex moving picture I encountered in the field. Fredrik Barth's (1993, 2002) transactionalism theory and anthropology of knowledge have been important guides in crafting ways to adequately describe diversity while also recognizing places of coherence in the American movement of contemplative Christianity.

Disheartenment, Pluralism, and the Draw of Centering Prayer

Not knowing when the dawn will come,
I open every door.
—EMILY DICKINSON[11]

Father Thomas Keating, an American Cistercian Trappist monk, is one who has been at the forefront of guiding those who yearn for unitive knowledge with the divine. In his mid-nineties at the time of publication, Fr. Thomas began noticing in the 1960s a surge in the burning desire of spiritual seekers in the United States. The Abbot of the Roman Catholic Trappist monastery, St. Joseph's Abbey, at Spencer, Massachusetts, from 1961 to 1981, Fr. Thomas wondered why so many young Americans streamed past his abbey as they headed to a neighboring Buddhist temple, or why they went "to India by the thousands from all over the world . . . to satisfy their hunger for an authentic spiritual path." They could have stopped in at the abbey, the place Fr. Thomas himself had chosen in his youth to live out the very same kind of desire. After all, Trappists are devoted to silence and contemplative practices as a way to foster intimacy with the divine. Didn't they know this? (Keating, personal communication; 2002a: 11–12, 14).[12]

This was the era of the Second Vatican Council, which encouraged greater openness in the Roman Catholic Church (Wilde 2007). Fr. Thomas recalled how his monastery hosted the teachers of Zen Buddhist and Hindu practices, including then-popular Transcendental Meditation, in the new spirit of ecumenism that characterized the times. He himself visited a number of interdenominational and inter-religious communities and was struck that the great majority of members were former Catholics and Protestant Christians. "Many of them were disaffected from the religion of their youth because of the legalistic and overmoralistic teaching that many had received in their local parishes and Catholic schools; they now felt spiritually enriched [not by Christianity but] by their experiences in Buddhism and Hinduism." At that time in the 1970s and 1980s, most of the people to whom he spoke outside of the monastic environment did not even know of the great contemplative Christian traditions that spanned church history (Keating 2002a: 14–15, 17). The combination of their passion and lack of awareness of Christian spiritual forms prompted him to seek a way to make the contemplative teachings of his church more accessible to people outside monastic environments.

It was in this sociocultural moment in American history that three Trappist monks from St. Joseph's Abbey developed a form of Christian meditation called Centering Prayer. Fr. Thomas Keating, Fr. William Meninger, and Fr. Basil Pennington sought a way to free contemplative Christian spirituality and practice from the confines of the monastery. The Trappists understood that the demanding twenty-four-hour monastic cycle of prayer and work was too much for the average person living out his or her life of social relationships and economic responsibility in American society. How could they help ordinary people create a sustained contemplative rhythm without imposing a schedule that was unmanageable? They drew from canonical scripture, the fourteenth-century English mystical classic *The Cloud of Unknowing*, ancient monastic prayer practices like *lectio divina* ("divine reading"), the writings of late Trappist novice master and well-known author Thomas Merton, and the meditation formats of Buddhism and Hinduism. After experimenting with forms, they settled on a contemplative technique of silent "consent" and "self-emptying" to the divine. Ideally practiced for twenty or more minutes twice daily, Centering Prayer is a form of meditation in which a practitioner chooses a single word to use, not as a perpetual mantra, but as a brief touchstone of "return" when the mind wanders (Keating, personal communication; 2002a: 15–16). Its practice is the common thread linking the people with whom I did ethnographic fieldwork.[13]

Thomas Keating's observations of fifty years ago corroborate the stories of the disheartened abandonment of Christianity that I heard during ethnographic fieldwork in the United States. Most of the people in my research had an upbringing in the Roman Catholic church or mainline Protestant Christian denominations like Episcopal, Lutheran, and Methodist churches. A lesser number came from the evangelical and charismatic churches and from other religions. Many told me that their childhood experiences with religious institutions did not satisfy their deep hunger for intimacy with the divine. They felt undernourished and overly confined in "the barren environment of ordinary parish life," as Eva, a former Catholic in my research, described it. A consequence of Calvinistic prejudice against ritual, the non-liturgical, pro-literalist environments of many American Protestant churches did little to capture or encourage the wonder and yearning that these people told me they felt. A similar tenor existed in many American Catholic parishes. While addressing some important problems of ecclesial power relations and exclusivities, the changes in post-Vatican II Roman Catholicism at the same time jettisoned much of the ancient contemplative practices of parish liturgies.

This research describes how people like Fr. Thomas Keating and his fellow monks have worked to show another face of Christianity to those disheartened seekers. Some were monks and nuns, some were priests, some were scholars, others were committed and learned practitioners from a variety of other professions. My research followed several monastic communities and leaders who were devoted to teaching contemplative Christianity. One such teacher was Cynthia Bourgeault, an Episcopal priest and medievalist scholar who studied at length with monks like Fr. Thomas Keating. Cynthia Bourgeault was an example of the new contingent of non-monastic teachers who have worked for years to reintroduce contemplative practices into the Christian liturgical palette through publications, online teachings, public lectures, and retreats. Cynthia Bourgeault described her globally dispersed body of contemplative students as a "congregation of brokenhearted Christians" who would like to find their way home.

Some Christians with contemplative leanings retained an affiliation to institutional churches, particularly the monks with whom I worked, but many others retreated from what one man in my research, Roland, called the churches' "rigid soullessness which has more to do with social status and behaving properly than love or union with God and people." Some managed to sustain and augment their Christianity by broadening and enhancing their worship with other religious traditions, but "the unbearable dryness" that Roland and some others experienced drove them away to seek alternatives that would better address their desire for an intimate connection with God. Their deep longing spurred them to join the stream of disaffected Christians who pursued other spiritual paths, such as Zen and Tibetan Buddhism, Vedanta Hinduism, Taoism, Sufism, and the spiritualities of some North American First Peoples.[14] Nevertheless, by learning of the mystical traditions of Christianity through the writings and lectures of contemporary teachers like Keating and Bourgeault, by stumbling upon websites devoted to contemplation or the vast but lesser known body of historical Christian mystical literature, or more rarely, by finding their way to a church or monastery that offered liturgies grounded in silence and contemplative practices like chant, these religious boundary crossers found a way back to Christianity, often bringing the teachings and practices of other traditions with them.

Brigid, whose eloquent lines about spiritual yearning opened this chapter, is one who merged the territories of multiple religions. Though her mother was a Methodist, Brigid was raised in her father's tradition of Roman Catholicism. In her teens, her parents decided to move to another state, so a Jewish rabbi and family in whose household Brigid had sometimes worked kindly offered to take her in so she could complete her studies at the Catholic high school. Brigid's appreciation for Judaism and the Jewish community prompted her to later work and serve at the Jewish student center on her college campus. "Through these 'lived experiences' of interfaith understanding and compassion, I found my heart opening to an expanded understanding of religious traditions and a spirituality of interconnectedness," she wrote in her ejournal. Brigid went on to study and practice Sufism, t'ai chi/qigong, and Reiki healing, all while being an oblate at a Roman Catholic Benedictine monastery and keeping classic Christian contemplative practices like *lectio divina* and *statio*, and newer ones like Centering Prayer. Ultimately her yearning prompted her to leave her profession as a schoolteacher and take a master's degree in world religions with a focus on mystical traditions. At the time of my research, Brigid worked at a Midwestern interfaith spirituality center as a teacher and spiritual director.[15]

Another boundary crosser, Helen wrote in her ejournal about how the Christianity of her family of origin could not satisfy the strength of her spiritual desire. Helen grew up Episcopalian in the Northeast, but had a mother who was already seeking outside ecclesial boundaries by exploring meditation, Hinduism, and "esoteric Christianity" in the 1960s and 1970s. "She was considered quite weird by my family and our friends, but I always 'knew' what she was talking about," she wrote. Helen followed her mother's example. She taught herself Transcendental Meditation through books in early adulthood, then delved into a number of other Eastern philosophies and meditation techniques at retreat houses and ashrams and through personal study. As a psychotherapist, Helen trained in and taught her clients Zen Buddhist–derived methods of mindfulness stress reduction. In the western New England region where she lived and worked, the psychotherapy profession was awash with Buddhists, she said, but she encountered no practicing Christians. Helen had all but abandoned Christianity herself until years later, when she became aware of its historical and contemporary contemplative practices, like Centering Prayer. "Cynthia Bourgeault's book, *Centering Prayer and Inner Awakening*, allowed me to return and go deep into my own tradition of Christianity," she wrote. In particular, "her teaching on the Wisdom Jesus has allowed me to find my place in my own tradition, with value placed on experiential knowledge of Jesus, not just belief in him."

These outward-looking impulses were not random wanderings of isolated individuals. Many teachers of American Christianity have similarly opened themselves to other religious traditions and then passed on their inter-religious learning to others. For example, Trappist author Thomas Merton (e.g., 1948, 1966, 1969) was a pioneer in inter-religious exploration, having traveled to India and East Asia to learn from Hindu, Buddhist, and Taoist communities before his death in 1968. Alongside distinctively Christian musings, he published his revelations about the teachings of other contemplative religions and their relationship to Christianity in books like *The Way of Chuang Tzu* (1965) and *Zen and the Birds of Appetite* (1968), which gained popular audiences.

Some of Merton's monastic students made similar forays beyond the confines of Christianity. After moving in 1981 to St. Joseph Abbey's daughter monastery, St. Benedict's in Colorado, Fr. Thomas Keating initiated the Snowmass Conferences on inter-religious understanding by inviting leading practitioners and "spiritual teachers" of world "wisdom traditions" to learn from one another, including varieties of Buddhism, Hinduism, Islam, Judaism, Native American traditions, and Christianity. Since the first meeting in 1984 at the monastery in a quiet Rocky Mountain valley, leaders of multiple faiths have gathered annually for dialogue and communal contemplative practices at different locations around the United States. Their intention has been to learn from one another and to establish relationships of trust and friendship (Miles-Yepez 2006; Cheetham, Pratt, and Thomas 2013).

These "leaders of wisdom traditions" agreed to honor their religious differences, yet after years of listening to one another they found that they could nevertheless discern substantial points of congruity in their religious knowledge and experiences. Thomas Keating wrote a summary of "points of similarity and convergence" in their ideas and practices, which included an acknowledgment that the divine is beyond ideological or doctrinal definition and that humans can foster their relationship with the divine through religious practice, nature, art, human relationships, and service to others. They also agreed that "disciplined practice is essential," while cautioning that "spiritual attainment is not the result of one's own efforts, but the result of the experience of oneness with Ultimate Reality" (Keating 2006: xvii–xix; Miles-Yepez 2006). In other words, they concluded that across traditions, beliefs bound by ideology and doctrine have limits in facilitating an understanding of the divine. On the other hand, the regular practice of prayer and service to others, along with a demeanor of humility and gratitude, they believed to be of primary importance.

Discovering these points of congruity, many Christian contemplatives found a greater affinity toward the so-called "wisdom traditions" of other world religions than with many expressions of American Christianity. While Brigid seemed able to hold Christianity alongside other traditions all along, Helen's story exemplifies the disenchantment that many contemplatives experienced with the churches of their childhood, which arose in part from a gap between belief and experience. A highly educated and outward-looking demographic, the American contemplative practitioners with whom I worked felt that many church institutions uphold simplistic and narrow beliefs which do not adequately address the complexity of our pluralistic, globalized society. Literalistic understandings of the bible, they said, do not give enough flexibility or breadth to the multiplicity and contradiction that people experience. Teachers of contemplative Christianity, who acknowledged the limitations of human knowledge and the inconstant nature of human sentiment, instead encouraged a commitment to practice. A scripturally grounded commitment to practice and service—rather than a reliance on unsteady belief and feeling—is the fulcrum of contemplative Christianity.[16]

Cosmopolitan and well-educated, this is a specialized community that is largely composed of Euro-American professionals from the upper middle class. In the communities where I did research, a considerable percentage were professors, scientists, priests, medical and social service professionals, artists, and students— in other words, a subsector of America's intelligentsia. Indeed, many were über-literate, with sophisticated theories of knowledge. They also tended to be well traveled and globally aware through their prevalent engagement with print media and digital communications. A telling statistic, 70 percent of participants held a doctoral degree at one retreat I attended, whereas the American national average of those who earned doctorates in 2009, for example, was 1.2 percent (Ryan and Siebens 2012). For the majority of this American subgroup, the Christianities they practiced in childhood could not bear the weight of the world's breadth as they knew it—neither the goodness and wonder of its expansiveness nor the burdens of its violence and contradiction.[17]

These are the very people whom some theorists of secularization predicted would reject religion. Yet rather than becoming secular in response to churches which they felt were at odds with worldly complexity, this group responded by taking up a seemingly paradoxical commitment to deepen knowledge while simultaneously allowing for doubt, ambiguity, and mystery in their understandings of the divine. For this community, the largesse of a chaotic world did not prompt clinging to dogmatic tenets, but instead inspired a creative bridging of knowing and "unknowing." This dynamic tension between scholarly knowledge, lived experience, and religious ambiguity suggests an epistemological embrace of a complex world that allows for no easy answers. Indeed, in counterpoint to secularization theorists who have depicted religion primarily as a defiant reaction to a profane modernity (e.g., Berger 1967, 1999; Finke and Stark 2005), my study shows a clear coexistence of modernization and religious observance (cf. Hann and Goltz 2010; Mahmood 2005).

As shown in the pages that follow, American contemplative Christians unabashedly crossed the boundaries between the so-called religious and secular by combining diverse elements like ascetic practice, intellectual learnedness, material wealth, humanitarian service, esoteric thought, personal achievement, monastic enclosure, and globalization. Regardless of the expectations of secularization theorists, these people have not found themselves encaged in a godless universe because of the alienating forces of modernity and bureaucratization, as in Weber's (1930) vision of a post-Reformation future for peoples of European descent. Rather, American contemplative Christians have found their way to a religious life that can bear human complexity, weakness, paradox, and doubt in an unfathomably diverse world. Of theories like those that oppose modernity with religious observance, Nancy Ammerman (2014: 5; emphasis in original) wrote, the "founding myths of social science have run their course. Rather than assuming that spiritual beliefs are irrational and religious participation is regressive, researchers are now asking *whether and under what conditions* different sorts of beliefs and spiritual practices have what kind of effects."

Richard Kearney (2010) is one who has attempted to understand the conditions in which people dwell at ease with modernity, pluralism, and religion. He coined a term for the lived theology of people like those in my study, ones who have abandoned the triumphalism of a Christian-centered universe in favor of a hermeneutical posture that replaces defensive certitude with humility. Kearney's *anatheism*, or "god after god," recognizes the need to adjust one's view of the divine in a world of immeasurable diversity, especially a world in which so many people suffer. Anatheists, wrote Kearney, are those who recognize their own ignorance. Rather than rejecting God in so uncertain and expansive a universe, they emphasize the need to welcome God in the stranger, thus taking on hospitality and openness as the central rubric in their stance of unknowing. Their primary concern is not to define a doctrinal list of facts about the divine, but to extend a hand outward, to practice anatheistic hospitality. In endeavoring to be open to a "stranger God" and to any stranger, wrote Kearney, they create a space for intimacy.

Kearney wrote that the orientation toward hospitality and service is born of a pluralistic outlook. Welcoming the stranger does not necessitate an abandonment of one's own scriptures or traditions, however, and is not even particularly novel in Christianity. After all, the tenet of hospitality is foundational to Benedictine monasticism, as taught in St. Benedict's sixth-century *Rule of Life*. However, compared with earlier Christian societies, we today have endless numbers of strangers at our fingertips: fast-paced globalization and instant-access virtual technologies allow us to look further and further afield while remaining in the solitude of our homes. With the entry of the Internet's global scope into private spaces, present-day contemplative Christians have embraced a world that is simultaneously expanding and contracting, a clear contrast to the ethos of some parochial Christianities which have had a significant voice in the history of American society (Ammerman 1987; Neitz 1987; Smith 1998).

Many adherents differentiated contemplative Christianity from more populist forms of American Protestantism, particularly evangelical and literalist Christianities, which emphasized belief and feeling over learnedness and ritual practice. But a blurring between formerly disparate genres of American Christian denominations has also become apparent, as Phyllis Tickle (2008, 2012) illustrated in her studies on "Emergent Christianity" (cf. Bielo 2011; Marti and Ganiel

2014). Such diverse religious responses to social and historical forces demonstrate that there is no monolithic or essentialized "American Christianity," as the project of the anthropology of Christianity has sought to show worldwide (e.g., Bialecki, Haynes, and Robbins 2008; Cannell 2006; T. Jenkins 2012; Lampe 2010; McDougall 2009; Robbins 2014).

A recent subfield, the anthropology of Christianity includes research on the relationship between local diversities and globalized institutions, like the worldwide Anglican Communion and Roman Catholicism, with which many have personal histories or current affiliations. While Barker (2014) reminds us that these Christian institutions have been effective globalizing forces and provide a basis for comparative study, Bialecki (2014) and Handman (2014) have noted that Christian organizations generally have a strong tendency toward schism because adherents regularly question whether institutional expressions adequately interpret, frame, and enact the ideals of scripture. The sixteenth-century European Protestant Reformation being just one regional historical example, Christianity's global history is fraught with the competing views and varieties that result from local differentiation and efforts at renewal. This propensity for schism is not exclusive to Christian institutions, but can be seen in many global religions (Bandak 2014; Robbins 2014: S164). However, the tendency in Christianity is particularly intensive in part because of the multiple versions of the Christian gospel, both canonical and non-canonical, not to mention the endless interpretations of those scriptures.

In the current era, people who envision and enact contemplative Christian alternatives have new varieties of social media that allow them to reach across the planet to others in unprecedented ways. Their desire to find like-minded others regardless of geographic proximity makes the organization, practice, and communication of contemplative Christians a globalizing, pluralizing social force that spans national and cultural boundaries (Halafoff 2013). Even when people struggle to transform them, Christian institutions have remained a vehicle for social organization and for the movement and transformation of ideas and behaviors around the globe (Engelke and Robbins 2010; P. Jenkins 2002; Robbins 2014). Those who practice Centering Prayer with a feeling for the larger community, whether local or distant, are part of a religious movement with a significant impact on the diversification and global spread of contemplative Christianity.

Contemplative Christianity's pluralistic inclination toward boundary crossing and openness has prompted an attraction to the ethos of certain ancient Christian expressions that accentuate the mystery and ambiguity of the divine. Return to thirteenth-century Hadewijch for a moment. Along with her writings on passionate union with the divine Bridegroom, she also described the paradoxical "Abyss of Omnipotence" in which the unknowability of God "cannot be put into words, since it is unspeakable" (quoted in Petroff 1986: 197). Maggie, one of the contemporary contemplatives who wrote ejournal entries for my research, described this ineffability as "that unknown place beyond what is." Eleanor wrote something similar in her ejournal: "Communion with God is an opening out into nothing. It really is *no thing*, something other than thing" (emphasis in original). Contemplatives often described the deepest point of union with the divine as boundlessness and nothingness, which nevertheless conferred what they called "experiential knowledge."

Despite their pluralistic perspectives and their openness, most of the monastic communities in which I worked held to the scriptures and liturgical practices, such as the Daily Office and the Holy Eucharist, that are distinctive to certain Christian institutions. Yet the monks and nuns in my research often focused on specific teachings about immanence, relationship, and personal responsibility, selecting from the historical breadth of Christian scripture and theology by returning again and again to specific genres like the works of the Desert Fathers and Mothers and the medieval and Counter-Reformation mystics. While a considerable number of monks and nuns I know studied the teachings of other religions alongside those of Christianity, their expressions of pluralism manifested primarily in the cultivation of a global consciousness of current cultural and political affairs and the subsequent practical care for others, especially the socially and economically marginalized.

One of the primary monasteries of my research, the Episcopal Society of Saint John the Evangelist (SSJE) in Cambridge, Massachusetts, was an example of a community with a pluralistic outlook and a dedication to hospitality. In 2012, SSJE sponsored a photographic exhibition that explored the reconciliation that was emerging out of the Rwandan genocide, held a liturgy of remembrance for homosexual youth who had committed suicide, hosted a gathering of "Kids for Peace" (an organization that brings together Islamic and Jewish children from Palestine and Israel to learn about and befriend one another), and facilitated a pilgrimage and retreat for homeless participants from Occupy Boston, the movement which protested the poverty they believed was brought on by the fiscal decadence of American financial institutions. The SSJE community's outward-looking stance and commitment to service was set in a highly formalized and semi-cloistered Christian liturgical context. The monks followed a daily round of four or five liturgies, intersected with periods of work and solitary contemplation, modeled on a fifteen-hundred-year-old Benedictine monastic rhythm.

The pluralism of those living outside of monasteries (whom I call "non-monastics") was frequently much more overtly inter-religious. Finding their way to the hidden door of this movement largely by individual study, word of mouth, and social media, they were drawn to a contemplative Christianity that has been strongly influenced by the monastic aesthetics of ancient European and Near Eastern churches; in the midst of silence, chant, icons, and incense, these returning Christians described a sense of relief that they had found a variety of their own religion to which they were attracted. "I had no idea from my upbringing that Christianity could be like this," wrote Daniel in his ejournal. "I had no idea it could be about listening in silence and feeling directly the touch of God."

With their return to Christianity, non-monastics often brought their inter-religious influences and flexibility with them. Some took up an association with Christian institutions, like those who attended contemplative Eucharists and med-itation circles at The Wellspring, a center for spiritual direction and contempla-tive practice led by non-monastic teachers and located on the grounds of a New England convent. I attended non-monastic liturgies that were often experimental, intercultural, and inter-religious, incorporating elements like neo-Celtic prayers from Iona, French chants from Taizé, Navajo adages, Zen koans, and the writ-ings of diverse literary visionaries like English medieval mystic Julian of Norwich, fourteenth-century Persian Sufi sheik Hāfez, and modern poets like Emily Dickinson, T. S. Eliot, Mary Oliver, Denise Levertov, Wendell Berry, and R. S. Thomas.[18] The nuns took part when their time allowed, and I remember well the response of one of them to the pluralistic references: Sister Cecilia, then eighty-five, was thrilled that she had been asked to read a poem written by fourteenth-century Sufi sheik Jalāl ad-Dīn Muhammad Rūmī. "Oh, Rumi!" she exclaimed clapping her hands, "He is *such* a delight!"

Although some practiced in groups and many had virtual and face-to-face networks of fellow contemplatives and teachers, a considerable number of these non-monastic boundary crossers preferred not to formally join (or rejoin) institu-tional churches. Indeed, while the historical and current global reach of Christian institutions is an important factor in the rise of contemplative Christian religious movements, the demographics of those religious institutions nevertheless can-not accurately detect unaffiliated, cross-denominational, and inter-religious con-templative Christians in the United States (or elsewhere). Of the actual numbers of people making up the amorphous group of unaffiliated practicing Christians, Phyllis Tickle (2008: 139) said, "Who knows?[19]

A retired advertising executive living in a Midwestern city, Zak was one non-monastic in my research who did not belong to any particular institution. Even so, he was dedicated to keeping the daily cycle of liturgies of the Roman Catholic Divine Office, including the office of Vigils for which he rose in the middle of the night, and also practiced the rites of several other religions. A decades-long stu-dent of world religions, he wrote tongue-in-cheek in his ejournal of the experience as an unaffiliated inter-religious practitioner:

I am without a "church" but not without spiritual influences, ancient and modern. I am without a real living human spiritual leader or guru and my practice is one that I've cobbled together from what I've gathered from doz-ens of sources over the years. You might think of me as playing "Abrahamic

Pinball." Under the glass-covered case are three bumpers: Islam, Judaism, and Christianity. I am the steel ball that gets bounced around from one bumper to the other, making revelatory lights flash and insightful ring-a-ding-dings sound. I pick up speed and points as I bounce along. Once in a while I roll down through the hole between the flippers at the bottom where there is a brief interlude of acedia[20] and then a new ball (me!) magically appears and a new round of Abrahamic Pinball commences— Oh, wait! I forgot about the Taoists, the Buddhists, and the Hindus. I love them all just as passionately, but I guess these days I hang more in the Abrahamic domains. I think under other circumstances in my early years, I could have become a monk . . . Benedictine or Franciscan . . . and could have become a single-minded dedicated Christian contemplative. But I am what I am . . . and what I am is f r a g m e n t e d.

"Under other circumstances" many of the non-monastics with whom I worked might indeed have been allied with a single religion or even a Christian denomination, but the contemporary milieu to which they have responded is a mosaic of unabated pluralism within the American cultural context of a strong drive for individual choice, amplified in recent decades by a heightened engagement with the world through the immediacy of digital communications.[21] We have seen that Zak's reluctance to join church institutions was not shared by all non-monastics, however. Consider the two women from whom we have already heard: In the past decade, Helen began leading contemplative liturgies and theological studies at her local Episcopal church in Vermont. She endowed the parish with money to build a side chapel dedicated to St. Mary Magdalene for this particular purpose. Brigid never left church participation, but expanded it to include other religious practices and teachings after her teenage exposure to Jewish hospitality and practice in a rabbi's home.

Ethnographic Fieldwork with American Contemplative Christians

The people who endeavor to follow contemplative Christianity with openness, hospitality, humility, and unknowing make up an unwieldy network. Describing contemplative Christians living in the United States as a community, as I do, definitely pushes the limits of a standard geographically based definition. Those who do not have a local community of fellow practitioners, as was true for many non-monastics in my research, are perhaps best described as a *non-gathered* community.[22] Their numbers appear to be growing, as we can see by increasing participation on websites, virtual newsletter memberships, book sales data, and the high demand for online and live courses and retreats. However, contemplative

Christians were widely but thinly dispersed across the United States and in other countries. They followed teachers through a plethora of books, virtual communications, and workshops, and to a lesser extent, at parish- or monastery-based liturgical gatherings. One who frequently participated in e-courses and online forums, Leslie succinctly described her experience of the global network of contemplative Christians in her ejournal: "We are all connected even if we never physically meet!"

I could not possibly draw in every aspect of this vast field, so I limited my research to the gathered and non-gathered communities who shared the practice of Centering Prayer in the United States. Whether avowed monastics, non-monastic church adherents, or unaffiliated individuals, the people in my study taught, practiced, or published on Centering Prayer, and often belonged to virtual organizations, like Thomas Keating's Contemplative Outreach, which promote it. With this definition of the community's boundaries, I have done ethnographic fieldwork at seven Episcopal and Roman Catholic (Cistercian Trappist and Benedictine) monasteries, twelve retreat centers, and three parishes, distributed among all of the major geographic regions of the United States except the Pacific Northwest.[23] By crossing the borders between monastic orders, Christian denominations, religions, and geographic regions, I hoped to convey the pluralistic breadth of the contemplative Christian movement in the United States.

The research community was made of practitioners living within as well as outside of monasteries. The monasteries and convents with which I had the fortune to work had clearly defined physical and social boundaries, but not so for the non-monastics who learned from them. Some lived in physical proximity to a monastic community or, more rarely, a contemplatively oriented church parish. Those few were able to gather with like-minded and like-practicing others. However, most non-monastics in my research were geographically dispersed, practicing contemplation in solitude or in small groups. The non-gathered practitioners with whom I worked were linked to the greater contemplative Christian community by virtual means and occasional retreats. I first encountered this portion of the community at retreats and met some individuals multiple times during my research. Those who agreed to write ejournals gave me a picture of how the non-gathered community lived and practiced outside of the retreat environment.

The socio-structural differences between monastic and non-monastic communities had their effect on my work as an ethnographer. Monasteries and convents were stable and permanent (though members did come and go occasionally for various reasons), so I was able to be with those communities repeatedly and for lengths of time. However, access to monasteries and convents was limited to me, a non-member, depending on how a community practiced enclosure and silence. Further, the quality of relationship differed. While monks and nuns were generally friendly, the expression of that friendliness was usually (though not always) much more formal than in non-monastic society, especially between genders. One attended monastic retreats, liturgies, workshops, volunteer work days, and meals as a *guest*, even if one had been asked to perform a duty. The obvious limit on the degree of participation—being a guest rather than a member—along with extensive practices of silence and enclosure, had an effect on the character of my observation (cf. Claussen 2001; Irvine 2010a; Lester 2005).

By contrast, there was no distinction between member and guest in the same way among non-monastics. Even though I had less frequent access to that non-gathered community and met individuals outside retreat or monastery environments irregularly, I was nevertheless able to fully participate in the ways they engaged contemplative Christianity when I was in their company. I was also able to make regular contact with non-monastics through digital means (much less so with monastics). Descriptions and discussions about enclosure, silence, and membership are the subject of Chapter 3, but the contrast of these strictures on the character of my participation and my subsequent knowledge becomes especially clear in the ethnographic comparison between monastic and non-monastic Holy Week liturgies in Chapter 4.

Particularly in its non-gathered manifestation, this community might be considered "imagined," in the theoretical sense proposed by Benedict Anderson (1983). In *Imagined Communities*, Anderson described how group identity can be constructed not only by face-to-face contact and geographic proximity, but also at a distance by individuals' identification with cultural forms through widespread media like newspapers. People conceptualize themselves as part of a greater community despite never having met others who similarly identify. However, in this case, virtual communications have transformed Anderson's original concept because, although they infrequently met one another in the flesh, many of these people not only adhered to the ideas of the contemplative Christian movement, but also had long-distance relationships with like-minded others through interactive media. Indeed, most of the spatially distant people in my research "gathered" online to teach or learn from one another, perform liturgies together, support each other through difficult times, and plan face-to-face retreats and meetings where they further cemented their social connections.

One of these non-gathered, Maggie wrote in her ejournal about discovering a "global community." For years she had meditated in isolation, but after taking an e-course she felt heartened by a new awareness that people around the world were practicing continuously through the time zones. Through an online Spirituality and Practice workshop on Centering Prayer taught by Cynthia Bourgeault in 2011, she saw that

> [h]undreds of people from all over the world were introducing themselves on the practice circle . . . and the feeling was pretty amazing . . . I found the practice circle on the e-course [to be] a place of shared experience and

community . . . all over the world were hundreds of people who were just learning, or had been practicing for years, all hungry for the practice itself and all seemed to so greatly appreciate knowing that there were others out there. Most people seemed to be practicing in isolation, even if they were within monastic life.

There was something new in that experience, having the sense of a world-wide body of connection, that included a small but steady and committed group of [my] personal friends. As if there was a bigger sense of the nest I personally rest in . . . . The connectedness of practice is happening on several different levels of community in my immediate and daily life and around the world [which] somehow makes it meaningful in a larger context . . . . So many are doing this very intimate and personal thing which touches the numerous small worlds of each individual . . . . That feels extraordinary, and I feel I am one of many.

While the intricate relations that physical proximity allow are fairly difficult to develop and sustain through interactive media, Maggie nevertheless said she had experiences of intimacy in the global context. Through interactive venues like Spirituality and Practice's Community thread and Practice Circle thread, these communities were less imagined and more interpersonal than they could ever have been in Benedict Anderson's era, just a few decades ago. Maggie's comments show the impact that electronic communications have had on creating a "community" of geographically dispersed contemplative practitioners.[24]

It is worth adding here that while my research focused on contemplative Christian practices and communities in the United States, the practitioners with whom I worked saw themselves as part of a global phenomenon, as Maggie clearly articulated. Confining this movement by national borders unnecessarily imposes artificial geographical, political, and cultural boundaries. Indeed, the globalized nature of a "world religion" like Christianity makes a concept of strict local boundaries problematic (Barker 2014; Peña 2011). Just like the Christian monastic institutions that inspired it, the contemplative Christian movement is transnational and transcultural, with inter-religious dynamics and a significant depth of history. Americans certainly had a strong role in the worldwide dissemination of ideas and ways, especially in the branch that practiced Centering Prayer, but there were significant voices from other global regions as well. After the anthropological convention of "ethnographic region" and for practical reasons of defining a research community (which was already extraordinarily difficult to hem in), I confined my study to contemporary manifestations of this movement in the United States, except for a pilgrimage abroad on which I accompanied American practitioners. Even so, I do not attempt to define what is "American" about this ethnographic picture, given that my research shows that the Centering Prayer movement is simultaneously an American subculture and a global phenomenon. The lives of contemplative Christians in the United States are influenced by complex cultural and historical factors, which draw from their engagement with multiple transnational sources.

One of the non-monastic subgroups of this movement that has significantly informed my research is "Wisdom Christianity," a particularly disciplined and devoted arm of the movement which draws from the teachings of canonical and non-canonical Wisdom literature, Christian mystics, and inter-religious contemplative texts and practices. Part of a growing movement of American "wisdom" leaders from different religious streams, teachers of American Wisdom Christianity were often priests or scholars with training in other contemplative traditions like Sufism or Buddhism. The Reverend Ward J. Bauman, whom I followed during fieldwork, illustrates the profile.

In 2014, Ward Bauman told me about how he found his way to Wisdom Christianity. Ward was born into an Anabaptist Old Order Brethren farming community in California, but his parents left to become what he called "Baptists of a very narrow sort." He began questioning the confines of his religious upbringing while attending an evangelical Christian university. Later, when he was studying toward a graduate degree in linguistics at UCLA, Ward was invited to work in Iran. He lived there from 1972 to 1977, where he ran a large English technical-language school in pre-revolutionary Tehran and established two more schools in other parts of the country. Ward wrote that in Iran,

> my faith was "lost" and rebuilt. I, for the first time, became open and questioned everything I had known. I studied Sufism there and encountered Evelyn Underhill's *Mysticism* which changed my life—encountering the Christian mystical tradition for the first time. Returning to the U.S. I studied Buddhism, and came under the spiritual direction of a Russian Orthodox Priest. I worked for seven years for [the Roman Catholic order of] the Christian Brothers, helping to run their retreat facility in the Napa Valley, CA. I then entered seminary in Berkeley. The breadth and depth of my life were changing incrementally. All this while, the contemplative arts were taking hold and the practices were forming my "intellect." I became an Episcopal priest and served several parishes before returning to retreat work once again at the House of Prayer in Collegeville, MN. Here it all came together for me and for the past twelve years I have encountered many people from many different traditions and backgrounds; seekers and teachers and mystics.
>
> The more I come to experience, the less I have to say about it. My primary teachers for the past 35 years have been Meister Eckhart, the Gospel of Philip, Jesus' Teaching on the Mountain (Matthew 5–7), Ken Wilber, and

a slew of others. I give much credit to Sufism, which cleared my path;
Buddhism, which cleared my mind; Evelyn Underhill, who cleared my
darkness; Jewish mysticism, which cleared my soul!

Teachers of Wisdom Christianity like Ward Bauman have promoted a re-
examination of and return to what they call Jesus' original messages, which
they say emphasize "teachings attuned to . . . spiritual transformation, 'right
action,' and compassionate presence in a pluralistic world."[25] Scholars and
innovative ritual specialists, Wisdom teachers have impacted the spread of
contemplative Christianity through their publications, experimental liturgies
and practices, online courses, and signature "Wisdom Schools"—intensive
residential retreats modeled on Sufi teacher-disciple mentoring relationships
(sohbet) and Christian monastic daily rhythms. At Wisdom Schools, participants
learned philosophies and techniques, which they believed developed their "contemplative senses" and a capacity for "unitive being," with the hope that they
might become a healing presence in the world. As in every form of American
contemplative Christianity I encountered, teachers had a key role in guiding
and supporting practitioners' understanding and commitment to an alternative
way of life.

   I have drawn my theories and conclusions from the ideas and practices of
all the people with whom I worked. However, there were some communities
with which I spent a greater amount of time and which became principal infor-
mants. Two monasteries became central in illustrating the roles of teaching and
formal ritual practice in this movement, especially the Society of Saint John the
Evangelist (Episcopal) of Cambridge, Massachusetts, where I spent the most
time among the monastics, and to a lesser extent, St. Benedict's Abbey (Roman
Catholic Cistercian Trappist) of Snowmass, Colorado. As these communities
have a strong public presence through websites, lectures tours, and print media,
I do not use pseudonyms for them so that I can properly cite their ideas. Unless
I use their published material (in print or online), I have endeavored to protect
the identities of individual monks or nuns. However, I do name public figures
like Fr. Thomas Keating, Fr. Richard Rohr, and Fr. Carl Arico. Among the non-
monastic communities, the greatest influence on my research came from the
Wisdom Schools of Reverend Dr. Cynthia Bourgeault, an Episcopal priest and
medieval scholar. With their permission, I also use the real names of Reverend
Ward Bauman and Dr. Darlene Franz, who led retreats and Wisdom Schools at
which I did research. I credit published material of other non-monastic communities where appropriate. With the exception of Helen Eberle Daly, who died at
the end of my research and whose family requested that she be named, individual participants go by pseudonyms. Any uncited material, including quotations,
derives from my fieldnotes.

The Role of the Anthropologist in Environments of Silence and Interiority

For my fieldwork I developed ethnographic methodologies that allowed me to work closely with groups and individual practitioners in both gathered and non-gathered communities. I investigated how contemplative Christians trained in and practiced their faith to learn about the similarities and differences within this minority religious movement as it was enacted in its diverse circumstances within and outside of the monastic cloister. My method was principally extensive participant-observation during which I visited, lived, and worked in the often silent contemplative environments of monasteries and retreat houses alongside fellow practitioners, engaging in monastic and non-monastic liturgies, meditation circles, seminars, workshops, and everyday tasks. I also held formal interviews and followed teachers and their adherents on the websites of inter-religious and Christian contemplative associations, monasteries, and teaching forums. In addition, I received by email the journal entries of twenty-five non-monastic contemplatives between the liturgical seasons of Advent and Pentecost in my last year of research (November 2011–May 2012). In these "ejournals," non-gathered contemplative Christians reflected upon their personal histories and home practices, information to which I would not otherwise have had access. My fieldwork spanned three and a half years, beginning in the spring of 2009 and ending in late autumn 2012.

Working with articulate people, some of whom were public figures and published authors, certainly took me away from the stereotypical role of the anthropologist as a discoverer of unknowns. Even so, this variety of Christianity is not well understood among anthropologists and other social theorists of American religion. For some readers, contemplative Christianity will not be at all familiar. Many people expressed surprise when I have spoken about my field sites, saying that they were unaware of functioning Christian monasteries in the United States. The prevalence of silence and interiority in these communities has perhaps been a factor in their concealment from the larger society. Doing anthropological fieldwork in mostly silent communities created particular challenges, which is the main reason I spent so long in the field. An extended research period helped me get past some of the barriers that silence and enclosure created. Although I cannot presume to know the inner thoughts of silent people, living and working with contemplatives over three and a half years helped me learn to hear what some of their silences meant.[26]

Questions about the effectiveness and accuracy of ethnographic methods are important for all anthropologists, as vigorous debates about theories of ethnographic writing and the anthropological lens attest (e.g., Marcus and Fischer 1986). These concerns are particularly relevant in environments of interiority in which people practice silence, stillness, and enclosure. Such conditions forced me to listen attentively to the Christian contemplatives with whom I worked, to explore and experiment with ways of learning among them, and to consider more carefully my place in their communities. To grasp what was happening in environments of silence and interiority, I found I had to ask the same questions of myself, the anthropologist, that I did of contemplative Christians' ways of knowing: How do human beings attune themselves to the subtle, the ambiguous, and the invisible? How do we know about the inner worlds of others? Are there ways of training ourselves to listen, see, and sense more acutely, in ways that may be beyond our experience, imagination, and even comfort level? The central anthropological goal has always been about trying to understand people who differ from us, but really, how well are we able to accomplish this task? And how far are we willing to go to learn about things we do not understand?

Clearly the questions one asks dictate the kind of research methods one uses. While outward behaviors, demographics, sociopolitical dynamics, and historical characteristics of the American Christian contemplative movement are obviously relevant to this work, my central question asks about the nature of communitas or phenomenological intersubjectivity, how it actually occurs, and how it forms experiences of personhood. I wanted to explore the ritual techniques that form personhood in relation to "unitive being," the intersubjective relationships of person, society, and practitioners' understandings and experiences of the divine.

Given that communitas and personhood are phenomenological and conceptual, observations of overt practices like liturgies can take an anthropologist only so far. The methods I used during my fieldwork needed to find their way to subtler places. Of course, when I was in environments that allowed conversations, I did ask people to describe what they know and experience, and this taught me a great deal. However, their verbal, rationalized representations of the phenomenology of self and other could not give a full picture of relational knowledge, especially when what they experienced was the "ineffable." Ineffable means, after all, unspeakable and inexpressible. As we heard earlier in Eleanor's words about apophatic union with the divine, this way of being is "something other than thing." Even when they want to, people struggle to adequately describe it. Add to this ineffability the practice of silence, the ethos of interiority, and the ethic of privacy, and we are left with a rather abstruse ethnographic field. Yet after a lengthy period of research, I can tell you something about the ineffable qualities of contemplative Christianity. How?

My approach was to fully take part in their world, to become one non-monastic student among many who closely followed teachers of contemplative Christianity, so that I might learn through profound emulation. An intensive version of anthropology's participant-observation methodology, this close-listening approach matured over the course of my research as I learned from (and was challenged by) the people with whom I worked. Good teachers draw in their students, as well as call them on their ploys of avoidance. The contemplative teachers I followed during research definitely challenged me on my initial tendency for remote observation. Their stance helped me realize that I could not possibly understand well enough unless I allowed myself to let down the methodological barrier of observer-observed, however lightly I attempted to hold it, and to seriously become a student.

In addition to more standard methodologies, I engaged in a form of watching and listening, not unlike the very attunement practices which Christian contemplatives themselves practiced, to be detailed in the chapters that follow. I have sometimes written myself into narratives of ritual action to illustrate this methodological technique and what it was able to teach me. After grappling with obstacles to understanding people in environments of silence and interiority, I concluded that contemplation was not only the subject of my research, but also needed to become an anthropological way of knowing. This monograph recounts the methods and lessons learned through such 'intersubjective ethnography." [27]

But how could I know whether what I experienced had any correlation with the experiences of others? My methods included training in contemplative attunement techniques of "listening" and sensing, then articulating what I experienced and understood in contexts like group seminars or one-on-one conversations with teachers and spiritual directors. Leaders and co-practitioners confirmed, contested, and augmented my observations. Teachers coached me about whether I was on the right track, whether the placement and quality of my "energy" in contemplative practices or my interpretations of esoteric ideas needed fine-tuning (or a complete overhaul, for that matter). As a way of forming generalities, I also listened to and compared other people's ruminations and inwardly measured them against my own understandings. [28]

But often, especially in monastic contexts, there was no venue for discussion. Intersubjective ethnography thus included sensing mood and group energy in a silent context and observing the subtleties of movement. As shown in the works of Erving Goffman (1959), people say a great deal through nonverbal communication such as facial expression, physical demeanor, and the pacing of movement and sound, but also through what some contemplatives in my research called "sensing energy." Durkheim's depictions of effervescence acknowledged and attempted to convey the unnameable, unspeakable, and invisible aspects of social communication, which even anthropologists might be savvy enough to notice if they tune in well enough. It is important to note that, where there was a general consensus that "something happened" in a group setting, there were sometimes outliers who "didn't get it." An anthropologist must be careful not to assume that intersubjectivity is uniformly experienced or felt by all in attendance. General acknowledgement of "indwelling" or "unitive consciousness" does not erase individual response. Indeed, variations in degree of experiential knowledge, as well as an acceptance that one must continually work toward greater understanding, were important ethnographic characteristics of this community.

I do not presume to have lost my bias by engaging in intersubjective ethnography. While I question the usefulness of an outsider's stance and the possibility of old-fashioned concepts of objectivity, I have nevertheless sought a critical understanding of the people with whom I worked. Indeed, by becoming more aware of my biases and attempting to shift them, and through incorporating what I know of others' biases, I have been able to hear something of what these thoughtful, interiorized people see and know, and have risked taking on an interpretive role, even among those with strong and able voices.

But in a context where the subjects are extraordinarily articulate (if often silent), what does an anthropologist have to add? My role here is multifaceted. First, I expand an ethnography of the socially powerful, a group that has been less often the subject of anthropological descriptions. This includes discussions about Christianity, which until recently anthropologists have avoided, perhaps because of its role in the colonization and oppression of peoples around the world. Their anxiety arising from a vestige of nineteenth-century "pure culture" concepts, some anthropologists seem to have felt that Christianity has sullied "real" pre-Christianized peoples and cultures (e.g., Comaroff and Comaroff 1991; cf. Robbins 2007). Many anthropologists of European descent may have also felt that Christianity is "too close to home" to be of ethnographic interest and that its study conveys a threatening evangelical intent (Cannell 2005; Robbins 2003).

More recently, studies featuring Christianity have increased. The anthropology of Christianity subfield has offered plenty of excellent ethnography and developing theory, but it has also focused primarily on the diverse manifestations of postcolonial Christianities and populist evangelical and Pentecostal forms.[29] Although this trend has begun to shift (e.g., Engelke 2012, 2013; Klassen 2011), there are still few studies of Christianities at the centers of power. The present study looks at Christianity among a mostly urban intellectual elite in the United States, a people commonly outside of the usual ethnographic categories. My choice to do research with mostly urban, university-educated, upper-middle-class American contemplative Christians adds to the ongoing conversations about modernity and secularization. Previously noted, theirs is a demographic that secularization theorists would peg as the very people who would not choose to follow a religious life. This work gives voice to the everyday realities of such people, those who live well in the mix of pluralism, modernity, and religion, regardless of the secularizing social forces which theorists have said should undermine their devotion.[30]

My primary theoretical focus is not secularization theory but pluralism studies, ritual studies, performance studies, and studies of knowledge and perception, particularly the characteristic of phenomenological intersubjectivity. In this work, I extend classic studies of ritual by offering detailed observations about how communitas can arise through the association of intensive psychic preparation and ritual practices, a dual aspect on which neither Durkheim nor Turner focused. My discussions about the relationship of intentional action and ambiguous "unknowing" also offer a closer examination of the interdependent roles of agency and habitus. In this way, my findings about contemplative Christians' ritual practice and the ritualization of everyday life add to two streams of recent scholarship: the theory of lived religion,[31] which attempts to debunk the classic dichotomized categories of sacred and profane that substantially colored earlier ritual studies, and the anthropological and phenomenological theory that illustrates the processes by which sociocultural diversity and cohesiveness are in perpetual relationship in any society.[32]

After Fredrik Barth (2002), I have chosen an epistemological frame to elucidate diversity, cohesion, and the phenomenology of lived experience. In detailing collective phenomenological experiences, I extend our notions of knowledge by exploring the capacity of people to engage multiple ways of knowing, including intellectual, experiential, and unitive. Learned contemplative Christians' gradients of knowledges clearly defy dichotomized renderings of rational and irrational and instead show knowing as a way of "being and becoming," as some people in my research described it: a moving process of the changing acuity of intellectual and phenomenological knowing, which is grounded in bodily experience. My use of clines and degrees in describing knowledge attempts to convey the diversity, multiplicity, and motion with which people live in any ethnographic context.

WE NOW STAND at the threshold. Sixteenth-century Counter-Reformation mystic St. Teresa of Ávila wrote *The Interior Castle* to allegorize Christians as travelers who enter a great house, moving through its seven rooms, coming closer and closer to the divine which dwells at its center. To learn more about these travelers, we too shall enter. Our edifice of encounter will not be a castle however, but a monastic chapel.[33]

At the Portico in this first chapter, we have already encountered the strength of yearning and desire that brought people to the door of contemplative Christianity. We have also looked at some of the qualities of those who came, their basic social and conceptual characteristics, as well as the practice of Centering Prayer that unified them and the ethnographic methods by which I have sought to understand them.

From here, we walk through to Chapter 2's Antechapel, the outer chapel where the community gathered. There, newcomers discovered contemplative alternatives and became familiar with significant principles like humility, non-attachment, and social responsibility. We learn more about their unusual relationship to theories of knowledge, which gave them a certain ease with the paradoxes of contemplative Christianity, its knowing and unknowing, being and becoming. Their solid ground came from discipline and ritual practices, which helped resolve dialectical tensions while also making space for the ambiguity of an apophatic stance in a pluralistic world. But the way could sometimes be challenging. Teachers offered stability, a key tenet of Benedictine monasticism, by showing the importance of defining and keeping one's intention and by encouraging people to take up the steadying influence of monastic tools, like a schedule of practice, a rule of life, service to others, and a sense of humor, which helped lighten the burdens of having chosen a way that was sometimes demanding.

In Chapter 3, contemplative Christians encountered a barrier, the Grille that separates the Antechapel from the inner reaches of the monastery. The silence and enclosure characteristic of contemplation initially seem at odds with the Benedictine tenet of hospitality. Contemplative interiority protected an alternative way of life that required dedication and focus, but it also fostered a sociality which was not always apparent to newcomers. Silence, we learn, is a way of communicating welcome and acceptance. The Grille asks us to consider the paradoxical relationship of hospitality and interiority, as well as distinctions between member and guest. Through the welcome of monks and nuns to their daily liturgies, spiritual counseling, and other events which they host, we find that the monastic cloister takes on a porous quality.

The Gate is the way of entry through the wrought-iron Grille. Chapter 4 describes how people brought change and diversity across the threshold. In the United States, religious institutions do not have a great deal of social authority. We learn how teachers depended on their social and cultural capital to encourage others to join them as they walk through the Gate. I give particular attention to how leaders selected and interpreted Christian histories, how they presented the great lineages of Christian contemplation as a way of authenticating particular ideas and practices. To illustrate this movement's diversity, I show how the ethos of monastic and Wisdom versions of the same liturgy can be vastly different, from the despair of atonement to the eros of Bridal Mysticism. The differences highlight the relationship between liturgical conservatism and innovation within a particular variety of American Christianity, and how ritual specialists' intellectual capacities, creativities, public voices, charisma, and credentials have the potential to open the door to alternative renderings in religious institutions that can be slow to change.

By Chapter 5 we have deepened our wisdom and commitment enough to sit with attentiveness in the Choir. Here on the other side of the Grille, we learn the critical role of formal ritual and prayer—the *ora* of Benedictine *ora et labora*. We learn how the chapel is a place to develop the senses, to heighten awareness, and to listen for the divine through aesthetics and sensations. Contemplative

Christians considered the body itself to be a kind of temple, a vessel that invites divine indwelling. By keeping postures of ritual practice and a commitment to contemplative ideals and ways, practitioners attempted to prepare a receptive ground that could encourage a "flow of the divine." We begin to understand how practitioners combined agency and habitus by cultivating an intentional relationship between cataphasis, or action, and apophasis, or contemplation. Practitioners enacted silence, stillness, movement, and sound to strengthen their capacity for attunement and attention, a way of becoming more aware of the divine, which they believed was everywhere around them.

But those practices of keeping attention were not confined to spaces set aside for formal ritual. In Chapter 6, we learn that contemplative Christians sought to live a life of "ceaseless prayer." Therefore, the Sacristy—where contemplatives worked at everyday relationships and ordinary tasks—was as important to their efforts at fostering intimacy with the divine as were the ritual practices of the Choir. The Sacristy is the place of the *labora* in Benedictine *ora et labora*, where people brought intention and attention to every part of life, not only aspects that are obviously "religious." Both formal ritual and the ritualization of everyday life combined the posture of agency and the flow of habitus, which were inseparable partners in contemplative Christians' work toward "transformation."

The rites and ritualizations of the Choir and the Sacristy fostered varieties and degrees of knowledge, prompting some to take a place at the altar. Chapter 7 brings us into the Sanctuary, where we learn that one's degree of experience, intention, and knowledge can make a difference to how well one serves the community. I describe three kinds of knowledge particular to contemplative Christians: *performative knowledge* and *unknowing*, which, when brought together with intention, can create the experiential knowledge of *unitive being* or communitas. While contemplatives stressed that unitive being is something that depends entirely on divine will, they nevertheless believed that actively practicing attentiveness in every aspect of life was a necessary responsibility and a way of "deepening into the divine." Contemplative practice was like performing music. Some were ordinary players, while others had both a strong feeling for the music and the technical ability to perform. Sometimes these players became masters or even virtuosos, those with a kind of charismatic knowledge that people in my research said could bring the divine into the midst of the community. These adepts acted as "icons," they said—windows between people and God. Yet however much experience one has, contemplative Christians insisted that this kind of knowledge does not come from accreditation, social status, or individual merit. Iconic knowledge only exists in the moment and only at the behest of the divine, they said. Humility thus continued to be a foundational tenet, regardless of experience and capability.

The journey does not end at the Sanctuary's altar. In Chapter 8, we leave the chapel altogether and enter the innermost room, the monastic Cell. There we find ourselves faced with solitude. But the practicing and experienced contemplative Christian understands that solitude is not the same as isolation. We learn from the story of Helen Eberle Daly's illness that increasing enclosure can be extraordinarily challenging, sometimes pushing one beyond the boundaries of comprehension or capacity to endure. However, Helen's journey to the Cell also shows us the contemplative Christian perspective that in times of severe emotional and physical distress, a commitment to keeping intention and attention, the openness and ambiguity of unknowing, and a willingness to give everything over to the divine can become a catalyst for unitive being. The one alone in the Cell—which is really the cell of personhood—can experience a sense of communion with the divine, people, and all creation. The walls of the Cell become porous.

Having considered innumerable choices in a pluralistic world, contemplative Christians have found their way to the Portico of contemplative Christianity. Let us now join them as they enter the Antechapel.

Photograph courtesy of SSJE.

2

Antechapel

GATHERING AND GROUNDING CONTEMPLATIVE
CHRISTIANS IN A PLURALISTIC SOCIETY

> *The community gathers in the Antechapel. There, on the out-*
> *side of the cloister, teachers welcome newcomers and adepts*
> *alike, meeting them wherever they are on the long journey to*
> *learning the ways and ideals of contemplative Christianity. The*
> *Antechapel is the public space of the monastery, a place of begin-*
> *nings that is open to a lively, pluralistic world, yet it is also a*
> *place of focus, shelter, and support for those who make first ges-*
> *tures of commitment to sometimes challenging alternatives.*

AFTER PRAYING THE Magnificat at the Society of Saint John the Evangelist's office
of Evening Prayer one day in May 2010, Jeremy stepped forward to be clothed
in the habit of the monastery. The postulant wore all black, a T-shirt, pants, and
Birkenstock sandals. The monks in their cassocks (also in black) had already processed two by two to the altar and awaited him there in a semi-circle. Using the
scripted words of the Society's Clothing ceremony, the Novice Guardian presented
Jeremy to the gathered Brothers, who replied in unison with a formal welcome.
The young man asked to be received into the Society. The Superior reminded
Jeremy of the challenges inherent in entering a communal life of disciplined
prayer and service, then went on to encourage him by assuring that he would
have the support of the community. "We will help you understand the role of the
monastic way in the life and mission of the Church," he said. "We will open to you
the meaning of our Rule of Life and share our tradition and the teaching of our
founders." The Superior added,

> If you are truly called to our way of life, the novitiate will be a time not
> merely of adaptation, but of inner change and conversion of life. Expect
> emotional and spiritual trials, since stages of genuine transformation are
> marked by experiences of confusion and loss. The Brothers who have
> responsibility for the work of formation will help you face these times with

courage and gain insight into their meaning. All of us are here to encourage you in the stress of adjustment and change.

Jeremy confirmed his desire to become a novice of this monastic life, and the
Brothers collectively agreed to receive and support him.

Three monks in turn then gave Jeremy the pieces of the Brothers' habit, which
the Superior had called "a powerful sign of our common life and identity." The
most recently professed monk gave Jeremy the Society's bronze cross, bearing
Latin passages from the Gospel of John and a crucifix reminiscent of the whirling
stone carvings of a French Romanesque tympanum. Jeremy silently placed the
pendant around his neck. Next, the eldest monk presented him with the Society's
black habit. Jeremy took a little while to dress himself, while the monks and fellow
congregants attentively waited. He carefully stepped into the cassock and fastened
the metal clasps at neck and chest, then pulled the scapular over his head. (A long-
time congregant later mentioned to me how elegantly he managed this public
dressing; some neophytes in the past had noticeably entangled themselves, she
said.) Finally, the Assistant Superior offered the cincture. Jeremy wound the black
cord belt around his waist three times and knotted it, foreshadowing the three
vows of professed life—poverty, celibacy, and obedience—which he hoped to take
not long in the future. The Superior took hold of Jeremy's hands as the smiling
Brothers received and blessed him.

Jeremy's Clothing ceremony was a simple, formalized enactment and confirmation of the mutual commitment of the novice and the monastic society into
which he sought admission. The new novice professed a willingness to learn and
to take on the Society's rule of life, persevering through the hardships of transforming into the ideals of humility, gratitude, and compassion that are characteristic of monastic culture, and the Brothers agreed to teach and support him.

During the Clothing, waves of sound—applause, amplified speeches, and
laughter—filtered through the chapel's stone walls from the status-shifting ceremonies of a neighboring institution. Witnessed by his new community and a
small gathering of family and friends, the quiet solemnity of Jeremy's Clothing
took place that day adjacent to Harvard University's Commencement ceremonies
at John F. Kennedy Park on the Charles River. Also dressed in robes of transformed status, though crimson rather than black, new graduates there celebrated
with exuberance their personal achievement of completing studies at an elite educational institution. Though both neophyte parties entered into rarefied, learned
communities that day, the contrast of sensibilities and intentions between the two
celebrations could hardly be greater: one of individual achievement and status in
the upper echelons of American society, the other an embrace of monastic poverty,
humility, and service.

THOSE WHO FOUND their way to the Antechapel were faced with learning the some-times challenging ideals and practices of contemplative Christianity. Teachers of the movement therefore had a crucial role. Like the monks who welcomed the new novice, Jeremy, into their community, they took on the duty to provide formation and stabilization to their students. Through various media, teach-ers guided newcomers in learning the ideas, ethos, and practices of Christian contemplation, which they felt could be quite different from the seemingly endless possibilities in the pluralistic United States, and they offered practical methods of grounding, sustaining, and developing those chosen alternatives. Their teachings thus proffered versions of a foundational tenet in Benedictine monasticism: stability.[1]

In a pluralistic society like that of the United States, people drawn to the divine have an extraordinary variety of religious sensibilities. Scholars of some American evangelical and fundamentalist Christianities, for example, have noted an incli-nation of members of those communities to prioritize belief and doctrine in response to the social and religious ambiguities that eclecticism inspires (Smith 1998). The American contemplative Christians with whom I worked tended to respond in another way: ideally, theirs was an ethos of openness that included the intentional cultivation of wonder as well as a welcome for "the stranger" and the unknown. Those who entered the Antechapel of contemplative Christianity were often thoughtful about the strengths and weaknesses of their own intellectual ability to interpret the world in which they lived, and they accepted the seeming paradox of committing to particular ways even while they cultivated an openness to a world that is full of other religious, philosophical, social, and political possi-bilities. American contemplative Christians fostered respect for the ambiguity and uncertainty that rises in such complex social spheres. Through their relationship with the world, they sought to become aware of the divine in every aspect of life (cf. Kearney 2010).

Even with their intention to see the divine in all things, the shifting ground of pluralism nevertheless had the capacity to destabilize contemplative Christians, especially in the non-gathered community outside of monasteries. Aspiring con-templatives rarely had the kind of community support Jeremy received as they worked toward a deepening commitment to contemplative Christian teachings. Feeling the absence of substantial guidance to learn and follow chosen alterna-tives, some identified certain "American norms" as potentially distracting, particu-larly individualist notions that constructed self-identity by way of achievement, acquisition, and preference. Learning to transform oneself into contemplative ide-als like humility and detachment, and to accept ambiguity rather than certainty as a condition of the contemplative way, required extraordinary reflexivity and a commitment to one's chosen intentions.

Contemplatives used discipline and other monastic tools as a way to foster "awakening" (that is, greater awareness) of self in the larger relational field of the divine and others. They also actively worked to reform their *habitus*, the term Pierre Bourdieu (1977) popularized for underlying cultural assumptions and ways of being that individuals acquire passively through societal interactions. Though Bourdieu's concept has been adopted by many theorists, these people's determined attempts at reforming thoughts and demeanors through intentional repetitive actions comes closer to the pedagogical Aristotelian understanding of habitus, outlined by Saba Mahmood (2005: 136) as "an acquired excellence at either a moral or a practical craft, learned through repeated practice until that practice leaves a permanent mark on the character of the person." She wrote, "Habitus in this tradition implies a quality that is acquired through human industry, assiduous practice, and discipline."

Though they were conscious of and committed to their intentions to a high degree, the people in my research were not unique in their efforts to subvert socialized norms. Phenomenological anthropologist Michael Jackson (2015: 296; emphasis in original) noted that many experience a struggle between the imperviousness of received knowledge and their desire to see past it. He wrote:

> Human beings are constantly renegotiating their relationships with objectified forms, invoking them to legitimate or explain their actions, resisting enslavement to them, adapting them to their individual needs. But whether accepting or rejecting these forms of more-than-life, we are never mere creatures of custom, assimilating ourselves to a world that has been constructed by others at other times; we are vital participants in a process of bringing the world into being . . . . Life both stretches *beyond* itself (toward transcendent or reified forms of thought) *and* involves making those extant forms responsible to our own specific existential needs.

The American contemplative Christian endeavor to identify and transform habituated thoughts and ways included learning to shift attention, both conscious and unconscious, from one's own concerns, emotions, self-importance, even identity. This desire to change underlying motivations and behaviors was reflected in Jeremy's Clothing ceremony: taking on the monastic *habit* was a symbol for Jeremy's intention to transform his *habitus*. The high-agency approach of subscribing to a disciplined and regularized life of study, practice, and service in the context of critical reflection reveals how contemplative Christians worked to bring unexamined habitus to conscious awareness (what Bourdieu called *doxa*) and then attempted to modify and normalize new, chosen ways. Learning to sustain the endless dance between conscious intention, critical thought, and contemplative practice was the groundwork of those in the Antechapel who hoped to someday approach the inner reaches of the chapel.[2]

A lifelong task, one's intention to learn a contemplative way of life was frequently more than non-monastics could manage without the everyday social-structural support of a community and well-grounded teachers. Their struggles, especially for those who attempted the Christian contemplative life in isolation from other like-minded and like-practicing others, could undermine even the most devoted of disciples, sometimes to the point of giving up. Ultimately, students had to make a choice to commit and to continually renew that commitment, regardless of unsettling emotions like loneliness and doubt. In committing to a disciplined life, they intentionally chose not to be drawn away by the distractions of their own inconsistencies or other cultural possibilities (cf. Mahmood 2005). Unlike the variety of commitment in which "individual interests become attached to the carrying out of socially organized patterns of behavior" (Kanter 1968: 500) or which rises in institutionalization (Parsons and Shils 1962), non-monastic students who were unassociated or loosely linked with institutions had to find other means of grounding their choices.

Contemplative teachers, both monastic and non-monastic, were fully aware of the sometimes arduous nature of this alternative way of life, as we saw from the comments of the SSJE Superior at Jeremy's Clothing ceremony, and they were especially aware of the difficulties for those in the non-gathered community. These teachers used their uncommon level of education, critical analyses of self and society, rhetorical abilities, and epistemological theories to effectively voice their positions and get their messages and support out to people beyond the walls of the cloister. Thus negotiating the tension between their ideals of humility and a professionalism and learnedness that carried a certain amount of social power and authority,[3] they encouraged practitioners to take up "monastic tools" like the stabilizing rhythm of a rule of life, the outward-looking activities of social action and service, and a sense of humor, which helped to lighten a demanding journey. Especially important was a notion of discipline as a positive force rather than as a form of institutional oppression, a way that assisted one in keeping freely chosen intentions and finding a way to stability, even outside of the sheltering environment of the monastic cloister.

Choosing Monastic Alternatives: Detachment, Humility, and Ambiguity in American Society

The American contemplative Christians with whom I worked tended to be learned, professional, and cosmopolitan. Even with their tendency toward open-mindedness however, they often felt their community's ways of being, thinking, and living (as varied as these were) contrasted with underlying societal norms. Teachers used rhetorical juxtaposition to get across their movement's ethos and values of detachment, humility, and ambiguity. Three examples from teachers in my research illustrate their diverse ways of expressing the movement's distinctiveness, as well as its breadth: they come from different American geographic regions, show different kinds of expertise and social circumstances, and employ different media and genres to convey their messages, sometimes with humor, sometimes with wonder, sometimes with a tinge of despair.

Sandra Mattheson,[4] for example, was a visual artist and teacher from the Southwest. She had been raised a Roman Catholic, but became disillusioned with institutionalized religion by her mid-teens. In early adulthood, she traveled to southern India, where she spent a year in an ashram. Some years later, Sandra discovered the contemplative aspects of Christianity and took an advanced degree in comparative religion. By the time I met her during fieldwork, she was part of an art cooperative and had an established practice as a spiritual director, workshop leader, and t'ai chi instructor. Sandra wrote a blog, and also used her Facebook page as a medium to spread ideas about the contemplative ways of Christianity, Vedanta Hinduism, and Taoism. In August 2014, she posted a *New Yorker* cartoon that poked fun at the trouble Americans had in letting go of

"This week on 'The Amazing Race to Enlightenment,' can Jim and Suzy achieve right mindfulness? And will Barb and Candy be eliminated for relentless clinging to the self?"

New Yorker cartoon by David Sipress, reprinted with permission from Condé Nast publications.

competitive self-identity, even in their contemplative endeavors. Sandra wrote under the cartoon, "What part of 'non-attachment' do you not understand?" [5]

Another teacher of Christian contemplation whom we encountered in Chapter 1, Ward Bauman, was an Episcopal priest who ran the House of Prayer, a retreat center located on the grounds of a Midwestern Roman Catholic Benedictine monastery where I did fieldwork. At the Episcopal House of Prayer, Ward Bauman and his guest teachers ran many kinds of retreats and Wisdom Schools on topics like Benedictine monasticism, yoga, cooking, poetry writing, and inter-religious contemplation. Ward clearly saw great value in ways of knowing from different cultural and religious schools, but also understood the potential instability created by the overwhelming number of choices in the "spiritual marketplace" of pluralistic America (Roof 2001).

Ward Bauman understood that the basic Christian contemplative tenets could be difficult for Americans to grasp, even for those who professed a commitment. In one of his monthly email newsletters from the House of Prayer, Ward acknowledged practitioners' struggle to transform their "acquiring hearts" and to embody an ethos of detachment and humility, which he considered to be radically different from ubiquitous American norms (W. Bauman 2013b). He wrote,

> One of the primary practices of all spiritual work is detachment, the learned behavior of "letting go" and not clinging . . . . The great paradox is that we cannot find it by grasping it. In other words, going to another conference, reading another book, or hearing another teaching will not ultimately be the knowledge that we seek and need. This is perhaps one of the hardest lessons of the spiritual life. We in the West do not get it. It is so antithetical to everything we've learned. But this is core to coming to spiritual truth. It also points to the heart of our spiritual malady, pride. True wisdom comes only through true humility.

Addressing a community of contemplatives, some of whom tended to be "retreat junkies" always in search of just the right teacher with just the right teaching, Ward Bauman said the insidious orientation of "the West" toward achievement was difficult to shake.[6] Paradoxically, people were transformed through detachment, not acquisition, he said, by letting go of the very things they seek.

By "detachment," Ward did not mean lack of care or emotional aloofness—indeed, learning to love without condition was the highest ideal for contemplative Christians. Detachment was rather a practice of "letting go," or *kenosis*, which stepped away from a concern for establishing one's personhood through identification with objects, statuses, behaviors, or tightly held categories of thought. Ward's point was that the American cultural temperament of seeking identity through acquisition and achievement, even when employed with the good intentions of changing oneself for the better through work and study, cannot bring people to the contemplative ethos of humility, which was the place from which "transformation" could begin.

Another teacher in the American contemplative Christian movement, Br. Curtis Almquist, SSJE, also used the motifs of detachment and humility to get across the contemplative Christian ethos. Through them, he showed how the intentional cultivation of ambiguity and paradox can prompt people to see past their usual boundaries. Br. Curtis Almquist was the Superior at the Society of Saint John the Evangelist (SSJE) when I first began fieldwork.[7] A priest, monk, and well-respected author, teacher, and speaker, he had been brought up in a Midwestern Lutheran family of Swedish origin. In contrast to the primacy and status of positive intellectual knowledge forms taught by his Ivy League neighbor, Harvard University, the importance of monastic ambiguity and liminality was apparent in Br. Curtis Almquist's (2011) public lecture, "Poetic Splendor in Color and Light," which commemorated Dr. Charles J. Connick, the artist who designed the stained-glass windows in the SSJE chapel at Cambridge, Massachusetts.[8]

In his lecture, Br. Curtis described how Dr. Charles J. Connick and the architect Ralph Adams Cram together created structural juxtapositions that fostered a feeling of liminality. Their work prompted those who entered the chapel to cross the *limen* (Latin for threshold) into another way of being, he said. When one passes over the threshold, one enters a "place of in-between," a "thin space" that brings together earthly and divine realms. This ambiguous place of "both/and" potentially acts as an "icon," he said, a kind of window or conduit through which the human and the divine make contact.[9]

Expanding on the notion that ambiguity and paradox have the transformative potential to take people beyond usual frames of knowledge and experience, Br. Curtis highlighted the chapel's contrasting architectural qualities. The paradoxical union of weighty stone and weightless light, for example, simultaneously fostered stability and effervescence. He said,

> Nothing could be heavier than a floor of undressed slate and polished marble, and the serene walls of granite. No matter how much you may feel your life is adrift, when you come into this space, you are grounded . . . [but] then the limestone Gothic arches, columns, pillars, and capitals lift your gaze to the light of the heavens with the beautiful rose window that crowns the antechapel, and the clerestory windows that line the choir.

Br. Curtis Almquist said, too, that the designers intentionally created an admixture of darkness and light in the chapel, which further expands a feeling of in-betweenness, unknowing, and wonder. Shadowy recesses contrasted with the danger of *too much* light, he said, the glare and exposure that he called "the wound of knowledge" after the words of Welsh poet, R. S. Thomas. Sanctification and holiness come through "an intermingling of light and darkness, enough of both," said Br. Curtis: the mystery of ambiguous "holy shadow" is as primary to awakening to the divine as the dazzle of overt knowledge.

Further, said Br. Curtis Almquist, Cram and Connick's decision to craft a small dark stone building alongside the gilt domes and "soaring beauties of neighboring Harvard University" sought to convey the paradoxical and unexpected power of humility. Their choice of austerity created an understated beauty by using the simple riches of stone and the "light and color in glass . . . as a medium for praise and prayer," a way of "transmit[ting] light to the soul," he said. Br. Curtis emphasized in particular the humility apparent in Connick's choice to design his windows as "handmaidens" of architecture, rather than to create showy works that would have overwhelmed the intimate space and placed the focus on the artist rather than the chapel's sanctity. Connick's gift to SSJE was an exquisite but humble beauty, said Br. Curtis, one which complements the stabilizing force of the chapel's architecture, creating a liminal realm of "stone and light" (SSJE 2010). By showing how a building's architectural design could open, suspend, and blend categories, Br. Curtis Almquist thus taught his listeners that ambiguity, paradox, and humility—indeed, detachment from one's conceptual and experiential frameworks—could prompt mystery and wonder. His words revealed how unknowing is an equal partner to knowledge on the contemplative Christian path.[10]

Kenosis and Consent: Limitation as Choice in Pluralistic America

Using different approaches, Sandra Mattheson, Ward Bauman, and Br. Curtis Almquist taught contemplative Christian ideals of detachment and humility, which can rise from of an ethos of ambiguity and unknowing. They thus encouraged their listeners to take up a demeanor based on the delicate and paradoxical combination of two foundational principles, consent and *kenosis*—that is, intentional, willing, and persistent engagement and the apophatic art of "letting go." Contemplative Christian teachers said that working toward "transformation" required consent to the divine and a long-term commitment to ways of knowing and doing that contrasted with what they saw as an underlying American focus on individual achievement, acquisition, and self-identity.[11]

Kenosis—what Ward Bauman called "not clinging" and "detachment" in his newsletter—was not about obtaining something, but about *releasing* something, about giving, relinquishing, and balancing the dialectic of one's responsibility to *do* with a willingness to *not* do. Leaders taught that the paradox of doing and not doing, knowing and not knowing, could open a way of seeing the divine in the world *despite* one's endeavors as well as because of them. At a winter Centering

Prayer retreat I attended in New York's Hudson River Valley, Fr. Carl Arico, a Roman Catholic priest and the vice president of Contemplative Outreach, advised his students that "letting go" was paramount. He said, "If Mother Mary *herself* comes walking across those ice floes on the river, you say to her, 'Not now, m'dear, I'm meditating.'"

Another teacher I followed during fieldwork, Cynthia Bourgeault (2004: 84–85, 88), described kenosis in her influential book, *Centering Prayer and Inner Awakening*, as "the core reality underlying every moment of Jesus' human journey." She noted that kenosis, which was made explicit in the apostle Paul's first-century letter to the Philippians (2:5–8), was Greek for "self-emptying" or "letting go." It was a gesture of "love made full in the act of giving itself away," which depended on the idea of a limitless flow of the divine. Following on the trail of Fr. William Meninger, OCSO (1997), Cynthia Bourgeault wrote that the practice of kenosis was foundational to the asceticism of particular varieties of Christian mystics, like the anonymous fourteenth-century English writer of *The Cloud of Unknowing* (anon. 1961), and is the underlying principle of Centering Prayer. "Apart from this grounding in *kenosis*, the practice of Centering Prayer may not fully make sense," she wrote. Along with a conviction that "sacred energy" has inexhaustible potential and bounty, contemplative Christians learn that "awakening" does not rise from inflexible vigilance or defensive renunciation, but flourishes through the outward-moving gestures of release, generosity, and hospitality—through "giving it away."

Cynthia Bourgeault and one of her own teachers, Fr. Thomas Keating, OCSO (1999, 2002b), thus taught that the primary method behind Centering Prayer is based on compassion for "the human condition." Acknowledging that people are distractible, the technique of Centering Prayer takes inattention as a part of the process of transformation. Teachers of Centering Prayer did not see distractions as something to avoid or reject, but instead framed them as opportunities to "let go and return." Their focus was thus on practitioners' repeated willingness to be attentive, rather than on their development of a capacity for rigorous steady-state concentration. Union with the divine begins with consent, taught Fr. Thomas Keating, not strident ascetical techniques that keep distractions at bay. Detachment was thus seen as a creative act, not one which impoverishes.[12]

These principles of kenosis, consent, detachment, ambiguity, and humility were foundational to American contemplative Christians' capacity for crafting and sustaining their religious sensibilities and practices in a pluralistic society. The combination of a compassionate view of human inconsistencies, "letting go," and a willingness to persist invited an open demeanor that attracted people who crossed all sorts of boundaries. In fact, at some of the Wisdom Schools I attended, Cynthia Bourgeault taught that this kenotic variety of contemplation was modeled on Jesus' own facility with crossing social and religious boundaries, as seen in biblical stories that show his detachment from any particular way of living. Cynthia said that he could move easily from the asceticism of praying alone in the desert for forty days to engaging with various classes of society, befriending and teaching both the marginalized and the powerful. The American contemplative Christians in my research took this scriptural model of boundary crossing, category mixing, and detachment from self-identification with particular lifeways as an ideal for their own lives. Those who took detachment seriously attempted to apply the art of letting go in every situation, which allowed contemplative life to fit well within the pluralistic context of American modernity.

The people with whom I worked thus approached contemplative life with a great deal of diversity, especially outside the monastery. Degrees of rigor in practice, discipline, and material asceticism varied considerably over the broad range of lifeways of those who practiced this kenotic, contemplative variety of Christianity. Some, like Br. Jeremy, did choose a monastic life, but the monastics I knew admired and encouraged non-monastic contemplatives. Br. Nathan, for example, said to a small group of congregants who were heading into the noisy fray of urban traffic after an evening Eucharist service, "I think it's much harder for you, staying centered in that. I'm not sure I could manage so well." Even so, the monks and nuns with whom I spoke emphasized that living in a monastery was not a way to escape society or close out other people. This became clear early in my fieldwork when I met Br. Philip on a city street and said by way of greeting, "Out in the world?" He lifted an eyebrow and replied rather pointedly, "Never left it." Entering a monastery or convent was just one model of contemplative life, albeit an intensive one. Among the semi-cloistered communities where I did research, monastic enclosure and devotion did not represent a "total institution" that excluded and rejected others (Goffman 1961) or that functioned primarily on techniques of renunciation (Kanter 1968), but was rather a way to focus attention and to find support and camaraderie in a sometimes demanding life choice, as we shall see in Chapter 3, which explores the role of silence, enclosure, and hospitality in contemplative Christianity.

People outside the monasteries followed Christian contemplative ways in the otherwise "ordinary," varied contexts of pluralistic American society. Though most were well educated and from the middle or upper middle classes, the contemplative Christians in my research nevertheless lived and worked in many different ways. Stephen, for instance, was a computer programmer, Zak was an advertising executive, Laurie was a counselor at a drug rehabilitation center, Sharon was a pediatrician, Ned was an English professor, and Liz was an activist and labor organizer of immigrant workers. Some were married, some were single, some had children, some lived in non-monastic intentional communities, and some were in same-sex partnerships. In addition to Christianity, nearly all of the non-monastic individuals with whom I worked had studied and drawn practices from one or more of the contemplative branches of other world religions (as well as some regionally specific ones), and many followed multiple contemporary teachers and philosophers through a variety of media. In this pluralistic American context, working toward contemplative transformation did require a commitment to learning and undertaking certain principles and practices, especially kenosis and consent, but it *did not* insist upon adopting a life way that renounced the world. Christian contemplative life of this variety clearly took many forms.

This pluralistic environment did have some undesired effects on contemplative life, however. In a complex, mobile society like the United States, with its dizzying array of potential lifeways, learning and developing the kenotic skills of self-emptying and non-attachment required discipline, self-direction, and conscious intention. Their high-agency approach of "consenting to the divine" relied upon a twofold practice: making an *intention*—that is, choosing and sustaining a particular way (or ways) from all the options—and paying *attention*—being alert or "present" to one's current thoughts and actions and ideally, as one matures, all of creation.[13] This chapter concentrates on the tools that practitioners, especially non-monastics, learned to help them keep their *intention* to live a devoted contemplative life. Learning the contemplative art of keeping *attention* is the focus of chapters to come, particularly Chapters 5 and 6.

Even though they valued pluralism, the more experienced practitioners with whom I worked recognized that too many choices could destabilize and distract from primary intentions. Rather than reacting unpredictably to covert "emotional programs for happiness" and self-oriented motivations, Fr. Thomas Keating (2002a) encouraged his students to act with deliberate intentions that focused on chosen ideals.[14] Adherents found that choosing to say "yes" to a contemplative life did indeed mean narrowing one's choices, while also learning to negotiate the tricky paradox of practicing detachment in a pluralistic environment without developing either hard-edged renunciation and judgment or a wishy-washy, undiscerning acceptance of everything that comes along. Ideally, kenosis and detachment in this community were neither a path to rejecting people nor an excuse to passively "roll over and die," as one retreat teacher said, but depended instead on learning "to live from a Holy Center" (Best 2005).

Ironically, the American freedom to intentionally limit one's choices to the ways of contemplative Christianity, whether within or outside a monastery, comes itself out of the cultural ground of pluralism. When he introduced his "New Paradigm" in response to secularization theory, Stephen Warner (1993) pointed out how the extraordinary diversity in American religion and a devotion to preference and choice came in part from historical reactions to British and European state-controlled religions. The American history of religious disestablishment encouraged religious vitality, as well as pluralism and voluntarism, in a kind of free market supply-and-demand model of religious choice. According to Warner, the characteristics of American history resulted in diverse and eclectic religious expressions, including contemplative varieties.

American history thus encouraged a strong underlying focus on choice in the United States, enhancing a prevalence of the related tenets of individualism, self-identity, personal freedom, and democracy. Paradoxically, however, the American *habitus of choice* had the potential to be at odds with this variety of contemplative Christianity, with its primary focus on detachment and letting go. While the open stance of kenosis can work well in pluralized environments, teachers emphasized that contemplative living nevertheless required discipline and dedication to its practices and principles. The very existence of a vast range of options made it more difficult to form and keep an intention to live a life based on self-emptying, detachment, and humility. Indeed, the factor of individual preference sometimes confounded the contemplatives with whom I worked, especially non-monastic neophytes who were easily caught up in the buzz of the next best teacher, the next best meditation technique, the next best book or app or website, the next best way to live, as Ward Bauman's newsletter (2013b) pointed out earlier in this chapter.

Trouble with the American habitus of choice was revealed in the writings of one of the people who ejournaled for me. Simon consciously grappled with the tension between choice and detachment as he continually struggled to settle into a sustainable rhythm of contemplative practice. In an ejournal entry, he described how new possibilities kept pulling him away from an established course. Simon had tried out a number of church denominations over the years, including Mennonite and Roman Catholic, and played with elements like daily poetry reading, journal writing, practicing *lectio divina* and Centering Prayer, spending regular time in solitary hermitage, studying numerous theological perspectives, developing liturgies at his parish, and attending retreats and Wisdom Schools. He often felt dissatisfied with how he managed and prioritized these activities, and shifted them regularly, like an ever-moving shell game. Simon also said he felt isolated, though he followed contemplative blogs and had online connections through social media, and would sometimes get "sidetracked" from his practices for long periods. Simon said he welcomed my request to write an ejournal because, even though he had then been practicing Centering Prayer for eighteen years, was an active member of his church, and met monthly with a spiritual director, he was dealing with a "disintegrating Centering Prayer practice"; he found that the task of writing for my research "prompted a timely re-examination of my contemplative life (such as it is)" and helped him to simplify. Simon's efforts to refocus by letting go of too many choices showed his commitment to the principles of kenosis and consent.[15]

Both monastic and non-monastic teachers in my research attempted to counter the destabilizing force of the habitus of choice and the desire for preference. They cautioned their students about the "seductive delusion" that more choice means more freedom, attempted to bring the cultural preoccupation with personal preference to *doxa* (conscious awareness), and encouraged them to cultivate a *habitus of detachment* through the stabilizing effects of self-discipline and regular contemplative practice. As an example of such teachings, the Society of Saint John the Evangelist (2013) addressed the habitus of choice with an online video series, "A Framework for Freedom," in which individual monks discussed the liberating benefits of committing to *less* choice by adopting simpler ways through a rule of life. This message came also in an SSJE sermon about voluntary poverty. In it, Br. David Vryhof (2007) encouraged his congregation to consciously opt for less as a way to challenge and transform American norms, which he felt were directly responsible for economic inequality in the world. He said,

> It is as if we are on a moving walkway. If we do nothing, we will simply be carried along by the materialism and consumerism of our culture. And if we do nothing, nothing will change. We have to be willing to turn around, to walk against the flow of culture, to push back against the assumptions and values of a . . . culture that refuses to see that its actions are having and will continue to have severe consequences for the entire world.

The non-monastic teacher Cynthia Bourgeault also set a gentle challenge to forgo choice at a Wisdom School in West Virginia in 2012. She said after a period of meditation and chant the first morning, "See if over the next few days you can work towards letting go of preference. Everyone is great at meditating after their morning coffee. Try *not* minding if you don't get it. See what happens." Many participants responded with confused expressions and blank stares, suggesting that Cynthia's proposition to let go of choice was unfathomable for some. Usually combining a daily Benedictine rhythm of *ora et labora* (prayer and work) with the study of a single theological or philosophical book, Cynthia Bourgeault's Wisdom School teaching techniques, like those of the monastics with whom I worked, drew on the transformational potential of concentrated sparsity. SSJE's similar dedication to simplicity was illustrated in the interactive forum called "Brother, Give Us a Word," a daily digital teaching adapted from the fourth-century Desert Fathers' practice of offering a single word on which novices could contemplate. Such teachers employed the catalyst of a single drop to prompt students to reflect on habitual thoughts and behaviors, like the desire for choice, which they felt could undermine one's intentions to live a contemplative life.

The minimalism of seasoned teachers contrasted with the enthusiasm for choice of one first-time leader at a week-long retreat I attended at a Roman Catholic Benedictine monastery in July 2011. The novice teacher loaded up his students with a three-inch binder, "Field Guide for the Way of the Heart," which included readings from a copious number of Kabbalist, Sufi, Tao, Buddhist, Hindu, Eastern Orthodox, Western Christian, and scientific neurobiological theories and

theologies. He then plied participants with hours of diverse, disconnected practices. Though he undoubtedly had good intentions and was working under the
guidance of a former priest who had decades of experience leading retreats, the
fragmentation and overload of his approach sent a considerable number of participants into tailspins of distress and even anger. Sr. Elsa, a Roman Catholic nun
of about seventy, remarked that the novice teacher had not yet fully learned the
monastic way of simplicity.

The eager new teacher's uncritical submission to American habitus of choice
was not that unusual among non-monastics, however. A fair number of retreat
participants I met, especially those new to contemplative Christianity, buried
themselves in mountains of books and blogs, and followed numerous ways. They
seemed to have trouble following the direction of experienced teachers to shake
off personal preferences and a concern for crafting self-identity through spiritual
pursuits. While a fair number of teachers encouraged pluralistic, inter-religious
approaches, most also recommended moderation and a commitment to the principles and practices of kenosis and consent. They taught that following through
with one's intentions to "let go" liberated rather than constrained, and proffered
a contemplative maturity that allowed one to go more deeply into a chosen way.

The Everyday Struggle of Working toward Contemplative Transformation

Wait
What grows tall and strong must also grow slowly and deep,
or it will tumble . . . . Depth takes time. God has all the
time in the world. Though we live in a culture that so highly
values instant access to everything, at least in the spiritual
realm, we can only bear a little at a time.

—BR. CURTIS ALMQUIST, *SSJE*[16]

No one is expected to transform to full maturity as a contemplative Christian upon
first entry into the Antechapel. Teresa of Ávila (1979 [1588]), a sixteenth-century
Spanish Carmelite Counter-Reformation mystic and one of only four female doctors of the Roman Catholic Church, famously described how a commitment to
prayer is a lifelong process that prompts one toward increasing contemplative
awareness. We learned in Chapter 1 that her book, *The Interior Castle*, described
a stately house with seven "mansions" or rooms as a metaphor for progressive
stages of consent, learning, openness, and connection with the divine. People on
this chosen path commonly move back and forth between the rooms, she wrote,
depending on multiple factors, including degrees of personal commitment and
knowledge, as well as divine will; the way is rarely, if ever, a linear progression.

However, while some people's depth of entry will arrest in one or another of the rooms (some may never move beyond the Antechapel), a few will learn to dwell more consistently within the inner reaches, their contemplative maturity signified in attributes like humility, patience, forgiveness, hospitality, gratitude, service, and compassion.

The call to engage the high ideals and paradoxical knowledge of contemplative monastic ways is a tall order, not easily fulfilled without considerable support. Teachers and non-monastic students told me that choosing to follow a contemplative life inevitably included struggle along the way.[17] On top of the potential fragility of committing to an intellectual framework of openness, ambiguity, and paradox, they acknowledged that they also had to deal with the cultural pressures of living an alternative life; there were many distractions that sometimes conflicted with the ideals undergirding their primary chosen intentions, they said. Indeed, Ward Bauman wrote in his retreat house newsletter that strong American sociocultural currents are so deeply engrained that those who choose alternatives may not always recognize their persistent motivation by the very values they hope to transform. He suggested that many contemplatives continued to live unaware of an underlying cultural habitus, despite their efforts to unlearn and disarm it. Yet through a high-agency approach of self-examination, long-term commitment, and a regular rhythm of study and practice, they believed that learning and living contemplative ideals was possible over time.

Fr. Theodore, a Benedictine monk in my research, described this process as a slow movement toward the embodiment of chosen ideals and ways of being that emerged from a commitment to specific practices and intentions. Fr. Theodore said, "For the longest time, you dress like a monk and you do things monks do. You study and you pray and you work, but it all feels a bit like playacting. Then somewhere along the line, years later, you realize that you *are* a monk. It's no longer play."

Contemplative teachers have depicted this transformational process in a number of ways. Fr. Thomas Keating (2002a: 86) used the image of a dynamic "Spiral Staircase" to convey the idea that "awakening" was something that developed in multiple directions and through time. Cynthia Bourgeault (2004: 104) described transformation as a shift in the way one perceives: like switching a computer's operating system, she said, new ways of seeing came from a totally different way of processing information. Br. James Koester, SSJE (2011), called the changes in perspective as learning to "get it." "Getting it" meant that one could see that "this is not about you" and your enlightenment, said Br. James in a sermon, but rather "about bringing in the realm of God." Not unlike what Frances Trix (1993) described as "attunement" in the teaching relationship between a Sufi master and his student, or what Loïc Wacquant (2004) called a "sense of movement" that boxing coaches imparted to their apprentices in the gym, "getting it" meant that lessons have been absorbed to the point that first impulses rise from deeply embodied values and ways of being to which one has committed, rather than from received, unexamined social norms.

Drawing from my fieldwork, I have also crafted a model of perceptual agency that attempts to show how contemplative Christians intentionally used formalized and everyday practices to effect an ongoing process of transformation. My model highlights how contemplatives worked toward changing perception through a relationship of agency and what I call "intentional unknowing," a simultaneous practice of doing and not-doing, or action and contemplation, which had, in the words of one teacher, "alchemical" properties that could prompt "awakening to the divine" (see Diagram 4 in the back matter of this volume). With dedication and perseverance, this practice could potentially shift perception, they believed, so that one could better sense the divine and see the world and others in new ways, especially with love and compassion; it was a way that fostered the knowledge of "unitive being," they believed.

My model uses the analogy of a convection current's flow of heating and cooling water to depict the process of transforming perception through both habitus and doxa, which contemplative Christians saw as part of "awakening to the divine." Using the metaphors of "upward" for greater doxa or awareness and "downward" for habitus or unconscious assumptions and ways, the movement toward contemplative maturity ideally flowed in continuous circuits of critical thought and contemplative ways of being. The doxa that resulted from reflexivity could be redirected and subsumed toward a renewed habitus of being and thinking by way of the disciplined enactment of kenotic practices like meditation, they believed. The idea is that over time, chosen ideals and intentions could become the undercurrent of a "new normal" from which first impulses rise.[18]

This "convection current," which transforms perception, takes its "heat sources" from a combination of personal agency, intentional openness to the unknown, and what practitioners called divine will or "grace." The people with whom I worked emphasized that the divine was the source of all change, yet individuals also had an important role in their own transformation. This personal agency, however, was an ambiguous factor. Engaging intentional practices and critical thought was seen as a primary responsibility of the contemplative; by training themselves in apophatic practices like meditation, as well as pursuing intellectual study and self-examination, contemplatives worked to shift their thought habits and behaviors toward chosen ideals. Despite the critical importance of personal action, they asserted humility as a key tenet. That is, in their view, personal capability and responsibility coexisted with human frailty and ineffectuality. Indeed, the contemplative way they followed was a paradox of action and contemplation, of responsibility and surrender. Morphing habitus and consciousness came degree by degree through a combination of doing and not doing, they believed, effecting subtle or substantial changes with each cycle of ascent and descent.

This rather intensive process of reforming one's habitus to monastic sensibilities and ways of being was difficult enough for residents of a monastery, as attested by SSJE's ritualized commitment of support in the Clothing ceremony for their new novice, Jeremy. However, the challenges were exponential for non-monastics, who often had little access to social-structural stability like that provided in a residential community. One of the primary differences between monastics and non-monastics was the level of social support for their pursuit of this alternative way of life. Besides having dedicated mentors and teachers, people who lived in the residential communities of monasteries had the everyday reinforcement of a like-intentioned and like-practicing community, which builds its life around the monastic Daily Office—that is, a group rhythm of Benedictine *ora et labora*, or prayer and work. Even when one falters, the rhythm of the community persists, and one is expected to take part whether one feels like it or not.

By contrast, many non-monastics did not have a physical, face-to-face community that practiced in the contemplative way, even if they belonged to church parishes (cf. Hann and Goltz 2010: 16–17). Despite the use of virtual communications to maintain a network of support, the non-gathered community's geographic scattering added to the already considerable challenge of learning and keeping a contemplative way of life. More than two-thirds of those who sent me ejournals described difficulties with keeping a consistent rhythm of Centering Prayer and other contemplative practices over the six-month period of writing. We have already seen this difficulty in Simon's ejournal contribution. Another ejournaler, AJ, was similarly transparent about the strain of her ongoing efforts to sustain a contemplative life. Though she often felt weighed down by the demands of her choices, she was nevertheless grateful for an inner tenacity that made her "always want to return if I stray." In an ejournal entry, she said, "I'm trying to live somewhat monastically in the world. I'm sure being in a monastery has lots of challenges, but . . . one of the challenges [of living] outside is that no one cares whether I do CP twice a day or keep my mind on God . . . . It's up to me, every day, to make it happen . . . . It is just me making my own schedule and priorities every day."[19]

Maggie also followed a solitary, self-directed contemplative daily rhythm. She wrote in her ejournal that she had lost the rhythm by inadvertently letting her practice slide over the Christmas holidays. "I let go of my usual 40 minute morning, 20 minute late afternoon or evening centering prayer, and only maintained a thread to it," she wrote. "Often I would touch in and do the prayer, but not in the way of my daily ritual. When I don't do it I miss it so." Part of Maggie's difficulty, like Simon's, was a feeling of isolation. Maggie felt very much at odds with her extended family. Her mother was cynical and judgmental about Christianity, and all but one of her siblings had no interest. They lived in an entirely different world from her, she wrote. Visiting her sisters in Arizona over Christmas brought up "the old history of being the weird and strange one, a label that comes with a long list of qualities that separated me from the family, and culminated in an old feeling of wanting to disappear." Feelings of isolation sometimes made keeping her intention difficult.

Liz, a young mother who organized and managed a fair-wage, cooperative cut-and-sew garment factory for immigrant women in North Carolina, also felt the pressure of the time, responsibility, and self-discipline it took to keep on track. Her considerable consternation at being pulled in too many directions was clear when she wrote in her ejournal, "How does the contemplative life play out in the first half of life—when there are children to raise, mortgages to pay, studies to be attended to. I understand why monks and nuns are single. It makes a lot of sense. But when you're called to be a momma and a worker and feel a longing for God that needs silence and stillness, . . . what do you do with all these pieces of yourself?"

Encountering this kind of discouragement and exasperation in his many years of teaching, Ward Bauman (2013a) described the depth of the dilemma as expressed by one man on a retreat:

> During an open discussion period, a person who was deeply involved in . . . spiritual formation made an honest, hard confession. "I am not up to this," he said. "This spiritual work demands more of me than I can do. I just can't do it." This was a turning point for everyone in the group. I felt the discouragement we all feel when we look at the contradictions in our lives in light of Jesus' own requirements for discipleship. And we each had to admit that we probably weren't up to the task.

These people's comments are telling. They illustrate how difficult it was for many practitioners to keep to the contemplative path outside of a monastery. Many felt isolated from other practitioners and had little or no face-to-face interaction with like-minded others. They felt a dearth of community support, which could have helped them sustain contemplative practices and ideals while they lived life "in the world," dealing with multiple social responsibilities, busy working lives, and the distractions of too much choice. The lack of community sometimes manifested in a loss of resolve and purpose, occasionally overwhelming even long-time practitioners to the point of withdrawal.

Stability in a Pluralistic World: The "Difficult and Costly Choice" of Discipline and Practice

How then did people persist in working toward a contemplative Christian life given the high demands of monastic ideals and the potential for disillusionment, especially when one lived outside of a supportive community? R. M. Kanter

(1968: 501–502, 1972) published a study that showed how social structures and their associated belief systems, ritual practices, and austerities were the "object of commitment" and the stabilizing force of utopian societies. In the loose affiliations of non-gathered contemplative Christians, we see a different picture. Rather than opting for strong social organization or the comforting boundaries of dogmatic constraints, non-monastic contemplative Christians turned to the steadying effects of discipline and practice. The structure of practice, including formal ritual and the ritualization of everyday life, was the basis of their stability (cf. Seligman and Weller 2012).

By contrast, many of the teachers in my research were monastics or ordained priests committed to church organizations. Nevertheless, none insisted on institutional adherence. Rather, they offered support to non-gathered, non-monastic contemplatives by promoting practice as an alternative to social structures like a monastery. Using a variety of electronic and print media, as well as face-to-face encounters, contemplative teachers taught specific, practical strategies for managing the sometimes hard reality of living social, philosophical, and religious alternatives. Their tools—like keeping a personal rule of life, subscribing to a daily rhythm of work and prayer, and acting in the service of others—were contemporary adaptations of historical Christian monastic disciplines, particularly those modeled on the 1,500-year-old Benedictine tradition.[20]

In the twenty-first-century context of the United States, contemplatives learned disciplined practice as a way to liberate themselves from unwanted habitual thoughts and behaviors. As suggested by the title of SSJE's teaching series, "A Framework to Freedom," contemplative Christians did not see discipline as an imposition of hierarchical authority, but rather as a method that fostered the capacity to follow demanding ideals. Contemporary Americans were generally under no social structural, legal, or cultural obligation to take on disciplined life as a Christian contemplative. As Warner (1993) proposed, Americans' participation in religion is largely voluntary, based principally on choice rather than governmental or church enforcement. Undoubtedly the Roman Catholic Church still retained some moral authority over its membership, even in the United States, and the leaders of Protestant denominations likely had some influence on the ground, as would family and friends. Even so, among contemplatives who had already strayed from more common forms of church life in America, the choice to follow an alternative religious path of contemplative discipline did not much derive from external impositions. Indeed, they saw the choice and commitment to keep a disciplined practice, though arduous at times, as a way to refine and concentrate their chosen intentions. Discipline in this context was seen primarily as a positive force, which constituted power *to* the individual, rather than a Foucauldian-style power *over* the individual (Foucault 1979).[21]

An example of one non-monastic who had learned the positive power of discipline and the steadying force of practice, Andrew described in his ejournal how monastic methods had helped him. Having learned some practical strategies from contemplative teachers over the fifteen years he had been practicing Centering Prayer and other contemplative techniques, he wrote during a period of instability when his marriage broke up and he moved across the country for a new job, "For the aspects of my contemplative life that aren't going the way I want them to, I know the answer is to put them on my schedule and follow through with them. Not in an unbending way, but in a 'this is what I want and I'm going to give myself these gifts' way." Andrew's perspective was that monastic-style discipline stabilized his voluntary choice to follow a contemplative life.

There were quite a number of "monastic tools" from which to choose. All of them sought to keep practitioners on the main goal: to work toward a life of compassion and love, which they said rises out of an intensifying awareness of one's relationship with the divine and with all creation. The primary tool was adopting a rule of life with its regular rhythm of prayer and work. Two others that were prevalent among the people with whom I worked were keeping a sense of humor and serving others, both of which similarly sought to turn practitioners' focus away from their own concerns and to foster a hospitable and caring demeanor.

Rule of Life

First we look at rules of life. Emerging centuries ago in early Christian communities, rules provided a sustaining rhythm that helped practitioners focus their chosen contemplative intentions, even in a pluralistic environment. Early founders of Christian monasticism had concerns about the zeal of those called to a religious life. In the sixth century, for example, Benedict of Nursia crafted the "middle way" of a communal rule of life in an effort to moderate the potential self-focus of religious ardor. His rule was not the first, but it has been the most influential in the history of Western Christianity. Benedict believed that community and a daily rhythm of practice could help temper the potential for individual self-centeredness and competitive asceticism in contemplative life. Though austere by current American norms, the *Rule of Saint Benedict* (2011) was moderate by the ascetical, martyr-oriented standards of early Christianity, allowing for comparatively adequate food, clothing, shelter, and rest in the daily mix of *ora et labora* (Chadwick 1993: 178–183).[22]

The stability that preoccupied St. Benedict was also a major concern for present-day American teachers of contemplative Christianity. Like Benedict, they recognized how easily the unmitigated passions of individuals could become an "egoic drive" for euphoric spiritual experiences and status. As Br. James Koester

(2011) reminded his congregation, "this is not about you, but about bringing in the realm of God." Attempting to counter the potential for an emotion-driven focus on "enlightenment" or "personal salvation," both monastic and non-monastic contemplative teachers with whom I worked encouraged their students toward adopting a rule of life, which emphasized regularity, rhythm, accountability, and service to others.[23]

Adopting a rule outside of monastic communities was not that straightforward, however. Indeed, most non-monastics had little exposure to rules of life when they first entered the Antechapel. SSJE (1997: xii–xvii), which undertook a communal process of revising their own rule in the 1980s and 1990s, helped familiarize their non-monastic adherents with the idea of a personal rule. They explained that, rather than being a restrictive list of uncompromising dictates, "rule" in the monastic context comes from the Latin *regula*, a word that suggests "a way of . . . *regularizing* our lives so that we can stay on the path we have set out for ourselves. A rule is like a trellis which offers support and guidance for a plant, helping it to grow in a certain direction" (Vryhof nd-a; emphasis in original).

While monastic communities usually had established rules of life, there were few models that were suited to the non-gathered community of American Christian contemplatives.[24] Teachers of contemplative Christianity recognized that established rules of life, like the *Rule of Saint Benedict*, were too demanding and inflexible for most people outside the monastery. Hence, some encouraged adherents to create their own rules. For example, the organization Contemplative Outreach offered assistance to non-monastics through its website and its publications, such as *Discipline of Prayer* (Best 2006), a workbook from its two-year distance learning Contemplative Life Program. An elegant, minimalistic booklet set with sepia-toned photographs and quotations from Christian mystics, *Discipline of Prayer* prompts readers to consider the ideals of Christian contemplation, the varieties of prayer types, and aspects of social and working life to help them discern a regular practice and personal rule that would be best suited to their particular life contexts. The authors call rules "a way of life to a heart of fire" and "a pattern of daily actions chosen" with the intention of "the continuous remembrance of God." Not until the fortieth and final day of the exercise do the authors leave readers to "[w]rite a simple Rule of Life for yourself. Know it will develop and change over time" (Best 2006: 88, 96).

At SSJE, Br. David Vryhof (nd-a) led workshops based on *Living Intentionally*, a booklet of exercises he authored that outlines steps people could follow to discern a personal rule of life. Br. David reminded his students of the central purpose of such an endeavor: "Designing a rule is not an end in itself, but rather a means to an end: namely, to live our lives for God with purpose and intention." He cautioned people to write rules that they could actually follow. Rules could be prescriptive, outlining daily practices and social responsibilities, and could also describe and identify the foundational principles and philosophies that underlie one's desire to live an intentional life. A serious commitment to contemplative life can be "a difficult and costly choice," Br. David Vryhof (nd-b) wrote. For those attempting to follow this way without the strong structural support of a monastic community, he said, "We strongly recommend that you keep [your rule] *simple*, and that the goals you set be *realistic and achievable* . . . . Like any spiritual discipline, adopting a rule should *help* you to live more faithfully" (nd-a; emphasis in original). If a rule was so idealistic and demanding as to be beyond one's capacity, it would soon be forgotten like so many New Year's resolutions, he said.[25]

A number of non-monastic contemplatives who wrote ejournals for me recognized the stabilizing and transformational potential of keeping an intentional prayer schedule and developing a personal rule. In a May 2012 ejournal entry, for example, Brigid told a story about how she found a way to commit to a daily rhythm of contemplative practices after realizing that her desire to commit to twice-daily periods of Centering Prayer and other practices like t'ai chi/qigong and *lectio divina* was frequently thwarted by the demands of a busy work and home life. She wrote,

> There were many distractions daily that arose . . . . One day, following a morning when I had chosen to answer the phone and meet a friend for tea instead of spending time in meditation, I was moved to drive to the store and purchase a pink marker . . . . I spent an hour going through my planner, prayerfully placing a pink "X" on each day's square—a reminder that this was sacred time (already scheduled) for being with my Beloved in prayer. Nowadays, when the phone rings or an email arrives asking for my time, I glance at my calendar and reply, "I'm sorry. I already have something on my calendar."

Following in the spirit of the Benedictine Daily Office, Brigid saw how a lack of commitment to a daily rhythm contributed to the erratic nature of her meditation and prayer practices. She viewed discipline as a positive choice, noting that "when I say 'yes' to one thing (spiritual practice), I am also saying 'no' to other things (whatever it was that I filled my time with previously). I continue to say 'yes' to spiritual practice, over and over and over. What is unnecessary in my life falls away." Thus, she effectively chose *not* to choose by restricting her options. Brigid's intentional method illustrates how Thomas Keating's principle of "consenting to the divine" can work in people's everyday lives.

Over a period of a year, Brigid discerned her call to become a Roman Catholic Benedictine oblate, studied the *Rule of Saint Benedict*, and developed her own personal rule, as required for her affiliation to the Wisconsin Benedictine monastery into which she was received. Following Benedict's guidance to "[l]isten with the ear of the heart," she said, "A Rule is not so much written as listened for." Brigid eventually came to a poetic and evocative statement of intent for a contemplative outlook in life, what she called "a little rule," to be observed in conjunction with the far more directive Benedictine rule:

> Be gentle with yourself and others.
> See the moss that grows in silent and unexpected places.
> Pray the space that lies between.
> And, through all, learn to love.

After becoming a spiritual director, Brigid herself taught the merits of intentional practice and rules of life, helping other non-monastics to discern their own rules.

AJ, another ejournaler, had a far more prescriptive approach in her personal rule. During a period of frustration, she went on a Jesuit retreat and had several talks with her spiritual director about not judging herself too harshly against monastic standards. AJ then crafted eleven practical points for an intentional contemplative life, which she felt realistically suited her personal situation of living alone with a physical disability and having grown up in a demanding but emotionally unsupportive Italian-American Roman Catholic household. In one of her ejournal entries, she outlined her rule like this:

1. Plan for a balance of life responsibilities with playtime, with full knowledge of your physical capacities, and be fully present to each.
2. Live in the present: live the life you have now, not the one you had, think you are supposed to have, or want in the future.
3. Don't try to make the house a monastery. Enjoy simplicity, solitude, and silence along with the opportunities of a secular life.
4. Don't procrastinate.
5. Consciously practice being present in everyday tasks just as you do during spiritual practice. Let everything be a doorway to God.
6. Take complete days off to play, relax, and be free.
7. Don't punish yourself for not living every day like you're on a strict ascetic retreat.
8. Let your body rest in God.
9. Go on retreat regularly.
10. Trust your love of God and commitment to the spiritual path. Stop watching over yourself with a big judgment stick and just live your deep knowing every day.
11. Simplify as best you can, while being consistently responsible to what you haven't let go of yet.[26]

A few weeks later, AJ refined these points with her optimistic, self-affirming, and exuberant "Radical Happiness Manifesto," a statement that made clear the primacy of overt intention, relationality, and self-consciously alternative choices:

I live a far-reaching, thorough, and fundamental embrace
of contentment and satisfaction, by consciously choosing
enlivening activities, habits, practices, and life-affirming relationships.
My lifestyle encourages personal and community resilience, interdependence,
health and wellbeing, and the deepening of spirit.
My choices enrich me, my community, and the Earth
and free me from my fear-based decisions
and the oppressive consumer culture's degradation
of mind, body, spirit, and Earth.
Through harmony with the Earth and my True Nature,
my life-path completely cures me of dissatisfaction with myself and others,
constant striving, loneliness, neediness, lack, insecurity, envy, longing, shame,
regret,
judgment of self and others, indecision, and emotional woundedness.
I emanate connectedness, unity, groundedness, contentment, joy, creativity,
gratitude, love, and fulfillment.

(italics in original)

Benedict of Nursia may not have recognized his own rule in AJ's manifesto. Indeed, the idea of a *personal* rule rather than a *collective* rule is very much a product of a post-Reformation individualist notion of religiosity. Nevertheless, the sociocultural diversity in pluralistic societies meant that individuals were faced with different kinds of obstacles to effectively following a contemplative path. Mentors knew that personal rules, if crafted in a spirit of service and "letting go of self," assisted people greatly in keeping their intentions. Living in a world of apparently endless choices, the people with whom I did research found that keeping a rule—whether collective, personal, or a combination of both—was a stabilizing force in their commitments to work toward contemplative alternatives.

Humor

Humor, a second "monastic tool" that helped stabilize contemplative Christian life, was not so much an overt form of discipline as an everyday rhetorical technique. Contemplative Christians often used humor to check any inclination toward self-centered spirituality and to lighten a sometimes rigorous way. Teachers sometimes made fun of themselves or jested good-naturedly about people's tendency to take themselves too seriously. We saw, for example, how Sandra Mattheson, the spiritual director from the Southwest, posted a *New Yorker* cartoon about Reality TV–style contemplation to satirize the trouble people had taking on the foundational values of humility and detachment in the American context. Br. David Vryhof (2013) also offered a good example in a sermon that opened with a story about the trials of monastic life. Br. David said,

> A young novice once approached an elderly monk, asking if he could speak with him about his prayer and life in the monastery. The old man consented. Things had not been easy, the young man admitted. His prayer often felt aimless and dry, he had underestimated the challenges of living in community, and he was struggling with loneliness and countless distractions. "Ah, yes," said the old monk, "the first fifty years or so are the hardest, but it gets easier after that."

The congregation broke into laughter at the idea that the contemplative road was just as long and embattled for monks as for people outside the monastery.

Fr. Carl Arico from Contemplative Outreach was well known in the Centering Prayer community for his amusing perspectives on the demands of reforming oneself to a contemplative sensibility. A "secular" (that is, non-monastic) Roman Catholic priest, Fr. Carl frequently made jokes during his teaching sessions at a retreat in the Catskill Mountains of New York State. There he told stories that played off people's tendency to judge. One described how hordes of people have come to him over the years with the complaint, "I could be a saint—if it weren't for *other people!*" He looked out at the group sardonically and said, "Remember: people have to put up with you, too."

At one of the thrice-daily Centering Prayer sessions, Fr. Carl noticed that some of us sat on meditation cushions and stools rather than chairs. He launched into a story about how at one of the first retreats he attended with Fr. Thomas Keating, he had followed other participants' example of taking up a yogic pose during meditation. He said that by the fourth day he was in excruciating pain, but he told himself, "I'm a priest. I ought to be able to do this. I have to keep up with the others!" He eventually confided in Fr. Thomas, who said simply, "Why don't you sit in a chair?" Fr. Carl protested that if the others could do it, so should he. Fr. Thomas just looked at him, raised his eyebrows, and said again, "Why don't you sit in a chair?" The next day, Fr. Carl, feeling like a failure, sat in a chair. "That meditation was endless: *Ya-da, ya-da, ya-da* in my head about all my faults." At the next session, four others were sitting in chairs, and more each time thereafter. "That was a lesson in humility," said Fr. Carl. Reminiscent of Sandra Mattheson's cartoon posting, he said, "Meditation isn't about keeping up with the Joneses; it isn't a competitive sport." Fr. Carl reiterated the need for forgiveness of both oneself and others by saying that we need to erase the mantra, "Everything I do I need to do perfectly," and replace it with "Everything I do I need to do *lovingly*."[27]

Fr. Carl Arico would likely have appreciated some of the entries Zak wrote in his ejournal. Zak noted that he greatly depended on humor to survive the isolation and spiritual malaise he has felt from time to time, wittily described in his metaphor of "Abrahamic Pinball" recounted in Chapter 1. He again showed playful self-mockery in his response to my suggestion that he should try publishing the thoughtful, amusing reflections he wrote for my research. Zak asked incredulously, "Who would read such a thing?" but then offered a few prospective titles, including "The Know-it-all's Guide to *The Cloud of Unknowing*," "Spiritual ABCs of Doing What You Please," and "How to Become Egoless . . . like ME!"

I was once at the center of such ego-checking humor at a Wisdom School in 2012 when I fussed a little too much about setting up a chapel for liturgy. My concern about just the right orientation of the Coptic cross and icons to the architectural layout of narthex and side chapels caused some eye rolling. It also inspired Cynthia Bourgeault and the retreat's music leader, Helen Daly, to begin chanting on the brand names of drugs for obsessive-compulsive disorder.

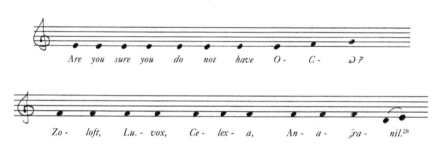

That definitely got me laughing about my own seriousness. For me and others, the "discipline" of humor and jest was an effective tool to help step back from self-importance and remember that the point was, as Fr. Carl Arico said, not so much working toward a human's-eye-view of perfection as acting with love.

Service

Social action and serving others, the third "monastic tool" I examine, shifted the focus away from individual spiritual concerns to the greater good, and at the same time helped to stabilize practitioners' choices to live contemplatively. As with humor and the discipline of a rule of life, contemplatives believed that kenosis must be the underlying principle of contemplative service and social action, which clearly showed that "letting go" did not mean "giving up" or acting passively in regards to human relations and social justice.

Br. Tom Shaw, SSJE (2013), who was the Bishop of the Episcopal Diocese
of Massachusetts from 1995 to 2014, felt that active service was an indicator of
grounded Christian practice. In a sermon, he said,

> It is easy to become overly concerned about our own piety. Yet prayer
> should lead us to activism. I knew a Roman Catholic spiritual director who
> used to teach that if somebody came to you for spiritual direction and, after
> eighteen months, still was not involved in any kind of active work of recon-
> ciliation in society, their prayer life had failed them.

Br. Tom Shaw thus taught that service and reconciliation are integral to contemplative life.[29]

Indeed, the co-observance of prayer practices and social action was so foundational to the Christian contemplative way of life that the Roman Catholic
Franciscan priest Richard Rohr, OFM, named his institution (in Albuquerque,
New Mexico) the Center for Action and Contemplation. The institution's mission statement said that the organization worked to encourage "actions of justice
rooted in prayer" with the intention of "teaching the transformation of human
consciousness through contemplation, and equipping people to be instruments
of peaceful change in the world."[30]

The organization Contemplative Outreach also taught the central importance
of social action. Contemplative Service, one of the forty-day practice booklets from
CO's Contemplative Life Program, guided people to approach service itself as a
form of prayer. Wrote the author and Contemplative Outreach president, Gail
Fitzpatrick-Hopler (2006: 8–9),

> Contemplative service is the way one consents and responds to the
> movement of the Indwelling Trinity in the interactions of everyday
> life, . . . according to one's gifts and calling within our family, work, com-
> munity and our global society . . . . Grounded in our daily discipline of
> Centering Prayer . . . and other contemplative practices, [contemplative
> service] is both prayer and action . . . . [It] is a manifestation of an inte-
> rior call—a prompting from the Spirit to activate our gifts and talents for
> the benefit of family, community, organizations or humanity. In this con-
> text, . . . service is more than helping or doing a task. It is a way of being—a
> disposition of the heart, with no beginning and no end.

In its mature form, added Fitzpatrick-Hopler, contemplative service is action and
"a way of being" that rises out of a connection to the divine, rather than a self-
serving imposition of one's goodness upon others, and functions on an idea that
working life and prayer life were not dichotomous, but integral partners. Action

in the world from their perspective is thus no less an avenue to "divine presence" than formalized contemplative prayer practices. Such teachings reveal that theoretical notions of segregated and dichotomized fields of sacred and profane inadequately depict how this variety of American Christians actually lved and worked toward what they called a "contemplative maturity" that acknowledged the divine in every aspect of life (cf. Ammerman 2007, 2014; McDannell 1995; Mahmood 2005; McGuire 2008; Seligman and Weller 2012; Turner 2012).

The monasteries at which I did research modeled a relationship between prayer and social action as being primary and essential.[31] Life at the SSJE monastery rested on a balance of *ora et labora*, in both individual and communal expressions. Alongside their daily schedule of personal contemplation and five communal liturgies, *The Rule of the Society of Saint John the Evangelist* (1997: 62–63) also delineated several aspects of the community's mission to serve, including teaching, offering hospitality, healing, giving spiritual direction, crafting liturgies and sermons, and serving "the deprived and oppressed" through social justice activities. Some of the monks' "special ventures in mission" at the time I did research included teaching at seminaries in North America and Africa; experimenting with Buddhist-Christian-inspired "Green Monasticism" and ecological farming techniques at Emery House, SSJE's country retreat (Mitchell and Skudlarek 2010); working on grassroots peace initiatives like Kids for Peace (both in North America and Palestine/Israel);[32] leading pilgrimages in Israel/Palestine and Egypt; creating online spiritual resources; and working with the deaf, homeless and HIV/AIDS communities in the Boston area.

Many non-monastic adherents of contemplative Christianity with whom I worked followed the example of this kind of service, integrating social action with contemplative prayer practices to various degrees. Some took the importance of service very seriously and had pursued careers in the helping professions. Among those with whom I did research were psychotherapists, teachers, addiction counselors, parish priests, managers of labor cooperatives, prison workers, nurses, occupational therapists, hospital chaplains, doctors, and spiritual directors.

Jennifer, for example, was a doctoral student at Harvard University who was considering a call to the priesthood in the Episcopal Church. She was actively involved as a "Protest Chaplain" at Occupy Wall Street and was one of the main organizers of Occupy Boston, a protest camp set up in 2011 to rally against homelessness, poverty, and the fiscal and social irresponsibility of American financial institutions.[33]

Sharon, a pediatrician from the Midwest, allotted much of her yearly vacation time for volunteer service in Haiti. Describing this voluntarism in her ejournal as "one of the fruits of my spiritual work," Sharon had been going to Haiti twice a year since 2006 to treat children and had established a year-round mobile clinic for two communities that would otherwise have had no access to health care. She said that having the courage to do this work was quite out of character for her. Sharon wrote in her ejournal, "I tell people that I am fearless in Haiti, not because I'm really a fearless person at all, but because there I feel in tune with God and my own inner wisdom."

Some practitioners worked at tasks that were not personally gratifying, but which they felt gave them an opportunity to consciously foster "divine presence" in environments of deprivation. At a Wisdom School in West Virginia, Charlotte told the group how she had been a social worker for many years, but had decided to take a management position at a municipal transit authority, the "Boston T," because she felt called to work directly among the kind of people she had previously served as a counselor. Charlotte seemed a little downcast by some of the difficulties she faced; she said that many of the people with whom she worked in that context were disempowered or abusive and angry, and though she found it extremely challenging, Charlotte spent her time consciously attempting to bring the divine into their midst by "staying present" and modeling respectful behavior that honored the dignity of others. The Wisdom School teacher, Cynthia Bourgeault, framed Charlotte's intentional work in both Christian and Buddhist terms, as a practice of sacrificing one's own desires for personal happiness in order to serve in the interest of a greater good. She called Charlotte "the bodhisat-tva of the T."

Some, however, really enjoyed the service they offered others. Having retired from his advertising executive position a few years before, Zak made volunteer service an integral part of his weekly round of practice by adopting a registered therapy dog, Sophie. He regularly took her on visits to "wonderful people" at places like nursing homes, a children's hospital, a psychiatric hospital, and an HIV/AIDS hospice. "My Therapy Dog visiting schedule is part of my practice," he wrote in his ejournal. Several times a week after his morning meditation and a run, Zak and Sophie would go to their Midwestern city's Roman Catholic cathedral to silently pray among the "regulars to whom I never speak" and pay homage at the chapel of St. Francis, the patron saint of animals. Zak wrote, "My prayer is always the same . . . to make me a channel, a conduit for God's will. May I be a healing presence to everyone I encounter at the hospital today."

In another ejournal entry, Zak offered a description that succinctly outlined how his work with Sophie attempted to combine service, selflessness, contemplation, and a monastic sensibility in his desire to bring divine "openness" and healing into the world:

In one of his books, Father Keating wrote about Contemplation being a great river bound by the two banks of worship and some kind of service to one's fellow human beings. One needs the outside practices of worship and service to shore up the flow of Contemplation. Sophie allows me to be of some service "out there." She is my Trojan Horse. I follow her into places I would never be able to go otherwise and meet people I would never encounter without her "leadership." My very focused intent is to bring a humble healing presence into the places we visit and the lives of the people we meet. I never speak of this intent to anyone and, of course, I don't in any way act "spiritual" or try to convert anyone, or any such nonsense. I only try to bring a heartfelt openness wherever we go and I have faith that somehow we are a channel for peace, healing, joy.

CONTEMPLATIVE CHRISTIAN TOOLS like service to others, humor, and a rule of life were varieties of discipline that helped people in the Antechapel learn how to stabilize chosen intentions. The way they integrated multiple spheres of a pluralistic society with a contemplative demeanor illustrates how social theories that dichotomize sacred and profane do not adequately portray the ideas and practices of this movement. Teachers guided both newcomers and old hands to learn humility and to "let go" of their impulses toward an eros of acquisition, achievement, and personal preferences. Yet even with their intentional narrowing of scope, American contemplatives sought to live with an openness and an appreciation for ambiguity that was compatible with life in a complex, multifaceted, globalized society. Even so, the Antechapel was very much a place of beginnings. Adherents began to deepen their knowledge as they persisted with contemplative practices. In Grille, the chapter that follows, we explore how contemplative Christians were inspired by Benedictine-style hospitality to embody the paradox that pairs humility and openness with the monastic practices of enclosure, silence, and solitude.

Photograph courtesy of SSJE.

3

Grille

SILENCE AND SECLUSION: CONTEMPLATIVE
ENVIRONMENTS OF INTERIORITY AND RECEPTIVITY

*The Grille is the monastery chapel's wrought-iron boundary that
cloisters a distinctive, intentional way of life. It creates a strong
container that allows those who dwell within to practice with
rigor and attention. Yet the Grille also reveals a surprising relationship between enclosure and hospitality. It invites those who
live on the other side to wonder, to peer in, and to listen for the
silence and sound that flow through the iron screen. The Grille
is a porous boundary that monastics open and close with care,
allowing them to keep attention and silence while also extending
a hand in welcome.*

A brother came to a hermit: and as he was taking his leave, he said,
"Forgive me, Abba, for preventing you from keeping your rule."
The hermit answered, "My rule is to welcome you with hospitality,
and to send you on your way in peace."

—SAYINGS OF THE DESERT FATHERS

ONLY A FEW had arrived to join the monks for the Noonday Office on a rainy week-day in March. The Brother Sacristan approached with a ring of keys and opened the wrought-iron grille, inviting me and the other guests to enter. We moved through the threshold between the antechapel and the chapel, bowed to the altar, and found a seat somewhere other than the monks' resident choir stalls. A long-time adherent to the monastery, Diane remained in the antechapel, sitting with eyes closed, alone and still. The rest of the monks made their way to their assigned places and set up their Daily Office books on the oak choir desks. Some quietly looked over slips of paper with the antiphons and responses assigned specifically to that date in the liturgical calendar. In an environment of stone, light, wood, and wrought iron, all rose with the Superior, then chanted, kept silence, spoke, and sang in unison or antiphonally.

This briefest of the daily offices concluded with the monks filing out of the choir stalls and processing toward the sanctuary two by two, faces impassive, looking at no one. They bowed at the altar, turned right, and passed through the door of the statio, disappearing into the monastic enclosure. The few guests stood silently watching their progress, then promptly returned their black-bound Office books to the shelves in their choir stalls, acknowledged the altar, and made their way out in the opposite direction through the grille's lattice of iron bars.

The Brother Sacristan reappeared with his keys. Quietly noting whether all had found their way to the other side, he secured the bottom latch of one of the grille's double doors, then swung closed its mate. With an open palm, he pressed the lock casement shut, releasing an emphatic *click* that in so silent a space reverberated around the granite walls. He disappeared once again into the enclosure.

I took a chair near Diane, who was still sitting with closed eyes in the antechapel. She surfaced in another ten minutes or so. Together we left the chapel, dipping our right hands into the stoup to collect a little holy water with which to cross ourselves. Once through the great oak doors of the portico and out among the robust movement of traffic, rowers, and dog walkers, Diane looked out at the river and mused, "You know, the sound of the gate closing—that 'click'?—it used to really startle me after being so deep into the silence. It really disturbed me. I'm used to it now though. Now I understand why they do it."

BENEDICTINE-STYLE HOSPITALITY IS one of the key tenets of contemplative Christianity. Even so, hospitality exists in relation to environments of interiority that do not always feel friendly or welcoming to those who have been raised in American society. In contrast to the emphasis in Chapter 2 on the outward monastic impulse to teach alternative values and sensibilities and to form and support community, here the ethnographic story turns toward the quietude of contemplation, particularly to how silence and seclusion can be enacted as both shelter and welcome. Environments of interiority, including silence, solitude, and enclosure, supported and protected an unusual lifeway that required a great deal of commitment, intentionality, and determination. Silence and seclusion are "strong containers," said one contemplative teacher; they impart a gravitas that provides a sustaining foundation for demanding alternatives. Yet rather than encouraging isolation from society, adepts taught and modeled the practice of contemplative silence, solitude, and enclosure as an alternate form of sociality and an empowering, transformative discipline that balanced the seemingly paradoxical principles of hospitality and interiority.[1]

Practices of interiority like seclusion and silence are notoriously difficult to interpret, especially across a cultural divide (Sajavaara and Lehtonen 1997). From the other side of the monastic grille or meditation-room door, an outsider may not easily perceive the potentially receptive gesture of contemplation, for interiority may appear to be a way of shutting others out, and it can indeed be a way of exclusion, depending in part upon the intentionality of the actors. Followers of contemplation found principles of interiority some of the hardest to learn and to keep, given their contrast with some common American sensibilities, like freedom of expression and talk-based friendliness (Bellah 1985; Hall and Lindholm 1999; Sampson 2003; Taylor 1989). When they first approached the Grille, some of the people with whom I worked found silence and seclusion daunting, isolating, and oppressive, even though, from the monastic perspective, they were ideally intended to be empowering forms of discipline.[2]

Despite monastic ideals, exclusivity did occasionally override hospitality among the Christian contemplatives with whom I worked. Perhaps because of their lesser access to social structural means of interiority like a physical cloister and communal frameworks of silence, exclusivist tendencies among a small sector of non-monastics in my research sometimes surfaced in their claims that the contemplative life was a higher calling that was not for everyone. In monasteries, both physical and behavioral boundaries overtly distinguished member from guest. Yet monks offered openings to their cloistered lives through liturgies, retreats, spiritual direction, and, at some monasteries, even social gatherings like communal meals and seasonal celebrations.

Ultimately, the line between exclusivity and hospitality in interiorized environments rested more on intention than outward gesture. Silence and seclusion could be a means of division, like a monastic chapel's iron grille, which physically segregates guests from members, or they could be a form of receptivity, acknowledgment, and welcome. This dialogical relationship between enclosure and hospitality becomes particularly clear in this chapter's final ethnographic sketch of a Maundy Thursday vigil in the monastic chapel of the Society of Saint John the Evangelist (SSJE). The events of that night in 2010 illustrate the play between openness and restriction, revealing how monasteries, even those that are cloistered, are *porous* rather than fully sealed. Indeed, while they may seem exclusive to the unpracticed eye, the monasteries at which I worked breathed an integrated rhythm of interiority and receptivity, creating a dynamic relationship between seclusion, silence, and hospitality that allowed the extension of a welcome through the grille.

QUESTIONS ABOUT INWARD focus, acceptance of others, and outright exclusion came up in a sermon given by Br. Robert L'Esperance, SSJE (2013a). His concerns are particularly interesting given that they came from one who lived in the environment of a semi-cloistered monastery.[3] Addressing the benefits and pitfalls of the human propensity toward in-group identification, Br. Robert said, "All

communities need symbols, practices, sacred song, and place." In his own community, he said, this included "the black habit, our daily rising at an early hour to
chant the monastic office together in this place, our sacrosanct hour of meditative
prayer, our common rule of life." While such markers help "to establish us and fix
us in the world we live in," Br. Robert L'Esperance acknowledged that

> there is a problem when we find ourselves stuck in that identity and unable
> to move on, . . . confusing the larger universal truths with . . . our group's
> mores and social preferences. Or even worse, when we limit our vision
> of the Truth to our particular way of viewing God's nature or our group's
> preferred ways of praying and worshipping.

In other words, clinging to one's identity—even an identity that one feels is an
expression of living well and faithfully—falls short of the monastic principle of
hospitality. Br. Robert concluded, "I am more and more convinced through my
own prayer, living, reading and study that Jesus came preaching a gospel that challenges . . . these constructs" about inclusivity and exclusivity. Rather, he invited
people "to move to a place that allows us to begin to live and breathe within a way
of seeing . . . that [is] not just limited to our particular group or identity but to
something capable of embracing more universal patterns of seeing and believing."

Even in the semi-cloistered social environment in which Br. Robert L'Esperance
resided, this idea and practice of opening oneself to a world beyond one's own
group—of welcoming the stranger—was a core aspect of American contemplative Christianity. Committed practitioners like Br. Robert taught that the sensibility of openness and hospitality is explicit in the gospels (e.g., Matthew 25:35)
and has been a counterpoint to ascetical orientations throughout the history of
Christianity. As shown in the quotation that opened this chapter, the desert hermits from the third and fourth centuries, for example, welcomed guests despite
their vows of silence and seclusion, illustrating how hospitality should ideally take
precedence over one's ascetic routines. In the sixth century, Benedict made hospitality central to his rule of life, saying that monastics should greet others as they
would Christ, yet he also instructed that they must live in silent cloister. Br. Robert
L'Esperance's outward-looking demeanor fifteen centuries later was representa-
tive of such Benedictine-style monastic hospitality.[4]

As we learned in Chapter 1, philosopher Richard Kearney (2010) has described
how there has been a recent flourishing of what he has called "anatheistic"
Christianity in the United States and elsewhere in response to pluralism and
globalization. According to Kearney, where the hostility of Crusade-oriented
Christianities rose out of certainty, triumphalism, and an "us-against-them" men-
tality, anatheistic (or "god after god") Christianities have emerged out of the ambiguity that comes from greeting the stranger in a pluralistic world. Truly welcoming

the other—listening and attempting to understand—can shake one's own conceptual foundations (including established notions of the divine), he wrote; a sincere engagement has required people to be open enough to make doctrinal tenets secondary and to try to perceive the universe without preconception, which creates a world of increasing ambiguity.

Seligman and Weller (2012: 25; emphasis added) have noted that ritual is one way to face the ambiguities inherent in a world of multiplicity. The repetition of ongoing, unending ritual cycles "allows us to *live* with ambiguity, not to remove it," they said, emphasizing ceremonial open-endedness itself as a kind of hospitality. Wrote Seligman and Weller (2012: 98), "Accepting the world's discontinuities and ambiguities means that the work of building and refining relationships will never end. Ritual, at least in its relationship to the rest of experience, is never totally coherent and never complete. Yet doing the work of ritual is one of the most important ways in which we live in such an inherently plural world."

Kearney also saw anatheistic responses as primarily relational and open-ended, based not on winning ideas and doctrines but on welcoming the other—divine, human, or something else. This anatheistic hospitality is a chosen stance, wrote Kearney, intentionally taken up in lieu of defensive entrenchment in the face of uncertainty. While Kearney (2010: 45) noted that anatheistic Christians value discernment (he said that they choose to greet the stranger "with eyes wide open"), their openness comes out of an acknowledgment of their own inability to fully know the divine or others. Such openness frames their willingness to accept unknowingness and ambiguity with receptivity, empathy, and wonder, rather than fear and rejection, and to face "encounter" as a place of learning, innovation, and renewal, while nevertheless keeping a discerning eye.

In a sermon about reconciliation, Br. Tom Shaw, SSJE (2013), demonstrated this impulse toward hospitality and a desire to greet the stranger. As a bishop, Br. Tom Shaw described what it was like to vote against a divisive resolution about homosexuality while seated among African bishops at the Anglican Communion's 1998 Lambeth Conference in London. "These bishops all around me started booing and stamping their feet when they saw my hand go up," he said. Outside he later "saw a young, gay English priest being chased by an African bishop who was insisting he be healed." Br. Tom said his response to this behavior was feeling that he needed "to get to Africa . . . not so that I can change their minds about homosexuality, but because I clearly don't understand them." Since then, Br. Tom Shaw repeatedly visited African countries, sometimes bringing Massachusetts college students along with him. He said he learned much from his African hosts, especially lessons about social action, forgiveness, and reconciliation. Going to Africa did not convert Br. Tom to an intolerance of homosexuality (he kept his discerning eye), but his willingness to engage with those unlike himself unmasked what he felt were aspects of the divine that had been previously muted to him. Br. Tom

Shaw said in his sermon, "We need to be able to hear God's voice in the other. God speaks through every one of us, even those with whom we disagree."

Varieties of Silence

Silence is God's first language.

—ST. JOHN OF THE CROSS

I woke at 3:30 a.m. just before the alarm was to go off, grateful because I didn't want to disturb my roommate. Audrey wasn't interested in quite so early a start. There was no time to lose for me, however; I threw the pile of blankets off the guesthouse bed, dressed in layers of wool and down as quietly as I could, then headed out the door to make my way across the mountain valley and down the lonely mile to the monastery for the office of Vigils.

Stepping into the frosty air, I gasped. The stars! At this altitude, in this cold, the stars really did have points, five crisp points just like a child's drawing. Except for the faint starlight, the earth rested silent in deep moonless dark. Periodic flashes from my light helped me keep to the unplowed gravel road. The beams caught the hoary frost, glittering, almost magical, on the sagebrush, grasses, and fence posts.

Entering the austere Trappist chapel, then edging my way to a side bench up against the brick wall, I moved into another variety of silence. It was dark except for a few starry votives at the tabernacle and icons. The monks, in hooded, ivory-colored habits, sat motionless on wooden benches in the antechapel. Their quiet seemed to blossom through space. A "pungent silence," our retreat leader, Cynthia Bourgeault, had called it on a previous visit. It had a kind of density, not accidental but filled with intention and potency.

With their initiation of the Vigil office, the monks approached the conclusion of that night's Great Silence. A clock chimed from the cloister walk outside. The monks rose, then the cantor toned,

The community used their thumbs to make the sign of the cross over their mouths, then responded,

Then bowing, the monks chanted together,

Glo - ry to the Fa – ther, and to the Son, and to the Ho - ly Spir - it

They stood again for,

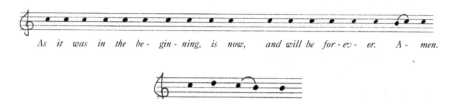

As it was in the be - gin - ning, is now, and will be for - ev - er. A - men.

Al - le - lu - ia.

The plainsong seemed to greet the silence rather than diminish it. Their words were inward, muted, and perfectly synchronized; the unified sound emerged from them effortlessly. It was not beautiful in the way of a stunning, magnetic performance of an accomplished concert choir, but was arresting in its simplicity and ease and intercorporeality. Their sound inhabited the silence as from a single body. White robes glowing in the votive candlelight, the monks then swept into the chapel choir, weaving light into darkness and sound into silence.[5]

After the office of Vigils and a lengthy period of meditation, I walked back to the guesthouse. The monks' intentional silence and sound made the quietude of the valley seem even more apparent. I heard not the slightest rustle in the frozen grasses. These two hours later, the air was colder and the stars had shifted, some constellations having set, others risen. My eyes adjusted to find that the sky had just perceptibly lightened. I could make out the edges of snow banks along the gravel road and discerned the slightly darker mass of mountains against the retreating night. I stopped to listen to the extraordinary lack of sound.

Just then, a lonely call cast itself across the valley from a high ridge. An interlude. Moments later, yips, howls, and yaps came bounding from an opposite hillside. I laughed at their versicle and responsory, cantor and choir Rocky Mountain style. A shooting star burst across the night sky as if in silent appreciation of the coyotes' early morning office.

Later that day, dressed in jeans and a plaid flannel workshirt, the bearded and slightly greying abbot of the Cistercian Trappist monastery greeted his visitors at the hillside guesthouse before the evening's Centering Prayer session. Sitting within the circle of retreatants and retreat leaders in the high-vaulted meditation room overlooking a panoramic view of Mount Sopris, Abbot Benjamin said, "The monastery and guesthouse are like a jewelry setting, but what good is a setting without gems?" He went on to say that we, the guests, were the jewels. "God is the raw force of nature that created the rough gemstones," he continued, "as well as the jeweler who picks and polishes the stones." He looked around the circle, saying emphatically, "God has placed you in this setting and therefore you are *most welcome*. Abolish any thought that you are intruding upon a rarefied Cistercian world! You are not only welcome, you are *wanted*!" Indeed, he said, the monastery's guests are cohorts in the monks' endeavor to enter deepening silence and prayer; we were their partners in "the way."

Yet the abbot's warm welcome was set against our physical segregation from the monastery. The guesthouse was a good mile uphill from the monastery's location in the valley. That separation indicated that the monks not only valued their seclusion, but also protected it. Even so, they had put significant thought and resources into building a beautiful space for visitors. A winner of a national religious architecture award, the guesthouse's design favored comfortable Colorado aesthetics of rough-hewn wood, wrought iron, and hand-painted ceramics with a layout that featured spectacular views of the surrounding Rocky Mountains. Overstuffed leather couches and armchairs in common living spaces emphasized communality and rest, while solitary hermitages and simple meditation rooms invited guests to engage with an environment of contemplative rigor, silence, and austerity that is unusual in much of American society. Although the monks retained their monastic boundaries, this guesthouse spoke clearly of the seriousness with which they took their ethic of hospitality and their desire to support the contemplative lives of non-monastics.

Continuing with the orientation of his monastic home, Abbot Benjamin confirmed what I had noticed in the early hours that same day: "This *particular* monastery has the deepest silence you may ever experience," he said. "I have been to every Cistercian monastery in the United States, and many overseas. They all have their sound backdrops: if it's not the flight path going into Atlanta, it's the frogs and crickets in North Carolina!" he laughed. Then he added more seriously, "You won't get a deeper silence than that of this valley."

In this way, Abbot Benjamin had encouraged us to appreciate the silence that was offered in this reclusive mountain setting, a silence that was fostered, perpetuated, and cherished by the Trappists, who are among the most silent of Christian orders. After Abbot Benjamin's talk, I listened even more closely on a walk the next afternoon. It was so still that I could hear the muscular flapping of a raven high above and the whistle of wind in closely shorn stubble of a hay field.

By teaching us to value this environment of silence, the abbot had encouraged us to keep silence without actually asking us not to talk. His tone was hospitable, rather than restrictive or didactic. After he left us, however, the non-monastic retreat leaders followed up with more overt strictures to help orient newcomers and remind seasoned practitioners of monastic etiquette. A former monk who was cooking and leading meditation sessions on this retreat explained that we could enter the chapel only for specific offices, for in this monastery not all services were open to the public. We were to go directly to the chapel without lingering in cloister passages or at the thresholds to restricted spaces of the monastery. The monks depended upon the honor system to keep the boundaries of their monastic enclosure; there were few locked doors during the chapel's public opening times. If we wanted to spend time in proximity to the sanctuary at other times, we could go into the separate public wing that housed a small meeting room, a restroom, and a prayer room that had a window looking down into the monastic chapel.

The retreat leader Cynthia Bourgeault then explained to us that there was an appropriate spirit with which one should enter and dwell in monastic environments. One should come with an "inner spaciousness" and stillness. Be aware of how one's own distractions send ripples through space to others, she said. "Quietly slip in, and don't draw attention to yourself." One should not only make no sound, but one should also move in a way that doesn't disrupt.

In the guesthouse, the retreatants were also to observe silence, speaking only in the communal sessions about our topic of study, religious philosopher Raimón Panikkar's *Christophany* (2004). However, Cynthia Bourgeault made it clear that we shouldn't be precious or judgmental about keeping silence. She understood that many participants had a steep learning curve before them in regard to silence; she was gentle with neophytes, but more demanding of "old timers." "Silence is not holy," she said, "Silence is *useful*." It is a tool, "a strong container" for our contemplative efforts to move toward "unitive consciousness and proximity to the divine," she said. It should have a "friendliness" to it, rather than a feeling of punitive abstention. "If you really need something, just quietly say so." Silence, said Cynthia, is not so much about full verbal restraint as it is a demeanor of interior quietude and spaciousness, which fosters an intensifying environment of reverence, attention, and reflection. Thus while a necessary spoken communication may be appropriate, noiselessly greeting another with facial expressions may well be a breach. While Cynthia Bourgeault did leave the degree of vocal interaction in dorm rooms up to their occupants, she wanted us to remember that retreatants may not have the same needs. Many come for silence, said Cynthia, while others really struggle with it. She encouraged us to "bear the silence" and explore where it could take us.[6]

IN A SOCIETY where many feel ill at ease with pauses in conversation, contemplatives' view of silence as a powerful and essential agent of positive transformation may be rather unusual. When non-monastics in my fieldwork first approached the world of contemplation, they often found the practice of silence confusing and difficult to sustain. Some did not seem to grasp its purpose and often found it tricky to understand. True enough, silence is notoriously hard to interpret; there are often gaps between what one intends and what another perceives ("illocution" and "perlocution"), especially in a pluralistic environment. I saw many instances during fieldwork that showed such disjunctures of communication. The resulting discomfort indicated how strange and unmanageable some neophytes found contemplative strictures on keeping silence.[7]

One example of a misreading of what was intended in an environment of silence, two women at a monastic guesthouse common room carried on a conversation. They "caught up with each other" in audible whispers, despite having received an orientation on monastic etiquette upon their arrival, as well as having a reminder notice perched on the coffee table between them, which clearly stated, *"Please Respect the Silence for Which Many People Come on Retreat."* Sitting nearby, some of the other guests looked visibly annoyed. One man had a furrowed brow; a woman near the window sighed, closed her book, and left the room. Did the women in conversation believe their whispers constituted silence?

In another part of the country, I gave Nick and Ruby a ride to the train station after a six-day Benedictine retreat. Neither of them had experienced an extended period of silence before. A clear example of Bedford's (2015: 140) idea that silence does not constitute a complete lack of sound, Nick said that he couldn't believe he had been expected to sit there during meals and "just listen to the sound of my own chewing." Nick seemed uneasy at dinner, looking around the communal table with wide eyes, unsure of how to get his neighbor's attention to pass the pitcher of water. Ruby also expressed discomfort, describing a feeling of panic that began to build on the first day of the retreat. She hadn't realized how much talking and busyness had distracted her from "paying attention to what is really in me," she said. "Why am I so scared? What do I think I'll find?" Ruby asked, then added with a little anxious laugh, "What if I don't find *anything*?"

The awkwardness these retreatants felt in the monastic context appeared to come from their unfamiliarity with silence. Their responses showed that they felt silence was contrary to what they expected of social engagement, especially certain prevalent aspects of American culture like self-expression (as in Nick's case), the verbal communication of friendliness and politeness through biographical narrative and inquiry (as with the two women in the guesthouse common room), and the social placement and identification of the self through "self-talk" (as revealed in Ruby's fear that in silence, she might find a vacuum where she thought her "self" should be). The idea that extended silences could be either positive or desirable seemed to confound them, even to the point of creating feelings of isolation and alienation. The practice of silence seemed to ask them to face themselves and others without the social identifiers found in "inner noise" and the talk-based sociality of story. In many sectors of American society, norms of sociability rely strongly on showing interest in the details of other people's lives and sharing one's own story. The practice of silence seemed to ask one to abandon this method of sociality (Bellah 1985; Hall and Lindholm 1999; Irvine 2010a; Taylor 1989).[8]

Many new to American contemplative Christianity thus had to learn the value and purpose of silence in contemplative contexts. Given the social and psychological importance of personal narrative, conversation, and "self-talk" in American society, it often took some time for new practitioners to grasp the ethos and ethics of contemplative silence. Adherents whom I met during fieldwork were at very different stages of enculturation and commitment. Some did not seem to understand the role of silence in the contemplative movement, and they struggled with giving up usual conversational modes of social connection.

It was not only neophytes who sometimes struggled with monastic silence, however. Some of those with long-time commitments recognized the potential for silence to reveal rough patches in power relations and community disharmony. A former Trappist monk who left his monastery to marry and form an intentional Buddhist-Christian community with several other families, William felt that silence in monasteries was not always beneficial and that contemplatives, especially non-monastics, often romanticized it. As well as a contemplative tool, he said that monastic silence could be isolating and oppressive, depending on particular contexts and how people used it. Reflecting on his own experience in a monastery, he said that sometimes silence just served to keep people in their places. Thus, while teachers of contemplation most often depicted silence as a positive discipline that assists in one's transformation rather than oppresses, power dynamics could vary significantly at the micro level of individual circumstances and transactions. Like any cultural phenomenon, silence never has a single meaning or motivation; its qualities depend on historical, cultural, and institutional contexts as well as individual enactment (Achino-Loeb 2006; Foucault 1978; Handman 2014; MacCulloch 2013).[9]

Despite some of these misgivings, many well-established followers of monastic or monastic-derived practices regarded silence as essential to contemplative life. Silence was seen as a way to foster relationality, a clear contrast to the view that it is isolating and oppressive. The practice of silence certainly had the capacity to insulate, protect, and distinguish minority ways of life like Christian monasticism. However, an equally important aspect was practitioners' intention to create community (Basso 1972; Saville-Troike 1985; Wichroski 1997).

The foundations for that community came in part from core teachings like the *Rule of Saint Benedict*, which shaped practices of silence among contemporary contemplative Christians, especially in monasteries. Quoting Psalms and Proverbs, Benedict's rule teaches that listening in a "spirit of silence" is the only appropriate or effective training ground of disciples. Modeled on the Benedictine way, all but one of the monasteries in which I worked practiced extensive daytime silence (though the details of their rules for silence varied), and they also kept the Great Silence, the rule of no talking between the final evening and first morning monastic offices. But for a few small exceptions around working life and hospitality, there was usually no conversation during the day, even at mealtimes, and the nights were completely silent. Silence thus continued to be of primary importance among contemporary monastics.[10]

Non-monastic adaptations of the practice of silence were often much looser. Without established communal codes of silence and solitude in their everyday lives, most non-monastics relied primarily on their own imagination and self-discipline to follow a course set by themselves in conjunction with teachers' recommendations. Taking on the formidable task of learning and establishing "inner silence" regardless of aural context was one way non-monastics could sustain their practices and commitments without the shelter of a cloister. Similar to Cynthia Bourgeault's guidance to retreatants about adopting a demeanor of "inner stillness" upon entering the Trappist chapel, Contemplative Outreach emphasized interiorization, supported by daily scheduled periods of silence and solitude, as the primary means of establishing an intentional contemplative life.[11]

The organization's Contemplative Life Program booklet, *Silence and Solitude* (Best 2006b), for example, acknowledged that non-monastics do not usually live in silent environments. It suggested an alternative, teaching practitioners to develop "the habit of silence," which did not depend entirely upon whether one refrained from talking or spent time alone in minimalistic soundscapes. Along with the recommended twice-daily practice of Centering Prayer, "the habit of silence" included the practice of *statio* or intentionally stopping, reflecting, and "stilling" oneself, and "being present" to the way one moves, breathes, and engages with others in an effort to quiet excessive "inner noise." These stilling practices were intended to help one "cultivate the disposition of interior space" in an effort to let go of "inner talking," as well as motivations like self-will, pride, and attachment, so that one could hear "God's first language . . . silence" (Best 2006b: 17, 32–33). Ultimately, learning to still inner noise was a way to help one cultivate what the booklet's authors called a "silence of being," which could exist regardless of aural, physical, or social context. Thus, while Abbot Benjamin was enthusiastic about his monastery's rare gift of an austere soundscape, guides of contemplation taught that "keeping silence" did not have to rely on a lack of sound (Bedford 2015).

During my fieldwork, experienced contemplative practitioners frequently expressed the idea that silence could exist in any circumstance. When Eleanor and Jamie joked around during kitchen duty at an eight-day silent retreat, for example, the young woman suddenly remembered herself, exclaiming, "Oh! We're not supposed to be talking!" Jamie paused mid-wipe of the kitchen island counter.

Raising his eyebrows and lifting a forefinger in jesting mimicry of some wise Sufi master or other, he replied, "Ah, but 'true silence is not the absence of sound. It is silence within.'" He cheerfully snapped the dishcloth in the air and added, "So we're okay!"

Conveying another example of "silence within," Liz used speech at a Wisdom School to communicate concerns about keeping silence during an evening discussion period about the day's events. The participants had been split into several work groups that day, some of which were permitted to speak during their tasks. She described how her liturgical work group was learning chant practices, which included lengthy periods of silence. She found herself agitated by the external noise coming from the gardening and building maintenance work groups outside. Liz said that in the middle of her frustration she had caught herself and remembered the principle that "everything belonged," including sound. "I realized I was fighting the sound and needed to let go of my annoyance. My own silence shouldn't be dependent on other people restraining themselves," she said. The retreat leader commended Liz, noting that in the midst of experiencing feelings of frustration, she had been able to recognize and stop her compulsion to guard silence as a kind of personal territory and object of veneration.

Silence as Hospitality

These ethnographic sketches of interiorized environments show the diversity of silences among American Christian contemplatives and how differences in experience affected understandings. Contemplative principles and practices of silence were not always easily learned or embraced. It took some time for practitioners of contemplation to learn the ethos and ethics of a silence that downplayed social categorizations and in some cases even seemed to be at odds with social norms of familiarity and friendliness. Adherents were at very different stages of formation and commitment. As practitioners became more fully acquainted with the ways of contemplation, they began to take on the idea that silence itself was a form of communication (cf. Wichroski 1997). Through the modeling and encouragement of their teachers, many began to see the practice of silence and seclusion as a positive and empowering (though not terribly easy) discipline that conveyed openness and relationality, both toward other people and the divine.

Especially prominent in monasteries, silence was often intended as a gesture of hospitality. Monastics considered the practice of silence to be a demonstration of acceptance of others' and one's own worth as human beings, regardless of personal preferences, statuses, achievements, failures, or affinities. Keeping silence, they believed, allowed people to be who they are without having to impress others with personal narratives or credentials. In effect, it was an ascetic act that stripped both sound and usual social categories, and offered support in their place. Consider, for example, a statement about idle curiosity from the *Rule of the Society of Saint John the Evangelist* (SSJE 1997: 54–55): "Only God knows [others] as they truly are, and in silence we learn to let go of the curiosity, presumption and condemnation that pretend to penetrate the mystery of their hearts. True silence is an expression of love." Here, contemplative silence is seen as a leveling agent and salve in a world that judges others. Details, especially details that predicate social status, are irrelevant and harmful from the perspective of the SSJE rule; here silence is a way of preserving human dignity.[12]

This Christian monastic perspective on silence as a form of solidarity and heal-ing is not unique. Michael Jackson (2013: 225) described the cultural meanings and intentions of silence in the context of postwar reconciliation in Sierra Leone. He wrote,

> Silence may be, as in Africa, a way of healing and reconciliation, and not a way of evading or repressing an issue. Indeed, it may be a consummate form of coexistence. To sit with a neighbor or friend, saying nothing, may seem like a negation of intersubjectivity, but among the Kuranko it is a form of exchange, an expression of solidarity. And if one's friend has expe-rienced loss, it is to acknowledge that loss, and what cannot be changed, at the same time as one affirms and demonstrates that the sufferer is not alone. Little is said, apart from the phrase *in toro*—you suffer—but in silence the social world is restored. Speech disperses the world, say the Bambara; silence reassembles it. Speech burns the mouth; silence heals it. The secret belongs to he who is quiet.

As Jackson hinted in his reference to intersubjectivity, the relational qual-ity of silence in these contexts goes well beyond restoring social categories. In Christian monasteries, the "secret" which belongs to practitioners of silence includes a cultivation of an existential stillness that can prompt an opening to phenomenological union with the divine and others. Ideally, personhood and community should not derive from one's social station, historical background, or intellectual faculties, many believed, but from connectivity and simple being. Thus, the contemplative alternative of silence emphasized that one's humanity comes primarily from coexistence (indeed, interexistence) with others, whether divine, human, or another aspect of creation. Fr. Thomas Keating (quoted in Best 2006b: 61) taught that this "silence of being" is first and foremost a "unitive way." In the contemplative Christian context in which I worked, teachers, adepts, and more advanced students saw silence as profoundly relational, socially as well as in the way of phenomenological intersubjectivity or unitive being, which is the subject of Chapter 7.

Varieties of Seclusion

The careful balance between silence and words,
withdrawal and involvement,
distance and closeness,
solitude and community
forms the basis of the Christian Life.
—HENRI NOUWEN, *Out of Solitude*[13]

Non-Monastic "Inner Circles" and Exclusivities

While silence and seclusion were often enacted in a spirit of receptivity and generosity, contemplative interiority could nevertheless occasionally tend toward varieties of distinction. In the non-monastic community, gradations of membership were informal, depending upon a participant's degree of experience and seriousness of commitment. Unlike the situation of monasteries, no one was ever really a guest in non-monastic venues, but one could certainly be a dabbler, a beginner, a serious student, an adept, or even a virtuoso. Such variation prompted the development of unofficial gradations in the non-gathered community. Subtle stratifications or concentric rings of participation and connection grew out of differentiation or distinctions in practitioners' intentions and knowledge. "Inner circles," as one contemplative teacher called them, formed from a sense of community among those with serious commitments. These inner circles were social groupings in which non-monastics could intensify and solidify their learning and practice in the company of peers. They were also a place of training for the next generation of teachers in the non-monastic community.

People noticed who was serious. The pattern in these communities was that the longer one persevered in practice and study and the more frequently one gathered with others (in person or online), the more deeply one penetrated this informal network of contemplative practitioners. Especially at the intermittent non-monastic encounters of retreats and Wisdom Schools, participants watched and listened to one another closely in seminar-style discussions. They quietly noticed who followed the path in earnest and who offered insights that demonstrated contemplative maturity. Through their irregular but repeated encounters, serious practitioners thus gradually established subtle in-groupings within non-gathered communities. In these inner circles, practitioners found companions who supported and reinforced their commitments to refine contemplative practices and knowledge. Often this included collaborating on ways to serve the greater community, especially as up-and-coming teachers in their own right.[14]

Inner circles were not sanctioned segregations or accreditations, but rather grass-roots affinities: people found their way to like-minded and like-practicing others. Usually the resulting stratification did not intentionally downgrade the worth of others. Instead, through them people recognized that those who "put in the work" could be trusted with their innermost motivations, commitments, and desires. In a way, the inner circles were an informal, social alternative for the social-structural and physical cloister of monasteries. Albeit rather amorphous, they functioned as social units that allowed people outside the monastery to concentrate intentions, disciplines, and practices toward a way of life that was not well represented in greater American society. Finding others with a similar determination helped non-monastics bear their isolation and keep on track; even at a distance, the sheltering "grille" of mutual support, affiliation, and friendship of other serious practitioners helped many continue to adhere to a contemplative way of life despite its sometimes difficult demands.[15]

Retreats and Wisdom Schools included people of mixed knowledge and commitment, however. There were often newcomers who arrived unprepared for the rigor of the schedule or the intellectual and spiritual demands of the teachings. At a week-long retreat taking place on the grounds of a Trappist monastery in December 2010, one woman confided to me that the retreat master's seminars on the metaphysics of Advent were wholly incomprehensible to her: "I have *no* idea *what* she's talking about. I am completely confused," she said. The woman was attracted to contemplation and she meditated at home, but this demanding seminar-style retreat was as yet too great a step for her, she said. A number of other participants seemed dazed and exhausted by the early risings for the office of Vigils, the multiple hour-long meditation sits, and the intellectually provocative seminars. The dictates of silence added to the intensity, especially if participants were new to the challenge of not being able to let off steam or satisfy curiosity by getting to know one another through ordinary conversation.

Coming to the inner circle was not just about having the capacity to keep silence, comprehend unfamiliar concepts, or master a demanding schedule of meditation and liturgies, however. Central to traveling this path was embodying the ideal intentions and behaviors that undergirded the philosophies and making them part of one's habitual way of being. In silent environments, adepts conveyed much of this appropriate behavior through modeling rather than overt teaching; the process of maturation included learning to listen, watch, and discern in an effort to emulate one's teachers and learned cohorts. One's ability to pick up on unstated cues and to interpret their intentions and meanings took one a long way into the inner circle.

Such appropriate behavior included learning "to keep attention in oneself" and to resist framing the work in terms of spiritual achievement.[16] Comparing how far along someone was on "the path," even if kindly and modestly meant to uphold another and belittle oneself, showed that one had not yet thrown off a concern for social status. An illustration comes from the same 2010 Advent retreat: Leila, a television director from New York City, emphatically exclaimed during a time of group reflection about how Audrey, the woman next to her in the meditation circle, "could sit like *no one else!*" Those acquainted with Audrey knew this to be true, for she had a practice of meditating at length several times a day and could easily sit perfectly still for more than an hour without getting up for the half-time "meditative walks" that the rest of us needed to make it through the sessions. True or not, however, Leila had shown herself a beginner by making a statement about another's contemplative prowess. Such hierarchizing narrative assessments came from values of achievement and status, learned practitioners believed, rather than from contemplative Christian principles of humility and detachment. In the silence that followed Leila's observation, a number of people shifted uncomfortably on their meditation cushions and looked a little embarrassed.[17]

Many are called, and few are chosen.

—MATTHEW 22:14

PERHAPS THERE IS a little irony that a desire to foster unitive consciousness sometimes created social distinctions. The inner circles of serious practitioners were subtle, informal manifestations of the like-minded and like-practicing, but in a few other non-monastic venues the expression of differentiation based on knowledge and commitment seemed to set the grille more firmly in place. Among the Christian Wisdom community in particular, a favorite scriptural passage was the Parable of the Ten Maidens.[18] The story is about ten female attendants who wait for the Bridegroom, only five of whom brought enough oil to replenish their lamp reservoirs as they watched through the night. When the Bridegroom arrives, five are prepared, greeting him with lamps alight, while the others are nowhere in sight, having scurried off on a last-minute search for more oil. Not having adequately prepared for the Bridegroom's coming, the door to the wedding feast is closed fast before those five can return. "Staying awake" and "keeping one's lamp lit" were thus key motifs in the contemplative Christian endeavor to learn to "keep attention" and live intentionally. Scriptural passages like these confirmed some contemplative practitioners' experience that many are either unwilling or unable to rise to the demands and challenges of preparing oneself for encounter with the divine.

This potential for exclusivity became clear to me at a gathering in Washington, D.C. There a dedicated group of non-monastic Christian contemplatives sponsored a retreat master to teach Seyyed Hossein Nasr's *Knowledge and the Sacred* (1989), a Sufi theological treatise based on the author's 1980–1981 Gifford Lectures.[19] This group called itself Wisdom East, a small network of Christians committed to the study of inter-religious contemplation who lived on the Eastern Seaboard of the United States. Among them were students of "world wisdom traditions" like Kabbalism, Vedanta Hinduism, and several schools of Sufism and Buddhism. Members of Wisdom East did their best to coordinate schedules and meet quarterly at someone's home, where they followed a Wisdom School format by bringing in a contemplative retreat master to explore esoteric texts and poetry in seminar-style gatherings and to practice liturgies, meditations, and chants in a rhythm that loosely emulated a monastic Daily Office. They said that their study of non-canonical Christian texts and the writings and practices of Eastern contemplative traditions was their attempt to recover knowledge of "the mystical core of Christianity," which they believed had become a minority voice as the result of historical assertions of power and misinterpretations of Jesus' original intentions.

The members of Wisdom East allowed me to join them several times during my fieldwork. In April 2011, our seminar-style discussions took place among the art- and book-lined walls of a stylish renovated home in an established leafy neighborhood of the American capital city. Three times a day, between meditating, chanting, and cooking, we energetically discussed the meanings behind Nasr's difficult text, which challenged the narrowness of contemporary definitions of knowledge and asserted the primacy of revelatory or "theophanic" wisdom. A few of the members were then actually students of Professor Nasr, who taught Islamic Studies and Perennial Philosophy at nearby George Washington University; they helped elucidate the text alongside the Texan retreat master, Michael, an Episcopal priest, scholar, and poet. Most participants had already come to Nasr's belief that the ultimate goal of all their practices and studies was *theosis*, or union with God, though many were still reeling to think that the sterile and impotent Christianity with which they felt they had been raised could hold such promise.

One woman called Joan had attended Roman Catholic parochial schools, but had later given up the Church, only to return to contemplative Christianity by way of Buddhism, Kabbalism, and Sufism. Joan said Nasr's indebtedness to the ancient Christian thinkers Origen and Clement showed her that, unlike the mainline Protestant theological tenet that "grace" rather than "works" is the only way to God, ancient forms of Christianity taught that people must make active efforts to become receptive to theosis. Joan said that during all her years as a Catholic, she had never known of the ancient Christian teachings on "pure gnosis," "received knowledge," or "full communion" with God, the "divine indwelling" and "direct transmission of wisdom" similar to that received by Muhammad when he wrote the Qu'ran. "What?!" she exclaimed, recounting her initial astonishment at this version of Christianity, "*These* are our roots?!"

I listened and participated in intense and vibrant debates about the meanings of Nasr's abstruse exposition. Some participants were clearly unsure of what to make of Nasr, while others in the group felt at ease leading. Ideas flew: people discussed the relationship of modernity and sacralization, debated whether attaining knowledge was a process or the product of an immediate divine encounter, considered whether Nasr was too authoritarian in his assertions and whether his mystical absolutism could coexist with Cartesian positivism, wondered whether adherence to "tradition" was mere idolatry, and expressed frustration and delight over Nasr's deliberate poetic obfuscation of concepts. Is the language a barrier or a manifestation of the divine, they asked, and is our willingness to wrestle with the text a way to push through to other ways of knowing that will open us up to transformation, bringing a "cardial space" to our intellection, or is it hopeless after all to think we could ever achieve the vision that Nasr here presents?

At one point, I questioned Nasr's assertions that knowledge of the divine was reserved for an elite class of seekers (e.g., Nasr 1989: 131). Was this view compatible with Christian principles of integral human worth and unconditional love? But Amelia had no conflict with this picture of exclusivity. Then auditing a graduate seminar with Nasr, Amelia had given up a career to fully engage in contemplative life: she taught yoga, worked as a church sexton, wrote poetry and icons, led contemplative study groups and meditation circles, and published a blog on interreligious contemplative wisdom. "Where does it say that it's open for all?" Amelia asked quite matter-of-factly in response to my concern about exclusivity. "Actually, it says, 'Many are called, and few are chosen.'"

Jamie, then a young seminary student who practiced Vedanta Hinduism and Mevlevi Sufism quietly on the side (now an ordained priest living in an intentional community), agreed that he was uncomfortable with the "seeming unfairness of it," assenting that "it is not as democratic as we would like." The retreat master, Michael, joined in by posing the question, "What does it mean if every person is created in the image and likeness of the divine?" He proposed that human worth is beyond our understanding, but noted nevertheless that it was obvious that not all people understood or cared about these things. "After all, here we are, doing the work. Where is everyone else?" he said. The comments of these participants suggested that the willingness and ability to do *effective* contemplative and intellectual work was a means (perhaps for a few, the *only* means) to one's transformation. Some clearly felt that not all were on that particular path or up to that challenge.

Until this gathering of Wisdom East, I had not come across overt expressions of exclusivity among contemplative Christians. Social frictions and segregations around gender, race, ethnicity, and sexual preference that have been historically common to Christianity, as we saw of Br. Tom Shaw's experience at the Lambeth conference early in his tenure as a bishop, were not evident in the contemplative communities in which I worked, despite biblical scriptures that could support them. And most teachers actively discouraged the "spiritual pride" that can foster exclusivist hierarchies of achievement, spiritual experience, or learnedness. Nevertheless, such teachers did not have any real authority to bring non-monastic contemplatives into line with an established body of ideas or practices. To be sure, unlike those in closely controlled institutionalized environments (Kanter 1968; Parsons and Shils 1962) or "total institutions" (Goffman 1961), no uniform conceptual establishment existed in the American contemplative Christian movement. Though there were core motifs and principles, ideas and practices varied considerably among Christian contemplatives, especially non-monastics.

The people of Wisdom East took their practice and study seriously, evidently believing that much depended on their dedication, elucidation, and persistence. For them it was a mistake to rely *solely* on "grace" to come into union with the divine. Any expression of exclusivity which arose in that context was unusual among the non-monastic contemplatives with whom I worked, however. More prevalent was the subtle differentiation of the "inner circles" that developed out of practitioners' varied degrees of experience, knowledge, and commitment.

Monastic Enclosure

When you pray, go to your inner room,
close the door, and pray to your Father in secret.
And your Father who sees in secret will reward you.
—MATTHEW 6:6

Monastic enclosure is a variety on the cline of contemplative seclusion and interiority. Enclosure connotes exclusion, yet the monasteries in which I worked, despite their architectural cloisters and gender-exclusive, graduated memberships and hierarchies, were often more intentional about inclusivity than some non-monastic contemplative manifestations of social-spiritual differentiation.[20] Compare the idea that contemplation was "not for everyone," which came up at Wisdom East, with a monastic expression of compassionate inclusivity: In one of the daily videos sent out to email subscribers during Lent 2013, Br. Curtis Almquist, SSJE (2013), said that he often hears people struggle with feelings of doubt about whether they are engaged in the right practices or disciplined enough to be worthy of God's love. He assured his listeners that "[i]t is not as if we have to get our act together, to get ourselves all ship-shape, before God will listen to us, God will attend to us, love us." We are never called "adults of God" in scripture, he said, but are instead "*children* of God," and "children are prone to getting their knees scuffed" on their way to maturity.

From our conversations, from listening to him give sermons over the years, and from attending Daily Offices alongside him, I know that Br. Curtis Almquist believed strongly in the contemplative tenet that regular practice and discipline hold transformative power. Inside their monastery, Br. Curtis Almquist and his fellow monks depended on the strict schedules of monastic prayer practices to assist in their self-formation and self-transformation, both in times of confidence and in times of doubt. Indeed, the remainder of the daily SSJE videos during Lent in 2013 were devoted to teaching non-monastics such practices. Nevertheless, Br. Curtis assured his listeners that all does not depend on "right practice." Rather, not unlike Thomas Keating's view of "consent to the divine," he taught that much depends on people's willingness to engage and persist. Br. Curtis thus mixed a strong dose of "grace" into his guidance on practice, the notion that the divine takes the greater part in bringing about *unio mystica*. Even though people must make an earnest effort to cultivate their own receptivity to the divine, Br. Curtis Almquist's picture allowed, even expected, humanity's imperfections to be an integral part of the journey (Elliot 2016).

That imperfect humanity, however, created a need for techniques and structures to help humans focus. Several monks with whom I spoke said they came to the monastery out of a longing for an environment that fostered and supported greater discipline in prayer and silence. Monastics used enclosure and a set daily rhythm of *ora et labora* as such a means. Understandably, there was a certain tension between the ideals of service and generosity and their practice of seclusion. Because their Benedictine-inspired Christianity demanded radical hospitality of their members, there was a built-in dialectic between the socio-theological ethic of openness and a desire for the concentrated silence and solitude that enclosure provides (cf. Irvine 2010a).

Referencing Matthew's decree to close the door of the inner room, the rule of Br. Curtis Almquist's community explained the play between solitude and community in monastic enclosure. The rule stated that, though sometimes arduous, an environment of seclusion was essential in helping the monks resist distractions from their deepening relationship with the divine. Yet enclosure alone would not adequately guide one to Christian maturity. The SSJE rule (1997: 52–53) said that solitude must be kept in balance with social responsibility and the need for community:

> Maintaining a balance in our life between solitude and engagement with others is not easy. We are subject to many pressures that deter us from experiencing solitude: the claims of work, the fear of loneliness, and the reluctance to face ourselves as we are in the company of Jesus before God. Without solitude we would forfeit an essential means of inner restoration and encounter with God in the depths of our own souls.

Enclosure is one way to assist monks in keeping attention and strengthening community. Some monasteries are fully cloistered, and their residents never encounter people outside their walls. The monasteries in which I worked were semi-cloistered, with varying degrees of contact with outsiders, depending on their particular rules. Whatever the degree of contact, significant energy went into maintaining the boundaries of the cloister by dictating where and when one may speak or have contact with others. Some monks emphasized that living in cloister, with its focus on intention and attention, was not an easy escape from ordinary life. This was an alternative form of community, not an easier one, they said. One monk described cloistered life to Diane, the woman who regularly attended liturgies at SSJE, as "living alone together."

When I spoke with him at his Colorado monastery in December 2011, Fr. Thomas Keating spoke to me about the deterioration of monastic enclosure, solitude, and silence. As the result of declining numbers of avowed religious, said Fr. Thomas, monks and nuns today do not live lives nearly as secluded or focused as did their predecessors. Monasteries can no longer perform all the tasks required to keep their communities functioning well. Not only does each monk or nun have a greater workload and busier schedule, but monasteries must also hire outside workers in numerous fields. Sure enough, just as Fr. Thomas Keating indicated, every monastery in which I worked had non-monastic volunteers or employees on their staff. They depended upon the labor of all kinds of specialists: people like cooks, farmworkers, builders, accountants, public relations specialists, librarians, custodians, and guesthouse keepers. Regardless of how well the monastic communities discerned whom they would allow into their enclosures, outside workers did not have a lifetime of training in the ethics, ethos, or aesthetics of the monks or nuns who lived permanently within. Some may have had only an economic relationship with the monasteries in which they worked. Certainly outside workers did not have an avowed commitment to their way of life, yet contemporary monasteries depended on them for their communities to function.

Along with the physical presence of outside workers, electronic communications also had the potential to disrupt the cloister. Though rather dated in its technological references, SSJE's rule (1997: 53) includes a cautionary note that monks "need to be disciplined in our use of the radio and recordings so that we use them as a means of enrichment rather than of empty distraction." Today, monasteries grapple with additional communications technologies—the Internet, cell phones, email, Skype, and social media like Facebook—which so easily allow others' virtual presence within the cloister. Many monks and nuns I knew owned cell phones and, while the extent of individual use of electronic communications inside monastic cells is unknown to me, the Internet had definitely become a key part of the working lives of many monasteries, especially in their management of a virtual public presence through monastic websites, online teachings, and blogs.[21]

Though the porous nature of monasteries did not necessarily detract from atmospheres of interiority, not all monasteries had equal access to environmental silence and solitude, as we learned from Abbot Benjamin. One monk told me about going on retreat at the rural Trappist monastery in Western Massachusetts where Fr. Thomas Keating was once abbot. He exclaimed that in that setting, "the quality of silence" was far richer than at his own monastery, which was located in an urban setting with an enthusiastic non-monastic congregation. The demands of serving the outside community sometimes seemed to challenge his order's balance between offering hospitality and maintaining the quality of seclusion, silence, and internal community cohesiveness. From time to time, the monasteries at which I worked canceled public liturgies and took retreat days to restore the balance. As much needed and befriended as outside workers and congregants were, and as useful as electronic communications were, their presence could evidently affect the depth of focus of resident monks and nuns. As Fr. Thomas Keating put it during our talk, "Our lives now are not so different from other people's as perhaps they once were."

A Porous Boundary: Hospitality and Enclosure at SSJE's Maundy Thursday Vigil

The presence of outside service providers and periodic openings for public ministry showed that the cloisters of some American monasteries were porous rather than fully sealed. This porous quality of monastic interiority was revealed in the vigil that the Society of Saint John the Evangelist hosted on Maundy Thursday in 2010.

SSJE was originally more cloistered than it is now, but the Society eventually opted for greater openness in order to better serve its non-monastic congregation. The monks began welcoming men for retreats in their guesthouse in the late 1920s. At first, the inner reaches of the Chapel of Saint Mary and Saint John were not open to the public at all; congregants sat in the antechapel on the outside of the locked wrought-iron grille. However, under the leadership of reform-minded Superior Paul Wessinger, the community began opening the grille in 1973 to allow congregants to participate in Daily Offices alongside the monks. Women were invited to stay on retreat at the guesthouse soon after, in 1975. Today visitors are expected to leave the inner chapel within a short time of a liturgy's completion, unless they have received a special invitation or are staying as guesthouse residents. The chapel physically separates the guesthouse from the monastic enclosure. Retreatants take breakfast in a guesthouse common room, but since the 1970s the monks have hosted all other meals at the monastery's refectory, which is otherwise a private space. Thus the boundaries of monastic enclosure periodically shift over the course of the day.[22]

Recent renovations, finished in 2011, were undertaken in part to better manage the balance of the monks' need for enclosure with their ministry of hospitality and teaching to people who live outside their walls. Before the renovations were completed, guests walked through the sacristy (rooms devoted to liturgical preparation) and the monks' common room to take meals in the refectory. A former outside cloister walk was glassed in to provide a sitting area and walkway that is now the route which takes guests directly from the chapel to the refectory without infringing on the privacy of the monastic enclosure. Guests can also view the monastic garden from that walkway, but it remains a private space of the monks.

Until the 2011 renovations were completed, the guesthouse washroom facilities were also open to the public during liturgies held in the chapel; from there, people potentially had access to guesthouse rooms and the monastic enclosure. The monks relied on people's integrity to honor the restrictions to those spaces. But during the renovations a washroom was built in a hallway just off the chapel, so that only registered guests would have access to the guesthouse. The monks still depend on the goodwill of their registered guests to preserve their privacy since there are no locked gates between the monastic enclosure and the guesthouse, only signs at the junctures between guest and monastic spaces stating "Private—Monastic Enclosure." The guesthouse and chapel are closed to outsiders over the Brothers' Sabbath, from Sunday Evensong at 4:30 p.m. until Tuesday Morning Prayer at 6:00 a.m. The 2011 renovations allowed a better balance of the monks' need for seclusion and their commitments to teaching ministries and an ethic of hospitality.[23]

This dialectic of enclosure and openness at the SSJE monastery created a *porous boundary* that supported and protected the monks' alternative way of life, while also allowing for relationships with non-monastic guests and the larger society. The viability of the relationship between openness and enclosure—between hospitality, silence, and seclusion—depended upon the monks' caretaking of that boundary, as well as upon the understanding and goodwill of their guests. In coming chapters, we shall see how the porosity of monastic enclosures emulates the contemplative understanding and phenomenological experience of intersubjective personhood and community, a kind of *porous self*. For now, the story of SSJE's 2010 Maundy Thursday vigil exemplifies the interactive dynamic of hospitality and interiority in a cloistered setting.

MAUNDY THURSDAY IS the first day of the Triduum, a three-day rite during Holy Week that begins with the commemoration of the Last Supper, follows with Good Friday liturgies in remembrance of the Crucifixion, and ends with the conclusion of the Easter Vigil on Sunday at daybreak. The Maundy Thursday liturgy commemorates the initiation by Jesus of the Christian practice called the Eucharist or Holy Communion, the rite that invites participants to "eat this bread" and "drink this wine" as a way of remembering, embodying, and committing to the founder of Christianity, his sanctity, and his principles.[24] Maundy Thursday's liturgy emphasizes the key importance of service to community in Christianity, symbolized in a foot-washing rite. At SSJE, the Superior initiated this liturgy by publicly washing the feet of his monks in the chapel, in imitation of biblical scripture's story of how Jesus washed the feet of his disciples.[25] After the Superior, all monks and those congregants who wished to participate also enacted this symbolic demonstration of their commitment to serve others.

A night-long vigil took place after the Maundy Thursday Eucharist service, demonstrating another key motif of Christianity, one of particular importance to contemplatives: keeping attention through "wakefulness." The story goes that Jesus asked his disciples to "stay awake with me" while he prayed in the Garden of Gethsemane after their "last supper" and before his incarceration, which would lead to his crucifixion the following day.[26] After the Maundy Thursday Eucharist, many Episcopal and Roman Catholic parishes included a silent vigil commemorating that time of prayer in the garden. People took part in various ways: remaining for a brief period, joining in a group effort to take turns over the course of the night, or staying in prayer until dawn. Participation in the vigil signified one's allegiance to Christ, and for contemplatives, a commitment to the practice of keeping attention or "staying awake" as a way to foster union with the divine.

On the afternoon of Maundy Thursday in April 2010, the SSJE Brothers and their overnight guests cleared pews from the "Lady Chapel," the neo-Romanesque side chapel dedicated to Mary, the mother of Jesus. There they placed carpets, prayer stools, and cushions and brought in pots of living palms to create an open, garden-like prayer space for the night vigil. This "Garden of Repose," which mirrored the garden of Gethsemane where Jesus prayed after the last supper, was to be the setting for the sanctified bread and wine, the object (to some, the subject) of veneration over the course of the vigil. The Brothers would keep the chapel open all night after the evening service. It was the only night of the year when people off the street had access to the monastery after regular opening hours. While the grille's central gate to the inner chapel was locked, a side gate off the Mary chapel was left open, allowing registered guests access to their rooms and outside visitors access to the restrooms, which at this time (before the renovations) were located in the guesthouse proper. The side gate thus also allowed access to the main chapel and potentially the monastic enclosure.

The Maundy Thursday Eucharist and foot-washing liturgy concluded in the flickering shadows of a candlelit recession from the high altar in which the priest, deacon, and subdeacon carried the sanctified elements of bread and wine through the grille to the outer altar of Mary's chapel. As they solemnly made their way, the schola led an a cappella Taizé chant, which continued for some fifteen minutes until all 250 or so congregants had followed, gathered, and composed themselves as best they could into the small side chapel. Their bronze, black, and red vestments glittering, the three celebrants placed the bread and wine at the center of a semi-circle of votive candles on the altar, then knelt with foreheads and hands to the slate floor. Miniature potted palms and golden light from pillar candles on their wrought-iron stands softened the austerity of gray granite walls. The cream and green marble altar was covered in a simple white fair linen, and on this night, the Mary chapel's elaborate gilded seventeenth-century Venetian reredos of saints was hidden by a plain linen screen so it would not detract from the visual focus on the sanctified elements. With the chant's conclusion, the congregation stayed in silent veneration. The church was then entirely in darkness but for the few candles around the Mary altar, the gentle warm pool of light focusing attention on the paten of bread and crystal flagon of glowing amber-colored wine. The recesses of the larger chapel were shadowed and still.

The three liturgical celebrants stood and withdrew, leaving congregants and monks to linger. Having already stayed some two and a half hours for the special Maundy Thursday liturgy, two-thirds of the congregation remained another twenty minutes or so, then left quietly through the large wooden portico door. There was no longer any holy water in the stoup with which the congregants could cross themselves upon exiting, as was the custom of many; one of the monks had soaked the water up with a sponge and taken it away in a basin while his Brothers silently stripped the darkened central chapel of all ornament. Icons, candles, flowers, fair linens, the sixteenth-century crucifix, and the seventeenth-century sanctuary lamps from the high altar and St. John's altar were all cleared away. The monks then washed the bare altars as though preparing the dead for burial. The usual repository of the sacrament, the tabernacle, yawned void.

The monks' task of thus emptying the church of signs of the divine presence marked the beginning of a time of ritual and theological intensity and barrenness as the community moved liturgically down the relentless road to crucifixion. The only exception from the stripping was an icon of Christ with the Beloved Disciple, placed on a wrought-iron stand behind the grille in reference to the faithful staying awake with Christ.

The feeling of intensity increased over the night. People sat in silence, some on meditation stools, cushions, or carpets, others on pew chairs. A few extended themselves in prostration, lying face down on the slate floor with arms stretched out in the shape of a cross or folded under their foreheads. The monks who were not engaged in stripping the church remained in the Mary chapel for an hour or more, then members of their community took turns over the night so that at least one monk was always in vigil with their guests. It was a long night. Some twenty people remained until two or three in the morning; some took a few hours' break then returned, while a handful stayed throughout the night. Some brought books—bibles, theological reflections, and volumes of poetry or prayer. Others wrote in journals. A university student wept on and off through the night, telling me later that in this vigil and at this monastery she had finally found a place that seemed to match the strength of her feelings of connectedness to the divine. Another man was a priest who had always wanted to keep watch for a full night at a Maundy Thursday vigil, but had been on duty for Holy Week every other year and could not afford to be overtired for the long services of Good Friday and Easter that followed. On sabbatical this year, he could finally stay awake all night. The monks, too, knew their limits given the number of services they would offer over the rest of the Triduum. One said it would be "hubris and unwise" for him or his Brothers to stay up all night while trying to properly serve their guests.

That Maundy Thursday night in 2010, a man who appeared to be homeless came into the chapel. As posh as it may seem, Harvard University attracted many homeless people from the greater Boston area, likely because they saw its potential for panhandling and because the well-treed urban parks provided some shelter at night. Perhaps this man had attended the service preceding the vigil; being one of the high holidays, Maundy Thursday brought in a number of people who did not regularly worship at the monastery. Or perhaps he noticed people coming and going from the chapel and found his way in from the cold. Dressed in work boots, grubby jeans, and an old oversized Harris tweed coat, this man tried at first to sit quietly in the pew chairs just off to the right of the Mary chapel, but he was soon leaning against a stone pillar and falling asleep. At about midnight he abandoned all pretense of praying, placed a hymnal under his head, and stretched himself out across three or four pew chairs (despite the upright prayer books in the chair dividers which broke the horizontality of his repose). He snored and grumbled rather loudly in his sleep. The quality of silence definitely changed, and I sensed a little anxiety in the small group of vigilants who had been very still until then. Br. Gabriel was keeping vigil at this time, meditating off to the side seated on the floor against a stone wall. When the man cried out in his sleep, "Which way? Left or right?!" Br. Gabriel gently smiled and went off, soon returning with a cushion. He offered it to the man, saying "There, now you can rest." Half asleep, the man accepted the cushion, tossed the hymnal from under his head, and settled down for the night.

At that evening's Eucharist, Br. David Vryhof (2010) had given a sermon, saying that Maundy Thursday reminds us to serve people out of love, not just duty, including the ones whom many reject. He reminded his congregants that one undertakes contemplation not for one's own edification, but so that one has the strength to act for others. As I watched Br. Gabriel attend the homeless man, I saw that he was enacting the spirit of that evening's sermon, merging contemplative prayer with active service by not being too precious about sacraments like the vigil that we were then observing. Later, Br. Gabriel told me that he had struggled over what to do in this situation, being torn between competing demands on his community's ethic of hospitality—his responsibility to preserve silence and an environment of reverence for those who stayed in vigil and his responsibility to care for the stranger who sought a safe and warm place to sleep. His choice to offer a little more comfort to the stranger bridged the demands, quieting the homeless man so that others could pray undisturbed.

Toward the end of the vigil, when multicolored light was already streaming in through the high clerestory stained-glass windows, another monk came in and noticed the still-sleeping homeless man. Perhaps he also felt the conflicting demands of sheltering the praying community and being hospitable to the one who slept despite the incipient stirrings of the chapel at dawn. He gently pulled the side gate closed without locking it, leaving access to the inner recesses of the monastery for those who were permitted within, but creating an appearance of closure for those who were not. ,

The unusual degree of openness to the outer community ended with the conclusion of Maundy Thursday's vigil on Good Friday morning. In the vigil's last moments, an increased number had gathered before the sanctified elements on the altar, though the amber wine no longer sparkled or glowed; the morning light paled those votive candles that had not yet burned themselves out. Some vigilants had returned after several hours' sleep to rejoin the few who had soldiered on through the night; others, close friends of the monks, came ready to help in the reassembly of the chapel in anticipation for Good Friday's services. Several minutes before the appointed hour, the Brother Sacristan came through the side gate, bowed at the Lady altar, then stood unobtrusively at a distance to the right. He checked the time on his cell phone as the vigil drew toward its conclusion. At 7 a.m., the Brother Sacristan approached the altar, bowed again, this time also genuflecting and touching the floor in reverence, then took the flagon of wine firmly in one hand and the paten of bread in the other. He walked through the grille to the passageway alongside the inner chapel, and shut the gate with a resounding *click*.

After a night of still and silent reverence, the Brother Sacristan's respectful yet pragmatic evacuation of the sacraments had a shocking effect. That *click* signaled the end of the "Garden of Repose," along with the atypical access to the monastery and its chapel. Other monks and a few friends had been waiting for the removal of the sacraments so that they could dismantle the Lady Chapel's vigil setting in time for the delayed start of Morning Prayer and subsequent Good Friday liturgies. Immediately people began lifting potted palms, rolling up carpets, carrying and repositioning pew chairs. The bustle of work roused the homeless man. Looking a little bewildered, he headed for the first opening he saw, a door into the private monastery garden, which had been unlocked so that workers could remove plants to the greenhouse. One of the monks smiled at the man and kindly but decisively redirected him to the main portico leading to the street. A little unsteady after his abrupt awakening, he hurried off into the thin morning light as people energetically attended their task of bringing the chapel into its usual form. Once they completed their work, the monks once again secured the gates and doors to the inner chapel and monastic enclosure. Having been placed by the Brother Sacristan in the monastery's Holy Spirit Chapel in the undercroft until Easter Sunday, the sanctified elements were no longer available to all. Thus the once-yearly expansion of monastic boundaries dissolved with the conclusion of the vigil, returning to the usual daily rhythm of alternating degrees of enclosure and openness.

Some of those who had been immersed in the vigil seemed startled by these transitions. One woman said that a full night of intensive prayer (and just the effort of staying awake) had pushed her past exhaustion into a kind of heightened concentration. She said that hour by hour she had moved into a highly energized and alert stillness. The change in atmosphere that came with the dawn was unsettling, she said, especially witnessing the pragmatic removal of the wine and bread on which she had been meditating. Like the soldiers' removal of Jesus from the Garden of Gethsemane, she said, moving the sacrament seemed audacious, "almost violent." So, too, a long-time congregant was crestfallen that she had arrived back that morning after the sacrament had already been taken away. A few others remained kneeling, hoping to continue their worship, but like the other two altars, the Mary altar had by then been stripped. The environment had been transformed.

This surprisingly quick transition between reverent vigil and the work-a-day tone of resetting the chapel for subsequent services revealed a principle of contemplative Christianity: detachment, even from the desire for union with the divine. The Brother Sacristan abided by the tenet of detachment by taking away the sacraments without hesitation when the time for their removal had come, as did the other monks and their guest-helpers by making a quick transition between overt spiritual practice to pragmatic work. By ending the vigil without lingering, moving directly to the next task, the Brothers taught non-monastic visitors by example not to be sentimental or precious about their spirituality and that prayer and work— Benedictine *ora et labora*—were of equal value. Their deeper unspoken lesson was that the possibility for connectedness with the divine does not exist only in silent adoration or beautiful liturgies, but in every moment of every task and in every place. Similar to keeping "inner silence" in environments of sound, learning the difficult skill of keeping equanimity regardless of context or activity was one of the contemplative's lifelong lessons and aspirations. In the transition from reverent vigil to ordinary work, the monastery's guests were also being asked to let go of their special access to the monastery, reserved only for Maundy Thursday, and to find their own interiorized space that, like the monastery, has the potential to always be sanctified.

THE MAUNDY THURSDAY vigil at the Society of Saint John the Evangelist demonstrated the paradox of receptivity and interiority on which the Grille of contemplative Christianity stands. Welcoming the stranger, whether a homeless man or an ordained priest, was a way of ameliorating the potentially divisive relationship of member and guest, of offering hospitality while also retaining the shelter which fosters an intensity that can deepen attention to the divine. The contemplative practices of silence, solitude, and enclosure were not easily understood in pluralistic American society, however. Newcomers often struggled to adopt the unfamiliar code, especially the idea that silence could be an inclusive gesture of welcome, which valued simple being over usual standards of social merit. Teachers guided non-monastics who lived outside of the stabilizing social structures and physical enclosure of monasteries to seek alternative methods of interiorization, especially in a commitment to the regular practice of silence and seclusion. Some who were serious about their commitments also found shelter in supportive networks, which occasionally showed an inhospitable tendency to exclude.

This ambiguous relationship between member and guest again rises in Gate, the chapter that follows. Those who find a way over the Gate's threshold to the inner chapel speak up, entering into a sometimes passionate discussion over the divergent interpretations of liturgies, scriptures, and histories that jostle for a place in the unofficial canon of contemplative Christianity.

Photograph courtesy of SSJE.

4

Gate

STABILITIES, INNOVATIONS, DIVERSITIES

The Gate is the grille's doorway to the inner chapel, a way of entering contemplative Christianity with seriousness. Opened or closed, the Gate is also a place of ambiguity, of hovering liminality, suggesting possibilities as well as potential contestations: What ideas and practices may one bring across the threshold? What historical understandings? Is every way accepted as a way of truth?

Illustration © John O'Brien from *Tales of a Magic Monastery*, by Theophane the Monk (1981). Reprinted with permission[1]

A FORMER EVANGELICAL Christian who turned to Roman Catholicism after discovering its contemplative side, Audrey was a woman I met repeatedly during fieldwork. I was setting off one evening from the St. Benedict's Monastery guesthouse to meet Fr. Thomas Keating for an interview at the abbey when Audrey pulled me aside to plead a request. "Could you—would you mind asking Fr. Thomas to come to Vespers tonight? We haven't seen him at all since we've been here." Fr. Thomas was to have co-taught our ten-day retreat with Cynthia Bourgeault, but his health was unstable so he was forced to withdraw. He hadn't been attending any of the offices or masses in the chapel either. Audrey had previously told me that after she had come across Fr. Thomas's books, which taught historical theologies and practices of "intimacy with God," she "could never again pray in the way [she] once did." Audrey spent at least two hours meditating every day ("I just love that dark cave," she had said) and was wistful that this was the most she could manage at home with family and work responsibilities. "It would mean so much just to be in his presence," she said as I turned for the door.

At the end of my discussion with Fr. Thomas, I relayed Audrey's message. A look of resignation came over him momentarily. He said quietly, "I'm not here to be on show, you know. It's not like I'm an animal in a zoo." But when we left the meeting room and headed back toward the monastic enclosure, Fr. Thomas responded to the request with hospitality by accompanying me into the chapel. I slipped into the seat Audrey had saved. When she saw Fr. Thomas taking a chair in the row in front of us, she whispered excitedly, just as if she had made a celebrity sighting, "Thank you, Paula, oh thank you!"

AUDREY'S RELATIONSHIP WITH Fr. Thomas Keating speaks to the power that has enabled teachers to guide practitioners. Through media like Thomas Keating's bestselling books (e.g., 2002a, 2002b, 2008), which highlight particular aspects of Christian history, teachers have helped shape *social memory* in the contemplative movement and thus have influenced people's understandings of the past, which then altered their engagement of Christian practice and thought in the present. Especially in the contemporary American religious environment, in which church institutions had little practicable authority, teachers of contemplative Christianity had to find engaging ways to persuade both new and committed adherents. Teachers relied greatly on their personal capacities—their social and cultural capital—as members of a well-educated stratum of society: they had a *performative knowledge* that came from their learnedness, rhetorical and literary skills, and liturgical artistry, the combination of which sometimes manifested in significant charismatic appeal, as illustrated by Audrey's feelings for Fr. Thomas. Their social and cultural capital also included knowledge about how to use various media to disseminate ideas and the credentials that backed the validity of their opinions.

This chapter discusses how teachers have spread contemplative Christian ways, despite the weakness of religious institutional authority in the United States, and focuses particularly on how they used selected histories to influence people's genre of Christian practice today. Their use of the old to inspire the new made this variety of American contemplative Christianity a kind of revitalization movement. They used aesthetic, scholarly, and liturgical interpretations of history to craft and authenticate social memory and to establish contemporary forms: American monasteries referenced early European architectural design, non-monastic rites included centuries-old iconic imagery and psalmodies, and authors relied greatly on the writings of mystics from medieval times and earlier. Their gestures toward the ancient and their interpretations and selections of the past brought innovation and diversity through the gate of contemplative Christianity.

Social Memory and Authenticity: Persuading Followers in a World of Faltering Religious Institutions

Although not exclusively, contemplative forms of Christianity have for the most part been historically rooted in the confined and somewhat rarefied environments of monasteries. Statistically, monasteries in the Western churches have experienced a decline, however, as have American mainline churches (Ebaugh 1993; Lantzer 2012; Wittberg 1994). In a movement that does not currently have a strong foundation of institutional authority, teachers have had to rely on other methods of leadership to persuade both potential and practicing adherents. For centuries, religious orders have offered guidance to non-members on a relatively small scale through sermons, pastoral care, letters, and publications,[2] but many monasteries have more recently widened their scope to address much larger communities.

An early popularizer of American contemplative Christianity was prolific author and Trappist monk Thomas Merton. Merton's first book, *Seven Storey Mountain*, sold over 600,000 copies in the original 1948 hardcover version and more than three million paperback copies by 1984 (Ostling 1984). His model of teaching to a broad public audience was handed down to the men who were his novices, including internationally recognized author and speaker Thomas Keating and some of the other first-generation monastic teachers in the Centering Prayer movement, like William Meninger (1997, 1998) and Basil Pennington (1983, 1987, 2000).[3] Some non-monastic contemplative teachers, like author and Episcopal priest Cynthia Bourgeault, also had significant followings around the world through print media, online, and at live teachings.[4] Whether they reached many or few, the teachers of contemplative Christianity gained followers more from the application of their personal learned skills and talents than from any authority associated with religious institutions.

The most effective teachers had the rhetorical artistry and practical skill to make themselves heard in imaginative ways, even in the context of the increasingly democratized cacophony of electronic communications in the United States. Most understood the ways and rules of society, government, and institutions like churches (or had the means to consult those who did), had the ability to fashion viable social, historical, philosophical, and theological analyses about them, and were proficient at dialogue and debate with other authorities. To varying degrees, their knowledge included understanding the effective use of rhetorical style and nuance, as well as the technical means of disseminating ideas in venues like liturgies, print and digital media, and lecture tours. By shifting their language of persuasion to the needs of particular audiences, they often had the capacity to craft creditable positions in the eyes of multiple communities, both local and distant, as well as to respond intelligently to their critics. Theirs was a kind of performative knowledge, a skill for communicating on many fronts.

Two young emerging teachers I met during fieldwork are perfect examples of this kind of skill. A professional musician with a doctorate in music performance, Darlene Franz specialized in teaching and composing chants especially for the non-monastic Wisdom Christianity community. She published print editions of liturgies as well as a quarterly digital newsletter, *Living Flame of Love*, about practice groups and events in the Pacific Northwest, and had a website dedicated to teaching and disseminating her chant compositions.[5] Darlene regularly co-taught Wisdom Schools with Cynthia Bourgeault and also led her own "Music and Attention" retreats in the United States and in countries as far away as New Zealand.

Another up-and-coming leader, Gregory Meyer was a young Baptist minister with a doctorate in religious history who taught spiritual formation at his parish in Georgia, including contemplative theologies and practices like Centering Prayer. He was also a member of a non-residential neo-monastic order that drew heavily from Islamic Sufi and Eastern Orthodox Christian teachings and practices. Gregory had co-edited a resource book on contemplative devotions for Baptist congregations, which was endorsed by a well-respected professor emeritus at an Ivy League Divinity School.[6]

This kind of social and cultural capital not only belonged to teachers in my research, but was also a characteristic of committed members of the contemplative Christian community at large. In an SSJE sermon on gratitude given to his Harvard Square congregation, Br. Kevin Hackett (2009) described individual talents as the gifts of society and God, and acknowledged that "[m]ost of us . . . are credentialed with a considerable body of personal and professional achievements. When it comes to the innate gifts which are here present this evening—everything from native intelligence to musical skill to scientific acumen to pastoral sensitivity—there is an embarrassment of wealth and riches." Of course, not all contemplative Christians' lives revolved around an Ivy League university, but Br. Kevin Hackett's point about the strength of social and cultural capital in the contemplative Christian movement was nevertheless sound for the majority of those with whom I worked. Even Peter, a young man who had been socially and economically disenfranchised during his youth as a homeless drug addict, began university studies in psychology and comparative religion during the course of my fieldwork in hopes of becoming a drug rehabilitation counselor.

The uneven distribution of knowledge in society and the centrality of agency among the people with whom I worked were important factors of the Centering Prayer movement. Fredrik Barth (2002) considered knowledge and agency to be keys to understanding social diversity and dynamism in human society. He noted that social diversity and coherence are in perpetual tension, and that societies are always in a state of flux. Transactions between individuals are the basis of this fluidity, according to Barth. Barth was not saying that there is no similarity in societies, of course, and has not argued that people are conscious of their every thought or action. Rather, he felt that disembodied, potentially reified concepts like "culture" do not have the necessary flexibility to account for the amount of diversity that actually exists in societies. Understanding similarities and diversities from the perspective of differential knowledge and social interactions allows us to incorporate this social dynamism in a substantial way, rather than as an aside. Barth felt that an anthropology of knowledge would help anthropologists avoid potentially stereotyping by depicting broad unified cultures or classes of people. An anthropology of knowledge is especially useful in complex, large-scale pluralistic societies like that of the United States.[7]

Pierre Bourdieu, by contrast, emphasized the power of class and social institutions. Using the French Roman Catholic church as his example, Bourdieu (1991) wrote that the authority of religious leaders' abilities to compel others came from their social and institutional status. The authority of such leaders' language, for example, derived from the credentials and social station of speakers who use qualified language in legitimate settings, he said. True enough, Christian contemplative teachers did use skills acquired through religious and educational institutions, and their credibility was definitely undergirded by those institutions. However, American religious and social diversity complicates Bourdieu's picture of the overarching, dominating power of institutional authority. Christian institutions in the United States have never wielded the social authority of European state religions on which Bourdieu modeled his theory (Verter 2003; Warner 1993).

An important theme in the anthropological study of Christianity, social friction between official institutional versions and local practices is common in varieties of Christianity around the world. Practitioners regularly confront institutional authority with internal critique, schism, and reform, at least in part because of the many interpretations that come out of a multiplex scriptural canon. Historically and in the present day, Christianity's propensity for group dissolution and reformation is born of people's disagreements about ideal Christian practices, social action, community models, doctrines, and theologies (Barker 2014; Bialecki 2014; Handman 2014; Humphrey 2014).[8] This dynamic of opposition and schism is especially apparent in the pluralism of contemporary American society with its multiple authorities and the democratization of voice in digital media, where power is rarely, perhaps never, concentrated in the hands of a few. There are *many*

American Christianities, including substantial diversity within denominations, showing how knowledge and agency at the micro level have had considerable social force in this environment. Contemplative Christians thus articulated their positions in a dynamic field of correlative and oppositional voices. Attested by the presence of their critics, leaders certainly did not have unqualified social authority, whether or not they were backed by institutions, for many of the institutions themselves were fraught with division and had declining memberships.[9]

Where people are discontent with the status quo and the structure consequently falters, charismatic leadership has a window to emerge as a stronger force. Charisma was definitely an important factor in the American contemplative Christian movement. Among Wisdom Schools, this charismatic expression rose as Weber's more revolutionary primary type, and among monastics, as his more institution-preserving secondary type, although both varieties turned to a "traditionalism" that was selected from particular cherished histories as a way to reform present-day Christian practices (Lindholm 2013; Weber 1978). People responded to the charismatic leadership emerging both from individuals, as in the cases of Keating and Bourgeault, and from groups, like the Society of Saint John the Evangelist. They voted with their actions by buying the books, following the social media, and attending the lectures, liturgies, workshops, and retreats of leaders who had the capacity to move them, not so much because of institutional authority. In Chapter 7, which describes the varieties and degrees of knowledge in the contemplative Christian movement, I discuss the charismatic effect of teachers' performative knowledge—what Charles Lindholm (2013) called their "extraordinary dramaturgical powers." Using liturgical examples of Holy Week, this chapter focuses not so much on charisma as on how contemplative teachers used the "genealogical method" of establishing authenticity (Lindholm 2008), an intentional selection of histories to demonstrate lineage, create social memory, and foster an identification with chosen contemplative sensibilities.

"Authenticity gathers people together in collectives that are felt to be real, essential, and vital, providing participants with meaning, unity, and a surpassing sense of belonging," wrote Lindholm (2008: 1). The appeal to history as a way of authenticating and renewing contemporary practices and knowledge made American contemplative Christianity a kind of revitalization movement. Teachers drew from the pool of available historical varieties to reintroduce, reinterpret, and prioritize parts of the Christian past as a true, viable (and, they sometimes argued, better) form. They distinguished certain ancients as having had a clearer vision of Jesus' original intentions and upheld them as sources of wisdom. This is one reason that the writings of ancient and medieval mystics played such an important role in explicating contemplatives' positions, as did the aesthetics of liturgies and material culture that referenced the past. While some adherents hoped for the survival of centuries-old institutional churches, others thought that a "return" to

contemplative Christianity may well manifest in different social-structural con-
figurations and were open to what might emerge. Some actively innovated social
alternatives, experimenting with forms like Wisdom Schools and various expressions of intentional living and neo-monasticism (Keenan 2002; Lindholm and
Zúquete 2010; Marti and Ganiel 2014; Tickle 2008, 2012; Wallace 1956).

The urge toward revitalization is nothing new, however, even in ancient institutions like Christian monastic orders. With their cloisters and monumental
churches, monasteries may appear stalwart bastions of authenticity and unbroken
lineage, but they too have repeatedly been places of rupture, innovation, and reformation. Thomas Keating's Roman Catholic Trappist order, for example, emerged
in the United States after the outlawing of monasteries during the French
Revolution. The original French Trappists (Order of Cistercians of the Strict
Observance [OCSO]) were the product of a seventeenth-century reform movement
of the Cistercian Order, which was an eleventh-century reform of the monasticism
founded by Benedict of Nursia (Order of Saint Benedict [OSB]) in the sixth century. Responding to the unpredictable times of Rome's fall, the Benedictines were
themselves a communal adaptation of the desert hermits who had withdrawn
in the fourth century to the wilderness of Egypt and Syria in search of a more
authentic way after Emperor Constantine had made Christianity a state religion
(H. Chadwick 1993; Frank and Lienhard 1993; Southern 1970).

So too, the Episcopal Society of Saint John the Evangelist (SSJE) was founded
on nineteenth-century impulses to revitalize the Church of England, itself a
product of the sixteenth-century English Reformation that instigated the destruction of Roman Catholic monasteries in Britain. Over three hundred years after
Martin Luther nailed his proclamation calling for religious reform to the door of a
German church, a group of Oxford scholars and priests banded together in agreement that something was missing from Anglican Christianity as it was then practiced. The members of this "Oxford movement" began publishing and preaching
on the complacence and ecclesial ennui of Victorian-era Anglicanism and looked
to the depths of church history for guidance on what might be a better way to live a
devoted Christian life. Part of the answer on which they settled was the reintroduc-
tion of "high liturgy" and the re-establishment of monasticism in England, which
included the Society of Saint John the Evangelist, a new Anglican monastic order
founded in 1866, which balanced Benedictine-style daily offices and contemplative prayer with social action. SSJE founder Fr. Richard Meux Benson described
them as "Trappists at home and Jesuits abroad." They established the order's
American chapter at Boston in 1870 (SSJE 1997: xiii; Faught 2003; MacCulloch
2005; Ollard 1932).[10]

These monastic institutions are thus historical products of reformations and
counter-reformations, a revolutionary process that has relied heavily on techniques which shape people's identification with particular pasts by crafting social

memory. For years, debates have been ongoing in the literature about whether social memory can have objective veracity or whether "traditions" are "inventions" for political and social ends (e.g., Hobsbawm and Ranger 1983; Pryce 1999; Sahlins 1993). There is no doubt, however, that people emphasize certain histories as a way of understanding their own circumstances, and sometimes they do this intentionally as a way of demonstrating the authenticity of certain ideas and ways. Lindholm (2008: 3–4) noted that the very concept of authenticity was born in the ambiguous mêlée of sixteenth-century European social transformations, including religious ones, which prompted people to assert new ways of living, thinking, and organizing as good and right, including their historical versions.

Moore (1992: viii) emphasized that people's memories are never "simply personal." Rather, memories "constitute our identity and provide the context for every thought and action." They are "learned, borrowed, and inherited—in part, and part of, a common stock, constructed, sustained, and transmitted by the families, communities, and cultures to which we belong. No human group is constituted, no code of conduct promulgated, no thought given form, no action committed, no knowledge communicated, without its intervention; history is both a product and a source of social memory." Fentress and Wickham (1992: 25–26) added that social memory is modeled and taught both intentionally and unintentionally, manifesting as culturally specific historical consciousness. They wrote, "Social memory is a source of knowledge. This means that it does more than provide a set of categories through which, in an unselfconscious way, a group experiences its surroundings; it also provides the groups with material for conscious reflection."

As we shall see clearly in the Wisdom School example of a Holy Week liturgy that follows, the teachers of American contemplative Christianity understood that their religion has a long history of contested stories and interpretations of the past. Indeed, the very fact that there are four canonical gospel stories (not to mention a plethora of non-canonical ones), which often conflict in their details about historical events, means that Christianity was created from multiple versions of the past. Historical arguments over interpretations, like those at the Council of Nicaea (325 CE), have persisted to the present, resulting in the great variety of Christian beliefs and practices around the world. Reflection on historical versions has always been a significant part of the picture.

Among the people with whom I did research, those histories were played out in part through commemoration. Many observed an annual liturgical calendar that celebrated selected historical personages and events, followed a lectionary which scheduled a tri-annual round of historical scriptural readings, and enacted commemorative rites like the Eucharist and the liturgical re-enactment of the events of Holy Week. Material culture like icons, vestments, liturgical paraphernalia, and church and monastic architecture further monumentalized history in chosen ways (Connerton 1989: 46–47; Oliphant 2016).

Perhaps it seems like an overstatement to depict these people as engaging in strategies that upheld chosen histories. My intention is certainly not to show them as calculating in a negative way, but rather to acknowledge the very conscious element of placing themselves within certain streams of history It is significant that almost everyone with whom I worked within the American contemplative Christian movement was there as a matter of conscious choice rather than birthright. Few of the people with whom I worked had been born into families that practiced contemplative traditions of any sort. Indeed, as we saw in Chapter 1, they often rejected their childhood Christianities and chose the contemplative Christian path after intentional searches. This conscious approach was particularly strong among monastics and ordained priests who undertook considerable reflection and formal study and went through a lengthy graduated discernment process before taking vows.

Monastic and non-monastic, ordained and lay, many of the people with whom I did research told me about their "Ah-ha!" moments, when they had come across alternative renderings of Christian historical thought that "spoke to them" and how these had shifted their interpretations of the Christian message and their subsequent practices. Their changed historical consciousness was sometimes universe bending, as we saw in Chapter 3 of Joan's new knowledge about the ancient principle of theosis, and of Audrey who said after having read the books of Fr. Thomas Keating, "I could never again pray as I once did." Making choices between the available varieties of Christian theologies, histories, and practices was a significant part of the process for all of the people with whom I worked.

To illustrate how contemplative Christian teachers in particular used historical forms to shape diverse sensibilities and ideas, including ones that were not majority expressions even within the contemplative Christian movement, I compare monastic and Wisdom Christianity versions of a specific Holy Week liturgy. Holy Week begins with Palm Sunday (the commemoration of Jesus' jubilant welcome to Jerusalem) and continues through to the events of the three-day Triduum: Maundy Thursday's "last supper," Good Friday's trial and crucifixion, and the resurrection on Easter morning. I turn to a lesser-known liturgy that occurs on the Wednesday evening of Holy Week, a service historically called Tenebrae, meaning "shadows" in Latin. Considered a kind of gateway liturgy that sets the tone for the Triduum, this rite is not universally celebrated, even in the more liturgically oriented denominations. It occurs most often in monastic contexts and some high liturgical parishes of Episcopal and Roman Catholic churches. I chose venues associated with the same denomination, the Episcopal Church, to have a baseline of structural comparability. Both versions appealed to ancient practices and scriptural roots that suggested authenticity and veracity. However, their liturgical renderings were distinctive. The monastic version employed the well-established Holy Week ethos of atonement, while the Wisdom version was overtly experimental, conveying an ambience of intimacy and eros that came from their focus on the historical genre of Bridal or Love Mysticism.

Before we look at the differences in these two liturgies, it is worth noting that the concepts of orthodoxy and orthopraxy are not particularly helpful in the context of American contemplative Christianity. In her discussions about emerging Christian forms in the United States, Phyllis Tickle (2008) described how American denominations have historically distinguished themselves by a focus on either orthopraxy or orthodoxy. Contemplative Christians definitely turned more toward right practice than right belief, but as Tickle made clear, how people actually live their Christianities smudges the line between these categories.[11] Recall from the previous chapter that Br. Curtis Almquist, SSJE (2013), counseled listeners in a video that all does not depend on "right practice." The Brothers at SSJE often advised people not to put too much emphasis on the transformative power of their spiritual practices, even though they themselves followed a daily schedule of five liturgies and set periods of private contemplation.[12] In a similar blurring of lines, the contemplatives with whom I worked did not ascribe to watertight doctrines, even though a considerable number recited creedal statements, such as the Nicene Creed, when they attended church services. Alan Jones (2014), the Dean Emeritus of Grace Episcopal Cathedral in San Francisco, wrote a blog article in the *Huffington Post* about the capacity of this variety of Christian to cross all sorts of boundaries, including seeing doubt as a form of faith.[13]

This blurring of lines and mixing of categories prompt me therefore to use the terms *orthodoxy* and *orthopraxy* rarely, and only in reference to the views of practitioners. From a theoretical perspective, these terms do not adequately convey the multiplicity that actually exists in the contemplative Christian movement in the United States. There is definitely no single "right way," either in thought or practice, and even pluralizing the terms to *orthodoxies* and *orthopraxies* retains a characteristic of monumentalism. The language of orthodoxy and orthopraxy is not nearly open enough to describe this movement, even in its monastic guises (Hann and Goltz 2010).[14]

The Society of Saint John the Evangelist: *Tenebrae—A Service of Shadows*

Even though monastic humility was a tenet they sought to practice, the Society of Saint John the Evangelist nevertheless had notable influence in the worldwide Anglican Communion. Brothers from the monastery have served in distinguished positions in the Church hierarchy, including Br. Tom Shaw's role as diocesan Bishop and Br. Geoffrey Tristam's role as Chaplain to the House of Bishops. A significant part of their work also included teaching and mentoring seminarians and ordained clergy, both at home and around the world. In other words, they were teachers of teachers as well as of laypeople. Since my first encounter with SSJE in 2005, the community had become increasingly well known through its web presence. The Dean of Boston's Episcopal cathedral noted their growing stature, saying to me when I ran into him at Assisi, Italy, in 2012 that he had watched the small monastery go from a "boutique" establishment with beautiful liturgies and teachings available to only a few, to a prominent institution in the international church. The Society's influence had magnified by its spiraling use of the Internet as a tool for teaching.[15]

SSJE's highly formalized liturgies, like the Tenebrae service I attended in March 2013, showed a conservative character of institutionally sanctioned rites, including an implicit conveyance of "orthodoxy." The establishment tone of SSJE's liturgies began with the monastic setting, an environment that suggested permanence, longevity, and authenticity. Ralph Adams Cram's design was a historical pastiche that employed architectural elements from different eras and places in Christian history: a small-scale adaptation of the basilica, one of the most ancient church forms, with a monumental bell tower and monastic enclosures. The chapel's interior included Romanesque- and Gothic-style arches, columns with stylized Doric and Ionic capitals, and a canopy-like baldacchino over the high altar in Renaissance style, including marble columns. Their Corinthian capitals were hand carved with scriptural symbols like the eagle, which is gospel writer St. John the Evangelist's historical attribute.[16]

The stained-glass windows also did their part: the rose window made reference to forms from early medieval churches in Europe, including the height of the Roman Catholic Church's power, which is still embodied in magnificent Gothic-period glassworks like those at the French cathedrals of Chartres and Strasbourg. The SSJE chapel's clerestory windows conveyed a particularly strong message about ancient lineage in their sixteen stained-glass portraits of monastic founders from the breadth of church history, from St. Anthony, the fourth-century Desert Father, to Richard Meux Benson, the nineteenth-century Anglican priest who re-established English monasticism by founding the Society of Saint John the Evangelist (SSJE nd). Liturgical paraphernalia like imported centuries-old sanctuary lamps, crucifixes, icons, and reredos, as well as elaborate vestments and simple monastic habits, further reinforced the historicity of rites performed in that setting.

With formalized practices like censing the altar, bowing, processing, prostrating, and making the sign of the cross, liturgies in such a monastic setting suggested immutability and permanence. While the Episcopal Church (1979) definitely had established liturgical forms set out in publications like *The Book of Common Prayer*, its authority structure nevertheless did not have a rigid grip on how rituals were performed on the ground; rather, authorized forms had a certain amount of flexibility built into them. During my fieldwork, Episcopal priests explained that technically one's bishop needed to approve any deviations from the written script, but in practice many parish priests often improvised and innovated in small ways. This was definitely true of SSJE, which was not under the authority of any diocese, according to Br. Gabriel, though they did have a "Bishop Visitor" who offered guidance. Even so, Br. Gabriel also told me that probably 95 percent of the liturgies SSJE performed fell well within the limits of established norms. More · inventive liturgies were created under the auspices of "An Order for Celebrating the Holy Eucharist," nicknamed "Rite III," a flexible liturgy which the Episcopal Church (1979: 400–405) developed to accommodate American congregations' desires to play more freely with content and style.[17]

The SSJE community was creative with the liturgical arts to the point of virtuosity. They used all the elements at their disposal—atmospheric, gestural, scriptural, musical, and rhetorical—to help guide their congregants toward certain sensibilities and frames of thought. SSJE's creativity sometimes took them into more experimental realms, such as a modified Compline liturgy they called Nightsong, co-designed and co-hosted in 2009 with a Boston Episcopal youth ministry group. A much less formal liturgy than was usual at SSJE, on this occasion the floor of the choir was strewn with carpets, cushions, and meditation stools. Nightsong used poetry readings, personal reflections, periods of meditation, Taizé chants, folk guitar music, and plenty of candles as a way to appeal specifically to the local college community. Yet most of SSJE's liturgical work (and play) lay in the realm of established ecclesial norms, albeit with a monastic sensibility, giving a tone of stability, historicity, authenticity, and "orthodoxy."

Following the form, intent, and much of the content of the published liturgy (Episcopal Church 2004: 75–92), SSJE's 2013 Tenebrae, "A Service of Shadows," indeed had a strong sense of this historicity and authenticity, and worked to convey an ethos of despair and darkness. A silent core of monks and monastery adherents (what Br. Philip called "the praying community") was in place before the gate opened at 7:00 p.m. to model the still and solemn ethos of the liturgy. As we saw in Chapter 3, teaching by example was a technique the monks used to guide people toward their liturgies' contemplative tone, a sensibility that was not common in American public venues, even in churches.

The modeling approach was not infallible, however. On that Wednesday in Holy Week of 2013, two women came into the antechapel about ten minutes before the Brother Sacristan opened the gate for the outside congregation to enter the choir. Clearly a newcomer, the older of the two women was taken aback by the very undemocratic presence of a monastic grille and locked gate. Although twenty or more people quietly sat in the antechapel in rush-bottomed chairs also waiting for the gate to open, she did not pick up the cue, but instead breached the silence by exclaiming her discomfort with being locked out. A few people— monks, guesthouse retreatants, and friends with liturgical duties—had already assembled in the interior chapel. This seemed to rattle the woman's sense of personal rights and freedoms. Rather than quietly watching and waiting, as did those around her, she expressed her dismay in full voice, "What are we meant to do? It is a very uncomfortable feeling, being locked out!" Once the Brother Sacristan opened the gate and the two women found seats to their liking, however, they quieted down. A number of the others who had waited also brought some of that frenetic "my-needs" energy through the gate, despite knowing enough to keep silence: under the guise of solemnity, they hurriedly sought out the perfect seat (something I've done myself), an act that seemed to prioritize personal desire rather than a community-oriented generosity of spirit, which the monks hoped to engender. The monks in their black habits persisted in modeling silence and stillness, however. The majority of guests were familiar with the ethos, and others soon picked up on it.

The chapel was dark, lit only by failing daylight from the stained-glass windows and a few flickering flames. On their wrought-iron pedestals, seven pillar candles burned at the foot of the sanctuary, and isolated lights shone from votives of the two seventeenth-century lamps that hung over the shadowed altars. Standing low at their center was the monastery's sixteenth-century Spanish crucifix, crafted from silver and ivory, a religious artifact from the time and place of the great Carmelite Counter-Reformation mystic, John of the Cross, whose likeness was among the significant historical monastics depicted in the clerestory windows high above. The monks, novices, and monastic interns took their places in their resident choir stalls, the gate flanked by the Superior and Assistant Superior, perhaps in reference to their symbolic roles as keepers of the community. Once the community had collected itself in silence for a length of time, a single monk approached the empty sanctuary and darkened altar to pour incense onto live coals in an earthy-hued ceramic bowl. Smoke curled upward in filigrees that swathed the crucifix and candles; its pungent fragrance crept forward, enveloping all with the scent that has for centuries symbolized and catalyzed passage into another kind of consciousness.

The congregation rose for the schola's polyphonic Latin anthem, *Christus factus est*, which the order of service translated as "Christ Became Obedient." The harmonies had the edgy, lamenting quality of the Eastern Orthodox Church. In the dusky light, all sat once more and listened to the schola sing psalms in raw harmony, the ancient poetry from the Judaeo-Christian tradition, here about despair and pleading, violence and destruction:

> Save me, O God,
>   for the waters have come up to my neck.
> I sink in deep mire,
>   where there is no foothold;

> I have come into deep waters,
>   and the flood sweeps over me.
>
> I am weary with my crying;
>   my throat is parched.
> My eyes grow dim
>   with waiting for my God . . . . [18]

After each psalm, a novice who had been recently clothed in the monastic habit rose from his choir stall with a brass snuffer, slowly approached the crucifix surrounded by its corona of candlelight, and extinguished a single pillar candle. As he returned to his place in the shadows, another monk struck a singing bowl, the sound of which lingered, then dissipated.

With the voicing of each psalm, the light thus diminished and the congregation sank into deeper and deeper stillness. Small points beneath the vast emptiness of a high-vaulted darkness, the candles had a mesmerizing effect. The assembly's concentrated focus seemed to intensify as the flames became fewer. After each psalm, cantors sang sober versicles and collects, to which the congregation responded in plainsong chant, reading from notation barely visible in their orders of service. Between the parenthetical clusters of psalms, three senior monks took turns to silently approach the ambo at center choir, bow to the crucifix, then chant one part of the Lamentations of Jeremiah, the Hebrew scripture that recounts the destruction of the Temple at Jerusalem in the sixth century BCE and the dispersal and degradation of the Hebrew people.

These Lamentations foreshadowed the Good Friday commemoration of the crucifixion of Jesus, who is cryptically described as the temple in the New Testament.[19] The symbolism of death, widowhood, barrenness, and shame also provided an extraordinarily powerful counter-image to the beloved bride in the Hebrew Bible's equally ancient book, Song of Songs, the scriptural basis of Love or Bridal Mysticism in Christianity, which recalls an earlier and happier epoch under the reign of King Solomon. In Lamentations 1, the City of Jerusalem is like a scorned and abandoned woman, widow of her ravaged spouse, the Temple:

> How lonely sits the city
>   that once was full of people!
> How like a widow she has become,
>   she that was great among the nations!
>
> She weeps bitterly in the night,
>   with tears on her cheeks;
> among all her lovers
>   she has no one to comfort her;

all her friends have dealt treacherously with her,
    they have become her enemies.
Jerusalem sinned grievously,
    so she has become a mockery;
all who honored her despise her,
    for they have seen her nakedness;
she herself groans,
    and turns her face away.[20]

The schola answered these Lamentations with anthems in minor key, building an ethos of despair. Toward the liturgy's conclusion, the ensemble sat at length in silent prayer as the darkness increased. The whirling smoke from the censer was no longer visible, but its evocative perfume enveloped the chapel. The final psalm, a "Prayer for Cleansing and Pardon" (Psalm 51), was chanted by a single cantor, beneath which the community hummed a minor-key drone line. Then they joined in with a plainsong response. which confirmed a sensibility of penitence: "Create in me a clean heart, O God, and renew a right spirit within me." A song of remorse said to be composed by King David after having another man killed so that he could have unsanctioned sex with his widow, this psalm again evoked the dark reversal of Bridal Mysticism. Yet the words ultimately offered hope of renewed and right relationship with the divine through atonement:

Have mercy on me, O God,
    according to your steadfast love;
according to your abundant mercy
    blot out my transgressions.
Wash me thoroughly from my iniquity,
    and cleanse me from my sin.
For I know my transgressions,
    and my sin is ever before me.

You desire truth in the inward being;
    therefore teach me wisdom in my secret heart.
Purge me with hyssop, and I shall be clean;
    wash me, and I shall be whiter than snow.

Let me hear joy and gladness;
    let the bones that you have crushed rejoice.
Hide your face from my sins,
    and blot out all my iniquities.[21]

By the service's conclusion, a single flame dimly lit the crucifix, and the clerestory windows were blind with night. All was still.

In time, the black-clad monks recessed in silence, approaching the altar in twos and bowing before the darkened crucifix before returning to their monastic enclosure. The guests then gathered themselves to leave before the Brother Sacristan locked the gate once more. Some moved soberly and quietly, sustaining the ethos of solemnity and despair that the liturgy had prompted; a few others bustled and whispered, clearly headed to their next undertaking.

SSJE'S VERSION OF the Tenebrae rite illustrates how the monks used their liturgical freedom to play with historical forms to establish specific sensibilities. Br. Gabriel told me a little about the process. He said that the Tenebrae was a mélange of the night and early morning Benedictine monastic offices of Matins and Lauds. It emerged in about the eighth century as a liturgical preparation for atonement-oriented Holy Week commemorations. Tenebrae's monastic roots are old, but the SSJE monks nevertheless experimented with liturgical details in an attempt to establish a fitting form for the non-monastic community they served. Br. Gabriel said that in the past the monastery had observed the entire liturgy, which lasted nearly three hours. By the time I attended their liturgies, the monks had cut the length by more than a third. In 2013, they chanted just two out of five poems of Lamentations and only six of a possible fourteen psalms. Other changes included the staging of diminishing light. They had seven candles rather than fifteen, in accordance with the fewer number of psalms. Also, at the liturgy's conclusion in former years the monks had taken the remaining lit candle and hidden it behind the darkened altar so that its flickering light was barely discernible. Br. Gabriel told me as well that the community previously ended the solemn service with a great crash, by rattling an aluminum sheet at the monastery chapel or by slamming a door at Emery House, SSJE's rural retreat. This ancient rite was meant to convey "foreboding and doom of the gathering storm," said Br. Gabriel, but the Brothers abandoned it because visitors were too badly startled by the sudden raucous noise after the liturgical cultivation of silence. Evidence of the pluralism that informed contemplative Christianity, the ringing of a Buddhist-style singing bowl was also a new addition in 2013.

Clearly there was room for play in the details of standardized rituals like the Tenebrae service at SSJE. Yet the tone and the message that the community fostered were less malleable. The monks' liturgical choices in the Tenebrae service worked to establish an affective quality of lamentation, atonement, and increasing solemnity, in keeping with certain historical forms. The deepening stillness I observed in the congregation suggested that those in attendance responded to this ethos (though among some, "street energy" quickly returned with the liturgy's conclusion). Descriptors in Br. James Koester's 2010 Wednesday in Holy Week sermon conveyed well the customary sensibility: cold, lonely, darkness, fear, betrayal. We approach the darkest hour in Christianity and must take courage, said Br. James, for only in relation to darkness can we fully appreciate the light to come: "We only know the relief of dawn when the terrors of the night have kept us awake" (Koester 2010). The Society of Saint John the Evangelist enacted the encroachment of night with their contemporary version of a centuries-old class of liturgy. In an aesthetic environment that cast an aura of establishment and authenticity, the Brothers used ancient liturgical elements like scripture, plain-song chant tones, discordant harmonies, and ritual gesture to encourage social memory toward specific Christian theologies and sensibilities. They used histori-cal forms to convey historical choices about the Episcopal Church's notion of the appropriate ethos for this time in the liturgical calendar.

History as Intimacy through Sacred Drama

The Society of Saint John the Evangelist's enactment of fear, foreboding, and shame in the Tenebrae service did not preclude intimacy. Whatever the senti-ment of any particular liturgy, SSJE worked to cultivate proximity with the divine by teaching what Br. Eldridge Pendleton called a "lived relationship" with the historical events of Holy Week.[22] In a sermon in 2010, Br. Eldridge, who was a history professor and a museum curator before taking vows at SSJE, encour-aged a contemplative approach to liturgies that commemorate the historical events that are so important to Christianity. He said that the way people choose to engage with Holy Week "offers us another chance to return" to God and "to immerse ourselves in the spiritual mystery of this holy season." In his sermon, Br. Eldridge Pendleton (2010; emphasis added) gave a little coaching session on how to engage:

> The events of Holy Week and Easter are *not merely annual re-enactments* of the tragic events of the life of an important historical personage. This is *spiritual mystery* on its deepest and most cosmic scale. Its *sacred drama* encompasses the depths of sin, human degradation and death, and then carries us forward to Jesus' triumph over death and resurrection to new life. These are mysteries we, too, struggle with daily all our lives and which remain beyond our comprehension.

Tenebrae and other Holy Week liturgies were part of a historical ritualization that enacted and embodied what many Christians understood to be a mysterious cycle of degradation, atonement, and redemption that people of every era must face.

In his sermon, Br. Eldridge Pendleton went on to offer two possible ways of attuning to Holy Week, both of which drew from contemplative techniques with lengthy histories in Christianity. The first was the time-honored monastic method of *lectio divina*, "an ancient Benedictine form of meditation" originating in the third century, in which one reads and contemplates scripture by setting aside the analytical mind to open oneself up to new meanings. Though he did not so identify it, the other technique seemed more akin to the imaginative self-entry into scriptural passages of St. Ignatius of Loyola's sixteenth-century spiritual exercises: "to fully enter into the Paschal mystery, to be there with Jesus, experiencing what the witnesses of those terrible events witnessed," said Br. Eldridge. He added, "Early Christians, in their worship, tried to enter into the events of the Gospel, to *actually experience* the drama of what was being recalled in their midst" (emphasis added). He encouraged his listeners to "risk" a Holy Week observance that was "more than a passive remembrance of the drama. Ask the Holy Spirit to guide you into the mystery." One can invite an indwelling of the divine by being "alert," he said: "be attentive and truly listen." Though its tone and interpretations of the events of Easter were quite different, the Wisdom community had a similar liturgical engagement with history, using dramatic renderings and other liturgical elements to foster an embodiment of and relationship with the historical characters of Holy Week.[23]

As Br. Eldridge Pendleton suggested, sacred drama as a technique of seeking a "lived relationship" with historical and divine persons has old roots in European forms of Christianity. Cynthia Bourgeault, a key advocate of sacred drama among the Wisdom community, told me that acting out scriptural stories first showed itself in the European historical record in the *Fleury Playbook* at L'Abbaye de Fleury in the Loire Valley of France. Before becoming an Episcopal priest, Bourgeault was a scholar of medieval theater who went to Fleury in the 1970s to study how the contemporary Benedictine community re-established its ancient Easter Vigil dramatization of the scriptural conversation between Mary and the angel at the empty tomb.[24] This dramatic rendering began in the ninth century as a plainsong chant, sung antiphonally across the choir, then morphed over two centuries into a fully staged liturgical drama. Scholars view the invention of dramatic presentation in liturgical context at Fleury as the birth of theater in Western Europe (Collins 1980; Kroll 2005; Ogden 2002; cf. Bourgeault 2010: 198).

One of the oldest religious communities on the continent (established ca. 630 CE), Fleury, like most monasteries in Europe, was sacked many times in wars and skirmishes and sometimes foundered with flagging membership and political scandal. With the eighteenth-century anti-Church activity of the French Revolution, Fleury was abandoned; the buildings of the monastic enclosure were destroyed, though the magnificent eleventh-century basilica survived by becoming the home of the local parish. Only in 1944 did a Benedictine community manage to fully re-establish itself there. Along with its reinstatement and the development of extraordinary monastic plainsong and choral devotion, the new community brought Fleury's old dramatic liturgical forms back to life in its own way. L'Abbaye de Fleury is an example, like SSJE and the American Wisdom community, of how discontinuity and imaginative re-establishment continually work together to create a dialogic between new and old liturgical forms in Western Christianity (Flannigan 1984; Saint-Benoît-sur-Loire nd).

We now look at how some practitioners of Wisdom Christianity, under the guidance of Episcopal priests Cynthia Bourgeault and Ward Bauman, used sacred drama and selected historical texts and practices in the Wednesday evening liturgy of Holy Week 2012 to craft social memory and historical consciousness of specific sensibilities and meanings.

"The Fire and the Rose":
Holy Week, Wisdom Style

Like monasteries, the non-gathered community of American Wisdom Christianity appealed to histories that helped establish the legitimacy of its theological tenets. Yet the Wisdom community focused on versions of history that introduced less prominent biblical interpretations. In the Wednesday evening liturgy of Holy Week 2012 at the Episcopal House of Prayer, the differences were striking. The sensibilities of darkness, defilement, and loneliness emphasized in SSJE's Tenebrae service contrasted greatly with those of the Wisdom community, whose liturgy brought together themes of death, beauty, surrender, and the eros of divine communion through texts and ritual gestures from the Christian genre of Bridal or Love Mysticism. In concert with study sessions of historical texts and contemporary theological interpretations, the community's leaders used liturgical experimentation as a way of shifting participants' historical consciousness. They thereby sought to "correct" what they considered errors of interpretation and practice that appeared early in the history of Western Christianity, especially the heavy emphasis on atonement taken up by the Roman church under the guidance of its first-century founders, Peter and Paul. Their alternative interpretation was of equal or perhaps even greater antiquity, they said, but was sidelined for sociopolitical reasons.[25]

The Wisdom community highlighted Christian Love Mysticism, which they felt was ideally demonstrated through the discipleship of Mary Magdalene, whom they called "the First Apostle" or "the apostle to the apostles." They were not isolated in their perspective; Love Mysticism was far from unknown in other contemplative settings, including monastic ones. For example, I once attended a workshop at SSJE on the intimacy of prayer that explored the idea of Love Mysticism, its historical expressions, and possibilities for contemporary practice. Even so, this genre has been a minority voice in Western Christian history. Here contemporary players used scholarly and liturgical tools to present that lesser known voice as a true manifestation of the original teachings, intentions, and practices of Jesus.

Holy Week 2012 at the Episcopal House of Prayer in Collegeville, Minnesota, was designed to foster attunement to both the divine and fellow members of the temporary residential community. The leaders, Cynthia Bourgeault and Ward Bauman, led the group in three or four Centering Prayer meditation sessions a day (of up to an hour each), as well as contemplative versions of Holy Week liturgies which they had developed over several years and had published the year before (Bourgeault, Bauman, and Franz 2011). They also gave seminars on theology and metaphysics, which showed the relationship of love and death, focusing especially on *The Mystery of Death*, written by a former Jesuit priest and student of Karl Rahner, Ladislaus Boros (1965), and on Bourgeault's book, *The Meaning of Mary Magdalene* (2010), about a contemplative model of Christianity based on teachings from "the First Apostle." Outside of liturgies and teaching sessions, the community observed silence and kept a work and prayer rhythm based on Benedictine *ora et labora*.

Participants had traveled there from all over the United States and were invariably committed practitioners of Christian contemplation. They were the lucky few: this Holy Week led by esteemed teachers of the Wisdom network took only twenty-five participants, a number that allowed for intimacy. There had been a very long waiting list of people hoping for a cancellation. This specialized temporary residential community contrasted with most lay congregations at monasteries or church parishes who come from all levels of commitment and expertise, especially during holidays like Holy Week, when many marginally committed practitioners show up. Those congregants go home to their everyday lives between liturgies and, while they may well attempt to "keep reverence" the entire week, most are obliged to engage in the everyday world of work and family commitments, which for some may detract from their intended focus. For most people in the United States, it is unusual to be fully surrounded by like-intentioned, like-practicing companions such as those at either Wisdom Schools or the residential monastic communities on which they were modeled.

Although it was temporary, the Wisdom Holy Week experiment was designed to emulate a monastic experience, at least in the sense of keeping a contemplative daily rhythm among a small enclosed and seriously observant community. The communal focus and ritual intensity of that week in residence was consciously intended to foster what Cynthia Bourgeault called the "merging of inner and outer," that is, a communal phenomenological intersubjectivity or "unitive consciousness." By observing concentrated forms of contemplative practices and liturgies, they hoped to dissolve barriers between people and the divine. The heightened intensity was a way to compensate for the temporary nature of these experiments among a non-gathered community, giving participants the tools, knowledge, and experiences that would assist their ongoing contemplative work at home.

Located on land granted from a Midwestern Benedictine monastery and university that has been instrumental in encouraging ecumenism and reform in the Roman Catholic Church, the Episcopal House of Prayer had a mandate to teach, practice, and experiment with contemplative versions of Christianity. The resident monastic community definitely influenced a Benedictine stance in the much smaller Episcopal institution. Though non-monastic and non-residential, the House of Prayer had itself developed a local, permanent rule-based society called the Contemplative Body, which came together weekly for communal contemplative practice and regular retreats. Members also took part in overseeing the mandate and activities of the retreat house. The director, Ward Bauman, felt that the depth of commitment and experience of the Contemplative Body provided stability to transitory retreat communities.[26] Unlike the Benedictine monastery on whose grounds it was located, however, the retreat house had strong inter-religious leanings, bringing in practices and philosophies from the mystical arms of other faiths to inform adherents' understandings and observances of Christianity.

This inter-religious influence could be seen in the design of its buildings. Ward Bauman told me that the architect designed the Oratory (chapel) to honor Native American aesthetics and principles.[27] Evocative of a sweat lodge or tipi, the Oratory was octagonal, with a three-tiered conical ceiling made from honey-colored wood that allowed natural light to filter in from hidden windows. The design also alluded to the indigenous understanding of the four directions, Ward said, seen in the recessed side chapels with semi-hidden windows at three directions, the entranceway being at the fourth. At the Oratory's center was a circle of granite masonry, which enclosed a patch of bare earth, then filled with sand, resembling the fire pit of a sweat lodge (see Diagrams 5 and 6, as well as images of the Oratory in the Photograph Gallery, in the back matter of this volume).

Although Ward said he had not thought of it in this way, I noticed that the buildings' design seemed also to give an architectural nod to female and male forms and their relationality. The Oratory the place of spiritual gestation, was round and softly lit, with a feeling of embracing enclosure, in clear reference to Native American symbolism of the womb-like sweat lodge (Bucko 1998). Oriented toward the Oratory, the main building was by contrast subtly phallic: long and thin, with bulkier rooms at the far end where *seminars* took place. The path that linked them was seeded with quotes from exemplary texts of the House of Prayer's distinctively inter-religious contemplative Christianity. Thus, in the very architecture there seemed to be embedded an implicit model of Bridal Mysticism, a genre that was overtly at work in the Wisdom version of Holy Week that I attended in 2012. Further, as do monastic architecture's interconnected living and liturgical spaces, the retreat house design pointed to the integral relationship between *labora*—the active work of intellectual seminars and physical work like kitchen duties and housekeeping that take place in the main building—and *ora*—its fruition through the contemplative work of liturgies and meditation in the Oratory. The architectural message was that the relationship of *ora et labora* is a foundation of life, that neither action nor contemplation could bear fruit outside of their partnership.

During the periods I spent at the House of Prayer over two years, the Native American aesthetic was not the major influence theologically or liturgically, however. Recall the inter-religious education and experience of the director, Ward Bauman, which I described in Chapter 1. Under Ward's influence, the House of Prayer experimented especially with the motifs of Middle Eastern and Eastern religions. The stone-encircled pit in the Oratory, filled as it then was with sand, was used more as a Buddhist sand garden than a sweat lodge fire, for example. This complex of flavors, along with the Christianities of fourth-century Desert mysticism, the non-canonical gospels of Nag Hammadi, particularly the Gospel of Thomas, and the writings of medieval and Counter-Reformation mystics, were then the major thrust of their theologies.[28]

The commitment to inter-religiosity was demonstrated in the stone inscriptions embedded along a winding pathway between the main building and the Oratory. One walked over five sayings engraved on granite slabs, ending with the words of the fourteenth-century Sufi poet and sheikh Jalāl ad-Dīn Rumi just before the Oratory's entrance. Beginning at the main building, they read,

You cannot travel the path until you have become the path itself.
—BUDDHA

True knowledge of God is that which is known by unknowing.
—CLOUD OF UNKNOWING

Come into being as you pass away.
—GOSPEL OF THOMAS

Be still and know that I am God.
—PSALM 46:10

This is a place where the Word is born in silence.
—RUMI

This inter-religiosity substantially influenced the liturgies offered at the House of Prayer during Holy Week. Like the monks at SSJE, the leaders and priests of this Wisdom version of Holy Week consciously sought to cultivate an ethos that nurtured transformation in relation to the divine, but by using Love Mysticism rather than atonement as its guiding theology. Their publication *Contemplative Liturgies for Holy Week* (Bourgeault, Bauman, and Franz 2011) provided an introduction explaining the theological and historical impetus for the "corrections" in these alternative liturgies, as well as detailed liturgical scripts for services from Tuesday to Sunday in Holy Week, including musical notation for chants, endnotes, credits, and lists of resources for further research. While retaining many core Christian liturgical elements, such as Maundy Thursday's foot-washing rite and the Easter Vigil's lighting of the Paschal Candle and recitation of the Exultet, the liturgists worked freely with sacred drama, silent meditation, chant, and dance, even blending some Sufi practices with Christian ones. Some rites were adapted from the liturgies of two French monastic communities that Cynthia Bourgeault had attended during Holy Week in 2005. They also omitted a number of elements, such as the customary Good Friday reading of St. John's Passion.

In her written introduction, Cynthia Bourgeault (2011: 6–7, 14) cautioned, "While they are not without their own complexity, [these liturgies] arise out of a ground of silence and are intended to be in counterpoint with that silence, not to displace it." She had concerns that the idea of "sacred theater" could be misunderstood as audience-oriented play-acting; these enactments were intended not as show, she said, but as a way to prompt people to become "deeply centered in the heart space opened up by intensive meditation." The liturgists had noticed in 2011 that the great amount of dramatic detail had distracted some participants, so in 2012 they worked to refine the rites. Cynthia increased repetition, depended on sources of rhythm like drumming, and simplified passages and dramatic actions in the hope that the liturgical "players" could spend their energy on "opening to the divine," rather than feeling overwhelmed with too much staging and too many lines.

When I asked Cynthia Bourgeault how she managed to be so innovative with liturgy, given the fairly conservative standards of the Episcopal Church, she, like SSJE's Br. Gabriel, directed me to Rite III in the *Book of Common Prayer* (Episcopal Church 1979: 400–405). She said that Rite III

> allows virtually complete innovation in the words so long as the basic structure is observed. The only caveat is that it can't technically be used at the principal Sunday service . . . . When I'm working in specialized situations—such as Wisdom Schools—where I'm not officially representing the Episcopal Church and the crew is ecumenical and often interSpiritual, nobody seems too concerned about what I do. I've had two bishops in attendance, and they love it![29]

Further, Cynthia said that if one were sensitive and didn't "back [church authorities] into the corner, they tend to love the low-key experiments. It keeps circulating new life through the cranky old system."

At the first evening's group discussion in the seminar room, Cynthia explained that this Wisdom version of Holy Week was an attempt to "change the modality" and "correct the tone" by exchanging "traditional" remorse and atonement with love and union. She said that atonement theology emphasizes humanity's "Fall from Grace" and the idea that Jesus' death was a way of compensating for human sin, thus creating an image of God as "a vindictive bully who must be paid off for slights against him." Cynthia said, too, that atonement orientations tend to set up barriers and oppositions, thereby downplaying contemplative views of humanity's intimate relationship with the divine and quelling the project to foster union.

Several additions and modifications aided the Wisdom community's effort to put forth their alternative. A significant change concerned liturgical form, which incorporated many hours of silent meditation over the week. Liturgies were also conducted in the round and adopted non-Christian influences such as Sufi-derived chants, poetry, and turning, the use of Buddhist singing bowls and chimes, and sitting on meditation cushions and stools. These were accompanied by monastic Christian elements, like ancient Gregorian and modern Taizé chants and Eucharistic rites. Intended as invocations of the divine rather than simple narrations, dramatic dialogue was crafted from selected scriptural passages, particularly from the Hebrew Bible's book of Bridal Mysticism, the Song of Songs, and mystical poetry from a variety of religious sources. Thus the liturgists did their best to cultivate an environment that encouraged the refinement of contemplative sensitivities and states of "unitive consciousness."

One of the major adjustments was the inclusion of women into the liturgical story of Holy Week. Cynthia pointed out that Mary Magdalene is prominent in the scripture that describes the events of Easter, but is nevertheless absent from the scripture used in standard Episcopal liturgies. She said that the readings in established Good Friday liturgies, for example, actually edit out Mary Magdalene's presence at the crucifixion and entombment of Jesus. In her book, Cynthia Bourgeault (2010: 207–208; emphasis in original) wrote that a first step to reclaiming Mary Magdalene is to "reinsert those authentic parts of the Passion story that tradition has conveniently excised, such as John 19:25: 'Near the cross of Jesus stood his mother, his mother's sister Mary, who was the wife of Cleophas, and *Mary of Magdala*'; or from Matthew 27:61: '*Mary Magdalene and the other Mary remained seated in front of the tomb.*'"

For the Wisdom community, Mary Magdalene's devotion as depicted in scripture had become a model by which contemplative Christians should live. In the experimental Holy Week liturgies at the House of Prayer, Mary Magdalene was brought to the foreground by focusing on her constancy, rather than on scriptures which describe the desertion of the male disciples, such as in the standard Episcopal and Roman Catholic Good Friday reading of the Passion of John.[30] This alternative rendering offered an ethos of warmth, intimacy, and loyalty by turning to scriptures and dramatic elements that overtly invoked the eros of divine union. While love, devotion, longing, and intimacy were not unknown in more standard Holy Week versions, as we saw in the depiction in Chapter 3 of SSJE's Maundy Thursday vigil, these sentiments were downplayed in liturgies leading up to Easter in comparison to an ethos of atonement. Indeed, the Tenebrae's use of Lamentations, which describes Jerusalem as a scorned and defiled widow, was in direct opposition to the honored and beloved bride in the imagery of Wisdom's Holy Week.

The Wisdom community's divergence from more established liturgical forms can be seen especially well in the Wednesday evening's Vespers Anointing Ceremony, the counter to the monastic Tenebrae service. The idea for this alternative liturgy came to Cynthia Bourgeault when she was on a Holy Week pilgrimage in France in 2005. At the Roman Catholic Communauté de l'Agneau convent in Paris, she attended a rite on the Monday in Holy Week based on the scriptural account of the anointing of Jesus at a gathering a few days before his death by the "woman with the alabaster jar" (Matthew 26:7) or a woman called Mary (John 12:3) who, in Christian tradition, is commonly thought to be Mary Magdalene. This is not a liturgy that comes out of standard enactments of the Triduum. Cynthia Bourgeault (2011: 7) explained how the French convent's addition of anointing rites by Mary Magdalene shifts the tone of Holy Week. She wrote,

> It is through his anointing at the hands of an unknown woman (whom tradition remembers as Mary Magdalene) that Jesus is sent forth to his death, sealed in the fragrance of love. And it is this same fragrance—borne in the same anointing oils, by the same set of loving hands—that awaits him in the garden on the morning of the Resurrection. With the Anointing Ceremony repositioned as the opening act in the Triduum drama, the entire shape of Holy Week shifts subtly but decisively. In this reconfiguration the meaning of anointing is itself transformed. It emerges as "the outward and visible sign" of the unshakable inner certainty that—in the immortal words of the Song of Songs—"Love is as strong as death." Thus, it becomes the sacramental seal upon all kenotic passage through those things which would appear to destroy or separate us, but in fact draw us more deeply toward the heart of divine love.

By adding anointing to the Wednesday liturgy, Cynthia Bourgeault was intentionally reclaiming an ancient rite. At a Sufi-inspired *sohbet*-style discussion that morning, she had described how olive oil was central to the Mediterranean culture. It was used for so many things, she said: cooking, cleaning, lighting lamps, healing, making love, giving birth, anointing royalty, consecrating the dying, and preparing the dead. She said, too, that in the first century, it was also used as a gesture of hospitality in the washing, drying, and application of oil to the feet of guests. Cynthia told us that, unlike the Eucharist, anointing was a sacrament that has never been restricted by the orthodoxies that grew up in Christian institutions. Anyone could anoint. In the Wednesday Holy Week Vespers service that Cynthia was then introducing, we would commemorate all the historical and cultural meanings around the anointing of Jesus at Bethany: its connotations included passionate love, welcome, kinghood, and immanent death, she said.

Cynthia had asked me to play the role of Mary Magdalene for the Wednesday Anointing Ceremony. Jamie, the young seminarian whom I knew from a Wisdom East gathering the previous spring, was to play Jesus to my Mary, the two dramatic roles for that evening's Vespers liturgy. That morning at 11 a.m., Helen (who was to lead the music) and a few others with liturgical duties joined Cynthia to rehearse their parts. Cynthia not only coached us in the staging, vocal presentation, and other technical aspects of our roles, but also guided us to discern, cultivate, and reposition "inner movement" and "quality of presence," a contemplative variety of performative knowledge that she said could prompt "divine flow" in the rites. Cynthia made it clear that our roles included working toward an invocation of "presence" or "spirit." Akin to the participatory sacred drama that Br. Eldridge Pendleton had described in his Holy Week sermon in 2010, we were not to "act" in the sense of pretending, but rather we were to "take on" those whom we represented. Thus, said Cynthia, playing these liturgical roles was not just about reading lines clearly and expressively, but was about "self-emptying"—getting ourselves out of the way enough to allow the historical-mystical persons of Mary Magdalene and Jesus to cross the barrier between realms and flow into the liturgy through us. We were to let Mary and Jesus dwell in us.[31]

Cynthia coached us further on the emotional tone we were seeking in the Anointing Ceremony. Drawing from classic motifs of Christian Bridal Mysticism, we were to balance ourselves between "firmness of being" and "ardor" as a way to bring out the eros of mystical union. This all seemed rather daunting, but Jamie and I opened up the liturgy book and spent the next hour trying to follow her direction. Cynthia offered pointers on liturgical arts like enunciation, the timing of our movements to Helen's frame drumming, the tipping point between evocative tension and lagging energy in dramatic pauses, and the sensate placement of what she called spiritual and physical energy in our bodies.

At the end of the rehearsal, Cynthia suggested that Jamie and I practice in the afternoon during the rest period between lunch and the mid-afternoon "double-sit" (hour-long) meditation. Given our assignment, we had license to break the prescribed silence. Sitting in Adirondack chairs out in the Oratory garden, we were not entirely sure how we were supposed to go about rehearsing and ended up bantering a little about "channeling" techniques. The joking tone arose from anxiety about our task, given that the liturgy used the erotic language of fourteenth-century Sufi poet Hāfez and the Hebrew Testament's Song of Songs. How *exactly* were we to practice this love-mystical connection? We felt a little uncomfortable. In the end, we mostly talked about other contemplative traditions and the challenge of drawing "flavors" and "modalities" out of world religions without watering them down or "cherry-picking" to use them to fit one's own purposes. Originally Pentecostal, Jamie had converted to the Episcopal Church in his early twenties, though he simultaneously practiced Medvedi Sufism and Vedanta Hinduism after having studied in India for a while. He was then also considering a Christian monastic vocation after he was to be ordained a priest later that year, though he wasn't sure celibacy was for him.[32]

While Jamie and I had been a little guarded about "rehearsing" mystical union in the light of day, that reserve fell away during the evening's liturgy. Ward Bauman had set the sand pit with numerous candles, an urn of red roses, and smaller vases of carnations, creating what the liturgy book described as the Song of Songs' "Mystical Garden of Love." The warm shimmering light and close duskiness of the Oratory fostered an atmosphere of intimacy. In this liturgical environment, the players were to encourage and cultivate the eros of divine union.

Having donned brown cotton robes over our everyday clothes, the twenty-five Wisdom School residents sat silent on meditation cushions or chairs in two concentric circles around the sand pit.[33] As the liturgy's presiding officiant, Ward sat at the eastern spoke of the circle with three singing bowls to his right. Seated in the inner circle, I faced him across the sand pit, and Cynthia and Jamie sat to his left. Helen was nearby with her frame drum. All present had experience with the contemplative practice of quieting their energy through silent meditation. When the group had settled into a collective stillness, Cynthia played a simple French medieval melody on her recorder, "Now the Green Blade Rises," whose lyrics (then unvoiced) associate death with "love come again like wheat that springeth green."[34] Ward then struck the mid-tone singing bowl three times.

The first reader opened with a canonical gospel passage about the fruitfulness of death, setting the tone for this version of Holy Week: "Unless a grain of wheat falls into the ground and dies, it remains a single grain, but if it dies, it shall yield a rich harvest" (John 12:26). Similar to the SSJE liturgy, this reading acknowledged that new life rises from death and darkness, yet the Wisdom liturgy primarily worked with meanings and sensibilities that emphasized light, warmth, openness, intimacy, and fecundity.[35]

Another reader then offered lines from the Sufi poet Hāfez as an "Invocation of the Mystical Garden of Love" and a directive to approach even death in beauty and hopefulness rather than in fear:

How did the rose ever open its heart and give to this world all its beauty?
It felt the encouragement of light against its being–
otherwise, we all remain too frightened.

Supported by Helen's frame drumming and using the four seven-bead "weeks" of the Anglican rosary,[36] the group then began four rounds of seven repetitions of Jesuit Thomas Hand's expansive, legato polyphonic chant "Slowly Blooms the Rose Within."

Slow - ly blooms the   Rose with - in,   slow - ly   blooms the   Rose with - in.

Thomas Hand.

Between each round, Jamie and I, as Jesus and Mary Magdalene, read from the Song of Songs, the Hebrew Bible's mystical love poetry attributed to King Solomon, which symbolizes God as Bridegroom and Israel as Bride. The rose refers to the gentle blossoming presence of divinity within, encouraged by the powerful eros of divine intimacy, and is often symbolically associated with historical representations of Mary Magdalene.[37]

Kneeling on a prayer stool at the western spoke of the Oratory's wheel and attempting to invoke Mary by being attentive to "sacred energy" and "spaciousness" in my body and voice, I said,

> I am the rose of Sharon,
> I am the lily of the valley . . .
> Let him kiss me with the kisses of his mouth;
> truly more pleasing is he than wine.
> I am my beloved's, and my beloved is mine.[38]

As Jesus, Jamie responded from across the circle with another passage,

> A garden enclosed, my sister bride;
> a garden enclosed; a fountain sealed . . .
> a garden fountain,
> a well of fresh water,
> flowing from Lebanon.
> Arise, north wind,
> and come, south wind!
> Blow upon my garden
> that its spices may flow.
> I have come to my garden, my sister, bride,
> I gather my myrrh with my spices.[39]

Using the rosary beads, the assembly chanted another seven rounds of "Slowly Blooms the Rose Within." I then concluded,

> Place me as a seal upon your heart,
> For love is as strong as death,
> its ardor as unyielding as the grave.
> It burns like a blazing fire,
> Like a mighty flame.
> Many waters cannot quench love.
> Rivers cannot wash it away.[40]

Repeated one last time, the chant's improvised harmonies arced through the close space: "Slowly blooms the rose within . . . . " There was definitely an erotic tone in the air, especially with the tingling bodily resonances from the free-moving chant and the Oratory's physically warm, softly lit atmosphere of circular embrace, scented by roses in full bloom.

The evening's second reader repeated Hāfez's dictate to open unreservedly and let go of fear. Then the congregation fell to silent meditation with the sounding of the mid-tone singing bowl.

Perhaps a quarter of an hour later, Ward lit incense and offered a paraphrase of the gospels of John and Matthew on the woman with the alabaster jar, who anointed the feet of Jesus, then wiped them with her hair and tears. In the story, Jesus upheld the woman's socially reckless impulse to join with the divine and defended her from criticisms that she wasted costly ointment: "Leave her alone. Was she not keeping it for the day of my burial? Truly I say to you, wherever the gospel is proclaimed all over the world, what she has done will be told in praise of her."

How does one describe a phenomenological density shaped from sound and motion? As I moved to begin my next part in the liturgy, the anointing, I could feel energy in my chest and lips, forehead and hands, weighty like something pressing against my skin, yet tingling with an enlivened sensation of openness and release. Simultaneously heavy and light, it had a concentrated feeling of expanding mass that manifested and intensified in the sound vibrations that resided in and emitted from my body as I spoke and chanted, and in my use of deliberately fluid, continuous movements which built energy, a technique similar to t'ai chi with which I was experimenting. Following the staging we had rehearsed, I lifted the shawl from my shoulders to wrap my head, took up the bowl of rose-scented olive oil that waited beside my meditation stool, and stood at my place in the circle. I felt that density of being increase as I circumnavigated the sand pit to kneel where Jamie/

Jesus sat. All this time, the group chanted spontaneous harmonies, undergirded by Helen's drum.

Place me as a seal u - pon your heart,   Place me as a seal u - pon your heart.

Cynthia Bourgeault.
Reprinted with permission.

The multitude of candles created a gorgeous aura of golden light; my movements cast shadows about the circle. Setting the bowl at Jamie's feet, I placed my hands together at my forehead and bowed to him. In the Sufi style, he gestured from his heart with the open palm of his right hand and bowed in reply. I kneeled, then dipped the fingers of my right hand into the bowl and lifted them dripping with oil to Jamie's forehead, saying, "Place me as a seal upon your heart, for love is as strong as death." I made the sign of the cross, then trailed my fingers down his nose to his lips, making another cross there. I refreshed the oil and made crosses on Jamie's feet and the palms of his hands, then returned to his face, soaking his throat and moving up to his cheekbone. He leaned into the pressure of my hand, eyes closed. After lingering a moment, I rose and bowed once more, as he did to me. Then I offered the bowl to another in the circle so that the anointing of all could begin. People continued to chant, "Place me as a seal upon your heart," as they moved one to the other with the bowl of rose-scented oil. I was the last in the circle to receive anointing.

The energy in the room was palpable: close, dense, warm, and quietly jubilant. When all had settled back in their places, another person read on the contemplative experience of "constant dying and rebirth" from J. G. Bennett, a disciple of G. I. Gurdjieff, "that we have no power to keep hold of our own life" and must give it freely. Introduced with a chant using the text of fourteenth-century English mystic Julian of Norwich, "All shall be well," a final reading from T. S. Eliot's *Little Gidding* also played with the sensate experience of Love Mysticism, which merges rose and fire,

> And all shall be well and
> All manner of thing shall be well
> When the tongues of flame are in-folded
> Into the crowned knot of fire
> And the fire and the rose are one.

We allowed those final words to disperse and settle, then remained in silence. In time, the liturgy concluded with Ward's liberal ringing of all three singing bowls.

Members of the congregation bowed to the garden at the center and withdrew or remained quietly to reflect in the candlelight.

Outside, people stood gazing at the stars that had appeared since we entered the Oratory. Some returned to the main buildings with the deliberate, praying-mantis-slow movements of a Buddhist-style meditative walk, passing over the five historical inter-religious inscriptions that encapsulate the Wisdom community's understanding of contemplative Christianity. One man had a rather troubled expression, but others beamed exuberantly. A few whispered passionately to each other about the power they felt from the liturgy, though we were officially to remain in silence outside of the Oratory. One said she could not describe the sweetness; another was overwhelmed by such a fiery entry into Holy Week. The following morning, Cynthia Bourgeault said that this year's version of the Anointing Ceremony had "hit it out of the ballpark." Clearly I was not the only one who felt the communitas, or "unitive presence."

APPARENT IN THIS liturgy for the Wednesday of Holy Week, Wisdom Christianity's approach to the re-enactment of the events leading to Jesus' death and resurrection differed significantly from the Society of Saint John the Evangelist's more standard liturgies. Both described the crucifixion of Jesus as "the Passion of Christ," but the tones of that passion—eros and despair—had quite different connotations. Even so, the color frontispiece for SSJE's 2013 Holy Week service bulletins called the Triduum "A Passion for *Living*": ultimately their emphasis was not death, of course, but the life that comes through death. We saw in the Wisdom community's Anointing Ceremony a similar sentiment in the opening reading from the gospel of John, the parable of the seed having to fall and die in the earth before coming to life, and there were definitely somber—even despairing—moments during the Maundy Thursday and Good Friday liturgies. But the Wisdom community's experimental rites came to the life of Easter by overtly drawing together eros and death, quite different from a more standard monastic version that marked the passage to life in part with betrayal and penitence.

These differences were clear in distinct liturgical "bookends" in each group's rites.[41] SSJE began Holy Week with a ritual diminishment of light in Wednesday's Tenebrae, the Service of Shadows, and concluded it with increasing light at the Easter Vigil when, in pre-dawn darkness, the monks kindled the sacramental fire from which the great Paschal candle was lit. People then spread the flame from taper to taper until the chapel was like a galaxy of stars. By the time the priest had proclaimed "Christ is risen!" some hours later, every light in the chapel had been turned on and daylight of the newly risen sun streamed through the clerestory windows. The entire three-day Triduum was thus ritually bracketed with Wednesday's light to darkness and the Easter Vigil's darkness to light. The light and darkness symbolized the people's journey through Holy Week as a passage of cosmic scale, in some way well beyond the imaginings and experience of ordinary human beings, despite the centrality of its very human story of betrayal and death.

While the Wisdom community also included this ancient "light out of darkness" rite with the lighting of the sacred fire and Paschal candle at the Easter Vigil, Cynthia Bourgeault (2011: 7) and her team of liturgists emphasized another kind of ritual bookending. The Anointing Ceremony on Wednesday in Holy Week was paired with Easter morning's gospel story of Mary Magdalene and another woman approaching the tomb to anoint Jesus' body. These ritual brackets are not the meaningful yet impersonal cosmic symbols of light and darkness, but the personal and intimate actions of sacramental touch at the hand of a devoted disciple, ritualized as gestures of cosmic significance. Focusing on alternative historical references (the scriptural accounts of loyal women anointing Jesus and anointing rites in general), the Wisdom liturgists hoped to reframe the Easter story from one of abandonment and betrayal to one of stalwart, attentive, and fearless passion. By highlighting different historical passages and using standard liturgical elements like sacred drama, anointing, and chanting in alternative ways, Cynthia Bourgeault (2011: 8) hoped to shift "the emotional epicenter of Holy Week from blame and guilt to freely offered transfiguring love."

I do not want to leave an impression that devotion and passion were missing from the monastic version of Holy Week. Far from it. Despair can certainly evoke its own varieties of intimacy, including strong notes of devotion, longing, friendship, and discipleship. We saw in Chapter 3, for example, how SSJE's Maundy Thursday liturgy and vigil inspired strong feelings of intimacy through commemorations of the foot-washing, supper among friends, and the long night watching in the Garden of Gethsemane in companionship with Jesus. Devotion was especially depicted in the relationship of Jesus with the unnamed Beloved Disciple, who in standard theological circles is usually thought to be John the Evangelist, SSJE's namesake (though, as we have seen, some Wisdom Christians have used biblical exegesis to claim that role for Mary Magdalene). In 2010, after they stripped the altar for the Maundy Thursday vigil, the SSJE monks set behind the wrought-iron gate a single remaining item: an icon of the Beloved Disciple with his head resting on the shoulder of Jesus. Contemplative intimacy was clearly a part of SSJE Holy Week liturgies, though there was certainly no hint of the erotic passion that Wisdom liturgies sometimes inspired.

These liturgical examples show how the contemporary environment of American pluralism opened the gate to innovation and play in contemplative Christianity. Facilitated in part by the weakened authority of religious institutions, teachers relied on personal skills and education to encourage both new and experienced contemplatives to follow their way. Teachers used selected scriptural, gestural, and architectural histories through media like ritual, spoken word, print literature, and online forums to shape collective social memory and identification with particular chosen pasts. Their efforts to persuade practitioners constituted a revitalization movement that turned especially to ancient, medieval, and Counter-Reformation mystical theologies and practices to craft and authenticate contemplative Christian ways in the present. Both monastic and non-monastic teachers used performative knowledge drawn from their social and cultural capital. This knowledge was undoubtedly gained in part from educational and religious institutions and was supported by their credentials, yet theirs was not so much an institutionally derived power as it was a learned population's capacity to influence through expertise, artistry, and technical skill, which sometimes manifested in significant charismatic appeal.

While this variety of American contemplative Christianity had strong unifying points, the movement also had internal diversity, as we have seen in the distinctive liturgical emphases of SSJE's "shadows" and the Wisdom community's "fire and rose" in a common Holy Week liturgy. With their "orthodox" tone, monasteries had the advantage of implicit authenticity in the weighty imagery of a substantial historical lineage, despite the reality of periodic stability, rupture, and renewal that has brought contemporary monastic communities into being. More overtly innovative, Christian Wisdom teachers like Cynthia Bourgeault and Ward Bauman worked at the grassroots level to encourage their versions of history by writing books, teaching online, and offering workshops, retreats, and Wisdom Schools all over the United States and abroad. One long-time practitioner of contemplative Christianity in my research marveled at how their determined efforts, practical skill, and "phenomenal knowledge" had "sown seeds all over the place to get the Wisdom network to grow and flourish."

Diverse, compelling teachers within the contemplative Christian movement prompted enthusiastic and committed followers, as we saw at the beginning of this chapter in Audrey's desire to be in the presence of Fr. Thomas Keating. Those like Audrey who ventured through the Gate next took their place in the Choir, the inner chapel where members turned to the serious practice of formal rites as a way to "listen" and "keep attention" to the divine.

Photograph by Diane Downs.

5

Choir

The Choir is the chapel's central place of communal worship, where contemplatives practice formal rites several times a day, year after year. The rituals of the Choir have a ceaseless rhythm, taking place regardless of individual enthusiasm or apathy, awakening in practitioners over time a steadying ground of attentiveness and a corpus of contemplative senses. Through the solidity and dependability of ritual posture, their practicing bodies—like temples themselves—offer a strong container for the ambiguous and creative flow of divine incarnation.

Guide us wak- ing, O Lord, and guard us sleep – ing,

That a - wake we may walk with Christ and a – sleep we may rest in peace.[1]

ON A BRILLIANT snowy morning in the season of Epiphany, I leaned heavily on the wrought-iron-hinged oak door to make my way in. Reminiscent of an eleventh-century French country church, the convent chapel had been designed in 1915 by Ralph Adams Cram, who specialized in creating evocative settings inspired by the great medieval architectural traditions of Western Europe. The understated chapel, close and intimate, was tucked away in a well-treed corner of New England. Sturdy whitewashed fieldstone walls, sheltering Romanesque arches, warm oak ceiling timbers and choir stalls, and deep-set, hand-glazed leaded windows gave a feel of rustic embrace. Uprooted from their original homes, a benefactor's gifts of ancient and modern *objets d'art* set the American convent into the great time span of both Western and Eastern Christianities. The interior space was enhanced with a pastiche of offerings: a stone baptismal font and pillars from early Roman Christendom, Coptic and Eastern Orthodox icons, a late-medieval bas-relief of biblical parables, an Umbrian-style rose window, and Art Nouveau brass plate engravings of women saints.

Here I was to attend "Awaken to Mystery," a twice-monthly contemplative morning liturgy of reading, reflection, and meditation. The space was so quiet that I wondered for a moment if I had mistaken the time or date. A rustle alerted me to the handful of people sitting in silence in a tiny side chapel, separated from the main sanctuary by a colonnade of pillars, including an ancient spiral column carved with salamanders and floral vines. One of the non-monastic "alongsiders" who ran the convent's contemplative outreach program called The Wellspring, Therese scrolled around on her iPhone for a while, then brought up the audio. She and her colleague, Ann, had taken care to create an environment of simple but inspiring beauty, just then enhanced by a download of Russian Orthodox chant. They had draped a low table with a beautifully patterned Kashmiri shawl and had set it at the center of a hand-knotted carpet. Floating in cobalt glass on this makeshift altar were white and golden chrysanthemums, the colors of Epiphany. A pillar candle burned, scenting the air with beeswax, and tapers sat in a pile ready for participants to light and wedge into a nearby metal basin of sand after voicing an intention or concern on which they would meditate that morning. Emblematic of the contemplative journey, a large spiraling nautilus shell nestled in the cataract of cloth that spilled from table to floor. Gathered around was an intimate circle of people on chairs and prayer stools. As a half-dozen more made their way in, crisp sunlight slanted through the wavy, bubbly hand-glazed window glass, sending sparkles bouncing about the unevenly textured stone walls. The newly arrived took in their surroundings. Rosy-cheeked from the cold and peeling off winter layers, they quietly joined the circle to begin the act of stilling themselves for an hour and a half of attentive listening and silence.

The Body as Temple

Often elegant but minimalistic, occasionally austere, the aesthetic environments of contemplative Christian chapels and meditation spaces set the stage for "awakening," honing sensitivity, and fostering receptivity to the divine through ritual practice. They provided places of shelter and prompting, especially important when people were new to contemplation or were in a time of difficulty. Akin to the enclosure and silence discussed in Chapter 3 that helped contemplatives direct their attention toward cultivating a "silence of being," the aesthetics of the choir—chapels, oratories, and meditation rooms—offered evocative settings in which people worked to develop senses for the divine through a regular schedule of formalized rites.

In practitioners' care for aesthetic settings like those at the "Awakening to Mystery" liturgy, there lies a paradox, however. Although people gave considerable attention to crafting contemplative environments, teachers often reminded their students that physical contexts do not really matter that much. Br. Curtis Almquist (2012; emphasis in original) said in a sermon that "we don't need a special cushion on which to sit, nor a special lamp to light, nor a special icon on which to gaze, nor special incense to smell, nor special prayer beads to finger . . . . None of that is in any way inappropriate. It may well help. It is simply not enough. What *is* enough is here and now." Ideally one was to work toward recognizing beauty and encountering the divine in any context because the real place of evocation was not the chapel, but the human body.

Keenly aware that scripture describes the human body itself as a temple and sacred space,[2] Christian contemplatives with whom I worked considered ritual practices and attunement exercises to be ways of establishing and sharpening their capacity to perceive divine presence through the senses. People engaged in formal ritual and the ritualization of everyday life in an effort to become more aware of an immanent divine in both their *individual bodies* and the *collective body*, that is, the practicing, observant community that the apostle Paul called "The Body of Christ."[3] In contemplative Christianity, the idea of incarnation and the development of *contemplative senses* thus underlay the importance of formal practice and aesthetics at the sites of ritual action. Chapel, person, and community were symbolically and phenomenologically linked.

This chapter and the following two chapters describe how paying attention to the human body individually and collectively transformed perception, heightened awareness, and attuned culturally specific senses to phenomenological intersubjectivity, or "unitive being." As the discussion develops, we shall see how "keeping attention" through formalized ritual and the ritualization of everyday life (or "intentional living") was a mode of perception that fostered culturally specific varieties of knowledge. Note that this separation of ritual, ritualization, and knowledge is a heuristic device: among contemplative Christians, formal rite and the ritualization of everyday life ideally existed cohesively as an arc of intention and attention in all aspects of life.[4] As practitioners matured, the formal rituals they enacted in the communal choir or private meditation room became integrally entwined with intentional living, a conscious contemplative outlook and responsiveness to life in the active world. So, too, knowledge—the *outcome* of ritual and ritualization—was inseparable from its source of intentional practices. Nevertheless, for the sake of clarity and analysis, I have segregated them. Think of these three chapters as a kind of Triduum, three parts of a single work, none of which can be properly understood in isolation. Chapters 5, 6, and 7 describe aspects of a single ritual process through which people work toward developing perceptual agency by combining intentional action and contemplative ways of knowing. Here, in Chapter 5, we begin with the regular, formalized rites that contemplative Christians saw as an active, responsible way to consent to the divine and to develop the skills of attention which they felt were a crucial element in the mystery of their transformation.

Attention: "The One Thing Needed"

Don't miss the moment.
The invitation for living life is in the present moment
where God is going to be most present to you and with you,
within you and around you.

—BR. CURTIS ALMQUIST, *SSJE*[5]

Phenomenological anthropologist Michael Jackson (2015: 294–295) described consciousness as fluid, complex, and "seldom stable. At one extreme, our thoughts are idle, arbitrary, distracted, and diffuse; at the other extreme, we become conceptually fixated, obsessed, abstracted, and simple-minded. We can be lost to the world one moment, and the next wholly engaged at the task at hand." Contemplative Christians understood this volatility of human perception and sought to direct themselves toward chosen ideals and ways by anchoring attention in the physical action of ritual.

Rituals can tell us many things about the communities that perform them, but the scope of the present discussion focuses on the role of attention in the phenomenology of unitive being. While teachers repeatedly emphasized that the divine was the primary actor in any contemplative encounter, practitioners nevertheless took a vital part in "co-creation" by actively "preparing the soil" through alertness and bodily attunement of the senses in ritual practice (Delio 2014; Hubbard 2014). Attuning the "spiritual senses" through the practice of attention has long been established in the history of contemplative Christianities (Dailey 2012; Elliott 2012; Gavrilyuk and Coakley 2013; Hamburger 2012).[6] Written in the early tenth century, for example, an article attributed to Symeon the New Theologian (1951) taught three methods of attention and prayer and cautioned that attention, if not combined with humility and devotion, may mislead. Sometimes called "serenity of the heart," the author noted that methods of keeping attention must be inextricably combined with an intention to follow God through prayer.

Eleven centuries later, Contemplative Outreach agreed that developing one's capacity for keeping attention is essential, but cannot be separated from an intention to love the divine. They called the combination of attention and intention "the one thing needed." The organization's Contemplative Life Program 40-day practice booklet, *Attention/Intention*, turned to the "prayerful listening attentiveness" of

Mary, who sat before Jesus at the dinner party in Bethany[7] for the archetypal form of "the one thing needed" that "allows us to be open and receptive to the Divine Indwelling" (Best 2005: 10). Apparent in the morning liturgy that The Wellspring community called "Awaken to Mystery," "awakening," "keeping attention," and "staying present" were key motifs in the formal rites among American contemplative Christians. Keeping attention meant focusing awareness on the present moment, especially by sensing the state of one's body in relation to one's environment, in which contemplatives included other people and the divine. Being present was a way of noticing immanence and recognizing that the divine was in their midst, indeed, in their very bodies.

Drawing from Ignatius of Loyola's "Foundation and First Principle" of his *Spiritual Exercises* (1991), Br. Curtis Almquist, SSJE (2012), called attentiveness a consciously chosen "posture." Before setting out to do anything, he said, "make sure you have the right posture. Get your bearings; find your center; remind yourself how to be. How do you wish to be?" *Posture* is both a consciously crafted intention and the "praxis" or practical form through which that intention is carried out. "For us to stay in touch with the presence that is present requires practice," said Br. Curtis. Such practice for monastics (and the non-monastics who learned from them) came in regular, repeated cataphatic rites like the Daily Office, which included ritualized silence, stillness, movement, and sound.

The dependable structure of recurrent cataphatic practices gave a stable form for its partner, the ambiguous, less biddable inner work of apophasis. Many contemplatives described the inner movements of self-emptying, apophatic prayer as a kind of "flow." *Flow* embodied the kenotic principles of contemplative practices, open to the wide-ranging creative potential of ambiguity, and a source of "transformation." Engaging this less visible aspect of formal rites depended upon individual agency and choice; it was the responsibility of the one who prays, yet was supported by the practicing community. Br. Curtis Almquist (2014b) encouraged his listeners on a YouTube video to choose a posture of openness that invites the inner movements of divine presence: "You are teeming with God's light and life and love," he said. "Don't grasp it. Don't squander it. Let it go. Let it go and let it flow." Experienced contemplatives believed that the strong arms of posture could support a flow of creative encounter. Both well-grounded intention and committed practice, posture could prompt one to refine perception, move past culturally normative strictures on thought and experience, and develop senses for a divine flow that "is really present in the ordinary present" (Almquist 2012).[8]

Using the work of Targoff (1997, 2001) on the post-Reformation standardization of public ritual in the Church of England, Saba Mahmood (2005: 133–135) found a resonance between the formal rites of Anglican and Muslim practitio-ners. She wrote that in both communities "external performative acts (like prayer) are understood to create corresponding inward dispositions." Mahmood's theo-ries highlight the importance of practice and rightly question anthropological assumptions about the priority of mental processes in prayer. The contemplative Christians in my research would certainly agree that repetitive physical acts of prayer have the power to form and transform selves. However, as we shall see in this Triduum of chapters, Mahmood's working distinction between the exter-nal and the internal is not a perfect fit in this ethnographic environment, for the Christian contemplative body in prayer takes on a porous, intersubjective qual-ity, a characteristic in which "external" and "internal" extensively intermingle. As illustrated in Br. Curtis Almquist's teachings, transformation in this community depends on the relationship between the posture of cataphatic, physical acts and intentions and the flow of apophatic, contemplative gestures. Physical and psy-chic actions, as well as agency and ambiguity, together instigate change; they are equally important.

In a sense, contemplative Christians' use of ritualized postures to encour-age flow was like offering an open invitation to ambiguity and its potential to inspire wonder. In a pluralistic society, embracing ambiguity is a way to address a world that is sometimes well beyond one's experience or imagination. Seligman and Weller (2012: 93) have explored how ritual's "subjunctive" character has the propensity to negotiate ambiguous conditions in a positive, relational way. They wrote,

> Rituals create a subjunctive space, a shared "could be" that constructs indi-viduals in relation to others. This is as true of religious ritual as it is of the rules of civility and etiquette. Ritual, in its formal, iterated, and enacted moments, presents a unique human resource for dealing with ambiguity and the multivocal nature of all relationships—with beings human and divine. Ritual defines and binds entities, times, and spaces. By creating such borders, it also links entities, times, and spaces to what lies beyond their immediate field.

The openness to possibility that rises out of ritual structures may be part of the reason that contemplative, practice-oriented, liturgically centered forms of Christianity—ones that use formal practices to cultivate attention and flow—are becoming more popular in the pluralistic environment of the United States. Perhaps more acutely for non-gathered contemplatives who have little access to face-to-face communities of fellow practitioners, the posture and flow of ritual encourages relationships to "what lies beyond their immediate field," whether human, divine, or some other part of their universe.

Benedict's Formula: Ora et Labora *and the Daily Office at SSJE*

The Daily Office takes us ever deeper into the incarnation.

—THE RULE OF SSJE[9]

Fifteen centuries ago, Benedict of Nursia (2011) began his *Rule* with the imperative, "listen with the ear of the heart." A way of encouraging "prayer without ceasing"[10] and developing contemplative senses over lifetimes, St. Benedict crafted his plan for a monastic *opus dei* through a framework called "the hours," a repetitive daily rhythm of *ora et labora*, or prayer and work. Every monastery at which I did fieldwork adopted some form of that ancient Benedictine rhythm for their own schedules and organizing principles.

At the Society of Saint John the Evangelist (SSJE), the daily round consisted of a rhythm of work and four daily offices plus the liturgy of the Holy Eucharist, except on its Monday Sabbath. Jamie Coats (2014: 21), the director of the Society's organization of friends and supporters called the Friends of SSJE, wrote an article describing the reasons for having liturgies throughout the day, which he encouraged his non-monastic readers to adopt in some form. He wrote,

> The Brothers, as is laid out in *The Book of Common Prayer*, publicly pray at least four times a day: Morning Prayer, Noonday Prayer, Evening Prayer, and Compline. I think of these prayers as follows:
>
> *Morning Prayer*: Center yourself as you begin your day.
> *Noonday Prayer*: In the thick of the day, offer all you are trying to achieve, all you see, to God. Be in awe.
> *Evening Prayer*: Stop work, be grateful, begin to recover a sense of peace.
> *Compline*: Have hope for the following day. Rest in God's peace.

"With these practices," Jamie Coats concluded, "we can try to keep our humanity in the busiest of worlds."

In the winter of 2011, Br. Matthew welcomed a group of high school students who were attending SSJE for the first time. In response to a young man's question about what it was like to live at the monastery, Br. Matthew outlined how the round of liturgies was integrated into the typical daily schedule at the monastery called the Daily Office.[11] He explained that the Brothers rose at 5 a.m. or so in preparation for the 6 a.m. office of Morning Prayer. After the first office, community members observed a private "sacrosanct hour" of meditative prayer in their own cells. On most days the Eucharist service came at 7:30 a.m.[12] The first hours of the day were thus given exclusively to liturgy and prayer, said Br. Matthew.

Breakfast and dish duty followed the Eucharist, then at 9 a.m. the community held its Chapter meeting in which they read and reflected on an aspect of their *Rule* and discussed the day's events or other business. The day's first work period extended from 9:30 a.m. until the Noonday Office at 12:30 p.m., interrupted briefly by the three triple-bell tollings at 12 noon, when the Brothers stopped individually to acknowledge the Angelus, the medieval prayer of encounter, consent, and incarnation, also said at the offices of Morning and Evening Prayer.[13] The main meal of the day came after Noonday Prayer, followed by washing up and the afternoon work period. Evening Prayer was at 6 p.m., after which the Brothers took a light supper. Following cleanup, they had free time until Compline at 8:30 p.m. The Great Silence began at the end of the final office, and the Brothers then retired to their cells for the night.

Br. Matthew's depiction of SSJE's daily schedule shows how deeply integrated are *ora et labora* in monastic communities, even those that are not strictly Benedictine. Through his instigation of the rhythm of formal prayer and work, Benedict intended to sanctify all aspects of life, including things that many may consider mundane: washing dishes, leading seminars, raking leaves, paying bills, holding meetings—ordinary everyday activities to be discussed in Chapter 6 as "the ritualization of everyday life." So, too, the morning "sacrosanct hour" of meditative prayer, which monks observed in their individual cells, was a cornerstone of community life. Br. Matthew said to the high school students, "Together we form a body of prayer, even though we are physically separate." Indeed, the community's *Rule* (SSJE 1997: 46) said, "Although we usually pray alone we are especially close in this hour, bearing one another up" with "a sense of unity." Brothers chose their own method of prayer for this hour—perhaps *lectio divina*, Ignatian exercises, icon gazing, or Centering Prayer—yet together, through "the radical simplicity of contemplative prayer," they ideally worked toward being "kindled by the Spirit within" and being "united in seeking to open our hearts." Life in the monastery thus integrated work and prayer as well as community and solitude. In the final chapter of this book, "Cell," I shall comment more on the important role of individual solitude in relation to community. This chapter, however, explores the communal aspects of *ora* or prayer through the monastic Daily Office and non-monastic adaptations, particularly in the cultivation of attention through chant and ritual gesture.

DESCRIBING THE HOLY Week Triduum, the year's most solemn rites at monasteries and liturgically oriented churches, Br. James Koester (2014 np) said, "Tonight, tomorrow, and Saturday are one long feast for the senses as we taste, touch, smell, hear and see God's love made manifest in bread and wine; in fire and oil; in water and towel; in word and action; in sign, symbol and sacrament." The chapel's choir was certainly a place for stimulation of the senses. The SSJE monks carefully crafted aesthetic environments for their communal worship, both the offices and the Eucharist, using ritual elements to enhance the quality and timbre of liturgical seasons.[14] Aesthetic environments were a way of nurturing practitioners' sensitivities through sound, touch, taste, scent and sight, and a place where rites fostered other "spiritual senses" that were not necessarily recognized outside of contemplative communities (Gavrilyuk and Coakley 2013).

Under the sheltering solidity of stone arches, the choir became a vessel that stirred contemplative senses by marking the shifting tone of liturgical seasons and by giving form to the ephemeral in sound, gestures, and objects. It was the place where monks created a ground of silence into which they sowed chant and spoken word. The choir offered the pungent aroma of frankincense, rising high in paisley helixes from simple bronze dishes, or in voluptuous billows from ornate silver censers as a priest blessed the altar for the Eucharist. It was the place where one felt the shock of cold on face and hands when the Superior made the rounds of the choir stalls at the end of Compline, showering the people with holy water, and where sharp wine helped dissolve a crumbly, sweet, oversized piece of unleavened bread. There in the choir, shifting medallions of color cast down from stained-glass windows to a checkerboard marble floor, and a monk's warm touch combined with cool, slick oil or gritty soot as he placed the sign of the cross on people's foreheads; candles, few or many, towered on the altar in silver, laid low on the floor in ceramic, flickered in jewel-toned glass high on granite ledges, or moved like a river of light in the hands of processing congregants. There one also felt the weighty Daily Office book, held in both hands and braced against torso, or set upon the smooth oak of a well-worn choir desk. Flowers added notes of color and scent: a handful of mauve lilacs at the statue of Mary in Ordinary Time, bowers of red peonies at the choir's center at Pentecost, or nothing, only their absence, in the depths of Lent. Add to this aesthetic world the sometimes wrenching physical effort of waking at dawn or earlier, then sitting, standing, bowing, and kneeling with the community's ceaseless tide of liturgy, ever moving regardless of one's energy, lethargy, engagement, or indifference.[15]

The aesthetic environment of the choir was magnificent at the high liturgies of feast days and holy days at the Society of Saint John the Evangelist, when the monks employed all the symbolic and expressive elements of their ritual artistry. Yet in my experience the everyday simplicity of the Daily Office deepened those senses the most, attuning participants to one another with liturgical rhythms and rites enacted repeatedly every day over the lifespan of the monks. *The Rule of SSJE* (1997: 36–37) described the Daily Office as the "heart of the Church," which "continually deepens our integration as a community, making us one with Christ." A ritual structure whose five liturgies punctuated the other activities of the day, the Daily Office was understood primarily as a way toward divine indwelling. According to the *Rule* (SSJE 1997: 36), it is a sustained act of union with Christ by which we participate in his unceasing offering of love to the Father. In reciting the psalms, singing canticles and hymns, proclaiming the divine word in Scripture, or lifting our voices in prayer, we are to enter more and more into the mind, heart, and will of Christ, and to be borne up by the Spirit in him to the Father.

Acknowledging the inevitable swings of human sentiment, the *Rule* allowed that from time to time, individual monks may be able to manage little more than "just showing up" for the formalized rites. Brothers must sometimes "accept being borne along by the corporate devotion of the assembly, remembering that the power of the sacrament is not dependent on our mental clarity or warmth of feeling," said the *Rule* (SSJE 1997: 35, 37; emphasis added), indicating that the established form of community "praxis" in the Daily Office had the capacity to override and subsume the unavoidable inconsistencies of individual monks. While "it is not possible for us to participate in the liturgy with intense devotion and awareness every time," fulfilling their "desire to experience . . . deepening communion" through the Daily Office nevertheless required taking on and "continually renewing" a posture of discipline, responsibility, and conscious effort; "for the office to be truly a means of our transfiguration we must cooperate by *continually renewing our inner attentiveness*, laying aside again and again the preoccupations and daydreams which confuse and tie us down," said the *Rule*.

Attentiveness clearly mattered at the Society of Saint John the Evangelist, even though the monks also believed that the divine acted with or without their conscious assistance. A paradox of doing and not doing, committing and recommitting to a posture of attentiveness, even in times of apathy or doubt, could help transform destabilizing sentiment over time, they believed. Central to their effort was "practice and preparation; the custom of taking our place in good time; stillness of posture; attentiveness to the readings; sensitivity and responsiveness to one another so that we can sing and recite together" (SSJE 1997: 37). Despite the fickleness of human sentiment, the monks of SSJE believed that unitive being was possible through the attentive ritual work of individual and community in cooperation with the divine.

Different from the more overt friendliness of the daily Eucharist services, the offices had a character of quietude and inwardness. Infrequently, monks might greet a long absent friend with a quiet smile across the Choir, but most often their gaze was lowered and their demeanor impassive; they appeared to keep attention in themselves, yet they were very attentive to one another and to guests in their common, unifying purpose of worshipping and encountering the divine. Entering from their cells or workplaces separately, some would arrange their sheets of music and prayer books. Most would sit in silence in their choir stalls for a period of time before the office, establishing a communal stillness into which visitors would enter. Once the office began, the monks took great care to observe a simultaneity of sound and movement. They were unified in ritual gestures like that which accompanied the chanted Gloria at the end of a psalm, bowing and crossing themselves in unison as they sang the first stanza.

Glo - ry   to the   Fa - ther and, to   the   Son,   and   to   the   Ho - ly   Spir -   it:

They then rose together to sing the next.

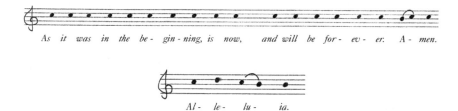

As   it   was   in   the   be - gin - ning, is   now,   and will   be   for -   ev -   er.   A - men.

Al -   le -   lu -   ia.

A participant in SSJE's Monastic Internship Program from 2011 to 2012, Rob Coulston (2012: 24–26) felt that one of the primary lessons of praying the Daily Office was learning "to listen deeply . . to be sensitive and discerning."[16] One of the regulars at the offices, Janice agreed, saying, "There is a surprising intimacy in not having to speak or greet others, but to just be in the presence of people you have prayed with for a long time. Even strangers who come for the first time seem to pick up on this. They listen and watch the community closely." Though the monks arrived for offices individually, they recessed as a community in silent formation, a notable gesture of unity. The ethos was one of transformation toward communal integration and sensitivity to the whole.

The backbone of the Daily Office was chanting the Psalms, the Hebrew Bible's book of ancient songs. Most of the Psalter of 150 psalms was chanted over a four-week cycle at the SSJE monastery (over six weeks at the country retreat, Emery House). The monks primarily sang Gregorian plainsong (unison) chant tones antiphonally or in full chorus, though they occasionally used polyphonic (harmonized) settings. Similar to a string quartet, there was no conductor. Instead, once the cantor established a tempo by singing the first stanza solo, a pulse emerged out of an internal rhythm of the community, developed over days, months, and years of chanting the same pieces together This flexible, communal non-mensurable pulse has no set time signature, but rises out of the community's feel for the rhythm of a chant's text. During antiphonal chant, the community separated into two, passing psalm verses back and forth across the choir, manifesting an ebb and flow of listening and vocalization that made silence as integral to liturgical responsiveness as sound. United again in full chorus, they redoubled the strength of their communal voice. Their seriousness of purpose in psalmody and chant was apparent in their *Rule*'s stipulation that they give the greatest care and attention "to the disciplines of choral prayer" (SSJE 1997: 36).[17]

Emphasizing the ambiguous flow that comes through the attentive enactment of chant, Br. Robert L'Esperance (2013b: 7–8; emphasis added) described his experience with communal psalmody at the Daily Office over many years: "Something happens in the body through the rise and fall of the chant pattern. What happens when we chant the psalms I cannot really explain in words. But whatever happens seems to both lull the body into a more relaxed state and heighten its attention at the same time." Quite different from speaking the psalms either liturgically or in the "very slow, deliberate, reflective reading" of private *lectio divina*, Br. Robert said, "[c]hanting evokes word patterns, repeated notes, and the rise and fall of the musical line. The words themselves, and their explicit meaning, seem to matter less than the body's experience of being caught up in the various patterns of the musical line's repetitions and cadences . . . . This type of prayer's quality is truly *visceral*—what we call *incarnational*."

Br. Robert L'Esperance noted that his observations and experience correlated with the studies of brain scientists. He said that neuroscientists have discovered that, unlike speaking, chanting the psalms engages "both left and right brain hemispheres simultaneously." Chanting the psalms is "a kind of 'prayer shock therapy,'" he said, "designed to break through dualistic thinking patterns and begin integrating prayer with life as we actually experience it, rather than as we might wish it to be." Br. Robert emphasized that this kind of prayer is not about being "nice," but about being "real" and "present." Br. Kevin Hackett (2013) agreed, saying that the effect of psalmody was "largely subliminal, as the texts work their way into the fiber of our being over the course of years." He said, "I have been shaped and formed by this discipline in ways I will never fully understand." When I spoke with Fr. Thomas Keating at his monastery in Colorado, he said something similar about the profound transformative effect of chanting the offices, adding that "science is just starting to catch on to what monks have known for centuries."

The SSJE *Rule* (1997: 36) concurred: "As we sing and chant deep levels of our being are involved." Indeed, the Daily Office's repetitive formal rites, like chanting the psalms, seemed to garner a heightened sensibility for communality and a phenomenological experience of unity, which an onlooker could sense in the cohesive flow of breath and pulse in both non-mensurable chant and in communal ritual gestures like standing, bowing, and walking in procession. The Brothers worked toward this kind of unification even when community members were not physically present; ideally, when for some reason monks were absent from the chapel and recited the offices in solitude, "the community remains united in the common offering of praise even when we are separated," according to the *Rule* (1997: 36). Br. Curtis Almquist (2012, 2014b) encouraged people to hold ritual action and aesthetics lightly and to focus more on the flow of divine presence "here and now." Even so, he and his community upheld the transformative potential of formal practice in a regular schedule. The monks felt that commitment to practicing formal postures in a regular rhythm strengthened one's capacity to sense the flow of the divine in the immediate present.

Learning Flow: Lessons in Attunement through Bodily Attention

You energize what you pay attention to.

—CYNTHIA BOURGEAULT

The SSJE Brothers taught contemplative sensitivities through the public enactment of communal rites. In the context of the Daily Office, this included things like establishing an ethos of attentive listening by intentionally seeding the chapel with individuals in silent prayer, by moving with quiet formality and keeping an inward gaze, and by chanting with still, communal interiority. Visitors primarily learned by emulating the monks' practices. Br. Kevin Hackett (2013) said that the monastery gave no lessons, not even to novices, on how to join into the sensibilities and techniques of chant at the Daily Office.[18] An exception to their hands-off approach was a page marker in guest editions of the Daily Office book on which was printed a brief passage asking visitors to be sensitive to the monks' dynamics and pacing in chant and spoken word. If a returning congregant persisted in singing without awareness for the communal form, at the conclusion of an office a monk sometimes (though rarely) offered gentle pointers on how to blend. Such direct methods were not the norm, however. Br. Kevin Hackett (2013; emphasis added) noted that people learned by taking part and tuning in: "The secret to singing the chant well, to praying together with one voice . . . verse after verse, is simply showing up, *listening carefully*, and singing as prayerfully as we can." He then added this important observation: "*Listening*, of course, is the key, and is a discipline that is central to monastic life at nearly every level."

One regular guest responded well to this indirect form of guidance. Sonja was a young poet and translator who grew up in the liturgically spartan milieu of a Norwegian-American Lutheran parish.[19] She said that as an adult she had not been able to stick with a religious institution for longer than six months until she came across SSJE. At first she had been taken aback by the monks' formality and the heavily structured Daily Office. She said, "I realized pretty quickly though that while the Brothers are very formal, they also don't care about it in a way that feels judgmental if you don't get it right. I'm not even sure how they get that message across because they're not talking to anyone or anything. It just comes through." Being present to the rhythms of the liturgy in a silently supportive environment, Sonja said that before long she saw the potential for creative inner movement in the monks' formal structure of practice. While the monks taught by example the benefits of orthopraxy, they were not unyieldingly "orthodox" about it.

Outside the context of their corporate rituals, the monks did teach contemplative attentiveness in the more direct genres of sermons, online forums, workshops, and video commentaries. At a Lenten Eucharist service, for example, Br. Geoffrey Tristam (2013) led a twenty-five-minute guided meditation exercise in lieu of a standard sermon. Adapting a spiritual exercise called "Prayer of the Present Moment" from the late Roman Catholic Jesuit priest Anthony de Mello (e.g., 1990), he invited his listeners to take up a still, but comfortable position. When silence and stillness were established, he guided people's awareness first to "inner bodily sensation" and then to sensation of the body in relation to its physical environment of clothing, air, floor, and chair. He encouraged the congregation to "think of how the atmosphere is charged with God's presence" and to consent to the divine by saying, "Come, Holy Spirit." Br. Geoffrey then invited his listeners to breathe in that "purifying presence" and breathe out the "impurities" of pride, anxiety, anger, selfishness: "Breathe out all the stuff that's built up over the day." He acknowledged how distractible are our "butterfly minds," but asked the community to persist in their concentration and presence: "As you breathe, don't think about anything else."

He allowed time for the congregants to experiment with these body awareness practices, then asked them to try extending the realm of sensitivity outward to the collective body: "Send out active praise and thanksgiving, forgiveness, and blessing to everyone in this chapel." At the end of the exercise, Br. Geoffrey Tristam told his listeners that "ninety percent of life is lived in the past or the future" and that the past's nostalgia or regret and the future's fantasy or anxiety are "the enemies of faith," a kind of prison that "stops us from living a life of abundance and joy" in the immediate presence of God. His exercise showed how, by consistently staying present and paying attention to bodily sensation in relation to others, people are able to hone a sense of connection both to humanity and to what he called "God's presence," regardless of the decentering ambiguities of past and future.

Such exercises fostered communal contemplative senses and physical simultaneity, what Wacquant (2004: 116–118) called "the synchronization of bodies." As Br. Robert L'Esperance phrased it, "something happens" through the communal enactment of "listening" in spiritual exercises and corporate rites. This "something" could occur even in very large groups. For instance, at the conclusion of SSJE's two-hour Maundy Thursday liturgy in 2008, the congregation of about 250 people processed in almost complete darkness from the choir to the Lady Chapel while singing a repetitive Taizé chant. The chanting continued at length as the congregation slowly moved to gather about the side chapel altar, where it developed into a cyclical, seamless pulse that flowed, swelled, and receded like the breath of a solitary creature at rest. The chant had a visceral quality, just as Br. Robert had observed on other occasions. Then, without any signal or leadership or cue, not even a slowing of tempo, every single person ceased the chant simultaneously. The contrast of the lulling, rhythmic, inward tones to the newly born silence was breathtaking. Utterly still, the assembly listened as reverberations of sound gradually dissipated into the rafters. Learning such unified attentiveness and attunement was wrought in the communal practice of formalized rites.

MANY NON-MONASTICS DID not have access to such provocative communal liturgies or to long-term immersion in the cycle of daily offices of intentional communities. They primarily practiced in solitude. Among these non-gathered contemplative Christians, spiritual exercises like Br. Geoffrey Tristam's "Prayer of the Present Moment" were a particularly important part of learning how practices could engage and develop contemplative senses and sensibilities. Some turned to Internet resources, like SSJE's "Brother, Give Us a Word" and online sermons and videos, or blogs and e-courses from Spirituality and Practice as well as Sounds True.[20] Some also relied on retreats and Wisdom Schools to augment their training and to establish their network of teachers and cohorts. At these non-monastic gatherings, important aspects were spiritual exercises that developed one's ability to keep attention, often taught in association with liturgies. The combination of exercises and rites was strongest at Wisdom Schools, which adapted the monastic Daily Office as a way to encourage people to take on the structures and rhythms of *ora et labora* as a stabilizing force for contemplative life at home. Learned techniques for keeping attention and attunement of the senses were a major emphasis.

A retreat in the pine forests on the ragged coast of Maine illustrates how non-monastics learned to "stay present" through body attention exercises. Sponsored by the Northeast Guild for Spiritual Formation, a local society devoted to organizing lectures, retreats, and regular meditation circles,[21] Cynthia Bourgeault had given a day-long workshop at a clapboard church on Mount Desert Island early in the summer of 2011. Twenty from that much larger group gathered down the bay at Kingfisher Cove Retreat House for a few days afterward. Cynthia had chosen chant as the theme of this gathering, focusing on the work of a Quaker musician, Paulette Meier, who had set some of her tradition's seventeenth-century mystical texts, like those of George Fox and Isaac Penington, to chants of her own composition.[22] Cynthia herself had gone to a Quaker school as a child, though her family was Christian Scientist, and remarked on the novel form these chants offered. Silent meetings were the standard practice of Quaker communities, she said.

A guest who specialized in chant had come to help lead this retreat. Clare, an English woman of perhaps forty, had lived in France until a few months before, when she had sold all her belongings and set off in search of a monastic home. Clare had a doctorate from Oxford in the history of mathematics and was an editor for a distinguished university press, as well as an accomplished pianist. For some years in Paris, she had studied ancient forms of Gregorian chant with a French mathematics professor of Russian descent, Iegor Reznikoff (2001, 2003, 2005). At Cynthia's request, Clare had taken time off from her monastic tour in the United States to share her knowledge with the group.

On the first evening at Kingfisher Cove, Clare described and demonstrated the chant technique. According to Reznikoff, she explained, Gregorian chant originally used just intonation, rather than the less flexible equal temperament, the tonal system that has dominated Western European music since the eighteenth century, because of the modal standardization required to tune a then newly popular instrument, the pianoforte. Singing plainsong in just intonation produces more intensive vibrations in the body than does equal temperament, she said, and has the capacity to create strong, clear harmonic overtones in a single voice. Reznikoff taught Clare and other students to feel and listen intensively to the sound vibrations they and their cohorts produced together, and to observe how the placement of sound in different parts of the body changes the quality of tone and sensation.[23]

Noting how difficult it is for the "Western ear" to hear just intonation, Clare admitted that she struggled with unlearning equal temperament. She had had a harder time than many of her fellow students to hear the tonal distinctions that the teacher demonstrated, but after half a year Clare's persistence brought her to a breakthrough when "something switched in me." Though she did not feel like an expert, she could now understand the just intonation modal system, not only through aural listening, but by listening through sensation, "by the way it inhabits my body." The intense physicality of this form of singing "lays me open," she said. Clare had not felt a religious affinity with Reznikoff's lessons until the "switch"; after that, she found her "spiritual way" in chant, she said.[24]

In the Common Room at Kingfisher Cove, Clare demonstrated just intonation chant. Clare asked the retreat house master to unplug the refrigerator and turn off the lights so that the pitches of their electric hum would not sway us. She then began to sing "Oh" on a mid-tone, demonstrating how the sound varied depending on physical subtleties like jaw placement, lip shape, position of the feet, and spinal alignment. Back in Paris, she said, Reznikoff might spend an entire two-hour class tinkering with the placement of a single tone, guiding his students in the art of fine listening.

Clare asked us to encircle her. She initiated a bass line tone, singing softly but with intense concentration. We listened for a long time, then she asked us to join in. People stood still, listening carefully with eyes closed, trying to respond to simple instructions about bringing the tone to the chest cavity, noticing the bodily sensation of pitch, and experimenting with vowel formation and the placement of vibration. Clare wanted us to experience how physical changes affected the quality of tone. After some twenty breath cycles, she asked us to shift the pitch to a hum, then she overlaid it with a Latin chant. As she sang, Clare visibly quivered with the intensity of the physical vibration, and yet the sound she produced had no vibrato; it was controlled and seamless, akin to what singers of Early Music call "white tone."[25] But Clare's tone had a significant difference: though as transparent and still as any of the best chant I have heard, Clare's plainsong was not at all plain; it was clearly harmonic. Like the deeper, throatier versions of Tibetan Buddhist chant, Clare was unmistakably producing several pitches. She was creating harmony through the bodily resonances of a solo chant. When Clare had finished her Latin verses, the rest of us closed the drone line together and stood in silence. The room itself seemed to be humming.

Practice sessions and discussion periods in the two days that followed showed that participants were at very different levels of understanding and comfort with chant. Eyes sparkling, face lit, Natalie said she was astonished at the energizing effects of chant. "No one has ever asked me to listen to the vibrations of sound in my own body," she said. "I had *no idea*." Jessie, on the other hand, had sung in choirs for many years, and had a strong feeling for the place of vocal sound in contemplative prayer. She said, "When a choir is really 'on,' it's not just that they're singing together really well or they're matching pitch and color really well. It's something else. The kind of concentration it takes to sing like that, it can move the whole group to another place." She paused, considering how to relate what she knew from experience: "They sort of *become* one another."[26]

Bourgeault nodded in agreement as she listened to Jessie, then described the choir as "the archetype for the ideal Christian community." She said that especially in communities that sing together multiple times a day, as they do in most monasteries, there is an "entrainment of individual singers toward a whole which constitutes 'community' at a different level." The fluidity of the Gregorian pulse mirrors "the dynamism of the cosmos," she said, allowing the choir to engage with the most expansive of rhythms. The choir's only metronomic dictate is to sense each other through pulse and tone. Pointing out that one-third of Benedict's *Rule* concerns singing the psalms, Cynthia said further that chant was a form of "Christian yoga": it was an intentional, communal discipline using regulated breath, non-mensurable pulse, and physical, tonal vibration as an "alchemical" method toward unitive being. She said, "We think of ourselves as particles, identifying people by boundaries of skin," but the experience of attunement in chant shows that "the vibrational reality of a person extends far beyond their skin" to "an interpenetration of being." Cynthia inferred that chant—primarily an aural/oral rather than a cognitive/literary experience—employs positive ritual attributes of ambiguity. She said that chant "helps us loosen the confines of dominating intellect and relearn the embodiment of love." Clare concurred, saying "true chant" is like the open window of an icon: "it communicates the divine and receives the divine."

Cynthia Bourgeault's practice had been formed by spending years in attendance at Fr. Thomas Keating's monastery, St. Benedict's in Snowmass, Colorado. She once told me that she had gone a four-year stretch without once missing the 4:30 a.m. office of Vigils. She saw such importance in the role of psalmody that she wrote a book for non-monastics, *Chanting the Psalms* (Bourgeault 2006: x), which says that chant's historical place in Christianity "goes all the way back to bedrock": Jesus "chanted the psalms as the native language of his own spiritual yearning," she wrote, and contemplative Christians' "favorite spiritual heroes have all chanted the psalms, from the desert fathers . . . to medieval saints and mystics . . . to [monastics of] our own day . . . such as Thomas Merton, Thomas Keating, and Joan Chittister." In the book, Cynthia described psalmody's role as a transformative tool, saying that the sound of Gregorian chant has "a sacred geometry so precise and compelling that it not only lifts the eye of the heart toward the sacred, but actually raises the level of being of the one who participates in it." Perhaps a model for SSJE's indirect methods of teaching chant, Benedict's *Rule* is "curiously silent" on "the actual technology of transformation." Nevertheless, wrote Cynthia, "My sense is that it's all right there, lurking just below the surface, in the Divine Office. The esoteric training was really accomplished in the choir, with Gregorian chant as the premier vessel for the actual rearrangement of conscious perception" (2006: 29). Given that most non-monastics do not have access to this kind of apprenticeship, Cynthia Bourgeault's book features a practical guide to help them learn and incorporate chant into their daily practice. Chanting the psalms, she wrote, has "an intentional and effective part to play in fine-tuning the instrument of spiritual transformation—that is, *you*" (2006: x).

By teaching chant in simple forms at retreats and Wisdom Schools, Cynthia Bourgeault brought this ancient monastic tool to the non-monastic community. She and other teachers had drawn from already established sources, like the intentional communities of Taizé in France and Iona in Scotland, who had been publishing simple chants for years.[27] Inspired by both Sufi and Christian forms of chant, American Wisdom teachers and students had also begun to write their own chants, which they named "Songs of the Presence," under the guidance and expertise of Lynn Bauman (nd). Their hope was to begin a groundswell of chant practice among contemplative Christians. This training was particularly intensive at Wisdom Schools.

In August 2011, a few months after the weekend retreat at Maine where Clare had demonstrated the vibrational qualities of just intonation, I attended one of Cynthia Bourgeault's Wisdom Schools, which again concentrated on chant.

Cynthia taught with the assistance of Darlene Franz, an oboist with a doctorate in music performance, who had for some years been developing a body of chant compositions to be used in Wisdom liturgies and gatherings.[28] Darlene independently taught chant as a form of contemplative practice, led a community of interreligious contemplatives in the Pacific Northwest, and had accompanied Cynthia to meet Iegor Reznikoff in France earlier in the year to learn more about his methods.

This was the fourteenth Wisdom School hosted by the Episcopal House of Prayer in the Midwest. The shape of the days was fairly rigorous. After an hour-long liturgy of meditation, readings, and chant at 7 a.m., we had breakfast in silence (taking turns on preparation and cleanup duties at each meal of the day). We broke the Great Silence at 9 a.m. at a *sohbet*-style study session that focused on William Segal's article, "The Force of Attention" (1987), Cynthia's newly published *The Meaning of Mary Magdalene* (Bourgeault 2010), and several other writings that explored what Cynthia called "the path of conscious love." After a short interval, we participated in a late-morning period of intentional work (gardening, kitchen work, and liturgical preparation), then took lunch and a break until 2:30 p.m. The remainder of the afternoon was divided into Darlene's teaching sessions on chant and listening practices, and a second liturgy with an extended hour-long meditation. After dinner, we gathered to discuss our reflections on the day's tasks, practices, and teachings, then had an evening liturgy of meditation, chant, and ritual gesture, after which began the Great Silence. Most people then retired for the night.

In the Common Room at the first evening's orientation, Darlene talked about chant as a tool for "transformation" and, similar to Br. Robert L'Esperance's observation, noted that in the context of contemplative practice, "it isn't about words, despite their beauty." "Breath and vibration sustain the deepest point of our existence," she said, before teaching us a chant written by one of her colleagues which set a version of 1 Kings 19 to a melodic fragment of a Sanskrit mantra: "Speak through the earthquake, the wind, and the fire / Still, small voice of love."[29]

Words: John Greenleaf Whittier, arr: Charles Rus.
Reprinted with permission.

Some people already knew the piece, and others learned quickly by listening. When the melodic bass line was established, people followed Darlene and Cynthia's cue in ad-libbing harmonies. Soon after, we walked over to the Oratory, its singing bowls and icons luminous with filtered evening light. We wrapped ourselves in brown cotton robes, settled into concentric circles around the sand pit, and incorporated the newly learned chant into the Compline liturgy.

In the days that followed, Darlene drew from Kristin Linklater's *Freeing the Natural Voice* (2006) to lead us in exercises that explored the relationship of sound, movement, and attention. She started with body awareness, saying, "Prayer is not so much what we do, but how we do it." That first afternoon session she had us stand around the Common Room performing simple movements like raising our arm from the points of wrist and elbow, or curling forward, "releasing muscular tension, vertebra by vertebra to gravity." Rather than resigning ourselves to move in "old accustomed ways," we were to listen closely to our bodies, to identify and isolate the working muscles and allow the others to rest. She was training us to distinguish between the body's "necessary" and "unnecessary tension." "Contrary to popular opinion," she said, "tension is not a bad thing." What most people call "tension" is anxiety manifested in the body; "relaxation" is actually "*necessary* tension," she said, a physical state in which we use only the muscles required to do a task. Could we tell the difference? Participants later talked about how strenuous simple movements were when attempted with the kind of attention Darlene asked of us.

Darlene invited us to bring body awareness to the production of vocal sound during the ninety-minute practice sessions on subsequent afternoons. Emphasizing the physicality of sound, she reminded us that vibration creates voice through the physical relationship of body and breath. "Breath transforms to sound when it sets the vocal cords in motion," she said. Like Clare, Darlene had us experiment by attending to vibrations in different parts of the torso and head. She also led us in experiments that varied the depth and length of breath cycles, first sighing "Ah, Oh, Oo, Mm"—then giving tone and pitch to all of the phonemes together: "Om." One participant commented on how the sound vibration made her feel anchored through the feet, "like I'm growing roots." Another, referring back to the morning's seminar discussion on "fractals" and "instantiation," described how the sound in his body felt like "a specific manifestation of the whole," like Julian of Norwich's hazelnut or T. S. Eliot's dewdrop, "in which resides all the world."

"Stillness is the ground from which the ability to attend rises," said Cynthia at another afternoon's session. Directing us in simple movements and tones, Darlene asked us to incorporate layers of attention by noticing how the perception of vibration shifted in the body with movement. How did the sensation of tone change with rolling down the spine, turning our heads, or walking? Where did the vibration seem to move in the body as awareness shifted?

Similar to Br. Geoffrey Tristam's teaching to send energy outward during the "Prayer of the Present Moment," Darlene then intensified the exercise by asking us to "expand the attentional field" beyond our own bodies. We stood in silence, taking some minutes to first feel "where stillness resides in you." Darlene initiated a mid-tone "Oh." We gave attention to the sound of our own voices, then layered in attention to the physical sensation of that sound in our bodies. Darlene then asked us to pay attention to the sound of someone else's voice. Could we then go so far as to feel the physical vibration of that voice? Afterward, Brigid remarked that she could not manage to expand to all these spheres of attention if she did not strongly feel the stability of her physical stillness first. A number of people voiced their struggle with keeping multiple layers of attention. It required extraordinary concentration. Cynthia encouraged them to set aside feelings of agitation and to persist by focusing on bodily sensation instead of a desire to succeed. "Having preferences, likes and dislikes, drains our ability to expand the attentional field," she said.

On the final afternoon of the Wisdom School, we moved from the Common Room in the main building to the Oratory.[30] Earlier in the morning work session, a group had embellished the sand pit with beautiful pieces drawn from the surrounding woods: they had threaded leaf skeletons onto the Coptic cross's trailing Pentecost ribbons, and set into the sand a trail of river stones, vases of field flowers, and a gnarled branch covered with lichen, toadstools, and vibrant green moss. As we stood in a circle around the sand pit, Darlene said, "Rhythms of the body are connected to renewal and transformation. Bodily enactment is key," not just "mental or spiritual" work. Such "embodied practice" included sensitivity to one's environment, she said: beings, places, and "external cycles like time and seasons in relation to the cycles of our own bodies."

Darlene then led us in an exercise in the "entrainment" of group rhythm. Gathering in fours at first, she guided us to "attend to the bodily alignment of rhythm with those around you" by sharing a tapped rhythm from person to person, palm to palm around the circle. Cynthia called this a way of "working the subtle metronome of the group." The size of the groups increased until the whole assembly of twenty-two was in a single circle around the sand pit. People kept their eyes closed in concentration for the most part, but also broke into laughter occasionally when the rhythm bottlenecked and crashed. Once the rhythm steadied, however, we overlaid the tapping with Cynthia's *Salve Nos* chant, which we had sung in liturgies during the week. The intention was to transfer the sensitivity of the group rhythm exercise to vocal expression. Darlene said afterward that at first there was a laborious "mechanical quality" of "thinking rather than embodying" the rhythm, but with time it became "normalized and entrained." Sharon added her sentiment: the "flow" of tapping and chanting in the large group "felt like pure love," she said.

These experiments in attention culminated that last afternoon with a liturgical exercise that brought together chant and ritual gesture. Darlene directed us
to make two concentric circles around the sand pit, apologizing to Cynthia for
not requesting permission to put gestures to her *Salve Nos* chant. Cynthia just
laughed, "This is a test of non-attachment." *Salve Nos* had three vocal lines. Lower
and higher lines of "Salve nos" pitched a third apart and repeated four times, and
a melody line with the words of consent which Jesus was said to have quoted from
Psalm 31, "Into your hands I commend my spirit / For you have redeemed me, O
God of truth."[31]

Cynthia Bourgeault.

Reprinted with permission.

Participants in the outer circle faced inward toward the Coptic cross that stood
at the center of the sand pit, raising and lowering their arms alternately on "Salve
nos." People in the inner circle took four steps counterclockwise on the first and
second "Salve nos," then, turning inward to the Coptic cross, they bowed with
hands cupped at heart on the third and fourth. Participants could step into the
space between these foundational circles to sing the melody line, "Into thy hands
I commend my spirit . . . . " One's choice to enter that in-between space depended
on group flow and necessity: Were there enough or too many singers of the melody? Did a space need to be filled? And were you the one to fill it? Darlene said that
those on the melody line could choose their gestures. Most ended up lifting their
hands upward or pressing hands together at their forehead in a *Namaste* gesture.

After ten minutes or more of enacting these instructions, Darlene rang one of
the singing bowls long and loud to get us to stop. She asked those of us who sang
the melody whether we felt we were being listened to. Cynthia gave an emphatic,
"No!" which others affirmed. People had been pretty absorbed in managing their

own actions, some heartily singing away, others vying for spots in the melody sector.

So Darlene added to her initial instructions rather emphatically, "We must *work together* so the main focus, the melody line, can be *heard*—if only one person is singing that line, then we all have to adjust and sing very softly. Remember this is an exercise in *all kinds of listening, including listening to sound.* Try to bring back that energy we found when we were silently tapping." She also reminded us of the monastic maxim that one should be able to hear those on either side as much as one hears oneself. "Try this: Imagine that your voice belongs to the people on either side of you, and you have their voice."

Darlene's prompting toward responsive listening worked wonders. People became much more attentive to the larger pulse, adjusting the quality of movement and sound. They "listened" spatially as well as aurally. Once people got the hang of it, the effect was lovely: people weaved in and out of spaces with a cohesive rhythm and the group gracefully reformed circles as individuals left or joined them. Aware of the moving whole, the group took on an agile attentiveness; the exercise's choreographed mechanics became more and more like dance. Occasionally the energy flagged when too many dropped the melody line, but then others noticed and stepped into that role, making the circle's energy surge again. People slipped into new vacancies as others shifted. They seemed less adamant about having their individual voices heard and instead blended to create a palette of bodily movement, vibration, and sound.

Darlene eventually brought us to closure. We sat there in our circles around the sand pit and had a brief post-mortem. Jack, one of the priests participating in the Wisdom School, exclaimed at how alert and responsive we had become. He observed how this kind of heightened attentiveness could have a significant effect on social responsibility; it had allowed for feelings of competition to fade and turned us instead toward listening and giving, he said. Margaret, also a priest, agreed, saying that at church she was always frustrated about how people did not seem aware of one another's needs, not helping with something as simple as finding a hymnbook for a newcomer. She said that watching people's responsiveness in this context "was very powerful." Margaret was amazed that, with just a little training, a group could become "spontaneous to seeing and hearing the needs of the community and just quietly step in."

Helen described the exercise more from a phenomenological perspective, saying that a week's worth of concentrated intellectual exploration, exercises in bodily attunement, and intensive liturgies and meditation had made participants extremely sensitive to one another. This final exercise in communal movement and sound made the group "a flowing, synchronous organism," she said.

Darlene and Cynthia smiled, pleased that people had discovered for themselves some of the characteristics that could rise from attentiveness to the body in community. Cynthia said that in twelve years of leading Wisdom Schools, she had yearned for a group that was "consciously able to step into this degree of attunement and subtlety," each member contributing to "an energetic unity." This work wasn't about acquiring information, she said, but about "forming and invoking the divine in real time." "It's not out there, but in here," she said gesturing to her chest. "It's the breath within the breath."

Judging from the responses of participants and my own experiences, intensive exercises like those at the House of Prayer Wisdom School in the summer of 2011 helped contemplative practitioners learn how to keep attention both in *one's own body* and *across a collective body*. Non-monastics in particular depended heavily on learned technique and group entrainment exercises as a way of compensating for a lack of communal practices like the Daily Office in everyday life. Rigorous rather than restful, Wisdom Schools intended to bridge the gap created from the isolation non-monastics experienced in social contexts where there were few like-minded or like-practicing companions.

AMONG AMERICAN CHRISTIAN contemplatives, ritual practices were ways of transforming perception by adopting a listening posture, keeping attention, and refining, even creating, senses. The theoretical way blazed by Steven Feld (1982) and Paul Stoller (1989), the anthropology of the senses has recognized that different cultures cultivate different perceptual strengths, prioritizing senses that other cultures may not even acknowledge.[32] American contemplative Christian communities that prized immanence and incarnation saw the human body as a temple, a sacred space of potential divine indwelling. They felt it was possible to perceive "divine flow" through a posture of contemplative listening in cataphatic rites. They also recognized and encouraged intersubjective senses that reached across the physical edges of the individual human body—senses that contrasted with some prevalent American cultural notions that individual humans are discrete, separate entities sealed in their envelopes of skin.

Part of a culturally specific vocabulary of perception, contemplative Christians understood senses as having the capacity to create a visceral intersubjectivity, and especially highlighted an expanded notion of "listening," which went well beyond the aural in these examples of formalized silence, stillness, movement, and sound. Their intersubjective ways of sensing interacted with their knowledge of historical Christian traditions of spiritual perception, creating a dialogical relationship between contemporary practitioners and past descriptions. Historical writers like Benedict of Nursia, who began his *Rule* with the imperative, "listen with the ear of your heart," both supported and shaped contemporary contemplatives' training, experience, and ways of knowing. Contemplative Christians also acknowledged the critical role of individual agency. God, they felt, was "here among us," and though they accepted the reality of human inconsistency, apathy, and doubt, downplayed the significance of emotion, and recognized the divine as the primary actor in every encounter, any barrier to "awakening" lay at least partly in one's own inattention to immanence. Formalized ritual and body attunement exercises were ways to consciously engage and to train one's senses for what Br. Curtis Almquist (2012) called the divine "presence that is really present."

As we have seen, the choir is a place of potential awakening to the divine in community. For practicing contemplatives, however, formal ritual was only one venue of encounter. The rites of the choir helped train a capacity for attentiveness and responsiveness to the divine in every aspect of life, they believed. We turn now from the Choir's *ora* to the Sacristy's *labora*, where contemplatives lived out their desire "to pray without ceasing" at work, in the home, and in greater society.

Photograph courtesy of SSJE.

6

Sacristy

PRAYER WITHOUT CEASING:
THE RITUALIZATION OF EVERYDAY LIFE

*The Sacristy is the room near the chapel where people work to
prepare for divine encounter. There they perform ordinary tasks,
things like the arranging, cleaning, and mending that support
formal ritual, indeed are inseparable from it. In the monastic
rhythm of* ora et labora, *intention and attention in the work
of the Sacristy can themselves be ways of staying present to the
divine. They reveal how contemplative life cannot be segregated
into spheres of sacred and profane.*

ILLUMINATED BY A near-full moon, three women and I went on a night walk
along a winding, stony path that skirted the forested coves of a lake. A half hour
of twisting climbs and descents brought us to a rustic altar and wooden benches
on a rocky outcropping above the water. We stripped to skin and scrabbled
down, laughing and talking. The black lake was mottled with rolling silver, and
islets and trees on the far shore were silhouetted against an indigo, well-starred
summer sky.

We leapt in and swam out. Helen responded to a loon's call and soon we were
singing away to loons, to trees, to rocks, moon, and stars, all the while laughing
and swirling. "Yes, let's whirl!" exclaimed Liz, lifting her right arm in the Sufi
turning posture while spinning herself around with her free arm and legs. So
we chanted and turned in a circle of friends, propelling ourselves about rather
noisily. Someone ventured to name our company of synchronized skinny-dippers
the "Whirling Water Dervishes." Could the Benedictine monks hear us in their
cells across the lake? Their Great Silence was well augmented that night by high-
spirited splashing and gleeful song.

Enlightenment, then the laundry.

—SIGN AT EPISCOPAL HOUSE OF PRAYER

Like these dervish skinny-dippers under a starry sky, contemplative Christians in the United States do not confine the sacred to formalized rituals or the architectural spaces in which they take place. Indeed, those with whom I did research worked toward having the "openness" to see the sacred in every situation and in every moment. Formal ritual and meditation practices were esteemed acts of devotion and entrainment, they believed, but they were not inherently different from their intentional, ritualized ways in everyday life. Rather, contemplative Christians worked toward making formal ritual and intentional living inseparable partners.

Matthew Wright (2014), an Episcopal priest who was a participant at some of the sites where I did research, wrote an online journal article that illustrates a contemplative view of a universe that is in every way sanctified. He described how three world religions, Buddhism, Christianity, and Islam, teach that there is no "dualistic separation of 'spirit' and 'world.'" He wrote,

> We have never been separate: not from one another, not from the Earth that holds us, not from the Infinite we long for . . . . We have misunderstood this longing as a defect—a symptom of our exile. It is instead the deepest sign of our belonging to the work of this world . . . . We have not been left unprepared for this work . . . . We see [a unifying divinity] forcefully in the rise of the Bodhisattva vow within Mahayana Buddhism: a shift away from individual enlightenment and escape into Nirvana, toward a pledge to remain in the phenomenal world for the service of collective awakening.
>
> We see it in the birth of Christianity, directly in the life of Jesus, who rejected a[n] . . . ascetic path in favor of one that fully embraced the world— he feasted, danced, and wept, all the while associating with those designated outcasts and sinners. He refused to recognize the expected divisions between sacred and profane. This full embrace of existence was enshrined in Christianity's core doctrine of the Incarnation—that "the Word became flesh" in the world "God so loved." . . .
>
> We see . . . its emergence in Islam and its mystical tradition, Sufism . . . . Islam's mystical path [was] based on the life of a prophet who was husband, lover, parent, warrior, and statesman . . . . Sufism pledged to keep the contemplative life fully integrated into the life of the world. It was in many ways the first wave of what many today are calling "the new monasticism." (2014).

Matthew Wright's article is an example of American contemplative Christians' inter-religious vision that the world is fully sanctified and that people living within it dwell in relation to an immanent divine, here and now.

In the world of social theory, Catherine Bell (1992) took up the term "ritualization" as a way to get past dualistic ideas that segregated thought from action and displaced "religion" and "ritual" from the contexts of lives lived by real people. The authors of *Ritual and Its Consequences* (Seligman, Weller, et al. 2008: 7–9, 11) agreed that a concept of ritual belongs "beyond the walls of religion," and added that "the work of ritual teaches us how to live within and between different boundaries," not within their confines. In place of a reified category of ritual, Bell offered ritualization as a historically and culturally contextualized process of action (rather than a conceptual category) that imbues all of life, including formal ritual and intentional everyday acts. First coined by Bourdieu (1977), "ritualization" is "the way in which certain social actions strategically distinguish themselves in relation to other actions" (Bell 1992: 74); it is "a simple imperative to *do* something in such a way that the doing itself gives the acts a special or privileged status" that is meaningful in specific social contexts (Bell, quoted in Seligman et al. 2008: 4). In other words, the idea of ritualization places formalized ritual, with its common features of fixity and repetition, squarely in the domain of the everyday activity that people approach with intention.

In the sanctified world of contemplative Christianity, formal liturgies were frequently a significant aspect on the cline of their ritualized lives. However, not everyone who lived with intention included formal rites in their repertoire of action, thus making their intentionality invisible to others. Among contemplative Christians, ritualization included repeating and persisting in the psychic actions—that is, the "inner gestures" and intentions they called "letting go" and "consenting to the divine"—that are potentially applied to any type of observable action. Practitioners may or may not include specific repeated physical actions in their ritualization of everyday life. Recognizing how people differently ritualize life helps us to better understand the great scope of activity that people employ to relate to an "Ultimate Reality," as Fr. Thomas Keating (2006) called it, even in communities that appear largely "secular" to social theorists. While dualistic theory has persisted, especially in conversations about secularization and modernity (e.g., Berger 1999; Finke and Starke 2005), scholars working on religion in the United States have begun to move away from sacred/profane distinctions in response to field research that has revealed how people integrate "religious" sensibilities and practices into their daily lives (e.g., Ammerman 2007, 2013, 2014; McDannell 1995; McGuire 2008; Peña 2011; Turner 2012).

Seeking to understand the integration of religious thought and action in the "modernity" of contemporary American life compels us to investigate how individuals engage with larger social forces. Along with her focus on agency, Bell's ritualization (1992: 78–80) also suggested something toward a *habitus* of ritual in relation to conscious action. Drawing from Bourdieu's practice theory, she described ritualization as individuals' habitual dispositions that take from and give shape to social and cultural conventions, both intentionally and below the level of consciousness. Based on the "socially informed body," including physical and culturally specific senses, a ritual habitus is an interplay between individual agency and hegemonizing social structures of cultural knowledge and practice.

As described in the previous chapter, the exercises that trained people in conscious attention illustrate how the role of agency is a crucial aspect of American contemplative Christians' efforts to craft and transform demeanors, behaviors, and thought in the context of unconscious, habitual fields of practice that are mediated by culture (cf. Mahmood 2005: 135–139). Contemplative Christians dwelled in a kind of convection current in which they analyzed and attempted through conscious acts to alter perception and to change habitual thoughts and behaviors, then subsume them through repetition in the effort to make the new ways and ideas a normal, assumed aspect of life. Contemplative Christian teachers recognized how difficult it was to move past ascribed cultural and social ways of being, which is why they insisted that discipline and repetitive schedules of practice were so important. They felt that one had little chance of working toward "transformation" if one depended only upon the inconstant whims of personal desire. Though situated in a cultural frame that understood human feelings, intentions, and endeavors to be inconsistent and God to be the primary actor, these people nevertheless felt that their own seriousness of purpose about transformation was a crucial factor, one which required work that actively challenged and changed underlying ways of acting and thinking.[1]

The chapel's sacristy is the place of life's work that is directly connected to formalized devotion, a place where one decants wine, cleans silver, strips away wax, takes inventory, logs sermon notes, arranges flowers, irons and repairs linens, and dons ritual vestments, all part of efforts toward a renewal of ritualized attentiveness that seeks relationship with the divine. In this chapter we follow Christian contemplatives to see how posture and intentional action in everyday American life was as crucial to the flow of divine indwelling as formal religious observance.

Monastic Teachings on Labora: *Learning Attentiveness through the Work of Everyday Life*

Rejoice always; pray without ceasing;
in everything give thanks.
—1 THESSALONIANS 5:17

One of my ejournalers, Rebecca, pointed out that the Society of Saint John the Evangelist's commitment to a balance of formal prayer and active life could be seen in three predominant circular stained-glass cameo windows set into the thick stone wall of St. John's side chapel. A Boston College doctoral student of early Christian history who regularly attended the 6 a.m. office of Morning Prayer, Rebecca said, "I've spent a lot of time looking up at those windows and I've come to the conclusion that they are meant to be read together." She said that, when seen as a single work, these three adjoining windows convey a key dialogic in Christian principles between action and contemplation. To the left is a window of St. John the Evangelist experiencing a vision of Lady Wisdom, or Sophia, while writing his gospel; at the right is a depiction of Jesus calling John from his fishing boat to join in active service. Each of these figures looks inward toward the center window, drawing the viewer's attention to a glasswork rendering of the ascended Christ surrounded by stars and lamps, a design convention for divine glory that John described in his Book of Revelation. As Rebecca observed, the windows teach us that together, contemplation and active work bring us to the enlightenment promised in scripture; one cannot find the way through dichotomization, by being *either* active *or* contemplative, but only through their union, manifested in a life that synthesizes, embraces, and practices both *ora et labora*.[2]

Following the pattern of St. Benedict's *ora et labora*, all of the monastics with whom I worked recognized that prayer and working life were integral partners in crafting a sustainable life of "ceaseless prayer." For example, in the chapter called "Prayer and Life," the SSJE *Rule* (1997: 44) said that, though it takes a great deal of courage and attentiveness, monks must resist "the tendency to restrict prayer to set times . . . [and instead] aim at eucharistic living that is responsive at all times and in all places to the divine presence." In the monastery's *Love Life* video series offered during Lent 2014, Br. Curtis Almquist (2014a) noted that he considered everyday occurrences "an invitation to participate in life, in God's life." He said,

> In a monastery, and it's probably true in your own life, a huge percentage of the day is tedious. We're not climbing the spiritual mountains: we're washing the dishes, petting the dog, cutting the grass, washing the clothes, getting from point A to point B. Most of life is that . . . . In those contexts . . . we should be asking . . . what is the invitation in this moment? It may be you're passing by people on the street, you're walking or you're on a bus or a subway, you're in commuter traffic . . . and you're seeing people sitting beside you or seeing people through car windows. What are you seeing? Can you put a blessing on them? Can you radiate God's light and life and love onto their being? . . . If God is really present to us . . . in every passing moment, what is the invitation now?

An example of taking up that invitation to love, Br. Robert L'Esperance (2014) described ways of transforming his responses in difficult relationships. Speaking of those who annoyed him in everyday life, Br. Robert said,

> I can spend so much time in my head demonizing them, which of course is a justification to myself for why I can be nasty to them, or why I'm in

conflict with them, or why they push my buttons . . . . That kind of thought
pattern is something . . . we have to catch ourselves in and that we have
to stop . . . . Augustine said, "Thinking can be sinful." . . . I think that this
is what he was talking about much more than . . . sexual desire . . . . Our
ability . . . to demonize others, to justify our own feelings about them.
And how do we stop that? . . . We catch ourselves in that kind of thinking
and we say, "No, I can't go there. I can't do that. I have to do something
else." . . . I think that there's a very sound spiritual practice for us.

Br. Robert taught that one must recognize aggressive, oppositional emotion in the
moment in order to transform it toward a chosen posture of love and communion.

Br. Robert L'Esperance's method of stopping, assessing, and transforming was
a classic monastic practice called *statio*. Statio is a practice in which one stops,
reflects, and reorients oneself toward the divine, especially by renewing and enacting chosen intentions (Chittister 1991). Just as the cameo windows in the wall of
St. John's chapel depicted principles about contemplation and action, the practice
of statio was also built into SSJE architecture: the monks who celebrate offices and
Eucharist services step from the sacristy into a small alcove called the statio before
entering the chapel's sanctuary and choir (see Diagrams 2 and 3 in the back matter of this volume). Adorned with hand-painted icons, bells, burning candles, and
a stoup of holy water, the statio has five doors leading to the numerous, divergent
activities of life. It is a liminal space to stop and gather oneself before moving
either to formal worship or to the tasks of ordinary life; it is a space of ambiguity
and transition, which links the chapel and the larger world.

Br. Robert noted that his practice of repeatedly asking and offering forgiveness
"has actually . . . become easier because I've had so many opportunities to practice
it." He smiled at his own hotheadedness, then added, "and maybe that's part of the
grace." Just as the potency of Centering Prayer is said to arise from one's need to
continually "return" because of inevitable distracting thoughts, the practice of statio
was a ritualized response to life's recurring adversities. Contemplative Christians
believed that the tensions of everyday life—when greeted with intentionality—
could actually become a source of change and transformation.

In his book, *Unwrapping the Gifts: The Twelve Days of Christmas*, Br. Curtis
Almquist (2008: 59–66) taught another form of statio when he wrote, "Humility
comes as a by-product of living a well-practiced life." Br. Curtis recommended
adopting a "posture of hesitation," an intentional way of enacting humility in daily
life by taking time before responding to others. "By hesitating, I am not talking
about being demure nor about being spineless. I'm speaking here of reverencing
those whom you find alien" (60). Rather than judging people because you find
them "uninteresting or ignorant or insufferable" for any number of personal or
cultural traits, one can stop and listen, considering them as "children of God" and

quite possibly "our teachers." Br. Curtis acknowledged that "judgment is necessary most every day" and "our 'critical faculties' are an essential part of life. Some
of this is simply pragmatic," he said, "like our judging whether it's safe to cross the
street," but it also extends to judging the thoughts, actions, and behaviors of other
people. Discerning one's position in relation to another's actions and assertions
is necessary, but "if we only go so far as damning or distancing ourselves . . . then
our judgment has probably not gone deep enough. Our critical faculties, used
unavoidably and essentially in life" must always work in relation to our awareness
of every person's connection to the divine, wrote Br. Curtis Almquist (62).

A posture of hesitation is a repeated, ritualized practice of awareness, what
Br. Curtis called "holy listening," which intentionally seeks to replace criticism
with compassion, reverence, and empathy. He said that the humility such efforts
engender comes out of "the conversion of our critical faculties from a rejecting
meanness to a generous mercy, the judgment of love and the grace of identification with others" (65). Through the repeated intentional practice of a posture
of hesitation, divisive critical thoughts and feelings can become what Br. Curtis
described as a "Pavlovian bell ringing in your soul" (64), a prompt to a reformed
embodiment of chosen ideals. Br. Curtis Almquist thus taught that consciously
chosen practices could be subsumed as a corpus of embodied responses, an example of contemplative Christians' belief that conscious thought and action have a
capacity to reform habitus.

Halfway across the country at his Colorado monastery, Fr. Thomas Keating
also talked to me about the necessity of intentional approaches to life, similar
to those advocated by the monks at SSJE. During a conversation in 2011, I asked
Fr. Thomas what he had learned about contemplative practices in the ordinary
lives of non-monastics during his years of teaching and mentoring. In answer, he
drew from some twenty centuries of history. Fr. Thomas first commented that the
sacred infuses all aspects of life. He said that Christian practitioners recognized
that "nothing could be more incarnational than God . . . divine love turning everything, even what *seems* opposite to itself, the most material of objects to the most
spiritual, not just jettisoning the material but integrating it or transforming it to a
spiritual-material reality." Even though some popular notions assume it is based
on a rejection of the world, he said, Christian asceticism was founded on a recognition that God is here among us and in all of creation, an idea that theologians
call panentheism.[3] The fourth-century desert hermits in Egypt and Syria learned
how to live everyday life with sanctity through "a century or two of experimentation," balancing contemplation, labor, and hospitality, the practices of which were
formalized into institutionalized monasticism some two hundred years later in
"Benedict's tripod of lection, *opus dei*, and manual labor," said Fr. Thomas.

This learning spread among laypeople over time, he said. A member of the
Dominican order that strived to regulate the sometimes uncontainable desire of

ordinary medieval Europeans to live integrated lives of devotion and active service in emulation of Jesus' original disciples, Thomas Aquinas recognized in
the Middle Ages that all people needed "balance between enough silence, solitude, and meditation or lection and a balance of other duties that you have to do,
whether these be the family or earning a living, or teaching," said Fr. Thomas.[4]
However, he believed that "the experience of most people . . . since the Industrial
Revolution is that the urgency of earning a living or the professional life . . . is
always encroaching." Without a balanced rhythm of work and prayer, people can
fall out of sync and become discouraged, said Fr. Thomas. In these situations,
people can no longer ameliorate "our natural weakness and our habits of thinking
that come from the ego . . . . These are constantly challenging our efforts to be
always in the presence of God."

Fr. Thomas Keating felt that contemporary sensibilities that reject hierarchy
and authority make the idea of monastic life or even church membership unat-
tractive for many people. There are few venues that capably teach contemplative ways, even church parishes, he said, so for those who have a deep draw to
the divine, "you're pretty much on your own." In his experience, non-monastic
Christian contemplatives often feel constrained and isolated in a cultural context
in which "24 hours a day you're hearing opposite values and the journey is deni-
grated as foolish, impossible, stupid." The intensity of the draw is hard to relate in
a culture that does not recognize "spiritual gifts or spiritual living": "Unless you
have some experience as a contemplative, you don't really know what the mystics
are talking about," he added. Indeed, Fr. Thomas said, without mentorship, social
support, or a "sound cultural frame," many people who have "spiritual gifts" can
become terribly confused.

Nevertheless, while for centuries the cloistered have felt that their communities of like-minded and like-practicing cohorts have given them focused environments, it is not impossible to follow a contemplative life in other contexts, said Fr.
Thomas Keating. He founded Contemplative Outreach and wrote many books to
support and teach contemplatives who live outside of the cloister. First published
in 1986, one of his most popular books, Open Mind, Open Heart, offers methods
that teach how to bring the kenotic principles of Centering Prayer to all aspects of
life. In association with a regular twice-daily practice of Centering Prayer, "There
are a number of practices that can help maintain your reservoir of interior silence
throughout the day and thus extend its effects into ordinary activities," he wrote.
Fr. Thomas listed ten practices and activities, including "Cultivate a basic acceptance of yourself," "Practice unconditional acceptance of others," "Deliberately dismantle excessive group identification," and "Join a contemplative prayer group,"
each of which was followed with a short discussion of how to practically adopt
these tasks (Keating 2002b: 123–124).

Two practices on the list of "Active Prayer" will serve as examples of Fr. Thomas's teachings in the self-reformation of habitus. The first, "Pick a prayer for action," is a method of repeating a short sentence during ordinary activities that do not require too much concentrated effort, like light housework or commuting. By repeating phrases like "Open my heart to love," "Into thy hands I commend my spirit," or "*Veni Sancte Spiritus*," one can endeavor to rework habitual thoughts ("the subconscious") so that they fall in line with one's chosen posture. Cautioning that one should approach this practice "without anxiety, haste, or excessive effort" (and if one has a tendency for compulsive behavior, "this practice is not for you"), the Active Prayer "has the remarkable effect of erasing old tapes [of unwanted habitual thought], thus providing a neutral zone in which . . . the Spirit of God can suggest what should be done," wrote Fr. Thomas. He emphasized the importance of repetition and the need for time and patience: "The old tapes were built up through repeated acts. A new tape can be established in the same way. It may take a year to establish one's active prayer in the subconscious. It will then arise spontaneously," he said (2002b: 124, 133–135).

A second example of Active Prayer from Fr. Thomas Keating's list of methods was "Practice guard of the heart." In this context, "guard" does not mean constraint or the rejection of others. Rather, it is another adaptation of classic monastic statio, a practice of stopping and "releasing upsetting emotions into the present moment" by "the prompt letting go of personal likes and dislikes." Instead of being derailed by something unexpected, practitioners adopted "guard of the heart" to develop an inner flexibility and openness in daily life. "The fruit of the guard of the heart is the habitual willingness to change our plans at a moment's notice. It disposes us to accept painful situations as they arise. Then we can decide what to do with them, modifying, correcting or improving them" (Keating 2002b: 125). The practice of guarding the heart requires attention to one's emotional responses and a conscious employment of the kenotic methods that one has learned and embodied through Centering Prayer.

In the mid-1980s, Mary Mrozowski, a "master teacher" and one of the founders of the Contemplative Outreach organization, developed the Welcoming Prayer from the principles of statio that Fr. Thomas Keating described in *Open Mind, Open Heart* and from the eighteenth-century writings of Jesuit priest Jean-Pierre de Caussade (1975). The Welcoming Prayer is "a practice of 'letting go' in the present moment" (Gursoy, Fitzpatrick-Hopler, and Koock 2005: 8) and "a method of consenting to God's presence and action in our physical and emotional reactions to events and situations in daily life." According to Contemplative Outreach (2009), its purpose is "to deepen our relationship with God through consenting in ordinary activities," to "dismantle" unconscious emotional reactivity, and "to heal the wounds of a lifetime by addressing them where they are stored—in the body.

It contributes to the process of transformation in Christ initiated in Centering Prayer."

The Welcoming Prayer method has three steps, which identify how emotional responses manifest in the body and help prompt their "release": (1) "Focus, feel and sink into feelings, emotions, thoughts, commentaries, or sensations in your body"; (2) Name and acknowledge the emotion by welcoming "the Divine Indwelling in the feelings, emotions, thoughts, commentaries, or sensations in your body"; and (3) "Let go" of divisive and constrained responses by repeating sentences such as, "I let go of the desire for control" or "I let go of the desire for security." The idea is that with practice, one learns how to recognize emotional tension in the body and release it to adopt a neutral posture, which allows one to approach people with openness, to make better decisions, and to take conscious action based on chosen principles rather than on emotional reactions. Said Mrozowski of the practice, "To welcome and to let go is one of the most radically loving, faith-filled gestures we can make in each moment of each day. It is an open-hearted embrace of all that is in ourselves and in the world" (Contemplative Outreach 2009; cf. Haisten 2005).

Practiced by many of the people with whom I did research, the Welcoming Prayer was taught face to face through workshops, retreats, and "intensives" all over the United States and in other countries. It has also been taught at a distance through publications like Cynthia Bourgeault's *Centering Prayer and Inner Awakening* (2004), through Contemplative Outreach publications, audiovisual aids, and teleconferences, and an e-course called "The Welcoming Prayer: Consent on the Go," taught by Contemplative Outreach leaders and the founders of Spirituality and Practice, the website that provided interactive online courses on many inter-religious subjects.[5] Cathy McCarthy, a long-time teacher of Centering Prayer who organized one of the retreats at which I did fieldwork, said that she felt the Welcoming Prayer was as essential as a daily routine of meditation. "Simply put, the faithful practice of both centering prayer and the welcoming prayer is the one-two punch that helps me to embrace God in every moment—in every event. The welcoming prayer is not understood in the head but experienced in the body," she said, urging her students to "practice, practice, practice" (quoted in Gursoy et al. 2005: 18).

The Welcoming Prayer, Br. Curtis Almquist's posture of hesitation, and Br. Robert L'Esperance's practice of forgiveness were teachings from the monasteries that encouraged people to live lives of "ceaseless prayer." At the end of his list of methods in *Open Mind, Open Heart*, Fr. Thomas Keating (2002b: 124) acknowledged that the rigorous monastic rhythm of *ora et labora* could not be easily adopted by those outside the cloister. He wrote, "the ordinary events of daily life become our practice. I can't emphasize that too much. A monastic structure is not the path to holiness for lay folks. The routine of daily life is. Contemplative prayer is aimed at transforming daily life with its never-ending round of ordinary activities." Inspired by such practices and theologies of monastic *labora*, intentional or "conscious work periods" became a kind of laboratory for observing how to best keep attention to the divine in every situation.

Wisdom School Conscious Work Periods: "St. Benedict Meets G. I. Gurdjieff"

Students of contemplation learned to keep presence in everyday life through experimentation with ordinary activities in the context of Wisdom Schools. As we have seen in previous chapters, Wisdom Schools emulated a monastic daily rhythm of *ora et labora*. Especially in examples of chant and liturgical gesture, rites and spiritual exercises in the chapel and meditation room trained people to keep attention in the body as a form of *ora* or prayer. Benedictine *labora* was adapted to the short-term learning environment of Wisdom Schools through overt experiments with "the practice of the presence of God" in a controlled situation of "intentional" or "conscious work." During work periods, teachers would offer guidance to participants in keeping attention during ordinary physical chores like gardening, cooking, or cleaning. Usually scheduled at mid-morning, the work periods did not have a logistical agenda of getting necessary jobs done, but were designed instead to give participants a chance to practice the art of keeping attention while doing ordinary life tasks. They were a way of learning to intentionally incorporate contemplative principles (that is, to ritualize) the activities of daily life, experimenting with attention, aliveness, and awakening in bodily movement to transform themselves toward lives of "ceaseless prayer."[6]

At the Episcopal House of Prayer Wisdom School in August 2011, Cynthia Bourgeault said, "Let's stop being pretentious and stop pretending that we are present" and instead really work toward learning *how* to be present. She taught that attention is an observable force, especially in work situations: "A job done with attention is better than a job done without attention," she said. One working with attention has "collected, directed subtle energy" rather than distracted and "mechanical, automated energy." The intention of work periods was to train people to understand the difference. Transforming old habits is demanding, she said, a kind of "purification by friction" in which we work through "like and dislike" to "confront our own automatic behaviors which put us to sleep." Indeed, said Cynthia, work periods can be most effective when you are doing unfamiliar things or things you don't like, a method of destabilizing the ordinary and habituated, and intentionally entering into an unknown, ambiguous space that can offer new perspectives. With perseverance, Cynthia said, such efforts could give practitioners a greater facility with staying alert and keeping presence, bringing them to "a place of rest that is alive" in any situation.

The idea of these conscious work periods was modeled on Benedictine rhythms as well as the methods of G. I. Gurdjieff (2002), an early twentieth-century thinker and writer (and guru) from Armenia who taught "conscious living." Cynthia said that Gurdjieff's instigation of "The Work" came out of a theory of three human intelligences that he called the Intellectual Center (mind, reason, information), the Moving Center (embodied knowledge), and the Emotional Center (empathic intuition, spiritual perception—not the same as sentiment or "feelings").[7] Balancing these three intelligences is necessary to "sustain presence," said Cynthia, adding that North Americans, with their sedentary lives and focus on sentiment and intellect, were particularly in need of developing their Moving Center. One's alertness and ways of knowing come through the stabilization of sensation, rhythm, and physical resonance, all aspects of the Moving Center, she said. Wisdom School work periods offered a controlled situation in which to experiment with the intelligence of bodily movement by keeping attention on one's physicality as a way to embody knowledge.

Cynthia Bourgeault explained the importance of embodied knowledge in a story about a young man who came to an Eastern Orthodox priest for advice on how to dislodge his spiritual ennui. The priest prescribed one hundred full-body prostrations a day. After a month, the young man returned with his face shining, no longer depressive or indifferent but full of wonder, Cynthia said. She followed that story with an example that most would understand from personal experience: "You can't learn to ride a bike by thinking about it or reading about it or talking about it; you have to *do* it to understand. The knowledge is in the body. The body carries affirming force to comprehend what the mind does not."[8]

For the mid-morning work periods at the House of Prayer Wisdom School, the larger company was divided into cleaning, gardening, kitchen, and liturgical work groups. Each day Cynthia gave us an "outer task" and an "inner task." The outer task was the work assignment—clearing paths, washing dishes, pulling weeds, setting up the Oratory for the evening's liturgy—and the inner task was the learning intention. Staying with themes similar to the afternoon chant sessions, on the Wednesday of that week Cynthia set the inner task of "keeping inner stillness by using only the muscles that are necessary to work the tools." Sharon's jaw dropped, exclaiming, "That's too hard! I give up!" Ward Bauman, the retreat center's director, humorously agreed, "I give up!" I then murmured, "That's good: giving up, letting go . . . . " Cynthia smiled, but said quite seriously, "Paula, giving up is not the same as letting go."

Cynthia then gave us a short primer on experiments with intentional work: "This isn't about getting anything 'done' but about finding how accustomed bodily postures associate with habitual thought patterns." Working with kenosis and exercises for keeping presence would help us to notice what "sends us to sleep" so we could break through habituations to form new patterns of attentiveness. "Just like practicing kenosis in Centering Prayer, you can expect to have to re-awaken 70 or 80 times over the work period." She then suggested that we try sensing inner stillness by feeling a vertical pillar through torso, legs, and feet, which anchors the body to the center of the earth, and from there experiment with the muscles necessary to one's given work.

Along with several others, I worked in the woods to decrease the fire hazard of built-up windfall. The rest of the "physical labor group" clipped overgrown vines, swept walks, or weeded flower gardens. It was heavy going, not just hauling logs and branches, but struggling to let go of distractions in an attempt to return to the inner task of noticing and isolating muscles at work. By the lunch bell, I was relieved it was over, and gladly returned my tools to the shed out back, straining all the while to do it with attention. It was so demanding that after lunch, I and quite a few exhausted others had to take afternoon naps.

Seven months later, on the edge of Saguaro National Park in Tucson, Arizona, I attended another Wisdom School in March 2012 at a Roman Catholic retreat facility, where I continued learning intentional work. Run by an order of Redemptorist monks whose prior had inter-religious leanings and a fondness for Japan, the center had its very own Zen Buddhist *zendo*, or meditation hall. We were there to study the fourth-century teachings of the Desert Fathers and Mothers, following again the usual Wisdom School schedule modeled on Benedictine *ora et labora*. The work periods were no less demanding than those at the House of Prayer, but by then I had attended several Wisdom Schools and had begun to better understand what was asked of me and what sensations of "presence" were supposed to be like. The outer tasks there were similar to other Wisdom Schools—gardening, cleaning, kitchen work, and liturgical preparation—and the inner tasks were designed, as before, to jolt people out of habitual behaviors and into the creative potential of ambiguity. They included things like "noticing when you've fallen out of presence" and working with one's non-dominant hand.

On the first day, Cynthia had taken aside a "core group" of ten people who were well acquainted with Wisdom practices and studies. She and Rosa, a specialist in Gurdjieff's methods, wanted to train new leaders of conscious work sessions. Rosa coached us, saying that our group had a threefold task for the week's work periods: staying present ourselves to the inner and outer tasks of the day, observing presence in other students, and "self-remembering"—that is, keeping an awareness of oneself in context of the greater whole.

One day's inner task was "change the tempo." This meant to still oneself enough to first discover what Rosa described as one's own primary inner pulse. Once we had gotten a feel for it, we were then to shift the speed of our movements in relation to that baseline pulse. Rosa explained to the core group that this primary pulse could act as an anchor for presence; if one were attentive to it, one could be flexible with other paces that an environment or work situation demanded, without falling out of presence. Quite in contrast to an idea of contemplation and concentration as a way of *narrowing* focus, this was a way of learning to "multiply attention," Cynthia said; that is, with practice one could learn to give full attention to more than one thing, even many things, rather than having the "divided attention" and distraction of "multi-tasking." Rosa then added a fourth task for the core group: "Be conscious of your left leg from the knee down, including the foot."

I wasn't sure if I had found my primary pulse or not and I frequently forgot about the left leg, but I did persist in my attempts to return to alertness. I also had a lot of fun playing with being attentive to the tempos of movement. Cynthia Bourgeault and I cleaned windows, I on one side of a pane of glass, she on the other. A way of observing and participating simultaneously, we began mirroring each other's actions, matching and shifting the tempo amazingly well. We tried to trick each other out of rhythm and ended up giggling all the way through. Cynthia later said that she didn't often have that much fun during a work period.

A few days later, the inner task was identical to the one at the House of Prayer the previous summer: to experiment with "inner stillness" by minimizing movements and using only the muscles necessary for the outer task, this time by weeding the garden. As part of the core group, I was to work these inner and outer tasks myself, while also observing others in the gardening group. I noted the sensation of keeping stillness by feeling a "center" deep in my belly, which seemed to root me earthward and made my gestures and words feel deliberate and intentional. I found myself attending especially to my physical center of gravity when changing between my postures of crouching to weed and standing to observe others.

Three women who weeded alongside me appeared to keep a concentrated stillness in their purposeful gestures. They moved slowly and intently, speaking with similar deliberation but only when necessary. They were clearly taking the opportunity to experiment with contemplative attention in their work. Further down the path, however, Candace and Frank seemed pretty task-oriented, apparently giving little conscious attention to their movements. They walked, dug with spades, and pushed wheelbarrows with plenty of bounce and extraneous motion, seemingly focused more on the work than on their own physicality of doing the work. Some men across the way were joking, tossing their heads and arms as they laughed and talked. They seemed more absorbed by their conversation than by sensing inner stillness or presence in their bodies through minimization of movement.

At the small core group's post-session discussion, I questioned my analysis of these observations, wondering if these people could find stillness in movements that did not appear to me deliberate, minimized, or consciously chosen. Yet, even if they had found another path to stillness, they definitely did not seem fully attentive to the prescribed inner task of using only the necessary muscles for their work. Marcus, an old hand at Centering Prayer and one of the founding members of Contemplative Outreach, then offered his experience of the session, saying that the combined work of observing and keeping multiple layers of attention on the inner and outer tasks "didn't separate me, but gave me a unified feeling." He said he had been buoyed by the communal body of intentional work and everyone's efforts to stay present, however well they actually managed. Working *en corps* was a form of "beneficence," he said, and a way of "deep listening." Alexandra added her thoughts. She said that the combined tasks of observing and staying present in our own work seemed to ask us to rethink boundaries we don't usually question, requiring us to move past the wall between self and other. She said, "We cannot be fully present and yet 'observe.' It's more like we need to listen to each other through interpenetration, not see from a distance."[9]

At the end of that day, the rest of the group discussed their experiences with the work session. Those on kitchen duty had a number of comments about learning to cut back on extraneous gestures. Suzanne, for example, remarked that she kept flour off herself better if she worked with attention. Gerald noticed how he triple-tapped his knife when putting carrots in a pot. He tried one tap and it worked just as well, he said, so he kept to the minimized action. Adele likened the deliberateness and attentiveness of her outer task to t'ai chi, which she had practiced for many years. She said, "Cleaning out the refrigerator with an economy of movement was as beautiful as t'ai chi—a real breakthrough. I see that if I did everything with the attention of my t'ai chi practice, it would all be beautiful."

By contrast, Claudia expressed real frustration with this work. She was restless and impatient, wanting to "surge ahead and get it done." She had spent a lifetime managing daily chores in order to move on to the things she'd rather be doing, she said. Without an agenda to complete the job, this work was really challenging to her and she felt angry with herself. "Why can't I do it?!" she fumed. Cynthia Bourgeault responded by steering her away from self-criticism and toward attention to bodily senses. "Turn your awareness to the sensation and you will learn why," she said. By self-condemning and resisting, she said "you likely feed the frustration." Instead, sit in the presence of the "energy fields" you consider "undesirable" so you can disarm them. "No labeling or analysis," Cynthia advised, "just sit with the beast." Louise, a woman who had come all the way from Wales with two others to take part in this Wisdom School, reminded Claudia of the Welcoming Prayer. Feel where the restriction comes from, greet it, and let it go, she recommended, acknowledging that this practice requires a significant amount of energy, but "when you learn to work from within" you will feel a "finer energy" that sustains you. Louise then mentioned her own way of assessing through contemplative senses whether her work was "right aligned" or not: "I can smell sourness when there's no flow; sweetness comes when the work flows well."

An older man, Jake, then described an instance when he felt he had "fallen out of presence." He had been taking a lot of photographs of desert landscapes as well as participants and Wisdom School sessions. That day, Jake had gone so far as to ask one of the retreat center's kitchen staff to take a photo of him chopping vegetables during the work period so he could show his wife back home. He now acknowledged that posing for the photo and his general concern for capturing photographic images seemed to draw him away from his inner task. Yet early the next morning I noticed him, heedless of the desert garden plants underfoot, skittering frantically across the stones to capture a shot of the sunrise from just the perfect vantage point. While he had noticed that the desire for external images drew him away from contemplative experimentation in the work period, perhaps he had not fully learned to apply this principle to his engagement of life in the world.

Beyond Exercises: "Conscious Living" Every Day

All shall be well,
and all shall be well,
and all manner of thing shall be well.

—JULIAN OF NORWICH

Midway through the Tucson Wisdom School, we had an opportunity to apply our efforts at conscious living and ritualization beyond the daily work period exercises. On the third day, people began falling like flies to the norovirus, a severe gastrointestinal flu-like illness that was then scourging communities all over the United States. Fourteen of sixty-three participants[10] became ill that first day, and the numbers increased until more than a third were confined to bed, including a bishop, some with severe symptoms of fever, vomitting, and diarrhea. One woman was hospitalized. Cynthia herself had milder symptoms, but she managed to keep teaching, feeling that she was "standing just by a thread" and that "heaven and earth were working" to keep her going. Those who kept their health continued on with the daily schedule as best they could while also attending to the afflicted. The well volunteered to care for specific individuals, checking in on them regularly to offer comfort and companionship, as well as bring fluids, simple foods, and medicine. The outbreak was so bad that the local public health office closed the facility for decontamination after we left.

Many took these rather dire circumstances as an opportunity, like any other, to engage contemplative ways of being. In a *sohbet* conversation to those of us she jokingly called "the predeceased," Cynthia Bourgeault said the norovirus had provided us with a "laboratory" on how to keep attention and stay "right aligned" in a situation that could inspire fear and panic. "Where do you go in your body that brings you back to steadiness?" she asked, suggesting that we find our "sensate centers of being" and let go of fear fueled by gossip, physical tension, and resistance. Keeping a steady center and an "intercessory disposition," we had the opportunity to transform the experience of these circumstances, she said.

Those who were ill also did their best to keep a contemplative demeanor. Alicia, the woman whom I assisted, was very ill indeed, passing out every time she vomited because of her low blood pressure. For the first two days, the most she could take was rice water, then slowly she graduated to white rice and crackers. A United Church of Christ minister who ran her own retreat facility with her husband in southeastern British Columbia, Alicia kept her composure extraordinarily well, even found some humor in it, sleeping and meditating her way through the illness until she shakily rejoined the group on the Wisdom School's final afternoon.[11]

To prevent a spread of germs in the sharing of bread and wine, Cynthia replaced the Eucharist liturgy on the first evening of the outbreak with a communal practice of *tonglen*. While some were already practitioners of tonglen, others had not heard of it. Cynthia described tonglen as a Buddhist variety of compassionate intercession or "transmutation prayer," a part of "free-flowing dialysis" of the world's pain, which could assist those who were suffering in and beyond our midst. The practice was a form of meditation in which one envisioned breathing in the world's pain and breathing out peace and blessing. Cynthia emphasized that it was crucial to keep humility, detachment, and "a surrendered heart" during this practice; it must be a pure gift, rather than a way of self-identification, she said. "There's no 'you' in it, no story, no drama, no 'I' in the practice of tonglen." It's not about an individual's cause and effect, but is instead consent to divine indwelling in and beyond one's physical boundaries, said Cynthia. One must have a "deadpan compassionate calm almost unknown in Christianity" that willingly participates in "a cycle that is bigger and more ancient than you," she said. After this, we practiced tonglen every evening.

With our mini epidemic, much of the daily discussions turned toward how we live with adversity. People tried to grapple with human-made horrors like the Holocaust and 9/11, and natural disasters like the 2004 Indian Ocean tsunami off Indonesia which affected people over a huge area of the globe. "The jaggedness of conditions of this realm cannot be smoothed over," said Cynthia. As an exemplar, she held up Edith Stein, a German woman who had converted from Judaism to Christianity in 1922 and took vows with Teresa of Ávila's Roman Catholic order, the Discalced Carmelites, in 1934. Edith Stein's convent could have protected her from the Nazis, said Cynthia, yet she chose to go to Auschwitz in solidarity with her fellow Jews. Stein spent her time in the concentration camp comforting and assisting those with whom she was incarcerated, said Cynthia, then was herself killed in the gas chambers.[12] While she cautioned that "goodness in outcome does not justify destruction," Cynthia said that we could choose "to make our hearts willing altars" of service to others in any situation; "a person's conscious choice to sacrifice liberates something into the planet," she said. Marcus agreed. Commenting on our group's passage through illness that week, he described a contemplative response to adversity as a chance to mature: "There are places in the heart that do not exist until suffering enters in."

At the end of the last evening's discussion, a nurse in the group held up a package of medication and addressed those wary of their long journey the following day: "If you're tired of 'letting go,' we have suppositories for that." The gathering greeted her "kenotic humor" with groans of laughter. Cynthia laughed, too, but before shifting to the week's final liturgy, she reminded us that staying present is not just for times when things are going well. "Pain and suffering are real and unavoidable parts of the conditions of life," she said. "Wisdom and contemplation are ways of responding to them with openness and attention, not ways of avoiding or denying them." She added, "It's all Wisdom School, whatever happens," but conceded that this hadn't been so much Wisdom School as "Wisdom Boot Camp."

Between Dallas and Boston on the last leg of my flight home, I too was hit by the norovirus. I decided to treat the situation as part of the Wisdom School laboratory of which I had just been a part and did my best to apply the principles of kenosis and keeping "right aligned" in the rather uncertain present moment. With the assistance of a very kind flight attendant, I managed the ambiguity of less-than-ideal circumstances without resorting to alarm or self-pity, all the time being attentive to the sensations in my body and pondering Marcus's words on the potential lessons of suffering, "There are places in the heart that do not exist until suffering enters in."

OF COURSE, THE ritualization of everyday life was not always so harrowing. The Sufi dervish skinny-dipping expedition that headlined this chapter was definitely a form of ritualization, as was Zak's intentional practice of visiting the sick and elderly with his therapy dog, Sophie, an ethnographic sketch of which concluded Chapter 2. In other ejournal entries, Zak offered advice about consciously adopting an "inner posture" of humility and "heartfelt openness" as a way to work toward living contemplatively in every situation. He wrote about how a conscious approach to life helped him notice the sacred everywhere around him, as in an ordinary conversation with an old woman he met walking down the street on his way to the Roman Catholic cathedral. "This was a beautiful woman with a beautiful open heart," he wrote, who, in the midst of a snow flurry in the busy, bustling city, "turned to me, smiled and said, 'Listen to the Q U I E T.' We parted and I will probably never see her again. Now, of course, I know with one part of me that she was just another person with aches and pains and cares and concerns like any other mortal. But another part of me knows for certain she brought . . . she was . . . an angelic presence" (ellipses and emphasis in original).

AJ also offered poignant examples of non-monastic ritualization in her ejournal, depicting how she used Christian liturgical seasons like Advent and Lent to prompt herself toward a contemplative approach to everyday life. AJ had founded and run a college in the Northeast that taught and certified alternative healthcare practitioners. After fifteen years of hard work, she decided to close the college in 2010 because of her own health crisis. She began negotiating the sale of the buildings and land that spring. Just before this, AJ had decided to give up worrying for Lent. Dealing with zoning restrictions and "codes enforcement people" was very stressful and she felt that "any moment an unforeseen issue could derail the whole sale. And there was nothing, absolutely nothing, I could do but wait. And worry." But using a form of statio, she would pause, recognize her impulse to worry, and stop herself. "Every time I started to worry, I'd say to myself, 'Ah! Wait a minute, promised Jesus I wouldn't worry!' And I would instantly stop worrying." It took a great deal of resolve to keep that promise, AJ said, but she found that "consciously not worrying for 40 days changed my relationship to worry; it broke the habit of worry and replaced it with letting go of what I can't control."

The following year, AJ gave up "rushing" for Lent. In her ejournal she wrote about her determined intentions:

> No rushing allowed. No cramming in that extra errand or item for my list for the day. No more scurrying dashing, racing, or breathlessly apologizing for being late when rushing didn't work . . . . The word, "dashing," means "attractive in a romantic, adventurous way." . . . Wasn't I just *dashing* when I was rushing? Not so much. I was actually harried, exhausted, and not at all present in the moment. I'd watch my racing mind during meditation and then get up and race through the day . . . . In a nutshell, I created a lot of unnecessary stress for the fake self-importance that busyness confers . . . . Giving up the option of rushing taught me about the culture of busyness, about how much I (and society) equate busyness with importance and meaning.
>
> I spent the 40 days of Lent choosing to organize every day around the tenet, "No Rushing Allowed." . . . The results I noticed were subtle but reached every corner of my life. I noticed first that I was more present in both meditation and interactions with others. I listened better, felt more grounded, prepared, and intuitive. I was more in tune with my surroundings, nature, and the feelings of others. I think the NO RUSHING credo unintentionally led to less multi-tasking, so everything I did became more focused, accurate, and thorough . . . . Rushing had been a way to avoid feeling, and slowing down to a sane pace allowed my mind to become present and my heart open, to myself and others. (emphasis in original)

AJ concluded her half-year of ejournal musings with an entry that reflected on "making a life." Even though her adulthood had been devoted to contemplative principles, she had been brought up with an atonement-oriented Roman Catholicism that had driven her to feel that she could never work hard enough to be a worthy person. She struggled to shake off the aura of guilt she called "the Catholic curse." Feeling unproductive and lonely after closing her college, AJ took her recovery time to seriously address her debilitating posture of "unreasonable self-expectation" and to reform herself by "just living a conscious life." Gardening was "my teacher," she wrote. Feeling rewarded by "every dirty, difficult task," she had been "completely consumed by the garden" at first, but she gradually incorporated a greater balance "as I let other responsibilities, including resting, into the mix." The intention to foster equilibrium and equanimity through conscious work became clearer and stronger with time. She said in her final ejournal entry from June 2012,

> In the midst of gardening the other day, I heard "Be happy within your-self." What it meant to me was NOT "be pleased with how you are doing" or the old "be OK alone." . . . It was more like: *Let happiness take root and blossom within you.* . . . What's most wonderful about that beautiful message is that there was no Do This or Do That kind of prescription. It was more like, *It's already there, just recognize it.* (emphasis in original)

What AJ used to think of as a "path" toward something yet unrealized, something to pursue and strive for, she began to understand as "a way of conscious living . . . . There actually is no path because there's actually nowhere to get to. I'm already there. Everyone is already there."

After my introduction to Wisdom School work periods in early 2011, I tried out some ritualization techniques to see how they worked in the isolation of one's own home, an ethnographic method I devised to experiment with participant-observation of the "non-gathered" contemplative Christian community. I chose driving as my "laboratory." The Boston area is renowned for its aggressive drivers and not without reason: I have seen a father with a toddler in the backseat drive on the sidewalk to get past a line of traffic at a busy intersection, fingering any driver who dared to honk in protest, and a man in an expensive suit once leaned out of his BMW to yell at me when I stepped onto a Harvard Square crosswalk with my two young daughters, "You fuckin' mothers think you own the road!" My time as a driver (and pedestrian) in Boston showed me numerous such incidents: repeated occurrences of drivers yelling, gesticulating, and driving in whatever way they thought would keep them ahead of the pack. I confess that Boston driving culture used to upset me.[13]

But my ethnographic apprenticeship among contemplatives helped me to realize that a response of anger (whether expressed outwardly or not) did not help the situation; rather, it increased the intensity of confrontational feeling and certainly did nothing to alter other drivers' behavior. People would do stupid things on the road whether I got mad or not, so I decided to try making driving a form of ritualization. I applied the principles of kenosis that I had been learning in ritual practices and awareness exercises during my fieldwork. I consciously made the choice not to get upset with other drivers, but instead to be alert, and to recognize and release physical tension when something unexpected happened. I needed to drive responsively to those who didn't follow the rules, but I didn't need to get emotional about it. I worked hard to stay conscious about this choice of ritualized driving, paying attention to both bodily and mental responses by keeping an open, relational demeanor. After a while, driving became almost like a dance with other drivers, like I was part of an active but seamless flow in a river of cars. I later joked with some Wisdom School participants that I would write an Op/Ed piece for *The Boston Globe* called "The Zen of Boston Driving." Zen, of course, is not exactly what most people think of when they get into a car in Boston. Nevertheless, having experimented with ritualization, I can better understand Br. Curtis Almquist's comments (2014a) that commuter traffic is an "invitation to participate in life" as much as any other activity, whether in the choir or the sacristy.

Why Ritual?
Posture and Flow in an Ambiguous World

Back at the House of Prayer Wisdom School in August 2011, Brigid had learned her lessons on keeping attention particularly well. Teachers and students alike recognized her as having an unusual capacity to employ ritualized postures as a way of attuning herself to the ambiguous flow of the divine. After a long day of silent meditation, liturgies, *sohbet* seminars, and work periods, Brigid (who began ejournaling for me later that year) sat a little off to the side of the Common Room's haphazard circle of chairs and sofas during the evening discussion period. A small woman in her forties, Brigid was soft-spoken and gave the impression of being shy. However, when she found an opening in the conversation to convey her experience of kitchen duty, she spoke so deliberately and with such focus that the whole room listened with uniform stillness. Brigid compelled the attention of others by carefully selecting each word, unafraid of lengthy pauses as she sought the right way to relay her observations. There appeared to be a concentration of meaning in each precise word, as though she were reliving the moments she had experienced earlier in the day. Her way of speaking itself seemed to be an act of attention and staying present.

Brigid told us that she had been assigned to kitchen duty for the week's experimental work periods. That morning Ward Bauman, the retreat house director, had asked her to chop vegetables for a dish to be served at the evening meal. Brigid described the cucumber, the wood grain of the cutting board, the weight and feel of the cleaver, the pressure of hand against knife and the positioning of fingers; she described the intensity of the cucumber's colors meeting in concentric circles of deep green skin, near-white inner flesh, and transparent innermost seeds: how the blade bit through resisting skin, then sank through the firm but giving inner flesh, its varied densities and leniencies. "Not the green *or* the white," she said pausing again and visibly shaking now, eyes bright with the immediacy of her recollection, "but in their meeting place—where they came together—was their place of surrender."

Brigid sat silently for a few moments but had something more to add. She said that because of the noisy kitchen bustle at the beginning of the work period she had been unable to hear exactly how Ward wanted the cucumber to be sliced. In the middle of the work period, Ward had passed by her side-counter station, had taken a quick look, and said, "Smaller." But Brigid had not wanted to cut the pieces smaller. She said, "I'd cut these perfect circles and stacked them three pieces high in perfectly aligned rows at the edge of the cutting board." Recalling a Sufi poem that praised seeds at the center, she had resisted Ward's request that she cut through the seed circle. Yet Brigid had sliced into them anyway, letting go of the desire to preserve a form that had meaning for her.

As she cut, her board had become wet with cucumber juice and the slices wouldn't stay put. "The cucumbers were slippery and the pieces went everywhere!" she said. In the midst of ineffectually trying to corral them, she had stopped with sudden realization: "Abundance!" exclaimed Brigid, "a gravitational outpouring of abundance everywhere around us!" She then returned to her measured, concentrated way, "I could see the beauty in the cucumber, but if I had kept to what I knew and what I *thought* I wanted, I would not have understood the abundance."

No one made a sound. All motion seemed to have been arrested by the intensity with which Brigid had conveyed her experiments with intentional kitchen work. The way she spoke and the intensity of her listeners' focus together profoundly changed the atmosphere of the room. Brigid's ritualized act of deliberate speech seemed to offer a glimpse of the divine that bound the community, even more than the details of her observations. The air itself seemed to shimmer. After a while, Cynthia said in almost a whisper, "Someone's paying attention, wow." Helen then glanced over to me and quietly said, "Our very own T. S. Eliot."

BRIGID'S CAPACITY TO use everyday forms like group discussions and kitchen work to foster unitive being illustrates how segregated categories of sacred and profane do not fit well in the ethnographic context of American contemplative

Christians. We saw how sanctity imbued life in the Tucson Wisdom School participants' response to the norovirus, in AJ's intentional postures of "no worrying" and "no rushing," and in Br. Robert L'Esperance's efforts to craft a forgiving and accepting response to people who annoyed him. A deeply held conception of divine incarnation was a primary motivator. Whether or not they felt compelled by emotion, contemplatives sought to work toward staying present to an immanent divine that they believed was everywhere around them. Along with their practices of formal rites, contemplatives used intentional postures and practices in everyday life in an effort to transform their ways of being and thinking to be "right aligned with the divine." Whether within or outside of the chapel and cloister, such intentional acts worked in the ambiguous place between the boundaries of reified categories like religion, ritual, sacred, and profane.

Ritualization's boundary-crossing characteristics were especially salient in the pluralistic world in which American contemplative Christians lived. Recall from Chapter 5 that in their book *Rethinking Pluralism*, Seligman and Weller (2012: 93) described the "subjunctive" power of ritual as "a unique human resource for dealing with ambiguity and the multivocal nature of all relationships—with beings human and divine." They added that ritual "presents a coherent and embracing way to live in a plural and hence also deeply ambiguous universe, one where order can never really be known, but still must be acted upon." In contrast to a dependence on the hard-edged belief and ephemeral emotion found in some manifestations of American Christianity, formalized rite and ritualization allowed contemplatives to foster an openness to the ambiguity ("what lies beyond their immediate field") that particularly abounds in the shifting pluralistic realities of the contemporary globalized world.

But, as we have seen, American contemplatives not only *addressed* ambiguity with ritualization, they also intentionally *created* it. Contemplatives used the liminality created from rite and ritualization as a method to transform phenomenological and intellectual categories of thought and being, both consciously and at the embodied level of habitus. Victor Turner (1969) wrote in his seminal work, *The Ritual Process*, that liminality is the primary catalyst for the intensive phenomenological intersubjectivity that he called "communitas." In Turner's theory, liminality rose out of rituals that created anti-structure, a temporary dissolution of the normal structures of society like status, class, age-sets, and kin groups. Turner's ideas derived from his ethnographic fieldwork among comparably cohesive, small-scale African societies, and though he did apply his theories to larger societies, he continued to rely on a model that opposed social structure with a ritual anti-structure.

An opposition of social structure and ritual anti-structure was not the primary impetus of unitive being among the American contemplative Christians with whom I worked, however. As we have seen, especially in Chapters 1 and 2, most non-monastic contemplatives lived within the ordinary social matrix of the United

States, with its extraordinary number of pluralistic possibilities, and though they sometimes went to retreats and Wisdom Schools that transformed the usual social order, their primary place of contemplative enactment was their ordinary lives. Monks and nuns, of course, fell outside of more standard varieties of American social life, but they had their own well-defined social orders, sometimes centuries old, which soon became quite ordinary for those who joined them. Recall Br. Curtis Almquist's comments about how monastic life isn't all about "climbing the spiritual mountains." Monks and nuns must work in a world of everyday relationships and activities, just like other people. In the pluralistic worlds of the United States, with their many social possibilities (cloistered and uncloistered), Turner's dialectical model of structure and anti-structure does not adequately explain Christian contemplatives' primary route to communitas or unitive being.[14]

Even so, liminality and ambiguity were indeed the basis of phenomenological union with others. How? And why ritual? Contemplative Christians crossed and dwelled between boundaries not so much by upending social structure, but by transforming categories of being and thought through consent and kenosis, as we saw with the methods that deliberately attempted to destabilize habitual ways in the intentional work sessions at Wisdom Schools. Ritual did provide a "subjunctive" framework to help practitioners negotiate the ambiguous realities of both pluralized societies and the divine, but among American contemplative Christians the "inner work" of apophasis and kenosis was as important as the "outer work" of cataphatic ritual form. That is, liminality and ambiguity arose from practitioners' intentional psycho-physical capacity to "let go" of the cultural and social norms that separate people, as well as the ideas, emotional responses, and the bodily sensations with which they are associated. Using rite and ritualization, contemplative Christians trained themselves to use sensation as a primary *mode* of perception to defuse their *categories* of perception, the aspects of embodied cultural knowledge they wished to reform. Among these people, the state of one's psychic being— one's attentiveness to keeping present and creating inner "spaciousness" through kenosis—allowed them to cross phenomenological and intellectual boundaries, indeed to hover between them. The ethnographic accounts of ritual and ritualization of these last two chapters illustrate how *psychic acts* of attention and openness made a difference to the phenomenological effects of *physical acts* like meditating, bowing, chanting, turning, or indeed, cutting cucumber. With greater attention, ordinary physical acts could become catalysts that opened people to unitive being and alternative varieties of knowledge. Even Br. Robert L'Esperance's and Br. Curtis Almquist's teachings on hospitality and humility were not so much about correct moral behavior as they were ritualization techniques that fostered *communion*, a phenomenology of unitive being.

American contemplatives thus created liminality through the partnership of posture and flow. As dialogical partners rather than opposing social forces, posture and flow combined chosen cataphatic rigidities—formal rites and demeanors—with an apophatic openness that in other contexts might well threaten chaos. Indeed, in the preceding ethnographic sketches we have seen how a regularized, stable practice of postures, enacted regardless of sentiment, could craft potent, creative environments of phenomenological and intellectual ambiguity that encouraged a refinement of senses and an ability to hear and see in new ways. Regardless of the unpredictability of self or society, posture and practice acted as "strong containers" that offered enough constancy to allow for the exploration of a potentially volatile world of endless possibilities.

The dialogical relationship of posture and flow helps us better understand the role of individual agency in ritual processes. While the terms themselves belong to a specific ethnographic context, American contemplative Christians' use of posture and flow shows more generally how individuals can differently employ social and cultural capital to consciously engage and alter the hegemonic forces in a given field of practice. Living into the paradoxes of *knowing/unknowing, expertise/humility,* and *doing/not doing* opens a realm of ambiguity and creative possibility that can thrust one past critical appraisal and into unexpected experience. Contemplative Christian teachers said that the extent to which one comprehends and enacts the cataphatic and apophatic elements of ritual has a significant impact on one's level of contemplative maturity. Degrees of dedication to ritualization and differing capacities to bear ambiguity created variability in the contemplative knowledge of practitioners. While contemplative Christians emphasized the primary role of the divine in bringing them to places of awakening, they felt that their choice to responsibly engage, commit, and consent was integral.

Contemplatives believed that their dedication to posture and flow prepared the soil for the seed of divine intimacy, inviting the knowledge it bestows to take root and flourish. In Sanctuary, the third in our Triduum of chapters, we explore varieties and degrees of intersubjective knowledge and how certain contemplatives, like Brigid or the old woman whom Zak encountered on a snowy city street, sometimes had the capacity to communicate that knowledge to the greater community.

Photograph courtesy of SSJE.

7

Sanctuary

THE PERSON AS ICON: AMERICAN CONTEMPLATIVE
CHRISTIAN WAYS OF KNOWING

*The chapel's Sanctuary is the place where contemplative
Christians evoke the divine. They serve the community by standing before the altar with humility and by using their knowledge, artistry, and wonder to bring a sense of communion to
all. Anyone may serve, but those with particular gifts of keeping
intention and attention may sometimes become an icon, a window through which others glimpse the divine.*

Jesus took with him Peter and James and his brother John
and led them up a high mountain, by themselves. And
he was transfigured before them, and his face shone like
the sun, and his clothes became dazzling white.

—MATTHEW 17:1–2

DURING HIS TENURE at Harvard University as a visiting professor in the early
1930s, T. S. Eliot attended the daily Eucharist services at SSJE. One of the Society's
most beloved anecdotes tells of an incident T. S. Eliot had in their chapel at the
time.[1] In that era of the Episcopal Church, priests consecrated the elements while
facing the altar, with their backs to the congregation. One morning after the
Eucharistic prayer, when the celebrant and acolyte were holding aloft the newly
blessed sacrament of bread and wine, they heard a loud thud behind them. The
priest whispered to the acolyte, "You'd better see what's happened back there."
The young man turned to find T. S. Eliot, the only visitor at that morning's service, out cold on the floor. He had swooned and collapsed, he said after reviving,
because of the intensity of an encounter he had had with the divine during the
Eucharistic prayer.

Decades later, in the current monastic chapel of SSJE, Br. David Vryhof (2014) gave a sermon called "A Mysterious Way of Seeing" about a much earlier historical encounter with the divine, Jesus' Transfiguration.[2] Addressing a learned Cambridge congregation, Br. David framed his teachings with comments that a "unitive moment" like the one in the Transfiguration story "defies logic" and "resists any easy interpretation." He said of divine encounters like these, "We have entered a realm where systematic, logical analysis does not apply . . . . It points to a mystery beyond our comprehension." Br. David said that one might better approach such stories by turning to the Christian mystics: "In the contemplative tradition of the Church, it has often been suggested that it was the *disciples* who were changed rather than Jesus. It was *their* eyes that were opened . . . [to] a glimpse of the divine" (emphasis in original).

Despite being difficult to apprehend or explain intellectually, Br. David said that the Transfiguration story

> reflects an understanding of the human condition that is common not only in the contemplative tradition of Christianity, but in other prominent religions as well. This understanding maintains that human beings live much of their lives in a state of blindness; that we do not see ourselves or the world in which we live clearly or accurately. According to this understanding, we bring far less than full awareness to our experience. Lost in past memories and hypnotized by future fantasies, we sleepwalk through life, oblivious to the sacredness of the world around us and blind to the sanctity of others and our own selves. (Vryhof 2014)

Yet despite this human tendency toward "blindness," said Br. David, contemplatives "acknowledge that God is everywhere present, that *in God* we live and move and have our being" and that people have "the possibility of regaining . . . sight" (emphasis in original). We have seen in Chapters 5 and 6 some of the ways contemplatives work to awaken "out of the blindness" by accepting and even embracing the ambiguity and unknowing which exists in relation to positive forms of knowledge. Those ways worked the dynamic between human agency and habitus to cultivate sensitivities and foster openness and consent to what Br. David Vryhof called the "God that is everywhere present."

Contemplatives were very much aware of the dialogic between their propensity and capacity to act and their understanding of human dependence on the divine. Br. David Vryhof emphasized that moments of "encounter with Divine Mystery . . . cannot be manufactured or sustained by the force of our own will. [They] defy logic and explanation, and [are] simply a gift of grace . . . [which] find their true value in lives of compassion and love." Contemplative experiences of unity with the divine and all of creation rise out of the paradox of doing and not doing, knowing and not knowing, a balance that asserted and accepted both the ambiguity and the clarity of contemplative ways of knowing.[3]

Chapters 5 and 6, the first two of our Triduum of chapters, focused on some technical methods of ritual and ritualization that engaged posture and flow as processes that honed contemplative senses. This chapter, "Sanctuary," turns to the knowledge that those processes created. Here we explore the chapel's chamber of transformation and transfiguration, and the variability of contemplative ways of knowing that can result from a ritualized life. Their forms of knowledge are themselves part of an ongoing process, not static, reified objects. In contemplative circles that emphasized "wakefulness" and the present moment, knowledge was ideally composed of immediate, enacted ways of perceiving that were responsive, receptive, and changing. Their efforts worked toward a kind of *perceptual agency.*

In the chapel's Sanctuary resides the altar, where learned contemplatives use performative knowledge, a kind of charisma, as a way of evoking divine presence. In the institutions of Episcopal and Roman Catholic churches, only ordained priests may approach the altar to perform the liturgy of the Eucharist, which is said to bring the divine into the elements of bread and wine. Even so, the contemplative tradition of Christianity teaches that anyone has the potential to foster union with the divine, not only ritual experts, and that some people (regardless of formal institutional training or rites of induction) show particularly potent varieties of knowledge and "grace" that can bring the divine into the midst of the community. From the contemplative perspective, this kind of *iconic knowledge*—acting as a conduit of the divine for others—is not about accreditation and cannot be taken for granted as a continuous ability or a product of individual merit. Rather, adherents like Br. David Vryhof see it first as "a gift of grace." Even so, practitioners can actively encourage such communion through attention and intention. They can create potent environments that invite "divine indwelling" through the conscious enactment of prayer and practices of attunement.

PARTLY INSPIRED BY Fredrik Barth's idea that an anthropology of knowledge (1993, 2002) can help explain diversity in complex, pluralistic societies, this chapter explores the variable palette of Christian contemplative ways of knowing. Practitioners acquire knowledge differently and thus range from simple "players" to learned "virtuosos." As in earlier chapters, I again introduce terms for two particular varieties of knowledge—*performative knowledge* and *unknowing*—which work together to encourage and invite a third variety of knowledge, *unitive being.*[4]

First, *performative knowledge* is a form of cultural capital derived from the technical skill to communicate and engage others contemplatively, whether in formalized ritual and liturgies or in ordinary life situations. As we saw in Chapter 4, the idea of performance here does not mean acting falsely to impress others, but is rather a learned repertoire of skills. Performative knowledge includes the learned skills of timing, pace, rhetoric, diplomacy, demeanor, the capacity to engage and to listen, as well as learned abilities to keep attention and employ contemplative senses: what to say when and how to say it, what to do when and how to do it, ideally enacted with compelling focus. These skills vary greatly from individual to individual. While social position, education, and class can give one a significant degree of knowledge, it does not tell the whole story. We all know, for example, that some people can give exhilarating lectures while others are infernal bores, even if they have similar social and cultural capital, such as doctoral degrees and twenty years of experience as professors. The same variability is true of Christian contemplatives. Some are virtuosos of the Sanctuary's altar, some are ordinary players, while others may even be "religiously unmusical" or "tone deaf." In the culture of contemplative Christianity, performative knowledge is an active, variable combination of intention and the capacity to draw on one's own resources, to engage cohorts, and "keep presence." [5]

Unknowing, on the other hand, is one's capacity for apophasis. Unknowing invites "flow" through an ease with ambiguity—that is, the degree to which one can evoke liminality through the practice of kenosis and consent to suspend established categories of knowledge in favor of trusting that the divine is at work well beyond the boundaries of one's imagination. Unknowing has two primary subcategories, which I call *circumstantial unknowing* and *intentional unknowing*. Circumstantial unknowing is what we don't know—our ignorance, that which is beyond the limits of our experience and imagination. Intentional unknowing is the conscious attempt to approach the world with openness, wonder, and mystery, rather than to immediately pre-judge and divide the world by known categories. Combining performative knowledge and unknowing is a way to shake off what contemplative Christians call the "blindness" that keeps them from an awareness of "divine presence" and a knowledge of unitive being.

This chapter explores perceptual agency—contemplative Christians' part in the evocation of unitive being, or phenomenological intersubjectivity, through the dialogical relationship of agency and habitus. Paradoxically, those who were most adept at contemplative ways were best able to use agency to "let go" and "surrender." Their performative knowledge and cultivation of intentional unknowing combined as crucial agents in fostering unitive being, the experiential knowledge of communion. To varying degrees, performative knowledge acted as a "strong container" for unknowing's capacity to encourage openness, receptivity, and a flow of self into the world—a quality of connectedness that contemplatives understood as a manifestation of divine encounter and the sensate experience of wisdom.

Performative Knowledge: Players, Virtuosos, and the Variable Knowledge of Being

I am not so much a flesh and blood mechanical object
but more like an event or performance.
—ZAK'S EJOURNAL

During my fieldwork, people described fostering communion with the divine as a way of living life as it was intended and the source by which people find the strength and clarity to do good in the world. Nevertheless, Br. Gabriel at SSJE said that experiential manifestations of a relationship with the divine (that is, "spiritual experiences") were a variety of "consolation"—indefinable and unbiddable mysteries that one must not expect or depend upon as a motivation for prayer. Among contemplative Christians, the ideal was to pray and express gratitude, regardless of desired or anticipated outcomes. Teachers like Br. Gabriel encouraged others to follow a disciplined schedule of prayer as an act of faith and devotion—a way to serve at the altar, rather than a search for personal gratification through spiritual experiences.

The contemplative Christians with whom I worked believed that regular practice strengthens a capacity for attentiveness and the liminality that sometimes opens a window to unitive being. Using a musicianship metaphor, practicing contemplative Christians were like players, some of whom excelled at their craft. Those who "practice, practice, practice," as Cathy McCarthy advised in the previous chapter, are better able to learn the ethos, genres, and techniques. Yet even with faithful practice, people still varied in their degrees of musicianship: some wrestled with musicality, some became competent or even masterly musicians, while others moved into the realm of virtuosity. Canonized saints are some who have been historically recognized as virtuosos, and the contemplatives with whom I worked said that such people exist among the living as well. But even virtuosos can have bad "performances." Their capacity to encourage unitive being depends on performative knowledge and intentional unknowing in any given moment, not on their social status. As Cynthia Bourgeault put it to her students, "There is no accreditation for wisdom. It only happens in present time, regardless of past or future." The shifting ground of individual and group attentiveness meant that contemplatives felt they lived on a moving gradient of intimacy with the divine and others; whether their task was to bless the sacraments at Eucharist, feed the hungry, do the laundry, or chant the psalms, their foundational work was to learn to dwell as consistently as possible in the liminal, kenotic space of doing and not doing, knowing and unknowing, where they believed the divine and wisdom reside.

In this section, I recount several liturgical situations where the degree and application of performative knowledge made all the difference to rituals that did not go so smoothly. In the words of Br. Robert L'Esperance, "something happens" or can falter, depending in part on the degrees of knowledge and attentiveness of the actors. Years of liturgical experience helped some practitioners bring formalized ritual and kenosis together, to gracefully merge the "doing" and "not doing" aspects of contemplative liturgy into paradoxical union. Three examples show how degrees and application of performative knowledge affected the outcome of ritual: two liturgical mishaps in comparison, one monastic, the other non-monastic, and a situation of more general disrepair in the Daily Office of a convent. The monastic "mishap" reveals how experience, liturgical artistry, and contemplative knowledge can turn any situation into a potential locus for unitive being, as we saw in the Tucson Wisdom School norovirus bootcamp. If those enacting the liturgy have the capacity to "keep presence" even in the face of unanticipated problems, then they may nevertheless help foster flow and phenomenological intersubjectivity among participants. In fact, mishap under these conditions can actually increase feelings of unity.[6]

First, however, I offer the non-monastic example. Though some had strong ties with churches or other religious communities and their liturgies, non-monastics generally had their greatest practical contemplative experience in solitary meditation. The teachers of Wisdom Schools endeavored to bring their students to a greater breadth of contemplative genres by expanding their repertoire of practices, including formalized rites and liturgies. In the closed residential environment of intensive practice and learning, teachers often used inter-religious and experimental rites, as well as more standard Christian liturgical forms, to "build energy" and foster "group entrainment." Their intention was to encourage participants' attunement to the divine and to one another over the week in residence, then send them off to take what they had learned out into the world. Intensive schedules of liturgies and group meditation created a heightened sense of unification and a feeling for what they described as a flow of divine energy.

However, many non-monastic participants' lesser familiarity with formal rites sometimes had a negative impact on the cohesiveness of liturgies, such as in the experimental form of sacred drama. The focus on contemplative experimentation and teaching in liturgical life was greatest at the Episcopal House of Prayer's Holy Week Wisdom School in 2012. We saw in Chapter 4 that there were plenty of evocative, intimate moments during that week, but there were a few liturgical mishaps as well. Some of the liturgies did not go as well as others.

On Good Friday afternoon of that week, the community observed one of the day's five liturgies, a "Solemn Commemoration of the Passion," which incorporated a session of tonglen in lieu of more standard Episcopalian and Roman Catholic observances like the Stations of the Cross, confession, and the Veneration of the Cross. Ward Bauman, the director of the Episcopal House of Prayer, presided. Well before the 4:00 p.m. start time, Ward had taken his place in the Oratory at the head of the inner circle, acting as a keeper of silence, solemnity, and still-ness. Just when most had settled into their places around the sand pit, a woman who was not part of the closed residential Wisdom School strode forthrightly into the Oratory. Brandishing a *Holy Week Liturgies* booklet, she stood above Ward and started talking. Ward was startled out of his meditation and looked up, open mouthed. He took a moment to grasp her questions, then shook his head: no book needed. The woman, who must have been a local adherent of the retreat house, made her way out again just as determinedly, then returned wearing a robe and carrying a prayer stool. She took a chair and set the stool down for a footrest, look-ing pointedly around at the others who, by contrast, sat still with an inward focus in preparation for the liturgy.[7]

The woman had brought an alien, almost invasive energy into the midst of the sensitive "being and presence" that the leaders and participants of the enclosed Holy Week gathering had been so carefully cultivating. The outside woman seemed to carry the fast-paced, utilitarian ethos of the ordinary world from which the group had been weaned over the past week. Though this was a liturgy meant only for those in residence, people accepted her presence without comment or question. The woman's disruption itself did not seem to immediately impinge on the gathering; people maintained their contemplative demeanor. Yet her insensi-tivity to the environment did seem to change the energy in the room, which may have contributed to a few hiccups—what J. L. Austin (1962) might have called "infelicities"—in the liturgy that followed.

Two women, Brigid and Naomi, played the roles of the "two Marys" in the experimental sacred drama and liturgies of Good Friday and the Easter Vigil.[8] In this crucifixion liturgy, as well as the "Entombment Liturgy" that would come later in the evening, Brigid and Naomi also acted as acolytes with specific liturgi-cal duties. Cynthia Bourgeault had rehearsed the roles with the two women, but during the actual liturgy, several times they seemed to freeze with stage fright and confusion. They forgot lines, were unsure of their blocking, and hesitated in their assigned tasks, such as retrieving the sacrament for the Eucharist. Darting, alarmed glances and bewildered expressions between the players let the assembly know that something was amiss. Helen, who was leading music for the week, quietly tried to get Naomi's attention to remind her to retrieve the chalice, but had no luck. The two women turned to Cynthia for guidance, who gestured prompts and mouthed directions from her meditation cushion in the inner circle while trying not to disrupt the liturgical flow. After the Eucharist, the women then for-got the next ritual action, wrapping the wooden cross in the altar cloth. In the end, all was accomplished, but the liturgical awkwardness and nervousness had restricted the formalized rite's capacity to cultivate "presence" and "build energy," even after a week's worth of intensive contemplative practices over Holy Week. Cynthia looked a little disappointed when the liturgy concluded, and I heard no whispered exclamations about beauty and synchrony on the walk back to the main building, as I had after liturgies on previous days.

The women's lack of performative knowledge had manifested as anxiety. Indeed, their state of nervousness detracted more from the intention to "build energy" and "keep presence" than did the imperfect execution of liturgical actions. Brigid, who had shown a great facility (even virtuosity) for an openness to divine indwelling in other situations, did not find her way so easily in one that was more foreign to her. Yet we saw in Chapters 5 and 6 that any action, antici- pated or unanticipated, has the potential to prompt contemplation. Remember the chant teacher Darlene Franz's comment that "it's not so much about what you do, as how you do it." Specific, formalized rites only served as a tool, albeit a potentially powerful, transformative tool; straying from "right action" did not necessarily deter practitioners from their efforts to "keep presence." Those play- ers who had a high degree of performative knowledge, contemplative training, and experience had a greater capacity to "let go," even in situations that were uncertain, giving them the *potential* to contemplate in any given situation: her- mits in solitude, professors in mid-lecture, taxi drivers in gridlock; so, too, in the midst of "flawed" liturgy and unexpected circumstances. In the context of formal rituals, liturgical adepts and virtuosos, ones well acquainted with the ground of formalized rite, could often manage awkward moments without detracting from the cultivation of intimacy.

Compare Brigid and Naomi's part in the Good Friday liturgy at the House of Prayer in 2012 with the Easter Vigil at the SSJE monastery in 2010. Ritual at SSJE is highly formalized and carefully crafted. Nevertheless, the monks tended to approach it with a light hand, which conveyed the idea that ritual itself is not the main point. In fact, Br. Matthew once said to me in a discussion about the role of liturgy, "Ritual matters and doesn't matter. Both are true." With their Benedictine rhythm of *ora et labora*, these men spend a significant amount of time in the chapel. Their experience gave them a real ease with liturgical expres- sion that infused their monastic formality with benevolence. As Sonja said in Chapter 5, their formality did not evoke an ethos of rigidity or remoteness, but rather one of warmth. In fact, accepting the little ragged edges when Brothers occasionally stumbled or when visitors did not know the protocol was an inten- tional act of hospitality: people and community mattered far more than a desire for orthopraxy.

The monks' conscious choice not to be too precious about ritual seemed to take the pressure off. Taking their rites seriously, but not *too* seriously, helped the monks to point congregants' attention to their understanding of the main inten- tions of liturgy: devotion to God, learning to love and serve, communion with one another, and divine indwelling. The intentional diminishment of self-importance and liturgical perfection paradoxically allowed them to engage well, whether the form of their actions was "right" or not. A freshness and sometimes even humor in their bearing (including in moments of seriousness or when things went awry) came from the experience and ease with which well-seasoned ritual officiants approached their craft. Yes, ritual matters (otherwise why would they devote so much time to doing it and doing it well?), but it is not the main point.

Here is an example of their ability to "keep presence" in the midst of imperfect liturgical conditions: At the monastery's 2010 Easter Vigil, monks and congregants assembled in the enclosed monastic Guesthouse garden at four in the morning. All lights had been ritually extinguished since the solemnities of Good Friday, so the community gathered in total darkness. During this liturgy, light was to be reintroduced as a symbol of the Resurrection. Vested in gold, red, and ivory, the presiding priests, deacons, and acolytes gathered in the sunken garden while some 250 congregants looked down from a slightly higher tier. In the dark and cold predawn of a New England March morning, the monks lit the "new fire," a bonfire kindled in a large cauldron-like brazier at the garden's center. The weather was wild. Wind thrashed around the confined space like a caged beast. After an extended delay and with considerable difficulty, the presiders managed to light the fire, the symbol of the unquenchable light of Christ in the world and his victory over death. The presiders' elaborate vestments flew about and I worried that someone would go up in flames at any moment.[9]

Every year at the Easter Vigil, a new Paschal candle is marked with the Greek symbols for alpha and omega and the current calendar year (the number of years since the birth of Jesus), and is studded with red wax pins in the shape of a cross, a sign of the "blessed wounds" of Christ crucified. The Paschal candle is then lit from the ceremonial "new fire." The SSJE candle was a massive white pillar, perhaps five feet tall, carried in procession by a subdeacon. The priests, deacons, and acolytes did their best to light the candle in the guesthouse garden, but the extreme weather made it impossible. They tried repeatedly, then finally gave up. The procession was to have followed the newly kindled "light of Christ" from the garden's ritual fire into the chapel's choir, where the rest of the three-hour-long liturgy would take place. Instead, we soberly processed behind an unlit candle. Having passed through the portico, the deacon turned to the congregation and stood before the Paschal candle to proclaim the first plainsong tone of the ancient incantation.

The   Light   of   Christ

The congregation (or at least those of us who were by then far enough inside the door) responded in like pitch,

Thanks be to God

Within the chapel, the deacon was then to proclaim "The Light of Christ" in ascending plainsong semi-tones each time the procession stopped at ascribed stations in the antechapel, at the gate, and in the lower choir, until it reached the candle's resting place at a garlanded wrought-iron stand behind the ceramic baptismal font at the choir's center, placed there during the liturgical season of Easter. But at this point just inside the portico, the candle was not yet burning with "the Light of Christ," so the company of ritual officiants paused, lit a taper with an ordinary match (rather than from the ritual fire that had been kindled outside), and got the Paschal candle to finally burn. They didn't fuss about it; they just did what needed to be done, all the while keeping the attentive energy of seriousness and solemnity.

Once the assembly had found its way to chairs in the antechapel and choir stalls, the Liturgy of the Word commenced. It recounted a scriptural history of the Hebrew people's relationship with God, interlaced with psalms chanted by the schola. In the midst of this, another mishap occurred. Before the readings, which took more than an hour, priests lit tapers from the Paschal candle, then "passed the light" to others, who turned to light their neighbors' tapers, until all held aloft their flickering flames, transforming the darkened chapel into a universe of stars. Halfway through the readings, I noticed smoke rising from the young man in the seat in front of me. In his early morning drowsiness, he had inadvertently let his order of service catch fire. Not wanting to make a scene, he was quietly trying to suppress the flames with his bare hands. Holding my lit taper in one hand, I leapt down from my choir stall and grasped the burning paper from the now startled-looking man, then quickly exited to a corner of the antechapel where I doused it in a water bucket set there for just such a circumstance. Over breakfast, I explained to the deacon what had happened. He responded simply, "Oh, that's what it was. I wondered what you were doing." My incongruous actions (not to mention the fire itself) had apparently not disturbed their countenance in the least.[10]

Perhaps an hour and a half after the fiery bulletin incident, the celebrant priest proclaimed the arrival of Easter in a chapel now fully lit by ceiling lights and the light of day, which then streamed through the stained-glass rose and clerestory windows. "Alleluia. Christ is risen!" he exclaimed, to which the community responded with jubilant vigor, "The Lord is risen indeed! Alleluia!" After the first Eucharist of Easter, the assembly then "brought in" Easter by singing the fourteenth-century hymn, "Jesus Christ Is Risen Today, Alleluia!" accompanied by fully unstopped organ accompaniment and pealing bells, both the great one in the monastery tower and hand bells which knowledgeable congregants had brought and which monks had earlier distributed among themselves and their resident guests. Standing before the altar, the three principal ritual celebrants were smiling, singing, and ringing in Easter when a great laugh went up from one side of the choir. The deacon stood with wide eyes and a bemused expression holding a bell handle without its bell. He had been ringing the bell so hard that it had jettisoned off into the congregation like a missile. Someone slipped up to his place in the sanctuary to offer him a replacement, which he rang with a wry, sheepish expression while the congregation laughed and beamed at one another through the final hymn.

The monks' years-long, five-times-daily leadership, participation, and experience with formal ritual allowed for this playful, light touch in the face of liturgical irregularities and unexpected happenstance. While the bell-ringing incident was certainly funny and came at an already buoyant moment in the liturgy, both occurrences of uncooperative fire had the potential to cause a rift in the crafting of communal reverence in a ritual that is the apex of the entire liturgical year. The lighting of the fire at the Easter Vigil is a particularly solemn rite with serious meaning: it represents the center of contemplative Christian cosmology, that Christ overcame death to infuse the world with divine presence. It is a key tenet of Christianity, symbolized in the ritual enactment of light emerging from darkness. The monks did their best to work the liturgical artistry of the moment, but the elements did not cooperate. Yet rather than depending too greatly on the proper execution of "right action," their performative knowledge made this awkward moment inconsequential. The world would not fail because the rite was not as it should have been. They kept calm and carried on.

Situational disrepair and faltering intention had greater consequences than a few liturgical rough edges, which came either from environmental circumstances, like the windstorm and faulty bell at SSJE's Easter Vigil in 2010, or from the inexperience, nervous tension, and stage fright at the Wisdom version of Good Friday in 2012. A third example of ritual "going wrong," which occurred at a women's convent in the Southwest, seemed to be the result of structural decline that had diminished the collective intentionality and contemplative attentiveness of the community. This community, like many Christian monasteries and convents in the United States, had been struggling to attract new members for some years. They had recently received a few new novices, but not nearly enough to bring their numbers up to the levels of the previous generation. In the months before I spent time with them, the nuns had been forced to divest some of their property and close several houses, including their main house in the Midwest. Twenty-eight Sisters were squeezed onto a small property and a few adjoining houses, which they had purchased to accommodate a population that was greater than the current convent could hold. The community was then searching for property to build a new facility that could properly accommodate all nuns from the former houses. The nuns were trying to keep their rule and way of life as best they could during the transition, and it certainly helped that there were women among them who were very experienced indeed, having written important theological works and mentored some of the most popular American spiritual authors of the latter part of the twentieth century.

However, after several years in this transitory phase, these women seemed to be in disarray. While they were bravely facing a new reality, they also seemed to be mourning the loss of their former convent homes and ways of life. The trauma of their situation showed itself in their cycle of the Daily Office. The Sisters appeared tired and lacking in concentration and enthusiasm, and not everyone showed up for the liturgies. In every monastery or convent I attended, there were often a few empty choir stalls at the offices because members were ill, went on trips, or had other duties. (In most cases, members were expected to perform the office on their own if they could, wherever they happened to be.) Some Sisters were away at a conference when I was visiting this convent, but a fair number did not attend offices even though they were in residence. At one Vespers office, only nine of twenty-eight nuns attended, some of whom arrived late.

More telling than numbers was the quality of attention of the Sisters who did participate. At one office, the lack of participants meant that a less experienced nun had to take the role of cantor. This community had a comprehensive breviary with musical notation for all the offices. Even so, the cantor struggled to lead the musical line and once actually stopped mid-psalm in exasperation: "Could we 'say' instead?" she asked (meaning, could the group speak the office instead of chanting it). On other occasions, individual nuns seemed very much disconnected from the proceedings. For example, at one Noonday Prayer service, an elderly Sister worked away at a crossword puzzle, another read a photocopied article, and a younger Sister seemed absorbed by a *Forbes* magazine folded open on her choir desk.

Having spent only one week with these nuns, I cannot claim to describe the shifting attitude of the community over time. But when I visited them, they seemed in a state of transition that had diminished their collective intentionality, serious-ness of purpose, and ability to keep attention. At least one novice who was there at that time did not choose to stay, and one fully avowed nun, Sr. Jane, said that the "half-baked canting," liturgical "train wrecks," and general low energy of the community were a source of real despair for her. The hallmark of contemplative communities—their intentional invocation of the divine through a seriousness of purpose and solemn ritual—was clearly impaired. Whether they had performative knowledge or not, they did not seem to be applying it to much effect during the short time I was among them. Sr. Jane, who had a long history with the Wisdom community, had brought in a Wisdom teacher to teach an evolutionary theology of the psalms, which are the foundation of most offices, and to lead Sufi-inspired psalmodic chant forms as a way to rejuvenate liturgical energy at the convent. Perhaps such alternative measures would help to recollect and revitalize the community, though some Sisters seemed wary or skeptical of the unfamiliar practices.

The precarious circumstances at the time of my visit illustrate the importance of *a critical mass of group intention and attention* to fostering the contemplative health of a community. The discouragement that can arise from decreasing monastic populations and the structural instability of closing houses and combining communities clearly has serious repercussions. The state of the convent's Daily Office, a tool of creating and sustaining contemplative attentiveness and a contemplative life, here revealed the damage.

Unknowing: "Chaos Birthing into Community"

Accept chaos and peace shall surely follow.

—RUMI

In November 2012, Cynthia Bourgeault tried another experiment with contemplative practices at a Wisdom School on the banks of the Shenandoah River in West Virginia. A Gurdjieff-inspired intentional community at a former plantation there had agreed to help introduce us to The Work, even though they usually only taught these practices and principles to those seriously committed to their philosophies and way of life. Cynthia impressed upon us that this was "a very rare opportunity for the uninitiated and unlearned to be allowed a glimpse of The Work." Their willingness to teach non-members was an extraordinary show of hospitality, she said. Cynthia herself had spent ten years working in Canadian Gurdjieff communities in Halifax and Toronto, but only a few of the participants at this Wisdom School had had previous exposure.

Cynthia directly addressed the group's unfamiliarity with Gurdjieffian practices and theories. She coached us to resist instantly slotting the unknown into established categories and asked us to instead "just sit with the ambiguity," even if we felt uncomfortable. In this context, unknowing took two forms: the *circumstantial unknowing* (in other words, ignorance) of being confronted with ideas, practices, and a sociocultural context that were new, and the *intentional unknowing* of apophasis, a way of approaching life with kenotic openness. The concentration and effort required to "sit with the unknown" as participants were thrust into unfamiliar, complex practices and philosophies made the week's work challenging, even for the most senior of Cynthia's contemplative Christian students. Their experiences offer us a glimpse into contemplative practitioners' variable facility with apophasis and kenosis, that is, ways of unknowing. We see how different people utilized their capacity for greeting and accepting something new (and even threatening) with "a kenotic heart" and what came of their acceptance or fear.

J. G. Bennett (2007), a former student of Gurdjieff (2002) and an author and spiritual teacher in his own right, had bought this old plantation to create a community based on The Work. The property had originally been given to horse breeding and included a huge rectangular horse barn with an octagonal barn attached at one end for exercising horses in winter. The former horse stalls were now a two-story wing of dormitories, meditation halls, dining room, kitchen, offices, and common living areas. The Wisdom School's *sohbet*-style seminars, meditation sessions, and liturgies were held in that wing's large common room, and conscious work sessions took place in various parts of the extensive grounds and buildings. The Movements sessions occurred in "the Octagon," part of which had been transformed into a dance studio.

About a hundred and fifty feet in diameter, the Octagon was a vast space, chilly in November. It was mostly unfinished, with a dance floor platform and grand piano in one sector, a screened-off tool storage area in another, and the rest left as open cement-floored barn. Natural light came through windows in a central coffered crown and in rows along the tops of the high white walls, like a rural version of monastic clerestory windows. Enormous sliding barn doors, rarely used now, mirrored each other on two opposing walls, and several ordinary doors allowed people to come and go from the residential wing or the grounds. Electric lights and radiant heat stations hung in clusters around the dance floor, a raised dais of about thirty by forty feet that was covered with well-sanded and varnished sheets of plywood. The matched seams between the plywood served as stage markings on which dancers aligned themselves when moving in formation.

We spent every afternoon during that Wisdom School learning and practicing the Movements. Our teacher, Marguerite, was very experienced, having taught Gurdjieff Movements for many years at this intentional residential community in West Virginia, at other locations in the United States, and in several European countries, especially Italy, Russia, and Ukraine. To us, the "uninitiated," Marguerite taught the basic formation of the Movements, the files and rows into which people align themselves in a grid pattern. Files were the working units, numbered right to left as dancers face forward, with the head of the file being the leader. Files were cross-aligned in rows, numbered front to back, so that the group worked in grid formation. We had six files of about seven rows. Some of the residents of the community and several non-residents who regularly attended Movements sessions joined us on some of the afternoons.[11]

The Movements required precise alignment and keen awareness of oneself in the context of people in motion. A key intention of practicing the Movements is to attune oneself to the group through simultaneous and complementary movements, which can be complex. If one is not keenly aware of the greater form of moving people, including the expansion and contraction of space between them, the collective endeavor will collapse into collisions and chaos. The Movements are reminiscent of symphonic music, with multifaceted harmonic relationships played by a large group to create a composer's vision of a "whole" comprising individual moving sound parts. At this Wisdom School, we had a week of afternoon Movement sessions. Cynthia Bourgeault told us that this work engages different kinds of intelligences—Gurdjieff's Intellectual, Emotional, and Moving Centers—"to refine our quality of attention and effort" and to "build presence."

Before we had our first Movements session, Cynthia also taught us how the community's founder, J. G. Bennett, described the kind of attention we were working toward. Bennett believed that there are three major categories of attention: "scattered attention," "sensitive energy," and "conscious presence." Akin to Bourdieu's (1977) passive variety of habitus, "scattered attention" or "common stream of consciousness" is the seat of assumed knowledge as well as distraction and "automatic behavior," according to Cynthia. We can sometimes rise to the second variety of attention called "sensitive energy," she said, a "euphoric fusion" in which one gets lost in an object of focus (Csikszentmihalyi 1997; Rappaport 1999). "This happens when one falls in love or is thoroughly absorbed in a compelling problem or idea," she said. This is also the place of ecstatic mystical experience during which boundaries between self and the divine disappear. By contrast, the third variety of attention, "conscious presence," is a keen, experiential recognition of oneself in relation to the complex whole of creation, including across time and space. She said the multiplicity of "conscious presence" (also called "witnessing presence" and "self-remembering") is not the fragmented attention of multitasking, but rather a "layered attention" that extends one's unified focus to an ever-expanding field as one's ability becomes more adept with training through exercises of "conscious work" like those which Rosa taught at the Tucson Wisdom School. The intricate group choreography of the Movements attempted to give participants experiential lessons in relational awareness, which could push people past chaos to create what Cynthia called a "unified field of attention that can hold all things gracefully."

With these theoretical preliminaries, Cynthia Bourgeault said that from the Movements can rise a "luminosity in heart and being," but she also warned us that people can get "pretty rattled" when first introduced to them. She advised us to draw on the contemplative skills we had learned in other arenas to "maintain presence" even in this unfamiliar territory, and to "stick to something you *can* do" if everything else feels like it's falling apart. "Be alertly, receptively present," draw from "the group's collective intelligence," and you may find "surprising possibilities," she said. Erin, a long-time resident of the community, added another simple imperative: "Relax and breathe."

The first sessions were fairly chaotic, just as Cynthia had expected. A lot of people chit-chatted and cross-talked despite having heard Cynthia's primer on Gurdjieffian *adab* (protocol and etiquette) for Movement sessions: suspend judgment; be silent and attentive; "re-spect" ("look twice"); allow energy to build, guarding against its expenditure through unfocused behaviors like chatter and fidgeting. And most important, "Movements teacher holds the post." In other words, no talking. The teacher's word goes without question. "If all is not clear, best to watch and wait rather than pester," she had said as a way to prepare us for our foray into something new. Cynthia had also said, "If you aren't accustomed to an environment of this kind of intensity and focus, remember that its seriousness is not the same as unfriendliness."

On the studio floor, however, a fair portion of the group had a hard time enacting these directives. When a little confusion or difficulty arose, many could not resist expressing themselves through physical squirminess and nervous laughter, or by voicing anxiety. In the first two days, there were moments of real din. Even some participants who were adept in other genres of contemplative training struggled to maintain the "inner stillness" and self-denial required to set aside insecurity and fear of getting it wrong. I myself felt this anxiety, especially when I unexpectedly found myself leading a file, knowing that the people lined up behind me were depending on my memory and accuracy of execution to follow me in the complicated choreography. I too rolled my eyes and grimaced before I managed to collect myself enough to concentrate on the work rather than succumb to feelings of inadequacy.

Marguerite introduced us to the Movements with Sacred Dance Three. I later learned that seasoned Gurdjieff practitioners considered this piece complex and not an obvious opener for beginners. The teacher had her reasons for starting us with a difficult piece, I realized upon reflection. Gurdjieff was known to use confusion as a tool for destabilizing the ordinary, a technique that potentially prompted openness for new perspectives. The sustained choreographic complexity "undid" us and ultimately forced us to either focus or dissolve into chaos. With impassive seriousness, Marguerite kept us onboard and moving to the unyielding piano accompaniment, regardless of the pending mayhem; we had little choice but to rise to the challenge. It was a difficult journey of letting go of the "critical mind," which Cynthia said was a little too slow-witted and mechanical for this work, and allowing "body knowledge of the Moving Center" to become the central engine of understanding and enactment. This was a prime environment for pushing us toward the contemplative tenet that Cynthia had taught on the first evening: "Wisdom cannot be studied; it must be learned by being formed in the energetic body, by living it and doing it."

Sacred Dance Three divided the group into two corps of odd and even files. The corps had distinct parts of angular but sustained movements that were choreographed to intertwine. Seated at her piano, wearing fingerless gloves and wrapped in sweaters and scarves, the pianist played haunting rhythmic music to which the odd and even files executed their complementary pieces. Halfway through, the two corps exchanged parts, finally ending in the position from which the whole had begun. Breath visible in the chill, Marguerite patiently taught us the movements for feet, step by step, until we had learned (though certainly had not mastered) the two sets of eleven steps of the choreography's complementary halves. On the second afternoon, Marguerite taught us associated head and arm movements, though in one week we did not get as far as learning the arms for the second half of the piece.[12]

In this work, more than forty people with varying physical and contemplative abilities had to coordinate memory, timing, quality of execution, and spatial awareness. It was extraordinarily demanding. Any little mistake was evident, causing people to collide with one another, threatening to throw off the composure of grid quadrants—indeed, of the group as a whole. It was challenge enough to get the mechanics of the dance right, but there was more to work toward in Sacred Dance Three than choreographic accuracy or even physical grace. A socially interactive contemplative body practice, the Movements are a method of increasing attentiveness to the present moment *en suite*, a hint of which we saw among participants of the *Salve Nos* chant and movement exercise in Chapter 5. The intention of the Movements was not to zero in on an isolated, deeply focused personal center, but to systematically expand one's focus by adding more and more elements—music and timing, spatial inter-relationality, the genre's interiorized ethos, facial expression, and very specific gestures of legs, feet, arms, hands, head, and eyes—to train the practitioners' awareness toward a focused multiplicity and breadth which they believed could push them toward a unified social field of "conscious presence."

For Sacred Dance Three to work well, the teachers said, each individual had to let go of fear and intellectualized memory, which often lagged behind the rhythm of the dance. The newness and complexity did not allow one to systematically think through to the next steps while moving in the present, propelled relentlessly by the juggernaut of piano accompaniment and group motion. The choreography had to be embodied, not rationalized, said Marguerite; *movement* was required, not static, objectified categories of knowledge. To enter into this way of intentional unknowing, one had to work in immediate time and integrate movement, sensation, feeling, and intellect, rather than prioritize one variety of knowledge over others. Just as we have seen in the monastic offices, a critical mass of attentiveness has the potential to create "collective group intelligence," as Cynthia Bourgeault called it, which can compensate for individual weaknesses and inattentiveness.

At one point, when chaos and nervous chatter threatened to overtake the session, Marguerite separated the group so that one half could observe while the other half danced. Those who headed files, myself included, did not have the opportunity to watch because we needed to lead, but the others seemed to benefit greatly from an external vantage point. Afterward, the whole assembly seemed better oriented and clearer on what was needed as a collective to make the movement flow. Later, at that evening's discussion, Joan, the woman from Wisdom East who was a long-time practitioner of Christian, Buddhist, Kabbalist, and Sufi contemplative rites, described Marguerite's tactic as an application of "Third Force," Gurdjieff's term for bringing an entirely different energy or idea to a place of conflict to redirect it toward a positive resolution and a new creation (Bourgeault 2013; Ouspensky 1949). Others with an understanding of Gurdjieffian metaphysics concurred. Cynthia commented that she was "struck that everyone recognized that something happened at the point when Marguerite broke the group in two." After this intervention, the group had indeed become quieter and more focused and was more able to address the demands of the work. Watching, then returning to the practice, seemed to help participants balance an objective perspective with ambiguity and the body knowledge of enactment, casting wider the circle of knowledges by integrating intellectual and sensorial, embodied ways of knowing.

Several afternoons are very few to go any distance in this training. Those sessions provided only a taste of what was possible if one were to become a long-term practitioner. Even so, as the days progressed, our confidence and ability increased, and at the week's end, Marguerite said that she was very impressed with how far we had come from our first anxious attempts at the Movements.

People told something of their experiences at evening discussion periods over the week, showing the variability with which they engaged the Movements. The larger percentage spoke in awe of the "energetic unity," "communal synchronicity," and "fine quality of aliveness" that they felt was created during their attempts with Sacred Dance Three. Brian from Arizona, for example, said that by "clearing the decks and abandoning the fear" he could feel that his "senses and energy were expanding outward into the group." Wes, a priest from Georgia, said that the Movements undermined our sense of solid ground and threatened chaos. Relying on the community is what allowed us to recover from our missteps, he said. Rita from Indiana commented that fear had had a paralyzing effect at first, but when we became more willing as a whole to give ourselves to the practice, she could feel that "body learning was happening and concentration was flowing through the group." Cynthia responded to them by saying that this kind of work allowed us to really see that "group intelligence is greater than me."

George, a man from Miami, noted how the Movements "pushed us to the point of fusion," creating "an intimate relationship between inner and outer." Val responded to this by saying that "there *was* no inner or outer—it was flowing right through us."[13] I myself said that step nine, a movement forward in unison that came after complicated wanderings, had a concentrated feeling of mounting communal energy, like a wave building and peaking, just ready to break on the shore. Fiona, another file leader, said things clicked when she stopped trying to "think it through" and instead "emptied myself and let the whole self take over." She said, "That great big blank barn door opposite me really helped. It reminded me to be blank too, to just stay present and go with the group rhythm. It was like letting the edges of myself go." Darlene Franz, the chant teacher, agreed, saying, "The quality of emptying determines the quality of filling."

Strong feelings of building energy and group unification were not unanimous, however. Harriet, an older woman who had followed The Work and other contemplative streams for many years, felt people sometimes "lost energy" when they let their attention lapse. She emphasized the relationship between the divine and human responsibility, saying, "Grace was holding us at that point which was tied to our attention. When we lost attention, we lost congruency." As Harriet suggested, I had similarly noticed what appeared to be varying degrees of attentiveness and willingness in the Octagon. Along with enlivened focus and seriousness of purpose, I also saw expressions of confused floundering, and even mild resentment and incredulity. After a few years of learning to engage contemplative senses, I could feel variation in what Cynthia Bourgeault called the "energetic unity" that the group was endeavoring to foster. Some moments felt exhilarating, powered by a collective inner pulse, while others had the quality of stodgy workhorse diligence or incohesiveness.

Penny told us of her experience, which seemed to be more of the workhorse variety. A retired counseling psychologist from the Midwest who had practiced meditation for decades, Penny was clearly flummoxed and expressed consternation about her "two left feet," her lack of physical coordination, and an inability to master the choreography. She felt a long way from experiencing "coherence" in the Movements, she said. Several people in the circle nodded in sympathetic recognition. Kim, a young professional musician and human rights activist from New York City who was new to contemplative work, was hesitant to publicly mar the group's general enthusiasm, but later in the shower room, she admitted to me and a few others that she really couldn't understand the point of the Movements. Kim seemed confused by people's observations and a little troubled to be on the outside of what others appeared to cherish. Kim's and Penny's comments showed how, even when many feel a strong sense of group cohesion, the experience was far from homogenous. Perception varies greatly within a group, even when many agree that "something happened."

In response to expressions of anxiety and confusion, Cynthia reminded the group that one's primary responsibility in contemplative work is to keep attention through kenosis, even if one finds the task difficult. She illustrated her point by telling us about a moment when she herself crashed because she had lost focus, dropping bodily attentiveness and "inner spaciousness" in favor of "a personal narrative." Cynthia said she had managed to execute a tricky move of turning and tapping in a short rhythmic space, and then promptly started congratulating herself: "I started saying to myself, 'I'm a musician and I have a strong sense of rhythm, so I could get that beat right and do that complicated turn,' at which point I lost it." Even adepts can "lose presence" if they drop a posture of humility and don't pay attention. No matter how much experience someone has, "presence" is never a given.

Cynthia then emphasized how the guidance of an experienced teacher can take a group to unexpected places in "building energy," even in difficult circumstances. Marguerite's clear intentions, contemplative knowledge, and sustained will increased the will of her students, she said, even when they were confronted with the unknown. Under her persistent guidance, the students were able to rise to the challenge of opening themselves to something foreign. Cynthia said that Marguerite had "midwifed" the group through lags in attention so that, even with our lack of experience, we cultivated a taste of "finer substance," which Gurdjieff called the immanent presence of divine energy. A pivotal moment came with Marguerite's decision to halve the group so we could observe Sacred Dance Three in motion, she said; that was the point when "group intelligence kicked in." Marguerite had shown extraordinary "grace, patience, and encouragement in chaos birthing into community," said Cynthia.

By our last Movements session, performing Sacred Dance Three seemed to give the group a feeling of strong coherence, even though a number of participants still struggled. During the week we had also learned a few other Movements, including one for which we sat cross-legged in grid formation, moving only our arms and head. Marguerite had us do this simpler Movement as a way to cool down, end our sessions, and focus on sensing what our work had manifested. At midweek, when we had finished and were seated still and silent, Marguerite advised us to cherish "the precious moments of the finer substance that has been created through your work. Sit in the presence of it," she said. People "listened" for that energy in silence; I myself could feel a dense, tingling sensation that seemed to be shared across bodies. Just before leaving us to contemplate, Marguerite added, "Don't squander it." These were the very words Br. Curtis Almquist (2014a) used a few years later when encouraging his listeners to "let God's presence flow." By the week's end, Marguerite quietly expressed how pleased she was that we had gathered ourselves out of distress and distraction to create what she called "something beautiful."

Transfiguration of the Turkey Carcass: Agency, Perception, and Unitive Being

Not my will but yours be done.

—LUKE 22:42

Abba Lot went to see Abba Joseph and said to him, "Abba, as far as I can, I say my little office, I fast a little, I pray and meditate. I live in peace and as far as I can, I purify my thoughts. What else can I do?" Then the old man stood up

and stretched his hands towards heaven. His fingers became
like ten lamps of fire and he said to him, "If you will, you can
become all flame."

Among contemplative Christians, there was a strong relationship between knowledge and agency or "will." With biblical quotes like "not my will but yours be done," .in which Jesus accepted his forthcoming incarceration and crucifixion after praying in the garden of Gethsemane, the centrality of personal will in Christianity may seem counterintuitive at first glance. Yet contemplative Christians straddled a paradoxical field of *personal will* and what they called *divine will* or "grace." Better explained, they used their own will to learn how to be in "right alignment" with divine will, thereby working toward what they saw as a *unified will*. Remember Br. David Vryhof's sermon on the Transfiguration in which he said that "unitive moments" were "a gift of grace," not something to be reckoned by "force of will." Yet, contemplative Christians, the SSJE Brothers included, honored the wisdom of fourth-century Egyptian desert hermits like Abba Joseph, who said to Abba Lot, "*If you will*, you can become all flame." At the West Virginia Wisdom School, we also saw in the practice of Gurdjieff's Movements how important the strength of the teacher's will was in bolstering the will of students in unfamiliar circumstances.

There is considerable difference between these two functions of will. "Force of will"—one's own drive and power—is not the source of spiritual outcomes, learned contemplatives cautioned, and one should not pray in an attempt to conjure desired effects. Contemplative teachers encouraged their students to instead direct their will (which they saw as always dependent upon divine will or "grace") toward "awakening" and attentiveness, *regardless* of outcome. Seeking "consolations," as Br. Gabriel called them, or "bliss," as Cynthia Bourgeault called it, is a mark of spiritual immaturity, they said. Attentiveness, on the other hand, they considered to be a primary act of responsibility that simultaneously requires kenotic ambiguity and an application of will. "Maturity is about quality of being, not ease of existence," said Cynthia to her students in the midst of the norovirus crisis at the Tucson Wisdom School. Like guidance from an experienced teacher, personal discipline and rules of life assisted practitioners to form and direct their will toward a chosen path, which they discerned to be in line with divine will, through study, practice, prayer, historical tradition, and sometimes adherence to local practicing communities.

Contemporary American contemplatives, ones who have *voluntarily* chosen this path, ideally understood adopting a posture of discipline not as undermining personal will, but as *training and intentionally directing* personal will so that one is able to sustain and bear the divine intimacy that allows one to serve others. Thus, from their perspective, Jesus' "submission" in the garden of Gethsemane—"Not my will, but yours be done"—is the responsible choice of an active agent, not an imposition from an outside authority. Opting to learn how to merge one's personal will with "divine will" is a form of responsibility and an intersubjective act, adepts believed, which is quite different from a variety of willfulness that is the product of an immature personal desire for pleasant experiences.[14]

Nevertheless, practitioners' attentiveness and willing application of performative knowledge and unknowing did indeed have some effect on "outcomes." Liturgies, sacred drama, contemplative exercises, and the ritualization of everyday life were all situations in which players chose to apply agency and knowledge as a way of working toward phenomenological intersubjectivity, group entrainment, and personal-collective transformation. First introduced in Chapter 2, then reiterated in Chapter 6, I proposed a convection current model of contemplative transformation that depicts the relationship between agency and habitus in contemplative Christians' attempts to modify perception. Again briefly, this model depicts American contemplative Christians' intentional process of crafting perception by analyzing and attempting to alter habitual thoughts and behaviors through conscious acts, then endeavoring to subsume them through repetition to become normal, taken-for-granted aspects of life. It is their method of working toward a transformation of habitual ways of being and thinking in chosen directions.[15]

This model draws from aspects of the work of Thomas Csordas, Saba Mahmood, and Fredrik Barth. Csordas's theory of embodiment (1990) offered an influential paradigm that described how habitus can create synchronous group behavior and experiences of phenomenological intersubjectivity. Possibly because of the ethnographic characteristics of his research, as well as a strong dependence on the class-centered theory of Bourdieu (1977), Csordas had a serious theoretical blind spot, however; he neglected the role of agency in favor of a dominating habitus.[16] Quite a different picture from Csordas's portrayal of unreflective ritual participants, agency and critical thought were significant elements in the process of embodiment, self-transformation, and phenomenological intersubjectivity among the American contemplative Christians with whom I worked. For this reason, Mahmood's (2005) theoretical adaptation of embodiment, which turns to an Aristotelian habitus that recognizes the key roles of intention and repetitive practice in self-formation, better suits the character of my high-agency ethnographic community. The people in my research used cataphatic and apophatic processes to shape and refine thoughts, actions, and ways of being, creating a kind of convection current that looped between habituated ways and conscious intentions and actions. Their intentionality, their great concern for the cultivation of knowledge, and their intensively relational pluralistic environment also led me toward the ideas of Fredrik Barth (1993, 2002). Barth's transactionalism and anthropology of knowledge downplayed theories of a unifying culture concept in favor of showing how an infinitude of social interactions, individuals' conscious choices, and an unequal distribution of knowledge create significant diversity in complex, pluralistic societies. My theoretical interpretations of American contemplatives' combined application of agency, kenosis, and habitus fit somewhere between the ritual embodiment of Csordas, the intentional self-formation of Mahmood, and Barth's strategic, differential ways of living and knowing.

Along with my convection current metaphor, I here add another model that shows how agency and a palette of epistemological types work together to create an environment conducive to phenomenological intersubjectivity. Performative knowledge (a communicative form of cultural capital applied to ritual and ritualization, including liturgical, rhetorical, intellectual, and contemplative skills and experience, particularly the ability to "keep attention") can act as an anchor for intentional unknowing (the capacity for ambiguity and openness, enacted through kenosis, humility, and consent). Together they can manifest the knowledge of unitive being, a "flow" that can create a kind of "porous self"—a self with permeable boundaries.[17] Though this flow certainly occurred among solitary contemplatives, practitioners acknowledged that the effect could magnify when persons with contemplative experience and "unified will" direct their attention to a common purpose by performing ritualized acts together. Cynthia Bourgeault's students pondered this phenomenon when she posed the rhetorical question at a *sohbet* seminar, "Why is it that meditation is so often more powerful in a group than at home alone?"

I have sketched this dynamic interplay of contemplative Christian varieties of knowledge as a kind of formula,

$$ub = xi(pkn + ukn)^g$$

in which *ub* is unitive being (or phenomenological intersubjectivity), *pkn* is performative knowledge, and *ukn* is intentional unknowing. These epistemological elements are dependent upon three wild cards: the semi-controllable variables of x (the degree of experience and knowledge of the person or group) and i (the degree of intention, will, or agency with which a person or group applies and sustains that knowledge), all of which they feel is completely dependent upon an uncontrollable variable, g (grace or divine will).[18]

This formula may at first appear to be a fixed structuralist representation of knowledge, and thus seems to fly in the face of the processual analysis of ritual that I have thus far applied to my research findings. However, as long as the "variables" are taken seriously (in all their ambiguity), it offers a plausible depiction of the conceptual framework for varieties of contemplative Christian knowledge in dynamic, dialogical flow, and interaction. As we shall see later in this chapter, the category I have called unitive being is itself variable and unfixed, manifesting in clines or degrees of knowledge and varieties of experiences. My formulaic depiction of changeable epistemological relationships suggests an applicability beyond the confines of my particular ethnographic community, especially in contemplative environments (Christian or otherwise) that emphasize the integral relationship between cataphatic and apophatic processes and principles, such as discipline, training, silence, ritualized practice, and ambiguity.[19]

This formula for phenomenological intersubjectivity thus gives a theoretical picture of how Christian contemplative practitioners engaged epistemological elements and variables to foster what they called "unitive being." But what is unitive being like? The ephemeral is always tough to portray, especially in academic prose. Social theorists have coined all kinds of terms in an attempt to describe intersubjective phenomena of this type: Durkheim's "effervescence" and "solidarity," Turner's "communitas," Csordas's "embodiment," Rappaport's "third level of ritual meaning" and "radical identification of self and other," Weiss's "intercorporeality," and Obeyesekere's "visionary experience" are just a few.[20] Theorists of the performing arts have also made attempts: David Blum (1986) called intersubjective phenomena among string musicians "the fifth player of the quartet"; Tony Bolden (2013) described it among American funk musicians as "the groove";[21] and Heider and Warner (2010) described it among American Sacred Harp singers as "bodies in sync." In the theater, Peter Brook (1968) called the unitive, reciprocal connection between audience and actors as "contact" and "quality of attention"; Erika Fischer-Lichte (2008) described it as "enchantment"; and Richard Schechner (1985) used the terms "transportations" and "transformations." For the most part, I have used culturally specific terms and explanations of the people with whom I have worked, calling these phenomena *unitive being, unio mystica, non-dual consciousness, conscious presence, theosis,* and *divine indwelling,* among other things. I have also used the more neutral and rather technical term *phenomenological intersubjectivity.*

These terms do little to convey people's experience of this kind of knowledge, however. An expression of phenomenological intersubjectivity that has become a kind of archetype for American contemplative Christians comes in a 1958 description by Thomas Merton (1966: 155–156; emphasis in original), the monk, priest, and prolific author from the Trappist Abbey of Our Lady of Gethsemani in Kentucky. Thomas Merton wrote,

> In Louisville, at the corner of Fourth and Walnut, in the center of the shopping district, I was suddenly overwhelmed with the realization that I loved all those people, that they were mine and I was theirs, that we could not be alien to one another even though we were total strangers. It was like waking from a dream of separateness, of spurious self-isolation in a special world [of the monastery], the world of renunciation and supposed holiness.
>
> . . . This sense of liberation from an illusory difference was such a relief and such a joy to me that I almost laughed out loud . . . . I have the immense joy of being *man,* a member of a race in which God Himself

became incarnate. As if the sorrows and stupidities of the human condition could overwhelm me, now I realize what we all are. And if only everybody could realize this! But it cannot be explained. There is no way of telling people that they are all walking around shining like the sun . . . . If only we could see each other that way all the time. There would be no more war, no more hatred, no more cruelty, no more greed . . . . I suppose the big problem would be that we would fall down and worship each other. But this cannot be seen, only believed and "understood" by a peculiar gift.

The people with whom I worked often referred to Merton's epiphany at Fourth and Walnut in Louisville, Kentucky, as a benchmark of contemplative awakening. At monastic retreats and Wisdom Schools, people sometimes offered their own stories of unitive being, which they often described as a visceral feeling of union among fellow practitioners. While it is hard to pin down ("a bit like trying to nail water to a board," said Henry at one retreat), people nevertheless did find ways to express their understanding and experience of phenomenological intersubjectivity. Like those with whom I did research, people throughout Christian history have used genres like poetry, music, movement, visual arts, and metaphysical formulations to convey what they know and feel.[22] Many of the adjectives people used during my fieldwork to describe unitive being emphasized the senses, including words like *sweet, fiery, spacious, fragrant, dense, pungent, energetic, luminous, soft, visceral,* and *brilliant.* Unitive being was sometimes described in ambiguous terms, as when Br. Robert L'Esperance (2013) said, "Something happens in the body," or in apophatic terms of negation like emptiness, void, or in Eleanor's words, which we saw in Chapter 1, "an opening out into nothing. It really is *no thing,* something other than thing."

In silent environments, the primary form of expression was through minimalistic gesture. Gestural language expressed communal experience in unspoken demeanors of warmth and gentleness, in an interiority that showed itself in the averted gaze and stillness adopted by whole communities, in small signs of recognition like the almost imperceptible bow of one's head to others, or the press of hands together at the lips or forehead, or the light cupping of the right hand at the heart then its extension toward another. Especially in monasteries, practitioners often did not attempt to outwardly communicate these things at all, but instead "sat" with them alone or in community. Such verbal and gestural forms attempted to convey phenomenological experiences of what many described as a physical feeling of connectedness, a diminishment or blurring of space between people, which simultaneously felt like an expansion of space within, and even a fusion between individual bodies: as Val said after working with Sacred Dance Three, "there *was* no inner or outer—it flowed right through us."

Frances and Angela's comments at Kingfisher House in Maine can stand for the many, many descriptions I heard of phenomenological intersubjectivity in a setting of group practice. At the June 2011 retreat, Frances said that she was "over-awed by the energy" she felt when she came into the main retreat house from her sleeping cabin. Each time she entered the common room, she felt physically struck by it, said Frances, and had to brace herself in the doorway just to get her bearings. "I have felt some kind of communion at my small meditation meetings, but with this number of people, never. And I have never felt it this strongly. You can *just feel* the bonds reaching between us during meditation. It surrounds us and embraces us all." Angela, a spiritual director and fellow retreatant who over-heard our conversation, said she felt it, too, agreeing that there is great power in groups with communal intention, especially when the participants have a sound understanding about how to keep attention and presence. Angela said, "I love that first moment when we close our eyes together, when we settle into that common purpose of contemplation." Together their comments seemed to answer Cynthia Bourgeault's question, "Why is meditation so often stronger in groups?"

Expressing themselves outside the context of the mostly silent collective environ-ments in which I did fieldwork, those who ejournaled for me in 2011 and 2012 gave more detailed and diverse descriptions of unitive being, some of which used classical Christian imagery. Sonja, for example, described a sensorial experience of contact with the divine while on respite from caring for a chronically ill family member. She said, "I could feel the wind from the awesome wings of the army of angels. No really."

Maggie, who was a dream therapist, had also had classic Christian visionary experiences since childhood. In one ejournal entry, she described these instances as being marked by strong feelings of relationship. She wrote, "I had such a sense of grace from the spiritual world as a child, though I considered these figures personal to me, in relationship. And I remember seeing God . . . in the sky, from the back of some kind of station wagon . . . . Driving by a Scott paper factory, flat country all around, and me back there, sort of amazed that God would choose to reveal himself in that particular spot, the middle of nowhere it seemed, not too much humanity around. But there he was, and I will never forget it."

Relational knowledge of the divine came to Maggie through adult contem-plative practices as well. When meditating on iconic images of the Madonna and Child, for example, Maggie said she had a vision she called "In the Heart of Christ." She wrote,

> I felt myself gasp at the impact. Suddenly receiving all the light of the upward turned eyes of the risen Christ in the midst of this incarnation story, the unfolding relationship between mother, child, and earth . . . . Is it possi-ble to convey that sensation? . . . Moments of impact, of meaning, that really have very little thought attached to them . . . . And then as I let it go and continued with the prayer I heard . . . "What about a direct relationship?"

Over the months she wrote for me, AJ also used classic Christian motifs, relational language, and sensorial observations to describe intimacy with the divine. She said she "knew love and grace deep in my bones" and sometimes felt "bathed in a profound inner knowledge of God's love," which was "overflowing." She added, "I can actually, viscerally, feel the letting go into God, into the emptiness as the presence of God—the spaciousness and calmness that blossoms in me during Centering Prayer."

Some of AJ's descriptions bring us back to the knowledge that comes from ardent Love Mysticism. One time she recounted a walk in the woods of western Pennsylvania where she said Christ sometimes appeared to her. In their conversation on that particular day, she expressed anxiety about whether all her attempts to love were acts of objectification, including objectification of the divine, which she felt rose out of her own neediness. AJ wrote,

> The other day, I met Jesus in the usual place, at the top of the dusty road, near the outcropping of rocks and the cliff overlooking the valley, village and beyond. I brought Him my worry, that I might be sabotaging my own healing efforts to move past "Lost without the love object." I asked Him, "What if I'm just making You the love object? Isn't that just as bad?" He said, "I'm not the love object. I'm the Love." "You're the Love," I said, "You're the Love Itself." And then He stepped behind me and merged into me, so that we were One.

For some two weeks afterward, AJ said that this passionate experience of unitive being sustained in her "the same physical sensations I've had in the past in kundalini experiences in yoga—a sexual aliveness as well as a feeling of floating . . . like the heightened sensations associated with falling in love. But in this case I think it is 'filling' with love, not falling!" Trying to understand the fieriness of divine intimacy and its sensations of vastness, AJ mused over Abba Joseph's teaching, "If you will, you can become all flame," and Mary Oliver's "ways to enter fire" in her poem "Sunrise" (1992), which rejects the need to categorize every corner of intimacy, and suggests instead abandonment to full entry. AJ concluded, "Fire, to me, represents deep communion with God" in which "I am alone but not alone."[23]

More often, the people with whom I worked did not offer classical Christian idioms, like visions of angels or conversations with Jesus, to describe unitive being. Zak wrote about many intimate encounters with the divine without using "God language." For example, he described seeing "colors and patterns" during meditation, which he interpreted as an indicator of conscious awareness. "I know when I am aware of these images . . . I am 'present,' " he wrote. In another passage,

Zak recalled "a spontaneous revelation" that shifted his relationship to the natural world. He wrote in his ejournal,

> I was sitting in a wooded area near my home in a sort of relaxed, medita-
> tive state. Suddenly it came to me that the tree directly in front of me only
> existed as an image in my brain. It's not exactly "out there" but, in a factual
> way, all that I know of that tree is from an image here inside my head,
> created by the apparatus of my eyes in miraculous concert with billions
> of neurons encased in a boney shell above my shoulders. This seed of an
> idea then flipped everything in my field of vision around in such a way that
> there was no difference between inside and outside of me . . . and "I" (as
> I had always experienced myself) disappeared! Just like that! I became just
> one more object in Awareness. This is a state of consciousness that I am
> now able to bring on more or less at will.

By integrating intellectual knowledge about the human physiology of perception with body/sensorial knowledge, he found himself moving from understanding "tree" as an objective category to an entity in intersubjective relation, the far-reaching, non-"I-centered" phenomenological understanding of relationality in the field of being in which Zak and tree were equal partners. This is perhaps an example of what Cynthia Bourgeault called "self-remembering" or "witnessing presence." After the first occurrence, Zak noted that he had a degree of perceptual agency in shifting his vision in this direction.

During my fieldwork at monasteries, retreats, and Wisdom Schools, my own participation in contemplative practices also prompted phenomenological inter-subjectivity. Back in Chapter 1, I said that to have any hope of understanding the inner workings of a community like this, one had to be willing to dive right in. Prayer—the "inner gesture" of ritual and ritualization—has been elusive to eth-nographers, who often focus on more easily described cataphatic rites, rather than the hidden subjectivities of ontological, relational being. Marcel Mauss (2008 [1909]), for example, eventually abandoned his dissertation, On Prayer. It may not have helped that he had not personally engaged in ethnographic fieldwork to investigate his subject, but instead relied on the correspondence of others in the field. The difficulty may have gone further than a lack of personal research, however. Whether research is first- or secondhand, prayer is a difficult thing to "observe," especially in interiorized forms like contemplation and monasticism.

Tanya Luhrmann (2012) and Rachel Morgain (Luhrmann and Morgain 2012) have more recently published on the subject of prayer among American evangelicals and came to some similar conclusions to my own about how dedi-cated practices of prayer can cultivate the senses and alter perception. Their "atten-tional learning theory of prayer" described how prayer cultivates inner senses to enhance imagination and spiritual experience. Observations about prayer like Luhrmann and Morgain's (or my own) rely on a significant amount of interpretation. Even a "dive-right-in" approach to fieldwork cannot let us know for certain what is happening in the internal lives of the people with whom we work. Fredrik Barth (1993: 160–161) was pragmatic about this ever-present ethnographic problem, writing, "There is no way we can enter inside the skin of another person, but this is an impediment inherent in the human condition, not a special difficulty of the anthropologist's task."

Yet years of scholarly work in hermeneutical theory, interpretive anthropology, and the "subjective turn" have by now taught us that despite our critical assessment and rejection of unproblematized attempts at objectivity, we humans (ethnographers included) can nevertheless learn something about others, despite the limits of our perspectives (Fabian 2012; Jackson 2005, 2012; Ricoeur 1976, 2005). "Anthropological attunement" is possible, wrote Barth (1993: 160–161), by immersing oneself in a society through "observation, reflection, conversation, and participation," by building up "a formidable inventory of cultural and social facts and a knowledge of the particulars that position a considerable number of different actors," and especially by engaging in *cultural practice*. It is in participation and cultural practice, he said, that we find the "keys of interpretation."

Like any student of American contemplative Christianity, I relied on a corpus of sociocultural knowledge, which included cultivating embodied knowledge and contemplative senses. Some specific ways helped me come to a closer understanding of contemplative varieties of relational knowledge, even in silent environments. In Chapter 1, I described my intersubjective methodological approach of exploring the inner worlds of contemplative Christians. To understand the internal gestures and dynamics of prayer in relation to the outer cataphatic postures of rituals and ritualizations, I did not confine myself to observing action and interaction or listening to what people had to say about it. That kind of research is extremely important, but it does not *alone* get so easily at the inner gestures, apophasis, or phenomenological intersubjectivity that were equal partners to the ritual action of American Christian contemplatives. Part of my research method therefore was to learn and to emulate the inner movements of contemplation as well as the outer ones. I did what they did, as best I could understand it, and learned whether I had come anywhere close to getting it right by watching and listening to teachers' and cohorts' responses to my efforts at participation. In my research, I took seriously Fr. Thomas Keating's comment to me in an interview, "Unless you have some experience as a contemplative, you don't really know what the mystics are talking about."[24]

During my research, I regularly felt something akin to the physical "bonds of energy" between practitioners that Frances and Angela described, but I also had

more specific and intensive, even visionary, experiences. The Wisdom School at
West Virginia resulted in particularly strong instances, prompted I believe by the
intensity of the Movements sessions. That Wisdom School was the final event of
my fieldwork, and by then I had begun to learn a certain amount about performative knowledge and unknowing, enough at least to have a sense of how to straddle
the paradox of simultaneous engagement/attention and letting go. Another factor contributing to that particular Wisdom School's intensity was that just before-
hand, a few participants, Cynthia Bourgeault and myself included, had taken part
in an anointing ceremony in Vermont to help prepare Helen Daly for her immi-
nent death from a fast-moving cancer. Helen died exactly a week afterward, when
the rest of us were still in West Virginia.

   In West Virginia, Cynthia had set tasks about paying attention to sensations
in the body, like identifying and using only the muscles necessary for particular work. She also layered in questions about the relationship of attention and
prayer. She qualified her instructions with the comment, "if it *interests* you," thus
emphasizing the central role of individual will and personal responsibility in
undertaking the work with seriousness. Prompted by these tasks and questions,
I began experimenting with ridding myself of extraneous sound and movement
as a practical way to hone attention. This manifested as a simplification of movement and sound, not as dilution, but rather its opposite: a concentration of movement and sound that inspired feelings of increasing energy in my body. This
conscious action resulted in sensations of a densification of energy that nevertheless felt spacious, light, and expansive. I sensed a fluidity and connectedness
in my movements, which made them feel as though they extended out past the
boundaries of my physical body, connecting with other entities, including other
Wisdom School participants. This variety of attention had the sensation of radi-
ating outward, while simultaneously feeling receptive of energies coming from
other sources. If I consciously "kept attention" and "presence," these sensations
not only continued through any activity I was doing—washing windows, performing Movements, listening or speaking at seminars, eating meals—but also
seemed to build in intensity.

   By Thursday evening, when I was on cleanup duty after an excellent
Thanksgiving dinner that the residential community had prepared for us, I could
not only feel "energy" but also actually see color and light shimmering around
me. As I removed a serving platter from the buffet table, the turkey carcass was
vivified with heightened, bouncing color; strong tingling sensations coursed up
my arms and into my chest and torso, seeming to pass back and forth between me
and the remains of the bird. I also felt vibrations in my lips and forehead, down
my arms to the palms of my hands, through my torso, and down my legs to the
soles of my feet and past them. These sensations felt like being on fire with energy,

creative potential, and alertness, and seemed to extend past turkey carcass into the space beyond, like an expansion of self into the world, a physical connectedness that was simultaneously emanating and receptive. It was as though my body had become porous to other entities and, as AJ wrote, it had a quality almost of "sexual aliveness."

As I have said, learning about and communicating the ephemeral, like these experiences that transfigured the turkey carcass, are a tricky undertaking for anthropologists. One way of confirming the accuracy of our hermeneutics—our interpretations of what others know and experience—is to listen to what one's research community has to say about one's own descriptions. I conveyed these incidents as best I could at discussion periods over a few evenings, describing the sensorial phenomena and changing quality of being through my experiments, and received confirmation that this was within the realm of what contemplatives experienced as conscious presence and unitive being. Using these observations, I answered Cynthia's Friday morning question, "Where is the intersection of attention and prayer?" I told the group that, if keeping attention was understood as being in concentrated conscious, phenomenological relationship with the divine and all creation, then there was no difference. Cynthia said, "I was hoping some-one would take up that task. That's right. There is no difference between attention and prayer."

After returning to New England, I met with Br. Gabriel at SSJE and told him about my experiments with concentrating energy in the body by being highly attentive and by eliminating extraneous movement and sound. I asked him to reflect on my experience in relation to how the monks enacted formalized ritual gestures in their liturgies. Did it make a difference how one physically executed silence, stillness, movement, and sound in the chapel? Did moving with atten-tion make a difference to one's awakening to the divine? Br. Gabriel pondered a moment, then nodded. "Yes, I think it does. I think attention to movement makes all the difference," he said.

Ritual is not magic—that is, formulaic actions that elicit set effects. There are no predetermined outcomes to ritualized gesture or sound, yet atten-tiveness in ritualization encourages certain possibilities. Minimizing action through highly focused sound and concentrated movements is one way that can create bodily environments for the intensification of energy and attentive-ness. The standardization of formalized movements of the priest during the Eucharistic prayer in the sanctuary, for example, offers the *option* of engaging attentively by using one's performative knowledge and capacity for unknowing to "keep presence," which contemplatives understand as a way to evoke inti-macy with the divine, both for oneself and for the community on whose behalf one dacts.

The Person as Icon: Degrees of Intimacy
in Intersubjective Knowledge

We talk a lot about human rights,
but not enough about human responsibility.

—CYNTHIA BOURGEAULT

Phenomenological knowledge of unitive being among American contemplative Christians manifests in a wide range. Ejournalers and retreatants have shown us that the types of unitive being are diverse, but so too are the degrees. Ken Wilber (1977, 1986, 2005), a popular American philosopher of science and religion followed by some of the contemplatives in my research, has described the difference between "states," or *temporary experiences* of altered consciousness and being, and "stages," or *permanent transformations* of consciousness and being. A few of the people with whom I worked distinguished between the temporary and the permanent, but most did not describe "transformation" as formulaically as Wilber does with his "integral theory." They certainly believed that persistence in practice and living with humility tended to bring people to greater wisdom, but their inclusion of the "variables" of grace and human inconsistency kept their theoretical constructs fluid.[25]

In a public conversation between the two teachers, Fr. Thomas Keating responded to Ken Wilber's idea that regular contemplative practice "helps move people through stages of awareness" and encourages "nearness to the divine presence" faster than cataphatic practices like yoga or psychotherapy. The Trappist monk politely listened to Wilber's views, then gently offered "a little precaution" by adding the all-important element of humility to the philosopher's treatises about stages of awareness. One could never assume permanence or depend on the effects of personal will, said Fr. Thomas.[26] To be sure, I heard no one in my study describe contemplative virtuosity as something one could take for granted, a place at which one could arrive and settle. While they believed that people did have the capacity to shift toward greater knowledge, one's quality of intersubjective "being-ness" was always in current time; they felt manifestations of *unio mystica* were very much dependent upon divine will and one's degree of attentiveness and willingness to consent in the moment.

Even with these caveats about fluidity and impermanence, contemplatives did describe unitive being as something that potentially deepens and can be increasingly intersubjective and potentially transformative to the point of seeing and experiencing one's relationship to the world in a profoundly different way. In Chapter 1, I wrote about St. Teresa of Ávila's metaphor of the Interior Castle (and indeed the literary structure of this book is modeled on it). In the sixteenth century, she said that the person is like a many-roomed house in which one roams about at a distance or dwells in closer proximity to the divine. At the dwelling's center (that is, one's *own* center), the person relates to the divine and others with the greatest intensity.

In this chapter we have already seen this kind of cline of intersubjective knowledge in the teachings of J.G. Bennett (2007). Contemplative students learned and worked toward Bennett's schema of deepening awareness types, and used them as a theoretical frame for things they already knew from personal experience. Bennett's three types of attention included the scattered attention that most people have in everyday life, the "sensitive energy" of blissful full union in which one loses consciousness of self, and "conscious presence" in which one is aware of oneself in union with all creation.

In the work of Ramón Panikkar, a Spanish-born professor of comparative religion and a Roman Catholic priest who died in 2010, Thomas Keating came across another model of a cline of phenomenological intersubjectivity that he felt reflected his own understanding about unitive being. He shared the find with Cynthia Bourgeault, and she suggested that they together begin incorporating Panikkar into their teachings. Fr. Thomas was hesitant because of the complexity of the philosophy and the significant potential for misunderstanding. Nevertheless, they went ahead with their first joint Panikkar teaching retreat in 2009 and have since led a few others for well-established students of contemplation.

I cannot here give a thorough description of Panikkar's ideas, but rather offer the briefest of summaries as they were taught to me and others at a special ten-day study and practice retreat in October 2011 at the guesthouse of Fr. Thomas Keating's home, the Cistercian Trappist St. Benedict's monastery at Snowmass, Colorado. Then almost ninety years old, Thomas Keating was to have co-taught with Cynthia Bourgeault, but an illness prevented his participation. Cynthia acknowledged in a letter before the retreat began that participants would be disappointed, but also said that Fr. Thomas's "presence during the week, carried in those deeper currents of silent prayer and heart communion, will be palpable, I can assure you!"

In that letter, Cynthia noted the challenging nature of Panikkar's book, *Christophany* (2004), which was to be our subject of study. She said that to begin to understand Panikkar's ideas, one must approach the text both intellectually and contemplatively. "Panikkar's brilliant vision cannot be touched through the mind alone, but only through mind/heart working together," she said. The retreat would be silent, except during teaching periods, and the days would be rigorous with demanding Centering Prayer meditation and seminar schedules, as well as attendance at some of the offices at the Trappist monastery chapel. She suggested that we find our own right balance: "In a stand-off between contemplative stillness and intellectual preparation, favor stillness!" she wrote. To assist in this balance, the ten days would include two "desert days" of unbroken silence with no teaching.

While the process of how retreatants grappled with Panikkar's philosophy with the help of our teacher was itself interesting, my concern here is more pointedly with the dissemination of ideas about degrees of intensity in phenomenological intersubjectivity. Cynthia assisted by talking us through the work, chapter by chapter, and also by writing her own "Cliff Notes" summaries of Panikkar's ideas. In the plainest of terms, Panikkar (2004: 25–35), who had an Indian Hindu father and a Spanish Roman Catholic mother, distinguished between the Advaita monism of Vedanta Hinduism ("Atman is Brahman" or "I am God") and the transcendent dualism of many Christian theologies ("God is other"), and said that Christian mysticism saw something different. Panikkar's work used the sixteenth-century visionary writings of the Spanish Roman Catholic saint Teresa of Ávila as a way of exploring another, more fluid option that rose out of the experience of unitive being among Christian mystics. Teresa of Ávila's vision of Christ saying, "Seek yourself in me, seek me in yourself"[27] is neither a monist nor a dualist perspective, but an intersubjective one. Panikkar used the term *theandric* to connote this "inter-abiding presence," which straddles immanence and transcendence in the "Christophanic experience" that is "neither the mere dualism of creatureliness nor the monistic simplification of divinization."

The theandric self is one that has gradually come to the knowledge that one is "the 'thou' of an 'I' "—that is, the recognition that, through the multidimensionality of concurrent intellectual, sensorial/embodied, and "pneumatic" (or "heart," in Cynthia's terminology) ways of knowing, one is able to know others "from within," as a "correlative being" where "[t]he 'other' has become your Self" (Panikkar 2004: 71). From this perspective, other and self are intersubjectively centered, rather than I-centered or other-centered, and are equal—indeed, potentially interchangeable. This theandric being is a way of knowing the universe in an "I-I" relationship, in which the "I" does not disappear into the divine, but which understands all I's "from within," through the experiential interpenetration of persons. Through contemplative practice and increasing knowledge, one can shift along the cline of perception from an "I-it" to an "I-thou" to an "I-I" perspective. Panikkar described the deepest relationality of the theandric I-I as neither first- nor second-person, but another category that bridges the two, where "one not only loves the Beloved, but loves what the Beloved loves"—that is, in which one *knows* the other as well as *experiences knowledge as the other experiences it*. Panikkar concluded that those who learn contemplative ways of knowing to this degree can become a kind of "mediator" between the "infinite" and the "finite" varieties of selves, where "Christ dwell[s] in the deepest center of our being" (Panikkar 2004: 20–25, 81).

In her seminars, Cynthia Bourgeault gave us a shorthand expression to summarize this deepest place of intersubjectivity as "not one, not two, but both one and two." Using the imagery of an American Sufi sheikh, she said of this variety

of being, "Where two stones cannot occupy the same space, two fragrances can."
She also added St. John Cassian's fifth-century depiction that this degree of unification occurs when monks together "sing the psalms as if they were composing
them." Contemplatives with whom I worked said that being "both one and two"
can occur to the extent that one experiences a phenomenological crossing over the
boundaries of distinct bodies, as we have heard in some ejournal descriptions, but
also over the boundaries of time and space, extending to what some contemplatives called "the realms," the dimensions in which deceased persons and other
conscious forms of being dwell. This phenomenological expansion across time
and space thus includes what contemplative Christians described as "the communion of saints," where death is no longer a barrier between entities, as well as the
realm of prophetic, revelatory knowledge, which practitioners sometimes called
"direct knowledge."[28]

Established teachers and thinkers like Panikkar and Bennett were not the only
ones to have theories about clines of intersubjective knowledge. Those who ejournaled for me also had theories of knowledge that depicted unification by degree.
Maggie described "deepening" through contemplative prayer as levels of revelatory knowledge that can lead to "a direct relationship" if one so chooses to engage.
She saw the process of intensifying intersubjectivity as a way by which

the unknown reveals itself. [It is] the way which the unconscious and
knowledge of the invisible worlds are constantly being unveiled, layer by
layer, piece by piece. I do not think it stops. I think there is always more
as long as we are embodied at least, more to sense into, to feel, to know,
to learn. There is always the mystery of what is not yet revealed, and this
little question: What about a direct relationship with Christ? I take it very
seriously.

For Maggie, "deepening" is ultimately about finding one's way to "a direct relationship" with the divine.

Zak coined the term "the Scale of Progressive Intimacy" to explain a tripartite
intersubjectivity. He said there is

a gross communion or concept stage . . . which progresses to a deeper condition of union . . . which progresses to actual identity. For example, I may
start out with a communal relationship to nature. I may see myself as part
of the great web of life, but at this stage it is just a concept; I don't feel it.
Then that relationship may deepen to a feeling of unity where the connection becomes stronger and in fact I start experiencing nature as a living
presence. That relationship may then deepen further to where myself and
nature combine, so to speak, in a radical oneness; an actual identity.

Different from both Bennett's and Panikkar's final "I-in-relation-to-whole" model, Zak's model can be seen in his "tree-as-self" experience, which culminated in an experience of "radical oneness," in which the boundaries between I and other "disappeared." Zak's experience of the deepest point on his Scale of Progressive Intimacy appears to be an example of Rappaport's (1999) "radical identification of self and other."

Rebecca's ejournal description of movement into deeper relationship with the divine is perhaps the example *par excellence* of this kind of principle. Though educated in Quaker schools, Rebecca converted to Roman Catholicism as a young adult and followed practices and theologies that were closer to classical forms of Christian mysticism. The years when I knew her, Rebecca was writing a doctoral dissertation on the history of early Christian martyrs, sang in the choir of a Roman Catholic church, and worshipped at SSJE's office of Morning Prayer almost without fail. Rebecca had no association (literary, digital, or face-to-face) with Cynthia Bourgeault or Thomas Keating, but her ideas and experiences nevertheless shared ground with them. In her 2011 ejournal, Rebecca told me about a personal practice that she had developed over the years, which included an understanding of degrees of unification with the divine. She warned me, "I find it dreadfully difficult to explain how I pray (in terms of concrete practices of contemplation)— mainly because it is something I developed almost instinctively as a young child during meeting for worship at my Quaker school and I have never really 'learned' any particular practice." Rebecca succeeded admirably in her explanation, however, describing a form of meditation in which she "consciously intensif[ied] the indwelling of the Holy Spirit and a radical awareness that all people are created in the image of God."

Then in her early thirties, Rebecca had for years persisted with a four-part practice in which she learned first "to locate and focus on the internal flame"—not an imaginary flame, she emphasized, but the flame of God that is "inherently present" in every person. Second, she learned "to concentrate on it and to focus on it growing and expanding until it was the only thing in . . . awareness." After this, she focused on "condensing" the flame "as though all of the energy of the large fire were compressed into a candle-flame." Finally, she learned to step back into "the space" created out of the flame's condensation. Rebecca wrote, "The open space created by the compression allowed a space to listen to the Spirit." When the flame was understood as the immanent presence of the divine rather than something of the imagination, she said,

> it becomes a way of entering into God's presence and forming a tangible connection with the indwelling Holy Spirit. Locating the flame and entering into it until it fills one's whole awareness . . . is itself an act of contemplative prayer, not just a preparatory centering exercise. And the act of

concentrating the flame has become a pulling back from the total immersion, while still maintaining the full intensity of focus and awareness of the connection.

Rebecca's cline of divine indwelling mirrors other Christian models that show varied intensities of intersubjectivity. It shows the profound relationality that is distinctive in this variety of Christian contemplative knowledge, especially in its aspect that the center point is not a dissolution of self, but a movement past full identification to heightened awareness of self in relation to other, which is not subject-object based, nor entirely the realm of subject-subject, but is rather an acute phenomenological understanding of the relationality of all things, oneself included. Rebecca's practice of identifying the flame, becoming engulfed by the flame, concentrating its energy, then stepping back to create "the open space" to understand oneself and all others experientially in the matrix of the universe is a classic expression of Christian mysticism—not an I-centered understanding, but an "all-centered" multidimensional understanding of creation.

Rebecca's model correlated with Teresa of Ávila's *Interior Castle*, Panikkar's "theandric inter-abiding presence," J. G. Bennett's "conscious presence," and Cynthia Bourgeault's "not one, not two, but both one and two," all of which straddle subject and object, immanence and transcendence. We saw this intersubjective knowledge, too, in Chapter 1's look at how desire compelled people to adopt contemplative Christianity in the first place. Recall that the thirteenth-century Beguine mystic Hadewijch wrote of herself and the divine Bridegroom, "they possess one another in mutual possession, their mouths one mouth, their hearts one heart, their bodies one body, their souls one soul, and sometimes one sweet divine nature transfuses them both, and they are one, each wholly in the other, and yet each one remains and will always remain himself" (quoted in Petroff 1994: 61).

THE DIFFERENCE BETWEEN a player and a virtuoso in contemplative Christianity comes in the degree of unitive being that one is able to bear and sustain in a given moment. This "deepest" place of phenomenological intersubjectivity, contemplative Christians have told me, is a way of being that invokes the divine. Through it, they say, a person can become a conduit between "realms," or, in Panikkar's terminology, a "mediator," illustrating what Br. David Vryhof (2014) said of the Transfiguration, that experiences of relationship with the divine are ideally acts of service that "find their true value in lives of compassion and love." Consenting to and working toward virtuosity can be an act of social responsibility and service in which a contemplative capably guides others toward unitive being, the ontological place that prompts hospitable, peaceful, and socially active living.

Contemplatives noticed the people who served their communities in this way, whether they were friends, strangers, teachers, priests, or ordinary practitioners.

Those who showed a frequent capacity to "bring the divine into their midst" had a charismatic quality. Charles Lindholm (2013), citing Sohm, noted that the term *charisma* comes from the Greek for "gifts of grace"—one who is imbued with *pneuma*, or spirit—and appears in the apostle Paul's first-century letters to early Christian communities. *Charisma* thus has a particularly fitting etymology in this ethnographic context. We saw a charismatic effect in Chapter 6 when Brigid held the attention of her cohorts while describing experimental kitchen work. So, too, Helen described Cynthia Bourgeault as having a charismatic quality that allowed her to convey "experiential knowledge" of the ephemeral, saying with simple assuredness that "Cynthia transmits the divine." Similarly, Ashona observed of a monk in one of the monasteries at which I worked, "He is really able to show us God; through him I know God's presence." This kind of charismatic virtuosity was depicted as belonging to groups as well as individuals. Some months after my fieldwork concluded, for example, one of Cynthia's most knowledgeable and experienced students, Audrey, visited me at Cambridge and together we attended SSJE's Eucharist on the feast day of Mary Magdalene. Audrey had not been at the SSJE monastery before, but afterward she said emphatically, "They brought Christ into our midst. Christ was *definitely* here among us."

Alicia, who was so sick with the norovirus at the Tucson Wisdom School, described such persons as *icons*, those who act as windows between the divine and all of creation. In Roman Catholic and Episcopalian doctrine, a priest is said to play this role of mediator between humanity and the divine when performing the Eucharistic prayer at the altar in the sanctuary. The priest serves the community by bringing the divine into its midst by sanctifying bread and wine, adherents said. But among contemplative Christians, iconic presence is neither a given, an accreditable state, nor the exclusive domain of ordained priests or any other religious expert. Virtuosity in unitive being and phenomenological intersubjectivity has much to do with one's degree of contemplative experiential knowledge, that is, wisdom, in a given moment. Though they believed it required the deepest humility and was entirely dependent upon divine will, the variable knowledge of unitive being was also an enactment of perceptual agency, which combined performative knowledge, unknowing, and one's capacity to sustain intention and attention.

After the public cultivation of unitive knowledge in the Sanctuary, we now move to a place where not every practitioner has the desire or courage to go. We leave the chapel altogether and enter the monk's Cell, the innermost place of solitude, which can thoroughly test a contemplative's resolve. Yet if one persists, the Cell can become a place of iconic being where a paradoxical relationship of solitude and communion finds its apex in a self with permeable boundaries, a porous self that serves community, regardless of physical segregation.

Photography by J. Eileen Scully.

8

Cell

THE POROUS SELF: COMMUNITY AND
INTERSUBJECTIVITY FROM THE INNER ROOM

*The monastic Cell is the inner room where contemplatives work
toward maturity and seek union with the divine in solitude. Its
demands for interiority require courage, yet keeping intention
and attention, the one in seclusion finds that interiority transforms to community. The one in the Cell is not solitary after all,
but is emanating and receptive. The walls of the Cell are porous,
and the one within is in communion despite physical barriers.*

The cell will teach you all things.
—ABBA MOSES, SAYINGS OF THE DESERT FATHERS

Lessons in Compassion from the Umbrian Countryside

Heading to a pilgrimage led by Richard Rohr's Center for Action and Contemplation
in May 2012, I had arranged by email to meet up with Marjorie, a Hildegard of
Bingen scholar and the "house mystic" at a church in Salisbury, England. We were
to connect at the Leonardo DaVinci airport in Rome so that together we could find
the central train station and make our way to Assisi, the hometown of the thirteenth-century Roman Catholic saints Francis and Clare. Marjorie and I managed
to miss each other at the baggage carousel and only crossed paths a few hours later
when we were already on the moving train. She picked me out by the book I was
reading (an English translation of one of Thomas of Celano's medieval biographies of Francis) and seemed very relieved to find me.[1]

Marjorie was clearly nervous about this trip despite the arrestingly gorgeous
Italian countryside zipping past, its red poppies and amber stone farmhouses
glowing like jewels in lush green barley. The train didn't zip for long, however. We

slowed and stopped, slowed and stopped, until we had traveled (or at least occu-
pied train seats) for six hours of what was supposed to be a two-and-a-half hour
journey. We were not even halfway there. Announcements intermittently crackled
and spat from the PA system in Italian, a language neither of us spoke. My fellow
traveler looked aghast and kept muttering, "This is rubbish, this is absolute rubbish!" and "Nothing ever works in Italy!"

I confess that I felt impatient with her. We weren't in a situation of peril, after
all, just late (very late) for our connecting train at Foligno. Marjorie's anxiety set
into relief the possibility of an opposite response: an embrace of kenotic openness
and unknowing. I did my best to let go of the impatience and tension. As I had
been learning over several years of fieldwork, I tried to make space for the potential wonder created by the ambiguity and uncertainty of our situation, for being
present, and more important, for feelings of compassion for my fellow traveler.
I was fine with the unexpected conditions of the trip, but struggled with accepting
the anxiety of a self-declared "house mystic."

A kindly woman called Giana noticed my companion's distress. As a former
university teacher of English and French, she capably translated for us: there
had been strong earthquakes in the northern region of Emilia-Romagna the day
before, she said, and damage to rail lines had caused extensive delays throughout
the country. Traveling all the way to Rimini on the northeast coast of Italy, Giana
herself was resigned to a very long journey indeed. She used her own mobile
phone to call the hotel in Assisi and alert them to Marjorie's late arrival, which
seemed to relax my companion considerably. After answering Marjorie's innumerable logistical questions, the Italian woman calmed her by chatting amiably.
Watching her example, I attempted to better adopt Giana's posture of compassion.

It was still some hours and long past dark when we arrived at Foligno. There
Marjorie and I learned that another train would not be coming to take us to Assisi
for several more hours. Faced with an empty train station and a dark night in the
now pouring rain, Marjorie's panic returned. I suggested we hail a taxi to take
us the last short leg of twenty or so kilometers, but the street outside the station
was deserted except for one other traveler, an Algerian man who was trying to get
home to his Italian wife in Perugia. We communicated in a mixture of English
and French. He was not entirely hopeful about a taxi coming our way on a Sunday
night. After forty-five minutes I began to consider searching for a hotel room, but
then headlights swung around in our direction. A taxi at last. The Algerian-Italian
man negotiated a ride for all of us, going considerably out of his way to accompany
us to Assisi, first finding Marjorie's hotel, then identifying the pedestrian-only
street where my *pensione* lay. He was about to leave the taxi waiting at curbside to
walk me and my bag all the way up the steep hill, but I assured him that I was fine,
encouraged him to get home out of the rain, and thanked him and the taxi man
profusely for their generous help.

Lessons from the Umbrian countryside for an anthropologist learning the ropes of contemplation and action: compassion in all circumstances. I closed my eyes for a moment, considering my attempts at emulating Christian contemplative practices and principles—persistent maybe, but far, far from ideal.

By the time I found myself on a cobblestone street outside the great arched wooden portal of my sixteenth-century *pensione*, Casa Franchi, I had been traveling over twenty-four hours and could not easily negotiate a lock and key. There I fumbled, soaking wet on the glistening stones under a wrought-iron lantern when I heard, "Paula, is that you?!" It was Helen Daly and her husband John, quite dry under their umbrella. They had arrived at Assisi the previous day and were returning from a late and leisurely dinner. My heart lifted. Seeing my state of exhaustion and near incoherence, Helen and John insisted on seeing me up to my room, where they left me to fall into a very deep sleep indeed.

Next morning the glory of Assisi revealed itself. A beautifully kept medieval Umbrian hill town of winding cobbled streets, salmon pink stonework, billowing flower boxes, and magnificent chapels, churches, and basilicas, it clearly deserves its United Nations World Heritage Site status. I dressed and headed through the streets down a confusing but charming maze of stone staircases to the conference center where the pilgrimage meetings were to take place. Distinct from its surroundings, the venue was modern and efficient, built to accommodate some of the multitudes who gathered in Assisi every year. In the main hall, there was a stage and lectern set up before rows of about 250 chairs, conference style. A wall of windows opened onto a terrace and garden, allowing a view of the fields on the Umbrian plain below. I spotted Helen in a row toward the back and headed her way.

The American Franciscan teacher Fr. Richard Rohr and the staff from his New Mexico–based organization were running the show for now, though other contemplative teachers would contribute later in the week. After a barrage of logistical announcements and introductions, Richard Rohr talked for over an hour on Franciscan-style contemplation, covering some entry-level basics of the theology and practices, and offering his opinion on why anyone would bother persisting with them. Helen and I then realized we were in for quite a different experience from the intensive intimacy and demanding office schedules we knew from our time at monasteries, contemplative retreats, and Wisdom Schools. (Before she had moved to Vermont from Cambridge, Helen had been a regular at the Society of Saint John the Evangelist—indeed, she was a member of their society of non-monastic associates, the Fellowship of Saint John—and had sometimes visited Benedictine and Trappist monasteries as well.)

The introductory level of Richard Rohr's statements suggested that the majority of participants at this pilgrimage did not have a similar amount of experience with contemplation. They mostly consisted of a lot of expensively dressed older Americans and a minority of people from other countries like the United Kingdom, South Africa, Canada, the Netherlands, Germany, Hong Kong, and Japan. Other than Helen and John, I recognized just ten people from venues at which I had done fieldwork, even though I knew that other participants from retreats and Wisdom Schools had expressed interest in coming. Two years before, Cynthia Bourgeault and Ward Bauman had together led a pilgrimage to Assisi that was based on the intensive practice-and-study format they used in their Wisdom Schools. A few of its participants had returned for this gathering.

While I knew there to be some committed, long-time practitioners in the group, Richard Rohr seemed to be targeting curious neophytes who had come to learn more about his new institution, the Living School of Action and Contemplation, for which he was then raising funds. Indeed, the final day of the nine-day-long pilgrimage was devoted to PowerPoint presentations on what the school would be like, with figures and tables, including the sobering financial realities of setting up an institution of this type. It seemed to be an open fundraising appeal targeted at a wealthy crowd. True enough, an average American income earner could probably not afford either the time or the money to come on a journey like this. This seemed to be even more of a class-specific event than the retreats and Wisdom Schools at which I did research in the United States. Helen and I had not realized before we arrived that these meetings would be so clearly directed toward newcomers with money.

When Richard Rohr wrapped up his lecture on the basics of contemplative prayer, he suggested we give it a go. I naïvely thought we would somehow dissemble the rows of chairs and set up in a circle with prayer cushions. However, Fr. Richard merely suggested we make ourselves comfortable where we were. "Why don't we try it for seven minutes," he said. Helen and I gaped at one another incredulously, silently mouthing in unison: "SEVEN MINUTES?!" Accustomed to rather greater rigor, Helen and I felt a little disconcerted sitting among strangers in rows of stackable chairs in an institutional conference hall setting, listening to speakers talk about contemplation for hours instead of actually doing it. Later, a number of other committed practitioners expressed similar feelings that this variety of practice seemed foreign indeed. They also agreed that, of course, this was just another opportunity to be open to a different approach and to keep presence. Maybe, but after lunch my impatience got the better of me. Helen and I made a break for it; Assisi was beckoning and we responded to its call.

That afternoon Helen and I walked out of the towering eastern gate of the medieval walled town and headed toward San Damiano. I was sketchy about the story of Francis, but this much I knew: San Damiano was the little church that Francis had rebuilt from ruins when he first felt the call to a religious life. The story goes that in the rubble of a chapel ruin that was ancient in his own time, Francis was praying before the dilapidated altar when the crucifix hanging above said to him, "Repair my house." Francis took the imperative literally and restored San Damiano stone by stone, then later turned it into a convent for Clare and the women who followed her (Celano 1963).

The cobbled path took Helen and me down a hillside covered in gnarled olive trees. Some were so old that their trunks were nothing more than perforated husks barely capable of supporting their leathery silver-green leaves, so old that some might have been there when Francis himself walked that road 800 years ago. We passed a few trinket stalls, modest stone farmhouses with hand-lettered signs advertising *Olio di oliva in vendita*, a fourteenth-century iron-gated shrine displaying its candle-lit fresco of the Madonna and Child, and shiny outdoor escalators rising from a sizable parking lot for some of the many air-conditioned coaches that brought tourists and pilgrims to Assisi every day. During the forty-minute walk, Helen stopped several times. Her back was really bothering her, she said, probably due to the many hours of wandering around Rome for three days when they first arrived in Italy, after being relatively inactive at home in Vermont during a particularly harsh winter.

Signs requesting *Silenzio per favore—tenere in riverenza* told us we were getting closer. San Damiano appeared around the bend of a curving monastery wall and a line of cypress trees. It was tiny and simple, with a finely worked rose window, terracotta roof tiles, sheltering cloister arches, and a small stone piazza with banks of votive candles. Two bronze statues depicted Francis, one walking barefoot with staff in hand toward the church's portico and another meditating cross-legged on the hillcrest before an expansive view of the rural landscape below. How different from the magnificent thirteenth-century basilica, adorned by the likes of Giotto, Cimabue, and Martini, that was built later on the other side of town in reverence for (and also in spite of) Francis's simplicity and radical poverty.

Threading our way through a scrum of photo-snapping visitors and past a young black-bearded friar who was sweeping the outer courtyard's stone pavements, we entered through a side chapel, which featured a gruesome, life-sized Baroque crucifix, then made our way into the nave of San Damiano proper. Helen and I stopped in our tracks: the sanctuary's low plaster vault was so organically irregular, the dusky filtered light so pensive, the early medieval starry-night frescoes so intimately drawn, the rickety wooden choir stalls so clearly made by the hands of those who used them centuries ago. The floor tiles were worn glossy from the thousands upon thousands who had stepped through, and the plaster walls were seasoned with the touch of so many who had remained there in prayer. Above the diminutive altar was the painted, iconic Syrian-Christian crucifix that people all around the world, including those in my research, hold in special reverence.[2]

It seemed more than the evocative minimalist charm of early medieval Umbrian aesthetics that moved Helen and me, however. Wide-eyed, I turned to my companion to find her in tears. She was also shaking, then I realized the same was true of me. We stood at length in the middle of the chapel with people moving all around us until we finally eased our way through the throng to a place in the narrow wooden pews. A few of the visitors stayed in the chapel, but more surged by in a steady stream, first looking about, then heading on past the altar for a self-guided tour of the cloister where Clare and her adherents once lived. Meanwhile, my entire body shook, not a little but rather violently. I felt as though I were on fire, something I would feel again half a year later at the West Virginia Wisdom School. I placed my hands and forehead against the cool plaster wall to try to steady myself. This was rather unexpected.

We stayed there a long time, but finally got our bearings. Moving out of the chapel toward Saint Clare's cloister, I felt some return of composure. We stepped through the nuns' private brightly frescoed choir, where they would have performed their daily offices and received communion, and climbed narrow, turning stairs to an upper dormitory cell with low slanted ceilings and a wall of arched windows opening onto an enclosed courtyard below. There, sunny geranium-filled balconies had a settling effect on me. But Helen responded differently. One corner of the dormitory was cordoned off with silk rope. On the floor was a ceramic hand-painted plaque telling us that this was the place of Chiara's (Clare's) death. Helen's breath caught. She stopped and knelt there, gazing with bowed head and parted lips.

A group of Bolivian nuns came through, led by a priest who gave them tidbits of history in Spanish. The breach of silence annoyed me, but Helen told me later how moved she was by their devotion. A few of the nuns rubbed their rosaries over the place where Chiara had died, a gesture of sanctification that I saw many times at sacred sites in Assisi. When the black-habited women had moved on, Helen stretched her torso and arms forward until her forehead touched the ground in the Islamic-style posture of half-prone prostration. I went to sit in the window arch and wondered about the severity of sensation that had overtaken me when we first entered the chapel of San Damiano. It wasn't as if I had a devotion to Francis, or any other saint, for that matter. I knew very little about them. Below in the enclosed cloister garden, tourists milled about a stone well and flower beds. Helen remained some time in prayer.

Both of us left San Damiano feeling a little shattered. We spoke with astonishment about the strange, visceral, and unexpected response. Helen said she deeply felt the presence of Francis and Clare, but that an especially strong sensation of connectedness came over her in Clare's cell. "It was like Chiara had her arms around me in sanctuary," she said. "Something *big* happened here," said Helen, looking out at the Umbrian plain. "And it's *still* happening."

On the way back up the hill, Helen stopped to take some ibuprofen for her back pain. She mentioned that she had been diagnosed with a benign spinal tumor eight years earlier, for which she had had surgery, but that it hadn't troubled her in ages. Halfway up the hill, the pain was bothering her so much that she opted for the outdoor *scala mobile* that went from the bus parking lot up to the city gate. Back in town, we stopped at Francis's childhood home. Inside there was a contemporary terracotta haute-relief sculpture of Francis with arms surrounding Clare in a sheltering arc. Helen found the piece arresting—it seemed to capture something of the experience of intimacy that she had just felt in San Damiano. She took out her iPhone and recorded every angle.

By the time she returned to her *pensione*, Helen was having considerable trouble with her back. From then on, pain and numbness increased until she could barely walk. Helen went to as many of the lectures as she could, lying on a bench softened with bed pillows and bolstered by pain medication and steroids prescribed by an American neurosurgeon who happened to be on the pilgrimage. Helen now appreciated the undemanding conference format that we had impatiently dismissed as too lightweight the first day.

Exploring Assisi was no longer possible for Helen, but I continued to frequent the places close to Francis and Clare. I had discovered that after the early morning offices, the friars at San Damiano kept the chapel open. Not many lingered, though, because locals had to get to work, and visitors could not tour Clare's cloister until it opened at 10 a.m. So I walked through the ancient olive groves to San Damiano every day just after dawn and stayed to meditate after the liturgies, for the most part in solitude. Then I roamed the streets of Assisi, or strode across the Umbrian plain, or ventured the five or so kilometers to the home base of Francis and his mendicant band, the minute Porzioncula church, reverently encapsulated (smothered really) during the Baroque period within a mammoth wedding cake of a basilica. With fellow conference truants (all people I knew from other retreat venues during my fieldwork), I also climbed Mount Subasio to spend time at the caves where Francis and some of his brothers made their hermitage.

From these wandering sojourns I brought back word pictures for Helen, who could no longer go out herself: the wild cyclamen in the hilly cloud forest, the dove grey limestone of the grotto hermitages worn butter smooth and lustrous by generations of seekers who passed there, the muted austerity of the basilica of Santa Chiara, the exquisite, jubilant frescoes of the basilica of San Francesco, and the crowded, edgy silence at the tomb of Francis himself. And back at what almost felt like home by then, the curious insistence of four out of five priests at San Damiano who placed the consecrated host in my mouth even though I approached the altar with the arms-crossed-over-chest gesture that signaled my non-Catholic status.

The pilgrimage's final gathering took place at La Chiesa di San Pietro, a vast Romanesque church of the Benedictine monastery that owned most of the land around Assisi in Francis's and Clare's time. Cynthia Bourgeault, who had offered some teachings at the end of the week, had been asked to come up with a liturgy on

short notice, since this was not Richard Rohr's specialty. Given the internationality
of the group, she asked people to simultaneously recite the Lord's Prayer in their
own language, creating a good-natured hubbub that made people smile. Cynthia
also included some simple chants, for which she had asked direction from Helen.
Having come the short distance in a taxi and shored up by pain meds and a cane,
Helen made her way up the steps to the sanctuary and stood at ease in leadership,
patiently teaching the congregation, most of whom had little or no experience with
chanting. It certainly was not the cohesive toning of an inter-embodied group of
long-time practitioners, but we players nevertheless created a warm resonance
that reverberated generously around the eleventh-century stone beehive dome.
Two and a half years later, a priest friend of Helen's told me that she had felt this
liturgy had marked for her the advent of a new leadership role in the Wisdom community, sanctioned by her own teacher, Cynthia Bourgeault.

After the service, Helen, John, and I took a taxi back up the hill for a final dinner with Cynthia and the dean of Boston's Episcopal cathedral, who just happened
to be spending his sabbatical writing in Assisi. He knew Helen because the year
before she had given some talks at the cathedral about neuroscience research on
contemplative practices. Between my companions' adventures in Umbria, their
common experience of New England living, and their years of following and teaching a contemplative path, we had a whole world to explore in conversation.

"O Maiden Wise": The Illness and Death
of Helen Eberle Daly

When was I less by dying?

—RUMI

The global breadth of contemplative Christianity that we experienced at Assisi was
soon replaced for Helen by the dimensions of the monastic cell. The day after she
arrived home in Vermont, Helen had a CT scan with alarming results. She was
rushed to Boston's Massachusetts General Hospital (MGH) for surgery to remove
a spinal tumor. The world-famous surgeon who had treated Helen the first time
around was about to publish a paper in the *New England Journal of Medicine* on
how this variety of tumor never recurred after surgical removal. He had to scrap it.

Helen had a rare malignant peripheral nerve sheath sarcoma, which had interlaced itself with the spinal cord. The doctors had said she need not worry about
this tumor too much, even though they had not managed to extract it entirely. They
were going to try other treatments. She would have to return to Boston over the
summer for chemotherapy and pinpoint proton beam radiation, a highly specialized treatment developed by Helen's doctor at MGH and offered at only a handful
of other locations in the United States. But over the summer, Helen's condition

was unstable, and ultimately worsened. The tumor was not as easy to control as the surgeon had expected.

Because I lived fairly close to the hospital, I was able to visit Helen a few times after her surgery in June. Once she asked me to bring bread and wine so she could have communion. Helen believed that the Eucharist should neither be limited to consecration by ordained clergy, nor restricted by religious or denominational exclusivity. In the hospital room, she herself blessed the bread and wine with a few well-chosen prayers and chants, then shared it with me.

Afterward, she told me something about how her contemplative practice had transformed her experience as a patient from the last time she went through these medical procedures. The medical staff had been surprised at how well Helen managed the major surgery, she said. "'It's as if we've just clipped her toenails,'" Helen laughed, recounting to me the surgeon's disbelief at her post-surgical glow of wellness. Helen was a different person from the one who had had her first tumor symptoms eight years before. She said that in 2004, "I had a huge fight-or-flight response to the pain and could get truly hysterical—crying, panic attacks. I was hospitalized for five days and really freaked out. We just loaded me up with narcotics. It took five months to get the whole thing to settle down." Although Helen had not tolerated the assault quite so well during her first illness, it was the catalyst that had launched her on an intensive relationship with contemplation for the remainder of her life. This time, through all her treatments, she meditated, chanted, practiced the Welcoming Prayer, and did some forms of body prayer, like walking a labyrinth, while she still had some mobility. Keeping attention and being present to the moment through contemplative practices helped her shed pain and fear.[3]

Even so, the parameters of Helen's physical and social world contracted. Reminiscent of *The Body Silent*, in which anthropologist Robert Murphy (1987) documented his physical deterioration due to a spinal condition, Helen persisted in teaching through written observations of her own contemplative experiments and responses to serious illness. She kept her friends and family abreast of her condition and also described the ways she responded to the mounting challenges on a patient blog site called *Caring Bridge*. Through her blog posts, she remained dedicated to teaching the ways of contemplative Christianity, calling her interaction with serious illness a kind of "laboratory" for both herself and her readers.

Helen's blog emphasized themes of surrender. In the face of physical and emotional trials and considerable uncertainty during her five months in cancer treatment, Helen put into practice her knowledge of kenosis and the dialogical relationship of action and contemplation, doing and not doing. Though she was committed to approaching her situation as an act of service for others, she never-theless experienced increasing interiorization, partly by choice in response to her need to pare down, and partly due to the realities of bodily and social seclusion that come with such severe illness. As her condition worsened, Helen decreased her face-to-face and virtual social contact with others. Yet, as we shall see in her blog postings, Helen described her bodily and social interiorization as intersubjective, characterized by strong sensations of a flow of energy between herself and others, and a sense of connectivity despite the increasing confinement of her cell, the physical boundaries of both her living spaces and her body.

In an ejournal entry she wrote for my research some months before any sign of her illness, Helen described how "experiential knowledge" was teaching her "deeper and deeper ways" of contemplative knowing. Her participation in an advanced Wisdom School for those who intended to teach launched her into even more intensive territory where she had begun to understand "motion and flow" from her own experience, describing a new way of seeing "unconstricted, relational movement" between people as well as "loosened boundaries" and an "ever-flowing mutuality of giving and receiving." She had written that even as a practicing psychotherapist with a doctoral degree, she found the reading material for these advanced studies difficult. At one Wisdom School session in particular, the intensity of engagement with the other students and teachers

> opened a trap door in my being that I didn't know was there. I couldn't understand the [study] material until I got there and was in the energetic field of the other learners and Cynthia's transmissions of high understanding while she taught. By the third day I could understand the material and was filled with joy. The liturgies gave me an experience of the signature fragrance of Christianity, a warm-hearted, tender, intimate love which the whole group shared. This has stayed with me . . . [and] has affected the compassionate presence I am able to offer my psychotherapy clients.

These new ways of knowing, she wrote, were "carving me deeper into Christ like rings of a tree."

Helen's intentional approach to greeting illness with contemplative intersubjectivity is exemplified in a liturgy she crafted herself, "A Service of Surrender and Anointing," which she described on her *Caring Bridge* blog. Choosing people who "would understand the ritual potential" of the liturgy, Helen asked a dozen friends to be with her for a sacramental cutting of her hair on the night before chemotherapy would begin at Massachusetts General Hospital. Her intention was in part to "test drive" what she called the "neurobiology of we" by consciously putting intersubjective ways of knowing "into practice with a really tactile, embodied ritual of touch and oil." A few days earlier she had posted on *Caring Bridge* a request that friends far and wide "join" her in prayer for this service on July 8 at 7:00 p.m. New England time, which many did, judging from the number of people who posted affirmative replies.

Some of those who could not be with her in person later asked Helen to post a detailed description of the liturgy. Helen complied, noting at the conclusion of the lengthy post that she shared her experiences of the "healing power" of such a liturgy "because I want people to know this is possible and available to anyone who might find it meaningful." A few years earlier she had led a similar rite for a Buddhist man, she wrote, emphasizing that this kind of ritual "doesn't have to be Christian or any other faith, although it certainly could be . . . . How wonderful it would be if cancer patients, or anyone with critical and chronic illness, or going through any transition could be blessed and anointed and touched this way."

The service took place in Helen and John's southern Vermont living room, where they had sometimes held contemplative gatherings of chant and meditation. Helen printed up an "Order of Service" ("as that is what we Episcopal church types do"), which outlined the liturgical elements. There were several "worship leaders" of various types there, with a female Episcopal priest officiating. Helen wrote that she trusted in their expertise to sense the energy of the group for judging the timing between liturgical elements. The group began with an invitiatory chant from the French monastery of Taizé, inviting the spirit to come into their midst, then they sang the old Beatles tune, "Let It Be." Helen called this "a powerful hymn of letting go" that uses Marian imagery and which she felt captured the ethos of the evening's liturgy. With her strong affinity for the ways of Mary, the mother of Jesus, Helen offered a teaching moment in her blog:

> The words "Let it Be" correspond to the Latin word *Fiat* that is spoken three times in the Jewish-Christian story—when God creates the world, when Mary agrees to bear God in human form, and when Jesus agrees in the garden of Gethsemane to carry out his death on the cross as an act of conscious love on behalf of humanity. Let it Be means to assert to what is, to enter the present moment without agendas or expectations.

Helen added that in their singing, the ensemble had enacted an incarnational rite: "Mary was very present in this song," she wrote, "and in the sweet, sweet statue I have of her in a posture of surrender."

The liturgy of haircutting followed. Helen framed this experience for herself in sacramental terms with the story of Francis cutting the hair of Clare. That haircutting embodied "her act of surrender to the Franciscan way of life. Her shorn hair was what really got through to her horrified family that she was now not theirs . . . but God's."[4] But even with this saintly historical model, Helen struggled with the loss of her hair. Helen definitely felt a calling to the religious life, prompted by her first back surgery, but she acknowledged that she "needed some help from friends to continue to surrender with the forty radiation sessions and two five-day courses of chemotherapy" ahead of her. Helen's hair stylist, who had volunteered with cancer patients in the past, shaved Helen's head. "I started to cry," she wrote, "and a couple of women came over and held my hand or put an arm around me." But then "in a few minutes the energy completely changed." One woman whispered, "'Helen, this is looking really good—I love it.' We started to laugh, and I said I didn't know if it really counted as a sacrifice if it looked good."

Helen's friends had expressed their desire to help in practical ways like cooking, gardening, and doing odd jobs. They wanted to take action on her behalf, so at this liturgy Helen gave them a physical task that was also sacramental. "I gave them something really real and physical to do—use copious amounts of oil and rub it onto my body as I lay on a massage table with them all around me." The sacrament of anointing held a great deal of "healing energy" for Helen, she said. She wished that everyone could be the recipient of such care, being able "to look up and see a circle of people who really love you, ready to lay hands and anoint and speak blessing and intimate prayer." Taking oil from a blue crystal bowl ("Mary's color"), the woman presiding at the liturgy "started off with a huge amount of oil at my throat—she really showed [the others] the generous, radically abundant lavishness we were going for. One by one the bowl was passed and words of love, friendship, blessing were spoken as my feet, legs, arms, hands, face were held by loving hands and caressed with oil."

Part of enacting the liturgy was sensing the "spiritual energy" and knowing when to move from one liturgical element to another. While they "took time to extend the healing energy to others not present," the celebrant and other seasoned ritual specialists in the group together felt out an appropriate liturgical rhythm based on their performative knowledge, which assessed the dynamics of what Helen called "group energy." Helen noted that "sensing spiritual energy is something we don't talk enough about—it's a very explicit topic in the Wisdom Schools I attend, and I would love to explore that more with different groups doing prayer and ritual."

The liturgy concluded with several hymns, including one that Helen had sung on her way into surgery, and a chant set to the fourteenth-century words of Julian of Norwich, "All Shall Be Well." As she often did at liturgies and lectures, Helen had recorded the proceedings on her iPhone so she could listen to them again. Hearing the ensemble later that summer in the solitude of her room at a Boston rehabilitative nursing home, she said the healing power and the beauty of that communal Service of Surrender and Anointing "all comes back."

Helen felt buoyed by the community support and by the energy created through the ritual acts she herself had innovated from the historical palette of contemplative Christian liturgies. However, the pain from encroaching cancer and oncological treatments became increasingly harsh. After some weeks as a cancer patient, Helen's optimism began to flag. The tumor turned out to be unusually active; its rapid regrowth made the "weeks after surgery very scary and confusing as I got worse and worse, rather than better and better." Besides simply updating people about her condition and care, Helen used the *Caring Bridge* blog to ponder her spiritual state and to offer teachings on psychological and contemplative methods of managing pain and distress. "So this is really hard," she wrote in mid-July. Even though she had a long history of practicing Centering Prayer and teaching "mindfulness meditation" and Sensorimotor Psychotherapy for the management of chronic pain, including "centering, grounding, breathing," she was finding it harder and harder to come "back into what we call the Window of Tolerance, where I could tolerate the heavy sensations." She realized that "doing" wasn't the full answer. She found herself being thrown "back into lower brain, fight-or-flight survival states" and was faced with "the paradox of I can do something / I can do nothing."

Techniques, she realized, could only take one so far. Enduring nights of unbearable pain, she felt that even with practical knowledge of "pain-management tools," she "still felt incredibly beat up by . . . the morning. I was having the experience of being utterly and totally helpless, empty." Then so "utterly dependent on John and so many others," she realized that, rather than taking charge, her "spiritual learning task through this treatment is to continue surrendering, letting go," as taught by contemplative Christianity and the other traditions she had studied and practiced. Helen, in her isolation, felt she needed to surrender even more to the harshness of her circumstances and make herself "available to receive and experience the Flow/Divine Presence." She wrote, "My current vulnerable state removes the idea that I could be in control of things now. This morning and through the day I had the felt sense, the experience of that Flow coming toward me, especially in the love, thoughts, prayers that so many are sending . . . . People's love and prayers are palpable to me." Such divine flow, she wrote, is like the "word" in the scripture that says "Man does not live by bread alone, but by every word that comes forth from the Mouth of God."[5] In her distress, she "got a taste of that word" as a tangible "felt sense," a "vibration by which our deep inner life is fed," even when in solitude.

Helen continued intermittently to use the blog as a teaching tool, responding to her readers' desire to know how she could handle a major crisis with such grace. She reminded them that she had not always had the tools, but had been working on contemplative practices for years. Her illness offered "a big chance to practice" and "focus my attention fiercely right now." It would take a great deal of awareness and intention to bring that kind of energy to ordinary life, she said, then counseled, "Go easy on yourself—have compassion and love yourself for whatever you're able to do right now."

Using her scholarly knowledge and clinical psychotherapeutic expertise in trauma counseling, Helen then went on to offer a lesson on the neurobiology of meditation and mindfulness, describing the relationship of equanimity ("a

Buddhist term") with training the brain to become less reactive to either pleasant or threatening stimuli, and to create "Great Steadiness of Mind" and a "sense
of great spaciousness surrounding the objects of awareness." She said that
brain research on Tibetan monks in the act of meditation shows "stable and far-
reaching gamma-wave synchronization of billions of neurons across large areas
of the brain, rhythmically firing together." Meditation, she said, is a way to use the
brain's neuroplasticity to unplug from flight-or-fight survival responses of "the
ancient circuitry" of the limbic brain and to activate and strengthen responses
from the "higher brain" of the prefrontal cortex and anterior cingulate, which create "equanimous ways (not apathetic ways) of responding to the world," bolstering
warmth and compassion while simultaneously dampening "the Stress-Response
System." As Helen put it, "what fires together, wires together—you have to fire the
new pathways over and over and over. That's practice—daily."

How did this play out in Helen's experience of living with cancer? After years
of practice and study, her responses were quite different from what they were
when her first symptoms showed up in 2004. She wrote in the *Caring Bridge* blog,

> As I was in Assisi and the pain and neurological deterioration of my walk-
> ing hit, I was surprised by my response . . . . This time in 2012, I was
> appropriately concerned and worried, John and I took all the appropriate
> medical steps. But I was not panicked, angry at my vacation/pilgrimage
> being ruined, or sad. I was *surprised* to find myself *curious* about what was
> going on. This stance of curiosity is what we try to cultivate in Sensorimotor
> Psychotherapy too—rather than running the old story about what might be
> happening . . . , we set it aside and mindfully study moment by moment
> what's going on right here and right now . . . We minutely notice physical
> sensations, emotions, thoughts, memories, and movement impulses—
> how does the body want to respond? We investigate, we lightly experiment.
> (emphasis in original)

Helen pondered this process in her own situation, saying, "I've been curious if
my neural networks really have been rewired toward the direction of equanimity."
From her experience of "sharing awareness and emotional resonance with my
patients," she guessed that "the hundreds of hours of work with patients along
these lines" had their effect on her as well. She remarked again that her feelings
had significantly altered from her reactions to the earlier illness, and she believed
that her clinical work and contemplative practice had made her more aware of
the "flow of grace." She said, "It's obvious to me and others that there is a lot of
grace flowing toward me, from many directions, above, below and between all of
us. The practice opens that . . . the teachings say." In Helen's experience, meditation and other contemplative practices brought a sense of "expansiveness" and

"softening," which cultivate the "neurobiology of we," a term for intersubjective flow that Helen drew from the work of Dan Siegel (2008).

At the end of August, when she came home from Boston again to recover from intensive radiation and chemotherapy before beginning another round in October, Helen edited the status on her blog. "I am very blessed to have world class care at MGH, and the doctors are optimistic," she wrote. "This has been an amazing opportunity to practice surrender, to 'be with what is,' and to keep my heart open. This is not life threatening, and has not spread." Even so, Helen had finally reached "the end of my resources for coping." The physiological effects of such challenging treatments left her grappling with exhaustion, nausea, and despair, and she needed to withdraw further from normal socialization. A little while later she wrote, "I appreciate the space people have been giving me—I seem to need to go inward, and have a more private healing space right now."

Helen was being faced with the cruel realities of her illness. Contemplative surrender was clearly not all about bliss and peace, but included unbearable loss and pain. About a month after her temporary seclusion from writing, she explained in a blog posting how physical therapy had helped enough that she could begin weaning herself from some of the stronger pain medications. Even with the improvement, she nevertheless realized that she could no longer participate in "a very special spiritual class I was really looking forward to, a six-month Wisdom School . . . . It was a real disappointment, but it eventually became a reality I had been avoiding." Helen wrote, about living with austerity to this degree,

> I continue to peel away parts of my life, or have them peeled away for me. I try both to grieve that and explore what is life, and who am I, without the pieces that make me Helen, or myself. That's spiritual practice in all the mystical or unitive, non-dual aspects of religion. That's what I've been studying in Wisdom Christianity, and so far I really haven't experienced much other than how sad and unhappy I am when I can't walk the way I want to, drive, go to my job, look the way I want, e.g., have hair, live out my familiar roles in my life.

Despite her despair, she was committed to persisting in the contemplative practice and "psychotherapeutic techniques of 'welcoming' these experiences and emotions."

On October 11, Helen wrote an optimistic blog post during a surge in physical capacity and well-being, reporting on having gone on a "leaf peeping" expedition and choosing spring garden bulbs with friends. However, she "crashed" the very next day. An MRI on October 22 revealed the cause: tumors had seeded themselves up the entire spinal column to the base of her skull. Doctors were shocked, this manifestation of the cancer being extraordinarily rare, "1% of 1% of 1%." No treatment would stop its movement now, and Helen opted only for palliative care from that time on. Helen chose to tell the news to her friends in a final blog entry. She wrote,

> This is a huge shock, given how two weeks ago I was feeling the best I had since coming home from the hospital August 24. One of the doctors said this is how it goes—the nervous system has a high threshold . . . then abruptly the functioning drops, like mine did last October 12. My walking deteriorated, my bladder stopped working, and the pain increased . . . . This will be my last posting on Caring Bridge. You have been incredible in uplifting, praying, cheerleading, sending love and being in the Flow of grace with me.

Soon after this, I was scheduled to fly from Switzerland, where I had recently moved, first to Boston to check in at the university and then on to West Virginia for a final fieldwork expedition. Before I knew of the sudden deterioration in her condition, I had been in touch with Helen about visiting her in Vermont while I was in the United States. Helen briefly replied by email from her iPhone, saying that she and Cynthia Bourgeault were planning an anointing ceremony for the very weekend I proposed to come. She asked me to contact her sister-in-law for further details as she no longer really had the energy or physical capacity to communicate by email or text. She was losing the use of her hands.

The first weekend in November 2012 I made my way to Helen's home through the exuberant autumn foliage of Vermont's sugar maple forests. Helen had requested that people gather in silence to create an environment that she felt would help preserve the little energy she had and to foster another kind of energy, the "finer substance" or "divine energy," which contemplatives say can manifest in the communal rites of well-attuned practitioners. In the living room, fifteen people settled in a circle of chairs, sofas, and meditation cushions. Many were distraught. I knew a third of them from events during my fieldwork. The others were Helen's husband, brother- and sister-in-law, and friends who were part of her contemplative network in Vermont, including her frame drumming teacher, a Jewish friend, and the priest and a few members from the Episcopal church across the street where Helen had taught and led contemplative practices.

The service began in silence. Helen's husband, John, and brother-in-law, Roger (who was an ordained minister of the United Church of Christ), wheeled Helen in from the main floor room where a hospital bed had been set up. Later friends told me their distress had lessened when they actually saw Helen. She was obviously extremely ill, but her face was bright and she seemed very happy to see us. Helen sat in a wheelchair, able to sit, but she had little control of her arms and hands. She greeted us and thanked us for coming, her voice still clear, though slightly softened with the increasing paralysis, then she handed the floor over to Cynthia Bourgeault, who offered a teaching on the Hungarian Jesuit theologian Ladislaus Boros's *The Mystery of Death* (1965). Helen and I had studied this text at the Holy Week Wisdom School together in Minnesota eight months before. In his book, Boros described the spirituality of aging and death, how as one's physical acuity decreased over time in a downward arc, one's "intensity of being" had the capacity to increase in an upward arc. She also reiterated a teaching from Br. Rafe, the Trappist monk who mentored and befriended Cynthia for three months before his own death. Br. Rafe had advised her then, "You must find the place within you that already lives beyond death and begin to live out of it now." Cynthia called Helen "a sterling sister" and an exemplary student of contemplation, one who had moved through severe conditions to persist and even blossom into "presence of being." Her embrace of a "conscious death" showed that Helen had taken to heart the teachings of Boros and Br. Rafe that we had studied in the spring, said Cynthia.[6]

Cynthia then asked Helen to offer her own teachings out of her "direct knowledge." Helen's first comment was, "I don't see myself as any different from anyone else." She simply wanted to be a "model," "a study ground," and a "lab" ("Not a lab*rador!*" she quipped, "a labo*ratory*") for "all of us to learn and experience" what can come of a conscious, contemplative approach to death. She "wanted us all to explore [death] together and be curious about it and learn from it." She said that before she knew where this year would take her, Boros's teachings on death "kind of blew me away." Now seeing the "death transition" as a powerful, transformative process, Helen said a little breathlessly but with enthusiasm,

> I feel super-charged! Things that I couldn't do normally, I'm doing with great joy and great power. There's an energy in my dying that I had no idea—*oh!*—was there and that was certainly in the teachings from last spring, that the death transition is bigger than life—*bigger than life*—and that we are all participating in it. I can feel people everywhere participating in my death . . . . It seems very strange to me . . . but I'm learning that our death is bigger than us.

Helen admitted that difficult feelings had risen over the course of her illness, like the depression and anger she felt at losing her burgeoning role as a teacher of the neuroscience and psychology of contemplative Christianity. Helen explained how crucial the "incarnational potential" of kenotic practices and ritual had been in helping her cope with such feelings. She said that the experimental liturgies she had designed—the haircutting and anointing ceremonies—were a way "to change a funeral rite so that Christians can reclaim their practices around eternity and connectedness," regardless of distance or life or death, and they were a way to share these things even during terminal illness. She said, "I feel Jesus around *a lot* . . . he's here all the time, he's guiding everything." Helen concluded by saying, "So I offer myself for that study and teaching and learning . . . and I don't feel special about it. I just want to be an example for people to take a look at, and especially to do it in relationship and in community."

With that, Cynthia Bourgeault initiated the sacrament of anointing. While the group chanted "Slowly Blooms the Rose Within" to frame drum accompaniment, each participant in turn took the olive oil laced with rose essence and anointed Helen. Some bowed to her, some whispered to her, others kissed her, touching the oil in small crosses on her forehead, throat, palms, and feet, others smoothing the oil over her skin more lavishly. After a while, people began anointing her husband, John, as well. People were somber and some were crying. When all had approached and we had then shared the Eucharist together, Helen and John were glistening with oil and shining with emotion.

Most of us there would not see Helen again. She died the following week. As part of her commitment to service, she had bequeathed the entirety of her sizable family fortune to the psychiatric hospital where she had practiced, to the construction of a side chapel dedicated to Mary Magdalene, the First Apostle, at her Episcopal church, and to the Narthex Project, a foundation she had created to support the teaching of Wisdom Christianity. These bequeaths were some of the "big and bold" things that she had mentioned she "couldn't do normally" but had done "with great joy and great power" during her journey to death. Deeply grieving, John said to me by phone a few days after Helen died, "By the end, she was pure spirit. She was shining." Others thought so, too. A friend of Helen's who was a fellow contemplative and a Boston priest told me that even in the final days of her paralysis, "Love was projecting out from her." One of the many good-bye letters and cards that Helen received as she was dying said something similar. The note alluded to *Sleepers Wake,* J. S. Bach's hymn based on the parable of the Ten Maidens, half of whom slept while the others remained attentive with lamps lit, despite the late hour.[7] It said, "Beloved friend, the Bridegroom comes. O Maiden Wise, you have tended well the flame of your lamp. You now accompany him in peace and joy."

Illustration © John O'Brien from *Tales of a Magic Monastery*, by Theophane the Monk (1981).

Reprinted with permission.

Cell Theory

Long ago in fourth-century Egypt, Abba Moses taught his disciples that "the cell will teach you all things." In the process of dying in early twenty-first-century America, Helen Eberle Daly showed her fellow contemplatives something about intersubjective community from the seclusion of the cell. She revealed how in the world of contemplative Christianity, whether in the architectural confines of a monastic cell or the biological boundaries of skin and flesh, the solitary person is not necessarily isolated, but can be in phenomenological communion with other entities, humans included.

During her talk at the anointing ceremony, Helen spoke with wonder about "many realms . . . many dimensions, there are many mansions" of which she felt the universe was made, places which people have an opportunity to "deepen into." By choosing to embrace and enact a "conscious death," Helen's response to serious illness exemplified the porous self. Her way of dying showed how the increasing solitude of a diminishing social and physical world need not be a hindrance to intersubjectivity, but could instead be a catalyst for it. Helen's fellow contemplatives and teachers saw her death process as a passage toward contemplative maturity, transformation, even virtuosity.

Helen's story shows us the surprise of contemplative Christianity. The birthplace of divine intimacy is not the Sanctuary, but the Cell. Fine-tuning attention to the divine is a way that contemplative Christians awaken to the knowledge that one is never isolated, but always in relationship; from their perspective, solitude implies neither separateness nor self-oriented independence. Contemplatives thus understand the devoted hermit who lives in seclusion to be as communal and socially responsible as those who pray and work in groups. AJ illustrated this perspective in the previous chapter when she observed, "I am alone, but not alone," as did Cynthia Bourgeault when she framed Fr. Thomas Keating's physical absence from the Panikkar retreat as a "palpable" presence "carried in those deeper currents of silent prayer and heart communion." Even though American non-monastic contemplatives were often socially and geographically separated from their cohorts, they worked toward what they called the experiential knowledge of being in deep communion with each other, the divine, and all creation. The primary locus of phenomenological intersubjectivity among contemplative Christians, then, is not so much the altar where ritual specialists act as mediators in direct physical contact with their communities, but the monastic cell—the iconic, porous self—which is not segregated. The porous self is connected with others through contemplative, intersubjective ways of being and knowing.

As a biological term, *cell* was coined by Robert Hooke in 1665. Hooke examined slices of cork under a rudimentary microscope and observed tiny capsules that reminded him of clusters of the individual cells that monks inhabit in monasteries. This was the beginning of biological cell theory, which has recognized for centuries that individual cells are the structural basis of organic life. Biological cells do not function in isolation, but are permeable. Active and passive processes of osmosis and diffusion allow substances to move past the membrane wall of the biological cell so that it communicates with other cells. Cells work together to create a functioning whole, regardless of the physical barriers between them (Wolpert 1995).

The knowledge and experiences of American contemplative Christians turn Hooke's theoretical ideas back to their origins: the monastic cell is a metaphor for the solitary human person, seemingly isolated and with discrete physical boundaries, but which upon closer examination actually works in relationship to create a much larger whole. The formula for phenomenological intersubjectivity introduced in Chapter 7 shows how performative knowledge and unknowing can function together to cultivate a flow of unitive being, even when practitioners are alone. Those from whom I learned during research saw the individual person as not isolated after all, but as emanating and receptive, that is, permeable, porous, and a locus of dynamic, relational being, the basis of a sociality that is greater than the sum of its parts.

While contemplative Christians were acutely aware of the limitations of their own efforts in effecting what they called transformation, they nevertheless understood the importance of their practical role in such change. Through repetitive practices of attention and an interplay of knowing and unknowing, they attempted to foster critical awareness of their habitual behaviors and thoughts, and to subsume and normalize chosen alternatives. Committing long-term to cataphatic and apophatic practices assisted contemplatives in their development of a perceptual agency that prompted transformations toward compassion and an experiential knowledge of the interconnectedness of all things. Practitioners thus learned to see themselves—their human bodies—as temples in which the divine dwelled and flowed toward others. Their exertions undercut anthropological ideas about the phenomenology of perception as a passive process.

In the nineteenth century, Herbert Spencer (1891) similarly saw the individual members of society as part of a larger organism. However, Spencer's theory remained at the level of mechanical social interaction. The contemplative Christians in my twenty-first-century research certainly related to one another through standard social means of gathering, organizing, and communicating digitally and in person. Yet Christian contemplatives understood that training and dedicated practice could help them become increasingly aware that, similar to the biological processes of osmosis and diffusion, the physical boundaries of the human person are not a hindrance to connectivity with others. This awareness sometimes became a phenomenological manifestation in which distinctions like "inside" and "outside" lost their rigidity or even dissolved. This is nothing new, they told me. Indeed, the people with whom I worked said that Christianity has noted this kind of phenomenological intersubjectivity since ancient times, offering a first-century example in the apostle Paul's recognition of the organic interdependence of human-divine collectivity by writing that Christians together make the "Body of Christ."[8] Their contemporary cultivation of the porous self was thus a means of enacting historical ways of knowing. Durkheim's effervescence and solidarity, later expanded and refined in Victor Turner's notion of communitas, had a stronger feeling for the relationships between people in this phenomenological sense.

Recall that one monk said of his life in a monastery, "It's like living alone together." Ideally for contemplative Christians, the cell (monastic or biological) is therefore not a place of isolation, but one of solitude in community, a place of intimacy with the Beloved. The cell represents the phenomenological experience of a self that is emanating and receptive, a porous self in "visceral" relationship with the divine, humanity, and all creation. It is the most intensive point of intersubjectivity on the cline of Christian contemplation according to Rebecca's description of the "condensed flame," Panikkar's "theandric self," and Cynthia Bourgeault's "not one, not two, but both one and two." It explains how among Christian contemplatives, prayer and meditation—even in solitude—are relational acts.

Even so, for many the cell also depicts the sometimes hard reality of perseverance and personal responsibility in committing to the divine through contemplative practices, ideals, and ways of life. As a Facebook posting from the Society of Saint John the Evangelist cautioned, "The spiritual life is not a collection of spiritual calisthenics [but is rather] a way of being attentive in the world that is open to God and open to others."[9] Yet, a contemplative approach to Christianity required considerable discipline, and came with periods of doubt and loneliness, regardless of how far along the path one has come. At some point on the contemplative journey, however, a long-time practitioner may not be so much at the mercy of the swinging pendulum of affect. Tools like a rule of life, silence, enclosure, and non-attachment, along with the monastic ethics of humility and hospitality, helped ground practitioners and bring them to greater contemplative equanimity. Dedicated work over years had the potential to attune practitioners so that regardless of their circumstances, they could increase their agility in keeping presence and self-emptying, allowing them to return more easily to the connected, awakened self that ideally manifests in compassion and service to others. Years of ritualization in everyday life could potentially create a capacity for keeping presence despite context, even to the point of contemplative virtuosity and iconic being.

Diagrams

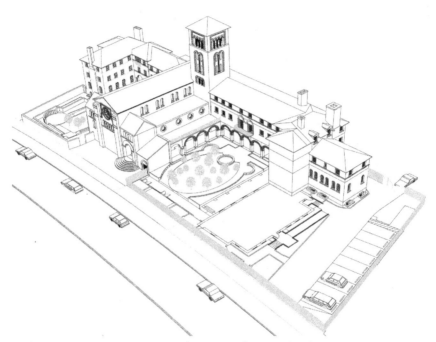

DIAGRAM 1. Monastic compound, Society of Saint John the Evangelist.
Diagram courtesy of the Society of Saint John the Evangelist (SSJE).

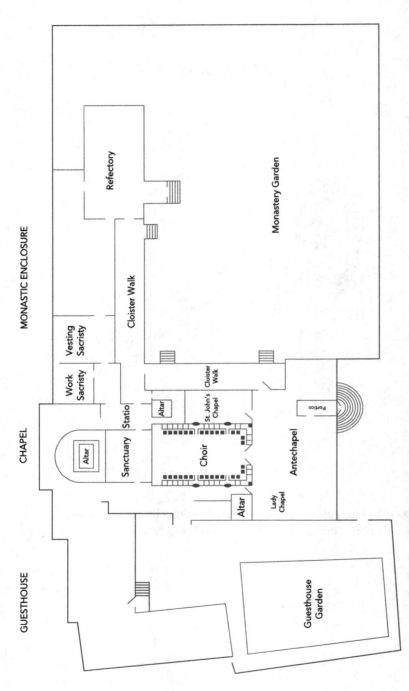

DIAGRAM 2. Monastery site plan, Society of Saint John the Evangelist. Diagram by Franziska Witz, after documents provided by SSJE.

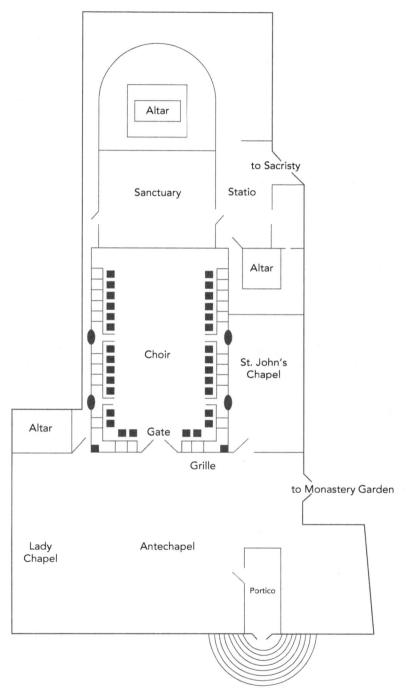

DIAGRAM 3. Monastery chapel, Society of Saint John the Evangelist.
Diagram by Franziska Witz, after documents provided by SSJE.

Diagrams

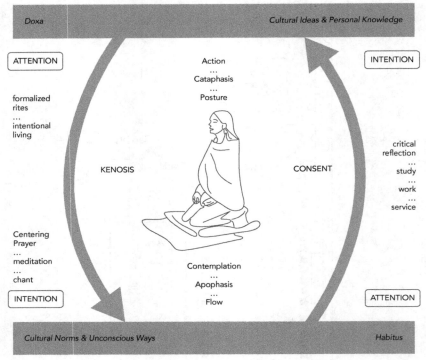

DIAGRAM 4. Contemplative transformation: Working toward perceptual agency through knowing and unknowing.

Diagram by Franziska Witz.

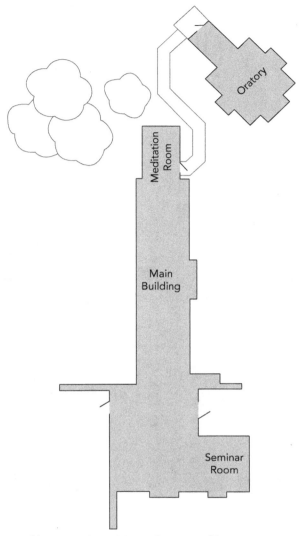

DIAGRAM 5. Building site plan, Episcopal House of Prayer.

Diagram by Franziska Witz, after documents provided by the Episcopal House of Prayer.

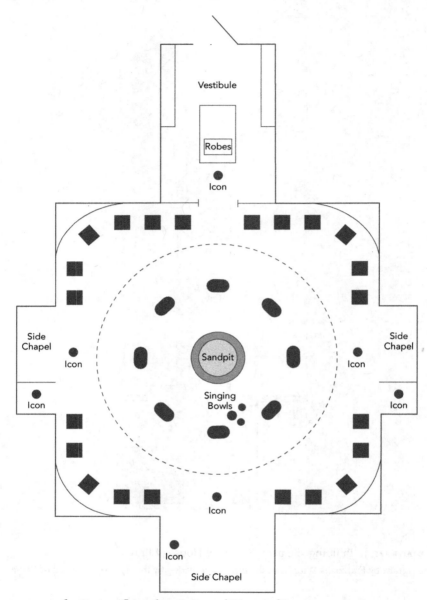

DIAGRAM 6. Oratory floor plan, Episcopal House of Prayer.
Design by Franziska Witz, after documents provided by the Episcopal House of Prayer.

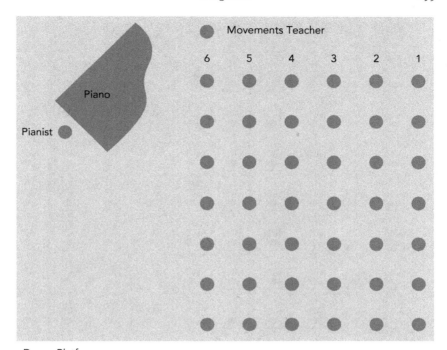

Movements Teacher

6 5 4 3 2 1

Piano

Pianist

Dance Platform

DIAGRAM 7. Gurdjieff Movements formation.
Diagram by Franziska Witz.

Formula for Phenomenological Intersubjectivity among American Contemplative Christians

$$ub = xi(pkn + ukn)^g$$

Epistemological Elements

> ub: unitive being (phenomenological intersubjectivity)
> pkn: performative knowledge
> ukn: intentional unknowing

Semi-controllable Variables

> x: the degree of experience and knowledge of the person or group
> i: the degree of intention, will, or agency with which a person or group applies and sustains that knowledge

Uncontrollable Variable

> g: grace or divine will

Photograph Gallery

A Few Places

The Chapel of St. Mary and St. John, Society of Saint John the Evangelist (SSJE).
Photograph courtesy of SSJE.

St. Benedict's Monastery, OCSO, in winter, and the monastery guesthouse in summer.

Photographs by Jill Sabella.

The Oratory at the Episcopal House of Prayer.
Photographs by Christian Korab.

The Octagon, where the Movements were practiced at the West Virginia Wisdom School.

Photographs by Regina Roman.

Contemplative Christian Aesthetics
Non-Monastic Settings

A labyrinth cut from pasture grasses.

The place of the leader in a contemplative circle.
Photographs by Robbin Brent Whittington.

A makeshift altar set for the Eucharist.

Cross and icon in the Sonoran desert near Tucson.

Photographs by Robbin Brent Whittington.

Buddhist singing bowl at the side of a Wisdom School teacher during a *sohbet*-style conversation with students.

Photograph by Robbin Brent Whittington.

Monastic Settings: The Society of Saint John the Evangelist

The interior of the Chapel of St. Mary and St. John, the Society of Saint John the Evangelist.

Photograph by Michael Blachly.

A votive candle stand at the statue of the Madonna and Child.
Photograph courtesy of SSJE.

A glimpse of the stained-glass artistry of Dr. Charles J. Connick.
Photographs by SSJE and Michael Blachly.

Icons and incense.
Photographs courtesy of SSJE.

Ora et Labora: *Prayer and Work*
Non-monastic Contemplative Practices

Lingering after the conclusion of a group meditation session.
Photograph by Robbin Brent Whittington.

Contemplative prayer at dawn in the Arizona desert.
Photographs by Robbin Brent Whittington.

Greeting the morning in solitude.
Photograph by Robbin Brent Whittington.

Moving prayer sessions at a Wisdom School in North Carolina.
Photographs by Robbin Brent Whittington.

Monastic Formal Rites and Contemplative Practices
Everyday Prayer

Contemplating the tabernacle in St. John's Chapel.
Photograph courtesy of SSJE.

Monks at prayer during the Daily Office.

Lighting incense for liturgy.
Photographs courtesy of SSJE.

The schola chants a psalm.
Photograph courtesy of SSJE.

Visiting congregants in the choir during a Eucharist service.
Photograph by Maria Arabbo.

Bowing before the altar after a liturgy of the Daily Office.
Photograph courtesy of SSJE.

Monastic High Liturgy

Thurifer leading a Palm Sunday procession with incense.
Photograph courtesy of SSJE.

Maundy Thursday foot-washing rites.
Photographs courtesy of SSJE.

Maundy Thursday Eucharist.
Photographs courtesy of SSJE.

Monks prostrating before the cross on Good Friday.
Photograph courtesy of SSJE.

Lighting the sacred fire and passing the light at the Easter Vigil.
Photographs by Diane Downs and SSJE.

Ringing in Easter.
Photograph by Diane Downs.

Intentional Living and Conscious Work

Eating in silence at a monastery refectory and a retreat house dining hall.
Photographs by SSJE and Regina Roman.

Wisdom School conscious work sessions.
Photographs by Robbin Brent Whittington.

Wisdom School conscious work sessions.
Photographs by Robbin Brent Whittington.

Daily work at the SSJE monastery.
Photographs courtesy of SSJE.

Grounds work at Emery House, SSJE's rural retreat.
Photograph courtesy of SSJE.

Teaching and Learning

Fr. Thomas Keating, OCSO.
Photograph courtesy of Contemplative Outreach.

Brs. Curtis Almquist and Geoffrey Tristam, SSJE, who had successive tenures as Superiors of the monastic order during the time of research.
Photograph courtesy of SSJE.

Cynthia Bourgeault.
Photograph by Robbin Brent Whittington.

Ward Bauman.

Darlene Franz.
Photograph by Robbin Brent Whittington.

Brothers lead a seminar with young adults.
Photograph courtesy of SSJE.

Cynthia Bourgeault gives a *sohbet*-style teaching session.
Photograph by Robbin Brent Whittington.

Darlene Franz teaches chant at a conscious work session.
Photgraph by Robbin Brent Whittington.

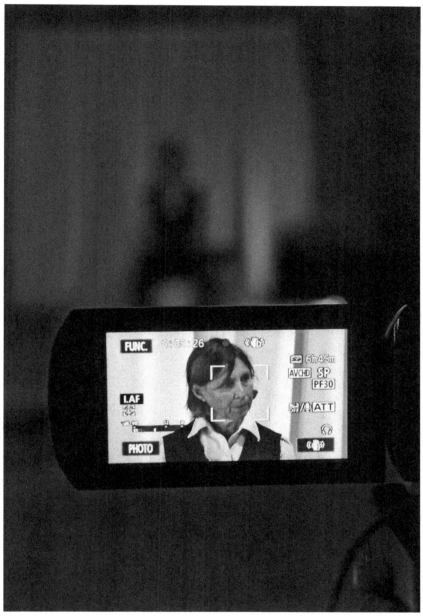

Recording a teaching session for online students.
Photograph by Robbin Brent Whittington.

Wisdom School students studying together.
Photograph by Robbin Brent Whittington.

Notes

1. This compilation of verses from Song of Songs (2:1; 1:2; 6:3) was used in a contemplative version of the liturgy for Wednesday in Holy Week in 2012 (Bourgeault, Bauman, and Franz 2011).

2. Twenty-five non-monastic contemplative Christians from different parts of the United States sent me email journal entries ("ejournals") in 2011 and 2012 on aspects of their personal history, community, and practices, an ethnographic method suggested to me by Professor Nancy T. Ammerman. They agreed to take on the task to assist me in understanding how contemplative Christians practice their faith at home after I met them at retreats that I attended during research.

3. Original sources quoted in Fanning (2001: 35, 129–130, 206, 233, 250) and Petroff (1986: 151).

4. Thomas Merton's essay, "The New Consciousness," in *Zen and the Birds of Appetite* (1968) offers a monastic view of the changing quality of Christians' desire for the divine through history. For an "anthropology of passion" in another (more adversarial) American context, see Desjarlais's *Counterplay: an Anthropologist at the Chessboard* (2011).

5. Marcel Mauss (2007: 51–54) introduced the Latin word *habitus* to stand for "habits that vary especially between societies, educations, proprieties, and fashions, prestiges." Pierre Bourdieu (1977: 78) adopted *habitus* from Mauss for his practice theory, calling it "history turned into nature." By this, Bourdieu meant that the ground of habitus is so much beneath the level of consciousness that people cannot perceive it. Habitual ways are thus unacknowledged, and are uncritically assumed to be "natural," even though they are actually specific to particular times, places, and social groups.

6. See the description of cataphatic and apophatic prayer in a publication of one of the contemplative Christian teachers in my research, Cynthia Bourgeault (2004: 31–41). For a historical overview of the terms, see Andrew Louth (2012). These ritualistic definitions differ from those used in the rhetorical arts, which describe techniques of persuasion using affirmation or denial.

7. See also Bernard McGinn's essay (2012b), "*Unio Mystica*/Mystical Union" in the same volume, as well as Schmidt's "The Making of Modern 'Mysticism'" (2002) and Bouyer's "Mysticism: An Essay on the History of the Word" (1980).

8. Contemplative Christians often used the problematic term *tradition*, which connotes unruptured longevity (Hobsbawm and Ranger 1983). Chapter 4 discusses how practitioners used selected histories to uphold chosen ideals and practices. Further, I do not question whether people have been able to develop "the capacity to engage reality directly," but rather, I explore this community's techniques and experiences in their efforts toward achieving this goal.

9. For more extensive discussions of wisdom in Judaeo-Christian history and contemporary expressions, see Hill (1996), Pramuk (2011), and Wisken (1975).

10. Other studies on the concept of religious conversion include Hefner (1993), Buckser and Glazier (2003), Mitchell and Ganiel (2011), and Rambo and Farhadian (2014).

11. Quoted in the orders of service of Christian meditation circles at The Wellspring, a New England Episcopal retreat house, which I attended over two years during fieldwork, 2010–2012.

12. The Order of Cistercians of the Strict Observance (OCSO) is a Roman Catholic order of cloister contemplative monks or nuns called Trappists or Trappistines after the French monastery La Grande Trappe, which led a reform movement of its mother order, the Cistercians, in the seventeenth century (Frank and Lienhard 1993).

13. Fr. William Meninger, OCSO (e.g., 1997, 1998), developed the first manifestation of this Christian meditation out of what he considered to be the core principle in the anonymously written *The Cloud of Unknowing* (anon. 1961): to silently cultivate "a naked intent directed to God." Meninger called it the "Prayer of the Cloud." Simultaneously, Dom John Main, OSB (e.g., 2002), the Abbot of a Benedictine monastery at Montréal, Québec, developed another form, which he called Christian Meditation. Currently, Centering Prayer and Christian Meditation are the two principal techniques of meditation in the Christianities historically connected to Western Europe. Both have worldwide followings. According to its website at the time of writing, the organization that promotes the practice of Centering Prayer, Contemplative Outreach (CO), had 120 active chapters in 39 countries, supported over 800 prayer groups in the United States, taught the methods of Centering Prayer to 15,000 people every year, and sent out 40,000 monthly newsletters (www.contemplativeoutreach.org/about-us; accessed November 28, 2016). In 2013, CO had 3,000 followers on Twitter, 400

people on the main Facebook page, and numerous Facebook pages of local chapters (Fr. Carl Arico, personal communication). For information about the alternate technique, Christian Meditation, see the website of The World Community of Christian Meditation (www.wccm.org).

14. See Tipton's *Getting Saved from the Sixties* (1982) for a look at social change and religious fluidity in the United States.

15. Spiritual directors provide mentorship to individual seekers, usually at monthly one-on-one meetings. Spiritual mentoring has a long history and many models in Christianity. In fourth-century Egypt, for example, novices sought the guidance of desert hermits. Some contemporary American publications about spiritual direction include Barry and Connolly's *The Practice of Spiritual Direction* (1982), which describes mentoring from a Roman Catholic Ignatian perspective, and Guenther's *Holy Listening* (1992), which comes from an Episcopal perspective. For more on contemporary practices, see the journal for professional spiritual directors, *Presence*, and the websites of Spiritual Direction International (www.sdiworld.org) and the Shalem Institute for Spiritual Formation (www.shalem.org).

16. See Hann and Goltz (2010) for ethnographic essays on Eastern Christianities, which also focus greatly on formalized ritual practice. Many of the people in my research studied the theologies and liturgies of Eastern Orthodox and Coptic churches.

17. It is important to note that the venues where I did fieldwork colored my perspective of the Centering Prayer movement's demographics. The community in the United States as I encountered it was largely formally educated, Euro-American, professional, and upper middle class. However, it was not exclusively so. There were Centering Prayer groups in the prison population (Coakley 2004), and homeless people attended some groups at inner-city churches. As well, according to my contacts at Contemplative Outreach, there was a significant population of practicing Hispanic Americans, especially in Florida. See the "Community" portal at www.contemplativeoutreach.org.

18. Iona and Taizé are contemporary ecumenical Christian intentional communities that have been influential in international contemplative Christian circles. Iona was founded and built in the 1930s by a Protestant minister as a way of offering meaningful work to unemployed craftsmen and seminary students during the Depression. Iona is located on the site of the early Christian monastery on a Hebridean island of the same name off northwest Scotland. The Taizé community, located in the French Burgundian countryside, was founded in the 1940s by a young Swiss man who offered shelter to war refugees. Taizé is modeled on Benedictine monasticism, and its primary members are avowed monks, now numbering in the hundreds, from about thirty countries. Taizé inspired the founding of many other ecumenical monasteries and convents, such as the convent of Grandchamp in Neuchâtel, Switzerland (www.grandchamp.org), and

an international non-monastic movement based on its ideals and aesthetics. For more information, see www.iona.org.uk and www.taize.fr. See also Moore (1970) on the Taizé experiment in ecumenical international living and Muir (2012) for an oral history of the founders of the contemporary Iona community.

19. Spirituality and Practice, an online educational forum for inter-religious practitioners, offered "e-courses" in which some teachers and students in my research took part. In a blog post called "Welcoming the Spiritually Independent," authors Frederic and Mary Ann Brussat used the term "spiritually independent" for the unassociated religious. They wrote, "Let's stop being so negative about the group that is transforming religion and spirituality in the 21st century. One-fifth of the American public—and a third of adults under 30—do not identify themselves with a religion . . . . In an attempt to label them, two terms have emerged: 'Spiritual But Not Religious' (SBNRs) and 'Nones.' We don't like either term. They categorize people by what they are not. We are interested in who they are. That's why we call them the 'spiritually independent.'" The Brussats go on to describe "interspiritual practitioners" as people who have gotten off "the tour bus of single organized religions" so they can get out and "directly experience" the land through which they have been traveling. They say spiritual independents are ones who "distrust . . . prepackaged beliefs, and also distrust religious institutions that are so often corrupt and hypocritical. Yet they value human spiritual heritage, often in great variety, and many of these people are more comfortable in a variety of religious settings than they would be in only one" [www.spiritualityandpractice/blog/spiritual-literacy/welcoming-the-spiritually-independent.com; accessed September 9, 2013]. See also the popular Jewish "wisdom teacher" Rami Shapiro's (2013) *Perennial Wisdom for the Spiritually Independent*. In September 2013, Rami Shapiro taught an e-course called "The Way of the Spiritually Independent" on the Spirituality and Practice website.

20. "Acedia" is religious apathy.

21. Defining the category "Christian" has been an ongoing topic in the anthropology of Christianity subfield (e.g., Robbins 2003; Garriott and O'Neill 2008; Jacobsen 2011). Hoskins's (2014) assertion that Christian divinities must be at the forefront of a pantheon for religious expressions to rightly be called a form of Christianity seems an unnecessary imposition of anthropological categories over people's own practices and conceptions. My own approach is to take people's self-categorizations, regardless of adherence to other religious traditions, in equal or greater measure.

22. The term "non-gathered community" was suggested to me by Professor Nancy T. Ammerman.

23. While I did not travel to the Pacific Northwest to do fieldwork, I did work elsewhere in the United States with practitioners and teachers who came from that region.

24. I followed e-courses on contemplative Christian subjects on the Spirituality and Practice website seven times, from four to six weeks each, and observed how

hundreds of individuals from multiple countries participated in discussions and developed relationships. While I have no way of knowing if other individuals had the means or interest to carry on these relationships in another context, some of the participants were people who knew each other from retreats at which I had done fieldwork. Some, like Maggie, mentioned how their co-participation bolstered their long-distance connections. I do not bring in details from the discussions that occurred on the Spirituality and Practice site because of a confidentiality code to which each participant must agree before taking an e-course. Spirituality and Practice had a significant reach; in 2013, it dispersed 60,000 monthly electronic newsletters.

25. Quoted from the Contemplative Society website: www.contemplative.org/about-us/our-program/; accessed September 15, 2013.

26. Claussen (2001), Irvine (2010a), Lester (2005), and Wichroski (1997) also described how silence in monastic environments posed challenges to their ethnographic fieldwork.

27. See Wikan (1991, 2012), Jackson (1996), Hollan (2008), Samudra (2008), Ram and Houston (2015), and Wynn (2015) for explorations of how "experience-near anthropology," "thick participation," and other phenomenological approaches to ethnographic fieldwork and writing can elucidate ephemeral subjectivities, like those associated with contemplation, including the role of the anthropologist's own perception. Throop (2010) might call my methods a kind of "ethnographic epoché." Desjarlais and Throop (2011) offer a good historical overview of anthropological uses of phenomenology, including in research methods.

28. This ethnographic method of serious, long-term apprenticeship was also taken up by Loïc Wacquant (2004: 6–11) in his endeavor to understand how young African American men trained in the subtleties of embodied knowledge in the field of boxing. He stressed the necessity of "surrender" as an ethnographer, emphasizing the practice of full immersion by calling his method "observant participation" rather than participant observation. See also Sarah Pink (2009) on "sensory apprenticeship" as an ethnographic field method.

29. E.g., Barker (1993, 2012); Coleman (2000); Coleman and Hackett (2015); Engelke (2007); Guadeloupe (2009); Harris (2006); Lampe (2010); Mitchell and Ganiel (2011); Robbins (2004). For critiques of the anthropology of Christianity project (and the disciplinary categorization of world religions generally), see Asad (1993a), Comaroff (2010), and Hann (2007). Using the work of Deleuze (1994) on the concept of the virtual, Bialecki (2012) counters these critics with arguments that revisit the appropriateness of universals, potentialities, and collective categories.

30. See also Elisha (2011) for an insightful ethnographic study of American evangelical megachurch communities, which work to negotiate their conservatism, desire to serve the urban poor, and engagement with pluralistic society.

31. E.g., Ammerman (2007, 2014); Bell (1992); Hann and Goltz (2010); Mahmood (2005); McDannell (1995); McGuire (2008); Peña (2011); Wikan (2012).

32. E.g., Barth (1993, 2002); Herzfeld (1997, 2004); Jackson (2002); Kleinman (1988); Mahmood (2005).

33. Teresa of Ávila (1979 [1588]).

The organizational framework of this book is a double metaphor: the image of a contemplative Christian moving toward the inner recesses of a monastic chapel refers both to the increasing spiritual maturity which the people in my research called "deepening into the divine," and to my own accumulating capacity to understand these interiorized people as an ethnographer, including my development of "intersubjective" research techniques. Mirroring the longterm project of contemplative (and ethnographic) work, the narratives and analyses in this book only gradually reveal the "transformations" of changing perception and the intersubjective experiences that can result from years of engaged and disciplined practice.

Diagrams 1 and 2 (back matter of this volume) show the monastic chapel of the Society of Saint John the Evangelist in Cambridge, Massachusetts, in context of the monastery as a whole. Diagram 3 offers a detailed floor plan of the chapel, which is marked with the different architectural areas that are the titles of my chapters: Portico, Antechapel, Grille, Gate, Choir, Sacristy, Sanctuary. The Cell is off-stage, in the privacy of the monastic cloister.

CHAPTER 2

1. See Forbess (2010) for another discussion on the intensive training in monasteries, using an ethnographic example from the Romanian Orthodox Church. Hann and Goltz (2010: 13) note the important relationship between monastics and laity that exists generally in Eastern Orthodox churches, calling monasteries "a strong magnet" for society as a whole. Luhrmann (2012) describes the central role of training and practice among American Vineyard evangelical Christian congregants in establishing relational spiritualities (see especially Chapter 5, "Learning from the Experts," for the function of the teacher).

2. Jen Tarr's (2008) ethnographic study of the Alexander Technique shows how dedicated practitioners consciously work to transform habitus in chosen directions. Compare also with Saba Mahmood's (2005) finding that, in an Egyptian Muslim women's piety movement, ascribed disciplined practices (including wearing symbolic clothing) can be co-productive of intentionality and self-formation, a subject that will be discussed at length in this chapter and chapters to come. See Kelman (1958) and Kanter (1968) for discussions on how "internalization" and "identification" with social norms and moral codes can work as motivators of commitment, including in alternative societies.

3. Ritual specialists have negotiated the paradox of status and humility in a variety of ethnographic settings around the world. See Victor Turner's essay, "Humility and Hierarchy: The Liminality of Status Elevation and Reversal," in *The Ritual*

Process (1969), which describes how the masking, reversal, and abasement of social status in ritual help create the social anti-structure that facilitates occurrences of communitas.

4. Sandra Mattheson is a pseudonym. In order to properly credit their published works, I have used the real names of the other two teachers in my example, Rev. Ward Bauman and Br. Curtis Almquist, SSJE, with permission.

5. *New Yorker* cartoon by David Sipress, republished here with permission from Condé Nast publications, which Sandra Mattheson posted on her Facebook page. It appeared in Robert Mankoff's August 7, 2014 article, "What Cartoons Can Do" in the *New Yorker* [www.newyorker.com/cartoons/bob-mankoff/cartoons-can]. Thanks to Mark Mealing for providing me with the original citation.

6. Ward Bauman's idea of "the West" will not here be problematized. Having lived, taught, and studied in the Middle East, he had practical as well as scholarly understandings of cultural differences between this region and the United States. See Edward Said's *Orientalism* (1978) and Tal Asad's *Genealogies of Religion* (1993), for example, for discussions about the history of the dichotomization of "East" and "West."

7. Br. Curtis Almquist was the Superior at the Society of Saint John the Evangelist at Cambridge, Massachusetts, for nine years. His tenure ended in 2010, when Br. Geoffrey Tristam became the new Superior. In 2016, the role of Superior was taken on by Br. James Koester.

8. The Charles J. Connick Stained Glass Foundation sponsors the annual Orin E. Skinner Lecture to fulfill its mission "to promote the true understanding of the glorious medium of color and light and to preserve and perpetuate the Connick tradition of stained glass." See the Education portal at the Foundation's website at www.cjconnick.org.

9. For more on SSJE's contemplative views of the icon, see Br. James Koester's sermon (2013), "Praying with Icons," as well as a teaching from their online resource, "Monastic Wisdom," at http://ssje.org/ssje/category/monastic-wisdom/praying-with-icons/. Rice (1972) and Weitzmann (1982) offer histories on the topic of Christian icons. Anthropological treatments of icon gazing include Hanganu (2010), Herzfeld (1990), Luehrmann (2010), Mahieu (2010), and Morgan (2005). Hann and Goltz (2010) remind us that icon gazing cannot be understood outside of a full social and liturgical context.

10. See the Photograph Gallery for images of the SSJE chapel, especially those in the section called "Monastic Settings: The Society of Saint John the Evangelist," under the heading "Contemplative Christian Aesthetics." See also the publication *Stone and Light: A Celebration of a Holy Place* (SSJE 2010) for additional photographs and reflections on what makes an architectural space holy. For a scholarly treatment of how architecture can prompt people to move across boundaries, see *Ritual and Its Consequences* (Seligman, Weller, Puett, and Simon 2008).

11. Gavin Flood's *The Ascetic Self: Subjectivity, Memory, and Tradition* (2004) offers a comparative study of concepts and practices of detachment in Christianity, Buddhism, and Hinduism. See also Naletova (2010) for an anthropological exploration of the principle and practice of kenosis in the context of Russian Orthodox pilgrimages.

12. The relationship of discipline and leniency in religious practice, as illustrated in the compassionate view of human frailty among contemplatives in my research, was the topic of a panel at the American Anthropological Association meetings in 2016 in Minneapolis (e.g., Elliot 2016; Malara 2016). Elliot noted that allowing a place for leniency is a key technique that assists in the stabilization of group discipline.

13. Cynthia Bourgeault (2004: 116) noted that the practice of attention has ancient roots. For example, a tenth-century essay by the Christian Byzantine mystic Symeon the New Theologian (1951) called it "attention of the heart."

14. Thomas Keating (2002a, 2002b) used a psychological model to describe how meditation can iron out the reactionary responses of individuals to their "emotional programs for happiness." He wrote that an attachment to preferences (even a preference for joy) can cause destabilization and that contemplative practices like Centering Prayer could foster greater detachment, helping practitioners to move toward equanimity over time, regardless of circumstance. Keating taught that ultimately the student of contemplation must learn that preferences should not influence or sway one's commitment, well-being, or stability.

15. Contemplative Christians could apparently use any avenue, even assisting in anthropological research, as a medium for self-reflexivity and renewal of commitment. The close engagement of my methods definitely made my research something that influenced and was influenced by others. See Carey (1967) and Chiesa and Hobbs (2008) for discussions on this so-called Hawthorne effect.

16. "Brother, Give Us a Word," SSJE's daily online reflection, posted December 1, 2013.

17. See Maguire's *An Infinity of Little Hours* (2006), which describes how those learning to live within monasteries—Carthusian, in this case—also struggled with adapting to the contemplative life.

18. This method of shifting perception is a kind of "phenomenological modification" (Desjarlais and Throop 2011; Duranti 2011; Husserl 1962; Throop 2009). Note a contrast with Bourdieu's view (1977, 1991) that few have the capacity to transform habitus as it requires significant cultural capital either to bring to doxa (critical awareness) or to change. In the pages to come, the role of cultural capital and varieties of knowledge will come clear in the process of transformation among American contemplative Christians. Although it gives agency a primary role and recognizes the transformative effects of intentional repetitive action, Mahmood's use of habitus (2005) does not include the positive, creative aspects of ambiguity in the transformative process which is essential to my model.

19. "CP" is Centering Prayer.

20. The idea of using monastic "tools" to sustain contemplative intentions was popular among contemplative Christians. See, for example, Sr. Mary Margaret Funk's *Tools Matter for Practicing the Spiritual Life* (2001) and Jane Tomaine's *St. Benedict's Toolbox* (2005). See also Tomaine's blogs "Cyber Toolbox" and "Randy's Corner" at www.stbenedictstoolbox.org.

21. I identified this positive variety of discipline as one giving "power to" individuals, rather than having "power over" them, in consultation with Nancy T. Ammerman. Coakley (2004) discusses the simultaneously empowering and oppressive aspects of silent meditation practices among African American and Latino American men in US prisons. (Thanks to Jason Byassee for alerting me to Coakley's article). See also Wacquant (2004) for an ethnographic account of discipline as a positive force among apprentice boxers. Similarly, the ethnography of Mahmood (2005) describes discipline as a means to positive self-formation in an Egyptian Muslim women's piety movement. Of course, Christian forms of discipline have also acted as a method of institutional control. For an anthropological analysis of Christian monastic discipline in the Foucauldian sense, see Asad's (1993b) "On Discipline and Humility in Medieval Christian Monasticism."

22. Forbess (2010) offers an anthropological treatment of how one Romanian Orthodox convent viewed their rule of life with some ambivalence, seeing strict adherence as potential hubris. They advocated a more active discernment of best practices by following the spirit rather than the letter of the rule. See Southern (1970) for an history of rules of life in Christian monastic practice. For popular teachings on the development of Christian non-monastic rules, see, for example, Chittister (1991, 2010), Casey (2014), and Guthrie (2000).

23. At the 2009 General Convention of the Episcopal Church, Presiding Bishop Katherine Jefferts Schori made a speech saying that there is no "personal salvation," but only salvation for all, stating that an "individualist focus is a form of idolatry, for it puts me and my words in the place that only God can occupy" (quoted in Virtue 2009).

24. Invariably more moderate than those for the avowed religious, some orders had rules for their oblate or tertiary adherents, which a number of the non-monastics in my research followed. See, for example, the rule of the Third Order of the Society of St. Francis, Province of the Americas (http://tssf.org/sample-page/our-rule/) and the rule of SSJE's Fellowship of Saint John (www.ssje.org/fsj.html).

25. During the 2016 season of Lent, SSJE again encouraged their followers to develop rules of life. Using both social media and print media over the forty days of Lent, they employed a metaphor of tending a garden as a way to guide individuals, parishes, and groups to "grow a rule of life" (SSJE 2016; see also www.SSJE.org/growrule; accessed March 11, 2016).

26. This rendering is slightly paraphrased for the sake of brevity and clarity.

27. See Fr. Carl Arico's article (2013) on the theology and practice of humor, titled "Are We Taking Ourselves Too Seriously?" as well as his book, *A Taste of Silence* (1999).

28. This rendering is an approximation. I was laughing too hard to grasp the exact text of their chant. Note that "OCD" is also a play on words: it not only stands for obsessive-compulsive disorder, but is also the abbreviation for the Roman Catholic Order of Discalced Carmelites, which was founded by Teresa of Ávila.

    This musical notation and other unattributed plainsong chant passages were drafted by Dr. Agnieszka Budzińska-Bennett.

29. As bishop, Br. Tom Shaw was called The Right Reverend M. Thomas Shaw, Bishop Diocesan. For overviews of his work during his tenure as bishop, see the sermon by the former Presiding Bishop of the Episcopal Church, the Rt. Rev. Frank T. Griswold (2014), and the *Boston Globe* article on the consecration of the new bishop, Alan M. Gates (Ortega 2014). Br. Tom Shaw died on October 17, 2014.

30. See www.cac.org/mission (accessed October 7, 2013). Richard Rohr established the Center for Action and Contemplation in 1986. Like the works of Thomas Keating, Rohr's many popular publications, public teachings, and retreats have been extremely influential in the American contemplative Christian movement and overseas. See, for example, Rohr (1991, 2003, 2009, 2014). For a Roman Catholic critique of Richard Rohr's ideas, see Sibley (2006).

31. For a historical overview of the relationship of action and contemplation in Christian contemplative practice, see Radler (2012).

32. See www.kidsforpeaceglobal.org.

33. See www.occupyboston.org and www.protestchaplains/blogspot.com.

CHAPTER 3

1. Hann and Goltz (2010: 13) also note a positive view of monastic silence and seclusion in Eastern Orthodox Christianities. They write that the people of those societies believe that monks, nuns, and hermits cloister themselves "for the world's sake. Their prayers in the wilderness sustain the world, and the other inhabitants of the world are well aware of their debt to this minority. These seeming 'unsocials' or even 'anti-socials' . . . are in fact the foundations of the social world."

2. Professor Deeana Klepper remarked that silence was not particularly easy in European medieval monastic contexts either. Many historical documents describe how monks and nuns got into trouble for breaching codes of silence. See Scott G. Bruce's *Silence and Sign Languages in Medieval Monasticism, the Cluniac Tradition c. 900–1200* (2007).

3. Christian monasteries and convents have varying degrees of enclosure, including complete segregation from outsiders. Although the details of their

boundaries differed, the monasteries and convents where I did research were all semi-cloistered, meaning that they had spaces that were reserved exclusively for their order's members, as well as some spaces that were intermittently open to the public on a regular basis.

4. Although he noted that a place for guests was "built in" to the structure of Christian monasticism, Irvine (2010a) also observed a tension between the contrasting tenets of interiority and hospitality at the English Benedictine monastery where he did ethnographic fieldwork.

5. Cynthia Bourgeault once described the movement of the ivory-clad monks from the antechapel to the choir during the office of Vigil at this monastery as "light overcoming the darkness." See also her description of this early morning office in the Introduction to her book, *Chanting the Psalms* (Bourgeault 2006: 1–3).

6. For a comprehensive historical overview of varieties of silence in Christianity, including the development of silence in monastic orders like the Cistercians, see Diarmaid MacCulloch (2013), especially Part Two, "The Triumph of Monastic Silence." Note that "silence" does not mean a complete lack of sound. Bedford (2015: 142) described silence as an "imperfect condition." Unlike the mathematical principle of zero, he said, "there is always something there" when it comes to sound, even if it is only the sound of the wind or one's own heartbeat and breath. See also John Cage (1961) on his experiments with creating "silent" soundscapes.

7. Sajavaara and Lehtonen (1997) describe the ambiguity of silences and their resistance to interpretation. See also Basso (1972), Saville-Troike (1985), Jaworski (1993, 1997), and Bedford (2015) for discussions about varieties of silence, and how their functions and expressions differ depending on the ethnographic setting. Basso's classic work, for example, identified silence as a culturally situated linguistic act rather than a lack of language, used among the Western Apache in situations of ambiguous social relationships. Coakley's article, "Jail Break" (2004), notes how intentional silence in meditation acted as an empowering "subversive activity" among mostly African American and Latino American prison inmates in the Boston area.

8. Charles Taylor's *Sources of the Self* (1989) emphasizes the primary role of personal narrative in constituting the self in modern societies.

9. MacCulloch's (2013) complex survey of positive and negative silences in Christian history is particularly useful for understanding the social circumstances of contemplatives in my research. For silences that have acted to conceal institutional abuses, see especially Chapter 8, "Things Not Remembered."

10. See Irvine (2010a: 228–232) for an ethnographic sketch of silence at an English Benedictine monastery.

11. Taylor (1989) offers an intellectual history of the development of the inward self, the basis of conceptual and phenomenological categories like "inner silence," which developed during the modernization of Western European societies.

12. Indeed, I found that the anthropologist's ethnographic task of uncovering as much information about people as possible was a misfit in this environment. After some uncomfortable incidents, I adapted my methods to this ethnographic environment by limiting questions, even when speaking was permitted. With time, the imperative of silence heightened my attentiveness to subtle nonverbal cues.

13. Quoted in the Contemplative Life Program's 40-day practice booklet, *Silence and Solitude* (Best 2006b: 75).

14. In the Wisdom Christianity community, the efforts to step up the training of new teachers intensified after my ethnographic fieldwork concluded. For example, Cynthia Bourgeault began asking some of her more advanced students to help organize and teach so that she could better respond to the high demand for introductory Wisdom Schools. With the assistance of a half-dozen apprentice teachers, she held a 2015 Wisdom School event in North Carolina with about 250 participants. In addition, advanced students practiced their work as teachers in an online forum, taking turns to assign weekly contemplative practices and intellectual teachings over six-week cycles.

15. In another environment outside of usual ecclesial social structures in which religious practitioners sought community, Russian Orthodox Christians developed a robust pilgrimage movement during the Soviet era, which provided a similarly amorphous but effective venue for informal networking and support. See Naletova (2010).

16. The idea and practice of "keeping attention in oneself" was drawn from a fourth-century desert monastic teaching of St. Anthony. See an explication of the subject in Cynthia Bourgeault's *The Heart of Centering Prayer* (2016) in the chapter entitled, "Centering Prayer and Witnessing Presence" (originally published as Bourgeault 2010a).

17. Wacquant (2004: 111) describes similar informal social stratifications of adepts and novices among boxers at a Chicago gym. As among Christian contemplatives in my research, he also observes that humility is essential to the learning process. He writes,

> To find and keep one's place in the pugilistic universe, one must indeed know and always take account of one's physical and moral limits, not let one's aspirations "take off" unrealistically, not seek to rise higher and faster than is reasonable . . . . This is why the trainer's instructions to his boxers frequently take the form of incitements to modesty, invitations to repeat the same gestures without shirking and without trying to overstep their capacities, to respect the seemingly stationary pace that he impresses on their apprenticeship. Through his remarks, his criticism, and his encouragement but also his prolonged silences or his attentive presence, [the trainer] lifts up those who, from lack of confidence or shyness, stoop below their worth . . . and takes down those who, elated by

their progress in the gym or by their success in the ring, start to bluster, thinking that they have "made it" and try to box beyond their capacities. Pugilistic pedagogy is thus inseparably a pedagogy of humility and honor whose goal is to inculcate in each the sense of limits (which is also a sense of the group and of one's place in the group).

18. Matthew 25.

19. Established in 1888, the Gifford Lectures are a prestigious annual series of lectures on religion, science, and philosophy delivered at Scottish universities. See www.giffordlectures.org.

20. In monastic orders, gender exclusivity was the norm, though there are a few American communities that take both female and male members. The Episcopal Church's Order of Julian of Norwich is one (see www.orderofjulian.org). Monasteries have long, graduated discernment processes, which allow both the community and the postulant time to decide if the relationship between them is the right fit. The monasteries in which I worked included the graduated membership of entry-level postulants, novices, first-vowed monks, and life-vowed monks. There were also different monastic roles within orders, including hierarchical ones like Novice Master and Superior or Abbot. How the dynamics of these hierarchies played out depended on individual communities' character, choices, and interpretations of their rules.

21. One public relations specialist at a monastery commented to me that the Internet could also work to enhance privacy and enclosure; since monastics could now teach online, they could potentially reduce the amount of time they taught non-monastics in person and thus increase their time in seclusion. None of the monks with whom I worked mentioned this effect, however.

22. See Diagram 2 (in the back matter of this volume) for a layout of the SSJE monastery, guesthouse, and chapel. Built in 1924 and extended in 1928 on land donated by Isabella Stewart Gardner, a Boston art collector and benefactor, the current guesthouse was the original monastic enclosure, called St. Francis House. It includes the Holy Spirit Chapel, the monastery's original chapel, in its undercroft. Construction of the current monastic enclosure and the main chapel, called the Chapel of Saint Mary and Saint John, began in 1936. They were designed by Ralph Adams Cram (SSJE 2010).

23. Occasionally the SSJE monks took long-term visitors, such as a scholar or student from a local university, who remained in the guesthouse over the Sabbath. Similarly, monastic interns, who worked alongside the monks for nine-month periods, resided full-time at the guesthouse or at Grafton House, the home for monastic interns at the Society's rural retreat, Emery House. See Jeffrey F. Hamburger's *The Visual and the Visionary* (1998) for a study about how efforts to provide monasteries and convents with seclusion and gender segregation prompted extraordinarily complex architectural designs in medieval Europe. For discussions about another present-day example of how a distinction between

guests and members is accommodated in monastic architecture, see Irvine (2010a, 2013).

24. The Eucharist or Holy Communion is the central weekly rite of many liturgically centered Christian denominations like Anglicanism, Episcopalianism, and Roman Catholicism. Monks and nuns of those denominations usually take communion daily. For images of a Maundy Thursday liturgy at SSJE, including the Eucharist and foot-washing rites, see "Monastic High Liturgy" in the "Monastic Formal Rites and Contemplative Practices" section of the Photograph Gallery.

25. John 13:1–17.

26. Mark 14:34; Matthew 26:38.

CHAPTER 4

1. *Tales of a Magic Monastery* (Theophane the Monk 1981) was written by Fr. Theophane Boyd, a Roman Catholic Cistercian Trappist monk who lived at St. Joseph's Abbey in Spencer, Massachusetts, and later at St. Benedict's Monastery at Snowmass, Colorado, where he was the choirmaster. He died in 2003.

2. Consider, for example, the twelfth-century public addresses of Benedictine abbess Hildegard von Bingen and Cistercian abbot Bernard of Clairvaux. Both were influential in political and social affairs. Similarly, religious orders ministered to the Beguines, a women's non-monastic movement that existed in the Lowland countries, the Rhineland, and parts of France from the twelfth to fifteenth centuries. Female mystics like Hadewijch of Brabant, Mechthild of Magdeburg, and Marguerite Porete were members of Beguine communities (McGinn 1994; Petroff 1994; Simon 2012).

3. Although William Meninger was the one who first devised Centering Prayer, Thomas Keating has been the most influential teacher in the movement. Besides having founded Contemplative Outreach, Keating has published twenty-six books and countless articles. Amazon.com reported that by 2006, his "best-selling spiritual classic," *Open Heart, Open Mind,* had "sold over half a million in the English language and has appeared in 10 foreign-language editions." Numerous video and audio recordings of Thomas Keating's interviews and lectures were also available. At the time of writing, YouTube videos like "Thomas Keating Centering Prayer Guidelines Intro" had been viewed nearly 200,000 times (accessed December 1, 2016). In September 2010, the Pitts Theological Library at Emory University in Atlanta, Georgia, signed an agreement with Contemplative Outreach to permanently house Keating's papers (*Emory Report,* September 23, 2010).

4. Cynthia Bourgeault's *Centering Prayer and Inner Awakening* (2004), originally published by SSJE's Cowley Press, has continually been a strong seller since it first appeared, and was #1 on Amazon's Anglican bestseller list when I checked it in December 2016. Although they would not give me the full sales statistics, the book's current publisher, Rowman & Littlefield, told me in 2013 that "*Centering*

Prayer and Inner Awakening continues to sell thousands of copies each year." Bourgeault's more recent books have been published by Shambhala. Sales data on the English versions of two of her nine books gives a picture of their reach. By October 2016, *The Wisdom Jesus* (2008) had sold 53,000 print books and 8,000 in the e-book version, and was #11 on the Amazon's Jesus bestseller list. *The Meaning of Mary Magdalene* (2010) had sold 35,000 print books and 5,400 e-books. Both had been translated into several languages. At the time of writing, she had just released a new book, *The Heart of Centering Prayer: Nondual Christianity in Theory and Practice* (2016). During the time of my research, Cynthia Bourgeault kept a rigorous lecture and retreat schedule that took her to Europe, Britain, Hong Kong, New Zealand, South Africa, Canada, and all over the United States. Bourgeault's retreats and Wisdom Schools were often fully booked two years in advance and had lengthy waiting lists. She also taught through online forums, including Spirituality & Practice, Sounds True, and YouTube, and was a teacher at Fr. Richard Rohr's Living School in Albuquerque, New Mexico (www.cac. org/living-school). A number of societies' websites were devoted to publicizing Cynthia Bourgeault's teachings, including the Contemplative Society (www. contemplative.org), the Wisdom Way of Knowing (www.wisdomwayofknowing. org), Northeast Wisdom (www.northeastwisdom.org), and the Wisdom Resource Center at the Center for Spiritual Resources (www.thecsr.org).

5. See www.wisdomchant.bandcamp.com. Because I use her chants and cite her teaching work extensively in later chapters, I use Darlene Franz's real name, with permission.

6. Gregory Meyer is a pseudonym.

7. See also Johannes Fabian (2012) for useful comments about knowledge as an analytical category in anthropology. Thanks to Denise Nuttall for the reference.

8. See also the anthropological literature about social tensions that arise because of differences between institutional authority, official models, and lived experiences in other ethnographic settings (e.g., Baumann 1996; Jackson 2002; Kapferer 1988; Kleinman 1988). Historical schism in Christianity is epitomized in the example of the European Reformation (O. Chadwick 1972; MacCulloch 2005).

9. For an example of significant denominational disputes, see discussions about the homosexuality debate in the Anglican Communion, of which the Episcopal Church is a part, in Bates's (2004) *Church at War: Anglicans and Homosexuality* and Brittain and McKinnon's essay (2011), "Homosexuality and the Construction of 'Anglican Orthodoxy': The Symbolic Politics of the Anglican Communion." For examples of populist critiques of the Centering Prayer movement, see Seventh-Day Adventist Howard Peth's *The Dangers of Contemplative Prayer* (2012) and Protestant evangelical pastor Rev. John D. Dreher's article (1997), "The Danger of Centering Prayer." The latter critique was re-posted on a Roman Catholic website, CatholicCulture.org, illustrating cross-denominational activity in genres of American Christianity besides contemplative ones.

10. For an example of a Greek Orthodox monastic revitalization movement in Antioch, Syria, from before the war that began in 2011, see Anna Poujeau's article, "Monasteries, Politics, and Social Memory" (2010). Poujeau describes the overtly political aspects of territorial reclamation through the re-establishment of Christian monasteries. American monasticism is not overtly territorial or political, although the monastic communities with which I worked tended toward what Americans would describe as "liberal" political perspectives.

11. Compare Tickle's integrated view of lived religion with the dichotomized theory of Harvey Whitehouse (2000), which splits religious adherents by their "modes of religiosity," either "doctrinal" (belief oriented) or "imagistic" (including a focus on practice). Similar to my findings, several ethnographic essays in a volume devoted to the study of Eastern Orthodox Christianity show that many people practice religion by intricately blending doctrinal texts, images, and rites (Forbess 2010; Hanganu 2010; Hann and Goltz 2010; Luehrmann 2010; Naumescu 2010). See also Bielo (2011) and Marti and Ganiel (2014).

12. For example, a posting on SSJE's Facebook page said, "The spiritual life is not a collection of spiritual calisthenics [but is rather] a way of being attentive in the world that is open to God and open to others" (July 12, 2014).

13. Thanks to Peter Elliott for bringing my attention to this article.

14. In the context of Eastern Orthodox Christianities, Hann and Goltz (2010: 15–16) also discuss the lack of fixity in so-called orthodoxy and orthopraxy in the way people actually live their religious lives. They observed that there is "a continuum between written canonical tradition and what believers have actually done," and that clear-cut categories of "orthodox" and "heterodox" are too oppositional to adequately describe and explain practices among the peoples with whom they have done research.

15. A few statistics help to show the extent of the community they served. The SSJE Brothers, together with a small team of public relations professionals, offered an extensive array of contemplative teachings through print media and online video and audio recordings of sermons and interviews under the heading, "Monastic Wisdom." The digital postings had significant followings. For example, the 2013 Lenten video series, "A Framework for Freedom: Living a Rule of Life," had up to 20,000 hits each day on Facebook. An interactive Advent calendar SSJE hosted on Facebook, Twitter, and Pintrest had over one million hits on a single day in December 2014. In 2013, SSJE had 6,500 subscribers to their daily digital reflection, "Brother, Give Us a Word," 5,000 people received print copies of *Cowley* magazine by mail each quarter, 10,000 received digital bi-monthly newsletters, and 2,000 people stayed in their two guesthouses. The Society's non-monastic companion order, the Fellowship of St. John, had about 1,000 members from around the world, both men and women (Jamie Coats, personal communication). Until 2010, they ran their own publishing house, Cowley Publications, now operated by Rowman & Littlefield.

16. See Irvine (2013) for another anthropological perspective on how monastic architecture supports notions of stability and continuity.

17. Note that the Episcopal Church's so-called Rite III is particular to the American expression of Anglicanism. The Anglican Church of Canada, for example, did not have a comparable liturgy in either their *Book of Common Prayer* (1959) or their more widely used *Book of Alternative Services* (1985). Cynthia Bourgeault, who worked as a priest in British Columbia for eight years, felt that liturgists were much more restricted in the Canadian church. The Episcopal Church (1979: 319–382, 435, 506) also allowed freedom for liturgical play by offering two versions of the "Great Thanksgiving" or Eucharist (Rite I and Rite II), as well as flexibility in marriage and burial services.

18. Psalm 69:1–3, New Standard Revised Version (NSRV). At the Tenebrae Service in 2013, the SSJE community sang psalms in two groups of three: 69:1–23, 70, 74, and 63:1–8, 90: 1–12, 143, plus The Song of Hezekiah (Isaiah 38:9, following). The groups of psalms were separated by the singing of the first two poems of the Lamentations of Jeremiah, divided into three parts.

19. E.g., John 2:19.

20. Selection from "The Deserted City" (Lamentations 1:1–2, 8, NSRV), sung in full by SSJE cantors.

21. Psalm 51:1–3, 6–9, NSRV.

22. Br. Eldridge Pendleton, SSJE, died on August 26, 2015 at the age of seventy-five.

23. See former SSJE Superior Martin L. Smith's *The Word Is Very Near You* (1989) for a guide on *lectio divina*. For Ignatius's original sixteenth-century writings on the spiritual exercises, see Ignatius of Loyola (1991) or a brief overview in O'Leary (2007).

24. E.g., Mark 16:5–7.

25. Their perspective about the suppression of alternative renderings of historical Christianities, including a school following Mary Magdalene, was founded in scholarship. See, for example, Ehrman's *Lost Christianities* (2003), Brock's *Mary Magdalene, the First Apostle: The Struggle for Authority* (2003), Jenkins's *The Lost History of Christianity* (2008), and King's *What Is Gnosticism?* (2003). Bourgeault (2010) draws especially from King's work in her own book on a Christian theology based on the life and ways of Mary Magdalene, *The Meaning of Mary Magdalene: Discovering the Woman at the Heart of Christianity*.

26. The House of Prayer website says that members of the Contemplative Body "are at the heart of our ministry." See www.ehouseofprayer.org/about/contemplative-body for a brief sketch of their rule of life.

27. I will not here discuss the sometimes contested term, "Native American," but use it as the people in my research used it. For discussions, see, for example, the works of Gerald Robert Vizenor (1999, 2012).

28. Dr. Lynn Bauman, Ward's brother and one of the instigators of the contemporary American Wisdom Christianity movement, was a scholar of both Islam and

Christianity with specialized knowledge of ancient Middle Eastern languages. He was one of the leaders I followed during research. Lynn published his own translation of the non-canonical Gospel of Thomas, as well as other ancient texts, like the psalms, to highlight the "unitive" aspects of their meaning. See Bauman (2003, 2008) as well as Bauman, Bauman, and Bourgeault (2008). Elaine Pagels's work (1989, 2004) offers more commentary on the Nag Hammadi texts.

29. Cynthia Bourgeault, personal communication via email, August 23, 2013.

30. John 18:1–19:37.

31. This kind of invocation and embodiment of persons beyond our own realm is not unheard of in ritual plays. In 1997, for example, I attended part of the Ramlila in India with New York University's Professor Richard Schechner (1993) in which young boys invoked (rather than "acted" or portrayed) Rama and other gods in the thirty-day dramatic rendering of the ancient Hindu religious text *The Ramayana*.

32. At the time of writing, Jamie had recently married, was living in an intentional community, and was working as a parish priest and an emerging leader in the Wisdom Christianity network.

33. See Diagram 6 for the Oratory layout.

34. See hymn 204 in the Episcopal Church's *Hymnal* (1982).

35. See Bourgeault et al. (2011: 25–31) for the text and music of this liturgy. The chants are reprinted with permission of Cynthia Bourgeault.

36. In the 1980s, Lynn Bauman (1989) and a contemplative group he led adapted the Anglican Rosary from the Roman Catholic rosary and Eastern Orthodox prayer beads. Besides Anglicans and Episcopalians, Lutherans, Methodists, Baptists, Presbyterians, and non-denominational Christians around the world now use this mnemonic device, according to the Wikipedia site, "Anglican Prayer Beads." See also Fr. Thomas Schultz's *The Rosary for Episcopalians/Anglicans* (2003) and Ward Bauman's *The Anglican Rosary: Meditating with the Mystics* (nd). A few dedicated websites include www.fullcirclebeads.com (Salt Lake City, UT), www.franciscan.org.au/anglican-rosary (Brisbane, Australia), and the Anglican Rosary's Facebook page (Cambridge, England), www.facebook.com/AnglicanRosary.

37. Not a terribly common observance in contemporary United States, the Christian manifestation of Love Mysticism came to an apex in medieval times with the sermons of St. Bernard of Clairvaux and Beguine mystics like Hadewijch of Brabant and Mechtild of Magdeburg. During their era, the bride as individual soul replaced the Hebrew symbol of the bride-nation or bride-people (Fanning 2001; Hollywood 2002; McGinn 1994, 2012). For an anthropological analysis of medieval Christian Love Mysticism from a psychoanalytical perspective, see Obeyesekere's *The Awakened Ones: Phenomenology of Visionary Experience*, particularly the discussion on Teresa of Ávila (2012: 186–216).

38. Song of Songs 2:1; 1:2; 6:3.

39. Song of Songs 4:12, 16; 5:1.

40. Song of Songs 8:6–7.

41. Cynthia Bourgeault (2011: 7, 15) drew my attention to the idea of liturgical book-
    ends when she referred to Bruce Chilton's observations (2005: 52) that anoint-
    ing begins and ends "the entire Triduum ordeal."

CHAPTER 5

1. Appealing to the divine for assistance in "awakening," the antiphon, "Guide us
   waking," brackets the *Nunc Dimittis* or *The Song of Simeon* (Luke 2:29–32), which
   concludes the night office of Compline. Musical notation by Dr. Agnieszka
   Budzińska-Bennett from an aural version sung at the Society of Saint John the
   Evangelist.
2. E.g., 1 Corinthians 6:19–20.
3. Romans 12:5; 1 Corinthians 12:27. For a compelling discussion on the historical
   cultural prejudice of anthropology toward the "reality" that individual bodies (rather
   than collectivities) are the primary basis of human existence, see Jon Bialecki's article, "Virtual Christianity in an Age of Nominalist Anthropology" (2012).
4. Chapter 6 offers a more comprehensive definition of "ritualization" and discusses the development of the idea, particularly through the work of Catherine
   Bell (1992).
5. Almquist (2014b).
6. See also Trix (1993) for contemporary examples of attunement in Islam. An
   anthropological treatment of attention in quite a different context may be found
   in Desjarlais's *Counterplay* (2011), which describes the phenomenology of
   playing chess.
7. Luke 10:42.
8. For a visual representation of the relationship of posture and flow in people's
   attempts to transform perception and behavior, see Diagram 4, "Contemplative
   Transformation: Working toward Perceptual Agency through Knowing and
   Unknowing" (back matter of this volume).
9. SSJE (1997: 36).
10. 1 Thessalonians 5:17.
11. Roman Catholics generally used the term "Divine Office" for the mix of com-
    munal prayer and work. Before Vatican II, they observed eight offices, called
    by their original Latin names: Vigils (or Matins), Lauds, Prime, Terce, Sext,
    None, Vespers, and Compline. Since Vatican II, many communities have modi-
    fied their schedules to be a little less rigorous. The Trappist monastery at St.
    Benedict's in Snowmass, Colorado, for example, shifted its earliest office from
    3 a.m. to 4:30 a.m. See Quigley (1920) for a pre–Vatican II discussion. See also
    David Landers's *Revolution in Time* (1983) for the historical importance of mon-
    asteries in the development of the clock and the mechanical measurement of
    time. Thanks to Charles Lindholm for pointing me to Landers.
12. The time of the Holy Eucharist service differed at SSJE on Tuesday (5:30 p.m.),
    Wednesday (12:30 p.m.), and Sunday (9:00 a.m.). The Sunday schedule also

differed from other days: Morning Prayer was at 6:30 a.m., Evening Prayer was at 4:00 p.m., and there was no service of Compline. For an ethnographic description of an English Benedictine monastery's daily round, see Irvine (2010a).

13. Recounting the story of the Annunciation when Archangel Gabriel came to tell Mary about her part in bringing Jesus to the world (Luke 1: 26–38), the Angelus prayer models contemplative ways of listening and consenting to the divine which can result in incarnation. The Angelus was part of the daily rhythm of prayer in much of Western Europe among both monastics and non-monastics by at least the thirteenth century, even though it was not fully standardized in the Roman Catholic Church until the seventeenth century (Thurston 1907). Located at the Musée D'Orsay in Paris, Jean-François Millet's mid-nineteenth century painting *The Angelus* shows how ordinary working people like farmers stopped to observe the prayer, the timing of which was marked by a village church bell. In twenty-first-century Switzerland and France, church bells continue to toll at the three historically allotted times for the Angelus, even in Protestant regions. On a recent trip to Burgundy, I noticed that locals still called the evening church bells the "Angelus" (though my host told me that people generally took this as the call to aperitifs rather than a call to prayer).

14. The liturgical year begins with the season of Advent four Sundays before Christmas in late November or early December. The year is composed of major and minor feast days, which commemorate saints and events in scripture, and includes seven seasons: Advent, Christmas, Epiphany, Lent, Easter, Pentecost, and Ordinary Time. Each season has its own sensibility marked by colors and symbols. For details of the Episcopal calendar, see the *Book of Common Prayer* (Episcopal Church 1979: 15–36). For a more colorful description, see Joan Chittister's Roman Catholic Benedictine perspective in *The Liturgical Year: The Spiraling Adventure of the Spiritual Life* (2009).

15. The "metaphor of narrative," like these literary attempts at conveying the sensuality of ritual, is a poor substitute for the actual embodied experience of ritual practice (Nancy T. Ammerman, quoted in Warner 2007: 185). See also Clifford's essay "On Ethnographic Allegory" (1986) and Samudra's "Memory in the Body" (2008) for thoughts on the problems of representing people's lives through the medium of scholarly narrative. Thanks to Denise Nuttall for alerting me to Samudra's work.

16. SSJE had a program for interns that offered "participants the opportunity to participate in the daily rhythm of prayer and work as lived by a contemporary monastic community of the Episcopal Church. Interns join the brothers in their daily worship and assist with various aspects of the ministry of hospitality and care of the houses, gardens and land. Interns engage in regular theological reflection guided by brothers and meet regularly with mentors of the SSJE community." The program took interns at both the urban monastery and the rural retreat and was open to women and men between the ages of twenty-one and

thirty-four. See www.ssje.org/internship (accessed August 10, 2013) for more information, including the interns' daily schedule.

17. As Bedford (2015: 138–139) has written, unmeasured music does indeed have rhythm, but does not have a prevailing rhythm imposed by set external dictates. The rhythm's flexibility is contextual, enacted and varied by the performers, according to historical norms and local aesthetic impulses. See, too, Ingold (2011a) for discussions about flow and temporality imbued by breath in vocalization. Neitz and Spickard (1990) also develop flow theory from their analysis of the bodily practices of singing and formal rite. Related studies include the sociological theory of music-making of Alfred Schutz (1964) and the psychological creativity theory of Mihaly Csikszentimihalyi (1975, 1997), though the latter's emphasis on "losing oneself" in practice is distinct from the attentiveness key to this contemplative Christian variety of flow, as we shall see in Chapter 7.

    To convey the plasticity of non-mensurable plainsong chant, Dr. Agnieszka Budzińska-Bennett wrote this volume's musical notation without time signature, bar lines, meter, or rhythmic note values. Scribes of ancient forms of plainsong notation used a number of different methods, all of which were devoid of rhythmic values. For some basics on plainsong chant in Western Christianity, see Hiley (2009).

18. Herzfeld's *The Body Impolitic* (2004) describes how nonverbal learning is valued in artisanal apprenticeships in which observation, imitation, and practice become the primary means of education. Particularly in the section entitled "An Implicit and Collective Pedagogy," Wacquant (2004) comes to similar conclusions about learning through performance and practice in *Body and Soul*, his ethnography about apprentice boxers.

19. Not all Lutheran practices are "spartan." The Lutheran denomination has a large range of liturgical forms, including some with a greater observance of formal rites. See Pfatteicher (1990).

20. www.spiritualityandpractice.com; www.soundstrue.com.

21. www.northeastguild.org.

22. Go to www.paulettemeier.com/spiritual-wisdom.html to hear her chants.

23. To hear examples of Iegor Reznikoff chanting in just intonation, see http://m.youtube.com/watch?autoplay=1&v=w1-5w3WYT5Y and http://m.youtube.com/watch?v=IFAB_aibwrU&autoplay=1. Whether Reznikoff is accurate in his findings and theories about just intonation and original forms of Gregorian chant is a question beyond the scope of the present work.

24. The difference between musical temperaments is a complex matter and cannot be addressed here in detail, though a few comments may assist non-musicians. Professor Robert Weller, a cellist, remarked that Clare likely struggled to distinguish between the two harmonic systems more because she was a pianist than because of her so-called "Western ear." String musicians in Europe and North America work with just intonation all the time, he said. Just (or "pure") intonation

is a flexible mode of harmonization that selects the pitches for intervals based on "pure harmony," that is, notes that do not cause a beat or thrumming effect when played together, but which generate sympathetic harmonic notes (Lindley 1980b; Angela Schwartz [former principal cellist, Synfonieorchester Basel], personal communication). Unfretted string instruments (and vocal sound) allow for easy manipulation of pitches and intervals to create this effect, whereas fixed-tone instruments like pianos have no such flexibility. The pitches and intervals of fixed-tone instruments are commonly based on a cycle of 12 identical fifths, with the octave divided into 12 equal, fixed semitones. This mode of "equal temperament" is now widely considered the "normal tuning of the Western, 12-note chromatic scale," according to Lindley (1980a: 218). Even so, equal temperament was originally developed in China as a way of seeking "the cosmically correct tuning for ritual bells," said Professor Weller. Vocalization is of course malleable in terms of creating pitch, but is also dependent on a singer's ability to distinguish variation in pitches, which is both a culturally influenced and individual capacity. Clare's challenges with learning just intonation demonstrate the aural "blindness" created by the learning contexts of specific cultural and instrumental milieus. For more on musical temperaments and their developmental history, see Donahue (2005).

25. At the meetings of the American Musicological Society, Dr. Melanie Marshall (2011), for example, gave a lecture entitled, "The Sound of Whiteness: Early Music Vocal Performance Practice in Britain." I myself studied how to produce white tone as a long-time singer of Gregorian chant and Renaissance choral music.

26. A powerfully intersubjective effect can also occur in choirs that do not have overtly religious intentions. Erick Lichte, a professional choral conductor, said of his rehearsals with his men's performance choir, Chor Leoni: "Life can be so full of the prosaic, and maybe just the hardscrabble of making ends meet in a city like Vancouver can be enough to get you down. But one of the blessings that I know I have, and that I share with the men of Chor Leoni, is that every Wednesday we get to close the doors on the rest of life and have a three-hour rehearsal. And maybe a couple of times in that rehearsal you'll be working on some bit of music and you are both completely inside your own body, and completely out of body. You are completely connected with your own soul, but you are completely interconnected with everyone else. Choral music can offer that to people—and, to me, that is grace" (quoted in Varty 2016).

27. See, for example, Taizé (1998) and Iona Abbey (nd).

28. See www.wisdomchant.bandcamp.com.

29. In Wisdom circles, the story circulated that this mantra was sung by the Dalai Lama to Vaclav Havel on his deathbed. Charles Rus, who adapted the melody from the Sanskrit mantra, paraphrased the words from a hymn by John Greenleaf Whittier. This notation was taken from Darlene Franz's own copy,

including her handwritten edit of the final word. She replaced "calm" with "love."

30. See Diagram 6 (back matter of this volume) for a floorplan of the Oratory.

31. Luke 23:46.

32. For some recent developments and debates regarding the anthropology of the senses, see Classen (1997), Howes (2003), Pink (2009), Howes and Pink (2010), and Ingold (2010, 2011b).

CHAPTER 6

1. See Diagram 4, "Contemplative Transformation: Working toward Perceptual Agency through Knowing and Unknowing."

2. Radler (2012) offers a historical treatment of the concepts of action and contemplation in contemplative Christianities. Go to the Photograph Gallery in the back matter of this volume to see images of St. John's chapel, which show the clerestory and cameo windows in photographs by Maria Arabbo and Michael Blachly.

3. Panentheism ("God in the world") differs from pantheism ("The world is God"). See Biernacki and Clayton's *Panentheism across the World's Traditions* (2014).

4. The Waldensians of the twelfth century are an example of the European lay mendicant movement devoted to emulating Christian poverty and service. The popularity of this manifestation of Christianity showed in the rise of Franciscanism in the thirteenth century. Not all versions were welcomed by Roman Catholic authorities, and the mendicant Dominican order, which officiated at church inquisitions, was created as a body to guide layfolk and to police heretics. See Grundmann (1995), Audisio (1999), and Evans (2003).

5. www.spiritualityandpractice.com. See also the Contemplative Outreach organization website for schedules of Welcoming Prayer retreats and intensives (www.contemplativeoutreach.org).

6. Using mundane tasks as a way to transform perception was certainly not unique to contemplative Christianity, either monastic or non-monastic. For other examples of ritualization and the cultivation of communal effervescence and phenomenological intersubjectivity through ordinary work, see Hirota (1995) on Buddhist tea practices, Wacquant (2004) on the apprenticeship of American inner-city boxers, and Mahmood (2005) on daily chores and social interactions among Egyptian Muslim women.

7. I cannot here offer a comprehensive description of The Work. For more substantial discussions of Gurdjieff's practices and ideas, see Webb (1980) and Nicoll (1996). See also Bourgeault (2003: 27–40).

8. Compare Cynthia Bourgeault's teaching on learning by doing to that of the head trainer who dismissed Wacquant's interest in books about boxing: "DeeDee screws up his face in disgust: 'You don' learn to box from books. You learn to box in d'gym'" (2004: 100).

9. Marcus's and Alexandra's comments about observation and intersubjectivity highlight the subtlety required to teach these kinds of practices. For me, this was an interesting experience of layering varieties of observation: observing as a contemplative teacher trainee, "self-remembering" (observing oneself as a part of the larger group/universe), observing the immediate work of personal "inner and outer tasks," and participant-observing as an ethnographer. The extra layer (and effort) of doing ethnographic fieldwork may have helped make me more conscious of the potential foibles and contributions of observation in general.

10. Sixty-three participants was by far the largest Wisdom School group that Cynthia Bourgeault had taught up to that time. During my ethnographic fieldwork, a more common group size was about twenty-five participants. Since then, Cynthia has taught much larger numbers by asking her advanced students to assist. In November 2015, for example, she gave an introductory Wisdom School for about 250 students in North Carolina, which she called a "mega Wisdom School" in playful allusion to the genre of American evangelical mega churches.

11. Alicia and her husband were Americans living in Canada. The United Church of Christ (UCC) is not a recognized denomination in Canada.

12. See Hamans and McInerny (2010) for a biography of Edith Stein. In 1998, Pope John Paul II canonized her as a patron saint of Europe. In Freiburg, Germany, where Edith Stein had been a professor of philosophy before becoming a nun, a Jesuit church has a side chapel dedicated to her.

13. See sociologist Jack Katz's humorous essay on road rage, "Pissed off in L.A." in *How Emotions Work* (1999), recommended by Professor Charles Lindholm.

14. Victor Turner (1969: 141–142, 145) did comment on special cases of people's attempts to create sites of "permanent liminality," which included monastic and mendicant Christian communities. He noted that in these situations, communitas tended to rise out of attention to "particulars" rather than a dependence on the generalities of institutional form, which coincides with my observations about monks' use of standardized practices as a way to pay attention to the immediate present. See also Turner's comments (1974: 292–293) about the relationship of instances of Christian mystical "detachment" rising as a social response to uncertain (liminal, ambiguous) historical times—that is, "anti-structure." Edith Turner (2012) expanded this work with her investigation of communitas in numerous social activities, both ritualized and non-ritualized.

CHAPTER 7

1. Br. Eldridge Pendleton, the SSJE resident historian who died in 2015, recounted stories of T. S. Eliot during my fieldwork. Now called the Holy Spirit Chapel, the original chapel is located in the undercroft of the guesthouse wing of the SSJE monastery.

2. Matthew 17:1–9, Mark 9:3–8, Luke 9:28–36.

3. See Alfred Schutz (1967, 1970) and Nancy T. Ammerman (2014) for discussions on how people's worlds consist of multiple phenomenological, existential, and social realities, as in this case of simultaneous "blindness" and "knowing."

4. *Performative knowledge* is a term of my own invention, whereas *unknowing* and *unitive being* are terms I have adopted from the contemplative Christian lexicon. Contemplatives also use names like *unio mystica, divine indwelling, incarnation,* and *non-dual consciousness,* whereas anthropologists use terms like *communitas* and *phenomenological intersubjectivity.*

5. Pointing me to the work of Max Weber (1946), Professor Charles Lindholm suggested the metaphor of virtuosity for exceptional practitioners of Christian contemplation. Obeyesekere (2012) also used the term for visionaries and mystics in *The Awakened Ones: Phenomenology of Visionary Experience.* The idea of ritual being an art rather than a purely technical act comes up in Seligman and Weller's (2012) distinction between interpretation and notation. William James (2004[1902]) preferred the term "genius" for the extraordinarily adept. As for the less learned, James used a musical analogy for religion and claimed that those with too great a reliance on rationalistic thought had a "psychophysical deficiency, like being tone deaf" (quoted in Ghosh 2008: 246). Max Weber described himself as "religiously unmusical" in a 1909 letter (quoted in Svatos 1998: 548), and a century later, Jürgen Habermas said in an interview that he was religiously "tone deaf" (Habermas and Ratzinger 2005: 11).

6. William James (2004[1902]) saw social breaks and ruptures as potential situations where religious experience and transformations could emerge.

7. See Diagram 6 (back matter of this volume) of the Oratory's spatial configuration.

8. Scripture tells the story that these two women, one of them Mary Magdalene, were part of the small group that remained with Jesus during his crucifixion; they were also the two who went to Jesus' tomb to find it empty and were the first to meet him there as the risen Christ (e.g., Luke 24, John 20). The day's liturgies, quite different from the range of established forms of Episcopal Good Friday services, included an "entombment ceremony" modeled on the contemporary rites from a monastery at Vézelay, France, in which the altar cloth became a shroud that the women used to "entomb" the wooden cross, the subject of veneration by the assembly at a Vespers liturgy that took place at 7:30 p.m.

9. See images of the Easter Vigil at SSJE, including the lighting of the new fire, passing the light, and ringing in Easter, in the "Monastic High Liturgy" section under the heading, "Monastic Formal Rites and Contemplative Practices," in the Photograph Gallery. Diagram 2 shows the Guesthouse garden in relation to the monastic buildings and Diagram 3 shows the floorplan of the chapel (back matter of this volume).

10. Easter and Christmas are the only days at SSJE when speaking is permitted in the refectory at breakfast. This Easter service took place before the renovations

that put kitchen facilities and a dining room in the guesthouse, allowing guests to take breakfast there.

11. See Diagram 7 for the basic grid formation of the Gurdjieff Movements at the West Virginia Wisdom School. Find images of the Octagon and the Movements dance floor under "A Few Places" in the Photograph Gallery in the back matter of this volume.

12. See a South Korean performance of Sacred Dance Three on YouTube at http://www.youtube.com/watch?v=uhMi3sGTjso (posted by dhyanprafuler, accessed April 12, 2016).

13. See Taylor (1989, 2007), as well as McGinn (2012a: 209), for a history of late medieval Christian mystics' understanding of bodily sensations of "inner" and "outer" as an indicator of "a continuum of conscious and progressive reception of divine gifts."

14. Compare these perspectives on will to Mahmood's discussions on the relationship between submission and agency in *Politics of Piety* (2005). See also Murphy and Throop's *Toward an Anthropology of Will* (2010).

15. See Diagram 4, "Contemplative Transformation: Working toward Perceptual Agency through Knowing and Unknowing" (in back matter of this volume).

16. Csordas has worked to correct this oversight in more recent publications. See, for example, Csordas (2011).

17. I developed this term, "the porous self," from my efforts to describe the emanating and receptive quality that I observed and experienced in my ethnographic research with American contemplative Christians. Only well after the fact did I realize (with the helpful nudging of Professor Richard Topping) that Charles Taylor (2007) had used this very term for the condition of pre-Reformation Christian Europeans in his Templeton Prize–winning treatise, *A Secular Age*. Taylor's porous self seeks to describe medieval Europeans as people who experienced a self with open boundaries that allowed for an influx of spirits and demons. The Protestant Reformation prompted Calvinist individual discipline, reflexivity, and moral agency, wrote Taylor, from which rose the modern experience of self-sufficiency, lesser dependency on a concept of divine omnipotence, and a sense of personal boundedness, which he calls a "buffered self." Taylor follows Weber (1930) in viewing this transformation as the initiation of a centuries-long progression of world "disenchantment."

    In my research among twenty-first-century American contemplative Christians, the phenomenology of a porous self did not depend on medieval-style unquestioning belief, as illustrated in the preceding discussions about their intellectual reflexivity and doubt. Rather, porosity was an experiential condition that occurred in relation to an acceptance of ambiguity, an intentional openness to unknown possibilities, a recognition of the inadequacy of human knowledge, a focus on bodily sensation rather than emotion, and a commitment to disciplined ritualized practices. The intersubjectivity that arises between these contemplative practitioners and other entities depends on a fluid conceptual and experiential relationship between inner and outer, the historical development of which Taylor (1989) elucidates in *Sources of the Self.*

The variety of a porous self that I describe among Christian moderns, therefore, exists alongside critical reflection and notions of inwardness, not despite them. These qualities coexist. In effect, contemporary contemplatives' devotion to practice and study (whether or not they experience feelings of doubt) was their method of training the self to allow for porosity, also called "intimacy with the divine," even when cultural norms encouraged an experience of a self-contained or "buffered" self.

18. Gratitude to Nancy T. Ammerman, Thomas Digby, Harry O. Maier, and Robert Weller (against his better judgment) for discussions that helped me refine this mathematical representation (a kind of visual poetry, really) of phenomenological intersubjectivity in contemplative societies. See Appendix, "Formula for Phenomenological Intersubjectivity among American Contemplative Christians."

19. This formula of epistemological interplay has some resonance with Jon Bialecki's (2012) concept of the "virtual," in which he explores the role of relational, overarching categories. Bialecki rethinks anthropology's reluctance to consider universals in favor of specificities by using Gilles Deleuze's *Difference and Repetition* (1994). Importantly, he emphasizes that his categories are not immutable "essences" but rather are historical, flexible "potentialities" that people transform into "actualities" through play and fusion. The plasticity of my three knowledge categories has some similarity to the "torsion" and "mutability of the idea" in Bialecki's formulation, especially in how these "virtual" elements are transformed through relational processes, resulting in "gradations of difference" in how people actually enact varieties of knowledge.

20. Durkheim (2001); Turner (1969); Csordas (1990); Rappaport (1999); Weiss (1999); Obeysekere (2012).

21. Charles Keil and Steven Feld are the founding scholars of "groove theory." See their seminal *Music Grooves* (Keil and Feld 1994).

22. See particularly expressive examples in the letters and visionary literature of Hadewijch of Brabant (in Petroff 1986: 189–200) and the illuminations and sacred music of Hildegard von Bingen (e.g., Hildegard 1994, 1996; Bobko, Fox, and Newman 1995; Fox 1985).

23. Mary Oliver, incidentally, has addressed congregations at the Society of Saint John the Evangelist and composed a poem for SSJE's capital campaign to help fund renovations of the monastery. It described the Brothers' "attention" in "their patterned hours of devotion and in their gifts to this nearly broken world." The poem was published in *Stone and Light* (SSJE 2010: 53).

24. See Mattijs van de Port's *Ecstatic Encounters* (2011) for an example of another ethnographer's method of full entry into a ritualized environment as a way to

understand its inner workings, and his attempts to describe them in scholarly narrative form.

25. See also Rich (2001), an anthropologist's interview with Ken Wilber on his concepts about the transformation of consciousness.

26. See the conversation on a YouTube video, "Spiritual, but Not Religious?" uploaded by Wilber's Integral Institute at https://m.youtube.com/watch?v=o4gdsFt_zDY (particularly minutes 12:00–15:30).

27. In Spanish, "Buscate en Mí, buscame en tí" (Panikkar 2004: 29–31).

28. See also Lester's "The Immediacy of Eternity: Time and Transformation in a Roman Catholic Convent" (2003). The Communion of Saints, whether living or dead, is based on the idea of Paul's "Body of Christ" in which all members of "the Church" are in mystical relationship (1 Corinthians 12). Benko (1964) offers a history of the development of the idea of *sanctorum communio*, or the Communion of Saints. Handman (2014) applies the term to colonial power relations in Lutheran Christian missions of Papua New Guinea.

CHAPTER 8

1. Just a few of the titles in the anthropological literature on religious pilgrimage include Badone and Roseman (2004), Coleman (2000, 2002, 2014), Coleman and Eade (2004), Dubisch (1995), Dubisch and Winkelman (2005), Eade, Katić, and Belaj (2014), Eade and Sallnow (1991), Margry (2008), Morinis (1992), Naletova (2010), Neville (1987), and Sallnow (1981). Relevant to the intention of this chapter's ethnographic narrative of journey, Coleman and Elsner (2003) also focus on the importance (and problems) of narrative in the explication of pilgrimage.

2. Four years after Clare died in 1253, the nuns of the San Damiano convent took refuge within the city walls of Assisi because of warfare and raiding between Umbrian hilltowns. They took the original eleventh-century crucifix with them, and it now hangs in the basilica of Santa Chiara in Assisi, the construction of which began in 1257 (Celano 1953). Though a later medieval reproduction of the eleventh-century original, the crucifix above San Damiano's altar has nevertheless captured the attention of pilgrims for centuries. When Lynn Bauman (1989) adapted the Anglican Rosary from Roman Catholic and Eastern Orthodox prayer beads almost thirty years ago, he chose a replica of the San Damiano cross to be its crucifix. The Anglican Rosary is now used by people in countries around the world.

3. Social studies on the relationship between religion and pain abound, starting with the classic work of William James (2004 [1902]). Norris (2009) has written an excellent overview article that contrasts biomedical understandings of pain as something to be avoided with cross-cultural understandings of pain and suffering as meaningful and even valuable, particularly for spiritual transformations. More specific to this ethnographic context, Corwin (2012) described how after

Vatican II, prayer in an American Roman Catholic Franciscan convent changed toward more "embodied" practices that fostered greater feelings of intimacy with the divine and transformed experiences of aging and pain. (Thanks to Charles Lindholm for drawing my attention to the two foregoing sources). See also *Pain and Its Transformations: The Interface of Biology and Culture* (Coakley and Kaufman Shelemay 2007) for cross-cultural and historical comparisons of the relationship of pain and religious experience, including Sarah Coakley's discussion on pain and transformation among sixteenth-century Carmelite monastics.

4. The spring that Helen and I were in Assisi was the 800th anniversary of Clare running away from her family after Palm Sunday services to join Francis and his mendicant band. When Clare arrived at the little church, Porziuncola, where the mendicants dwelled in the plain below Assisi, Francis sheared her head, just as he did for the young men who would become his friars. He then secured Clare refuge from her family at a nearby convent until he was able to set up a convent of her own at San Damiano (Celano 1953, 1963). In celebration of the anniversary, the Franciscans placed on the altar of Porziuncola a glass vessel containing the relic of what is purported to be Clare's blonde hair from that ceremonial act of surrender 800 years ago.

5. Matthew 4:4.

6. Quotations from this anointing ceremony were taken from a video of the event, the recording of which Helen Daly had requested so that it could become a teaching tool for other students of contemplation.

7. The hymn, *Sleepers Wake*, is based on the parable of the Ten Maidens (Matthew 25:1–13). Music: *Wachet Auf* by Hans Sachs (1494–1576), adapted by Philipp Nicolai (1556–1608), arranged and harmonized by Johann Sebastian Bach (1685–1750); words by Philipp Nicolai, translated by Carl P. Daw, Jr. (b. 1944)—who is, incidently, a congregant at the Society of Saint John the Evangelist and a professor of Hymnology and Curator of the Hymnological Collections at Boston University's School of Theology.

8. 1 Corinthians 12:12–14.

9. Posted July 12, 2014 on the Facebook page of the Society of Saint John the Evangelist.

Glossary

acedia Religious or spiritual apathy.

adab An Arabic word referring to Islamic etiquette and moral behavior.

ambo A lectern from which scripture is read in a church.

anatheism A term coined by Richard Kearney (2010) for an understanding of the divine that has been modified by interaction with pluralistic forces, especially multiple cultural understandings of God and atheism; literally, "god after god."

Angelus A Roman Catholic prayer of devotion to the Virgin Mary, which recounts the Annunciation (Mary's encounter with Archangel Gabriel; Luke 1:26–38). Initiated in medieval Europe, it was practiced three times daily by both monastics and non-monastics.

antechapel The outer area of the chapel between the portico and the choir; also called the nave.

anthem A musical setting of scripture or other religious text sung by a choral ensemble during church liturgies.

antiphon A spoken or sung response set within a larger piece, such as a repeated phrase set between psalm verses. Antiphonal music is created when two choirs sing alternating verses or passages.

apophasis Ambiguous contemplative aspects of ritual and prayer that foster "being-ness," "nothingness," and "openness to the divine."

baldacchino A ceremonial canopy over an altar, usually made of stone or metal.

bodhisattva A Sanskrit term from Mahayana Buddhism referring to an enlightened person who, for reasons of compassion, works to relieve the suffering of sentient beings and encourage collective "awakening" on earth rather than retreat to nirvana.

Bridal Mysticism A passionate relationship between humanity and the divine typified in the nuptial language of the Hebrew Bible's Song of Songs. Christians have allegorized the two lovers in the text as Christ and either the church or the Christian individual. Also called Love Mysticism.

breviary A book that outlines the services of the Daily Office in churches and monasteries.

canticle A passage of scripture, usually sung, that is a set part of a liturgy, such as the Nunc Dimittis and the Magnificat; also, another name for the Hebrew Bible's Song of Songs.

cantor A choral leader who initiates musical passages in liturgies, which the schola or congregation then join.

cataphasis Active aspects of ritual and prayer, including physical movement, vocalization, and thought.

cell The small room in a monastery or convent where an individual monk or nun sleeps, studies, and prays in seclusion.

censer A container, usually metal, in which incense is burned during Christian liturgies; also called a thurible.

Centering Prayer A Christian form of meditation using a sacred word, not continuously but only when one is distracted; developed by American Trappist monks based on scripture, monastic practices, and inter-religious techniques.

choir The part of the church between the antechapel and the sanctuary and altar; in monastic chapels, often enclosed or restricted to outsiders.

choir stall One in a series of fixed seats for ritual participants lining the sides of the choir of a church, often including choir desks for holding music and liturgical books.

clerestory windows A collection of windows, often of stained glass, in the upper story of the nave or choir.

cloister A monastic enclosure; originally referring to cloister walks, or the covered walkways within a monastic compound.

Clothing ceremony The monastic ceremony at which a postulant receives the monastic habit, thus becoming a novice, after which he or she studies and prays in preparation for taking initial monastic vows.

collect A short prayer passage to gather the congregation.

Counter-Reformation A sixteenth- and seventeenth-century Roman Catholic revitalization and resistance movement initiated in response to the Protestant Reformation.

crucifix A ritual object representing Jesus being crucified on a cross.

Daily Office A daily group rhythm of prayer and work in monasteries, including multiple liturgies at set hours and usually a daily Eucharist service; also called the Divine Office and the Canonical Hours.

EHoP Episcopal House of Prayer

Eucharist The ritual consecration and consumption of bread and wine in commemoration of Maundy Thursday's Last Supper; also called Holy Communion.

fair linen Uppermost ceremonial cloth on an altar, usually white.

gate The locked entrance way in the grille between the antechapel and chapel, separating public and private spaces in monasteries.

Great Silence The daily period of silence observed between the final evening and first morning liturgies in many monastic orders.

grille An architectural screen, often of metal, between the antechapel and the inner chapel which segregates public and monastic space; also called a rood screen.

habit The garment worn by a member of a religious order.

habitus A term introduced by Marcel Mauss and elaborated by Pierre Bourdieu meaning cultural ways of being, doing, and thinking that are so much beneath conscious thought that people do not acknowledge them, but instead assume them to be "natural."

icon A devotional representation, often a painting of a religious figure, used particularly in Eastern Orthodox Christian traditions.

intercession, intercessory prayer Prayer on behalf of another person.

kenosis A Greek word referring to a contemplative form of prayer meaning "self-emptying" or "letting go," derived from Paul's letter to the Philippians (2:5–8); along with "consent to the divine," it is a foundational principle of Centering Prayer.

Lady Chapel A colloquial name for a chapel dedicated to Mary, the mother of Jesus.

lectio divina A prayer practice originating among early Christian desert monastics in which one reads and contemplates short passages of scripture by setting aside the analytical mind.

Magnificat An ancient canticle derived from the words of Mary as written in the Gospel of Luke (1:46–55); an important element in Marian Christianity and evening liturgies in Western Christian monasteries.

monastic A person living inside a monastery or convent who has taken religious vows or who intends to take religious vows.

monastic enclosure An enclosed space in which monastics live, work, and pray; a cloister.

narthex A vestibule or enclosed porch at the entrance to a church or chapel; also called a portico.

non-gathered community A term coined by Nancy T. Ammerman for members of a movement who do not live in geographic proximity to one another.

non-mensurable chant A variety of chant with no set time signature, the pulse of which rises out of singers' communal feel for the text's rhythm.

non-monastic A person living outside of a monastery or convent.

novice A person who has entered a monastic community with the intention of becoming a full member by training and eventually taking monastic vows.

Nunc Dimittis The canticle or sung scriptural passage called The Song of Simeon (Luke 2:29–32), which concludes the night office of Compline.

oblate A person who has made a commitment to a religious order but who usually lives outside of the monastery and has not taken full vows; sometimes called a member of a Third Order.

OCD Order of the Discalced Carmelites, a reformed version of the Roman Catholic Order of Carmelites (O.Carm.), founded by Teresa of Ávila in the sixteenth century.

OCSO The Order of Cistercians of the Strict Observance, a Roman Catholic order of cloistered contemplative monks or nuns called Trappists or Trappistines after the French monastery, La Grande Trappe, which led a reform movement of its mother order, the Cistercians, in the seventeenth century.

OFM The Order of Friars Minor, also called the Franciscans, a Roman Catholic mendicant order founded by St. Francis of Assisi in the early thirteenth century.

ora et labora Latin for "prayer and work," the foundational principles of Benedictine monasticism.

oratory A small consecrated space usually for private devotions.

OSB Order of Saint Benedict, a Roman Catholic monastic order founded by Benedict of Nursia, ca. 529.

Paschal candle A large pillar candle used ceremonially during the liturgical season of Easter and during prominent rites at other times, such as baptisms.

paten A ceremonial plate used to hold the bread during the Eucharist.

plainsong Religious chant in unison using a pulse based on textual rhythm, originating in the early medieval Christian church; sometimes called Gregorian chant.

portico A vestibule or enclosed porch at the entrance to a church or chapel; also called a narthex.

postulant A person at the initial level of candidacy and discernment of a monastic profession.

refectory A communal dining hall in a monastery.

reredos An ornamental screen or decoration behind a church altar, usually with religious images.

rule of life (or rule) A written treatise that encapsulates a monastic order's ideals and intentions, as well as outlines practical aspects of communal life and individual responsibilities; recently, also an individual statement of ideals and intentions.

sacristy Chambers in a church located off the sanctuary in which ritual officiants prepare for liturgy and store liturgical items.

sanctuary The consecrated part of a church where the altar resides; also called the chancel.

sanctuary lamp A candle or oil lantern in the sanctuary that remains lit to represent the presence of the divine in the reserved sacrament (consecrated bread).

scapular A monastic garment consisting of a long rectangle of cloth with an opening for the head, suspended from the shoulders and worn over the habit.

schola Latin for a group of choristers in a monastery or cathedral; shortened version of *schola cantorum* (literally, "singing school").

sohbet A contemplative form of instructive conversation between student and teacher in Sufism which is said to transmit spiritual knowledge.

SSJE The Society of Saint John the Evangelist, a Christian monastic community for men founded at Oxford, England, in 1866 by the Reverend Richard Meux Benson, and the first Anglican (Episcopalian) religious order to emerge after the sixteenth-century English Reformation. The house in Boston was established in 1870.

statio A prayer practice in which one stops, reflects, and reorients oneself toward the divine, especially by renewing and enacting chosen intentions and guiding principles; in architecture, the vestibule in which a ritual officiant collects him- or herself before entering the sanctuary.

stoup A basin of consecrated water near the door of a church into which people dip their fingers and cross themselves upon entry and exit.

tabernacle A receptacle for the reserved sacrament (consecrated bread), usually on or near an altar.

Taizé An ecumenical Christian monastic men's community founded in the 1940s at Taizé, France; also, the simple harmonic chants and contemplative liturgies inspired by that community.

Third Order A non-monastic order of lay adherents in association with a monastic order, often having a modified rule of life and simple vows.

thurifer The acolyte who carries the censer of burning incense during a liturgy.

tonglen A Tibetan Buddhist meditation practice that acts as intercessory prayer, in which one envisions breathing in the world's suffering and breathing out peace and compassion; literally "giving and taking."

Triduum The three-day liturgy during Holy Week (the week leading up to Easter), including Maundy Thursday, Good Friday, Holy Saturday, ending on Easter Sunday.

tympanum In architecture, a decorated space over a doorway between the lintel and the arch.

undercroft The crypt or understory of a church.

versicle A short sentence spoken or sung by a liturgical officiant to which the congregation responds.

votive Something offered in fulfillment of a vow.

zendo The meditation hall of a Zen Buddhist monastery.

Bibliography

Achino-Loeb, Maria-Luisa, ed.
2006. *Silence: The Currency of Power.* New York: Berghahn Books.
Almquist, Curtis, SSJE.
2011. "Poetic Splendor in Color and Light." Orin E. Skinner Annual Lecture. The
Dr. Charles J. Connick Foundation. Boston. November 13, 2011. [http://ssje.org/
ssje/2011/11/13/poetic-splendor-in-color-and-light-the-connick-foundations-
orin-e-skinner-annual-lecture-br-curtis-almquist/, accessed April 7, 2013].
2012. "Living Gratefully: A Posture and a Practice." Sermon. Cambridge: Society of
Saint John the Evangelist. August 15, 2012. [http://ssje.org/ssje/2012/08/15/
living-gratefully-a-posture-and-a-practice/, accessed April 7, 2013].
2013. "Children of God." *Praying Our Lives* video series. February 16, 2013.
Cambridge: Society of Saint John the Evangelist. [http://ssje.org/word/?p=4411,
accessed May 20, 2013].
2014a. "Invitation: Identity." *Love Life* video series. March 19, 2014. Cambridge:
Society of Saint John the Evangelist. [http://ssje.org/ssje/2014/03/19/love-life-
identity/, accessed April 14, 2014].
2014b. "Vocation: Belonging." *Love Life* video series. April 7, 2014. Cambridge: Society
of Saint John the Evangelist. [http://ssje.org/ssje/2014/04/07/love-life-belonging,
accessed April 14, 2014].
Ammerman, Nancy Tatom.
1987. *Bible Believers: Fundamentalists in the Modern World.* New Brunswick,
NJ: Rutgers University Press.
2013. "Spiritual but Not Religious? Beyond Binary Choices in the Study of Religion."
Journal for the Scientific Study of Religion. 52(2): 258–278.
2014. *Sacred Stories, Spiritual Tribes: Finding Religion in Everyday Life.* Oxford: Oxford
University Press.

Ammerman, Nancy Tatom, ed.

2007. *Everyday Religion: Observing Modern Religious Lives.* Oxford: Oxford University Press.

Anderson, Benedict.

1983. *Imagined Communities: Reflections on the Origin and Spread of Nationalism.* London: Verso.

Anglican Church of Canada.

1959. *Book of Common Prayer.* Toronto: Anglican Book Centre.

1985. *The Book of Alternative Services.* Toronto: Anglican Book Centre.

Anonymous.

1961 [mid-14th c.]. *The Cloud of Unknowing and Other Works.* Clifton Wolters, trans. London: Penguin.

Arico, Carl.

1999. *A Taste of Silence: A Guide to the Fundamentals of Centering Prayer.* New York: Continuum.

2013. "Are We Taking Ourselves Too Seriously?" *Contemplative Outreach News.* December. 30(1): 6–8.

Asad, Talal.

1993a. "The Construction of Religion as an Anthropological Category." In Asad, *Genealogies of Religion: Discipline and Reasons of Power in Christianity and Islam,* pp. 27–54. Baltimore, MD: John Hopkins University Press.

1993b. "On Discipline and Humility in Medieval Christian Monasticism." In Asad, *Genealogies of Religion: Discipline and Reasons of Power in Christianity and Islam,* pp. 125–167. Baltimore, MD: John Hopkins University Press.

Audisio, Gabriel.

1999. *The Waldensian Dissent: Persecution and Survival, c. 1170–c. 1570.* Cambridge: Cambridge University Press.

Austin, J. L.

1962. *How to Do Things with Words.* Cambridge, MA: Harvard University Press.

Badone, Ellen, and Sharon R. Roseman, eds.

2004. *Intersecting Journeys: The Anthropology of Pilgrimage and Tourism.* Urbana: University of Illinois Press.

Bandak, Andreas.

2014. "Of Refrains and Rhythms in Contemporary Damascus: Urban Space and Christian-Muslim Coexistence." *Current Anthropology.* 55(10): S248–S261.

Barker, John.

1993. "'We Are *Ekelesia*': Conversion in Uiaku, Papua New Guinea." In *Christian Conversion: Historical and Anthropological Perspectives on a Great Transformation,* Robert Hefner, ed., pp. 199–230. Berkeley: University of California Press.

2012. "The Politics of Christianity in Papua New Guinea." In *Christian Politics in Oceania,* M. Tomlinson and D. McDougall, eds., pp. 146–170. Oxford: Berghahn.

2014. "The One and the Many: Church-Centered Innovations in a Papua New Guinean Community." *Current Anthropology*. 55(S 10): S172–S181.

Barry, William A., and William J. Connolly.

1982. *The Practice of Spiritual Direction*. New York: HarperCollins.

Barth, Fredrik.

1993. *Balinese Worlds*. Chicago: University of Chicago Press.

2002. "Sidney W. Mintz Lecture for 2000: An Anthropology of Knowledge." *Current Anthropology*. 43(1): 1–18.

Basso, Keith.

1972. "'To Give Up on Words': Silence in Western Apache Culture." In *Language and Social Context*, Pier Paolo Giuglioli, ed., pp. 67–86. New York: Penguin.

Bates, Stephen.

2004. *A Church at War: Anglicans and Homosexuality*. London: I. B. Tauris.

Bauman, Lynn C.

nd. *Songs of Presence: Contemplative Chants for the New Millennium*. (CD and booklet). Telephone, TX: Praxis.

1989. *The Anglican Rosary*. Telephone, TX: Praxis.

2003. *The Gospel of Thomas: Wisdom of the Twin*. Ashland, OR: White Cloud Press.

2008. *Ancient Songs Sung Anew: The Psalms as Poetry*. Telephone, TX: Praxis.

Bauman, Lynn C., Ward J. Bauman, and Cynthia Bourgeault.

2008. *The Luminous Gospels: Thomas, Mary Magdalene, and Philip*. Telephone, TX: Praxis.

Bauman, Ward.

nd. *The Anglican Rosary: Meditation with the Mystics*. Collegeville, MN: Episcopal House of Prayer.

2013a. "Newsletter." June 2013. Collegeville, MN: Episcopal House of Prayer.

2013b. "Newsletter." July 2013. Collegeville, MN: Episcopal House of Prayer.

Baumann, Gerd.

1996. *Contesting Culture: Discourses of Identity in Multi-Ethnic London*. Cambridge: Cambridge University Press.

Bedford, Ian.

2015. "Unmeasured Music and Silence." In *Phenomenology in Anthropology: A Sense of Perspective*, K. Ram and C. Houston, eds., pp. 138–149. Bloomington: Indiana University Press.

Bell, Catherine.

1992. *Ritual Theory, Ritual Practice*. Oxford: Oxford University Press.

Bellah, Robert.

1985. *Habits of the Heart: Individualism and Commitment in American Life*. Berkeley: University of California Press.

Benedict of Nursia.

2011 [6th c.]. *The Rule of Saint Benedict*. Cambridge, MA: Harvard University Press.

Benko, Stephen.

1964. *The Meaning of* Sanctorum Communio. Naperfille, IL: A. R. Allenson.

Bennett, J. G.

2007. *Witness: The Story of a Search*. Santa Fe, NM: Bennett Books.

Berger, Peter L.

1967. *The Sacred Canopy: Elements of a Sociological Theory of Religion*. New York: Anchor Books.

1999. *The Desecularization of the World: Resurgent Religion and World Politics*. Grand Rapids, MI: Eerdmans.

Best, Mary Ann.

2005. "Attention/Intention." *The Contemplative Life Program Forty-Day Practice*. Butler, NJ: Contemplative Outreach.

2006a. "Discipline of Prayer." *The Contemplative Life Program Forty-Day Practice*. Butler, NJ: Contemplative Outreach.

2006b. "Silence and Solitude." *The Contemplative Life Program Forty-Day Practice*. Butler, NJ: Contemplative Outreach.

Bialecki, Jon.

2012. "Virtual Christianity in an Age of Nominalist Anthropology." *Anthropological Theory*. 12: 295–319.

2014. "After the Denominozoic: Evolution, Differentiation, Denominationalism." *Current Anthropology*. 55(S 10): S193–S204.

Bialecki, Jon, Naomi Haynes, and Joel Robbins.

2008. "The Anthropology of Christianity." *Religion Compass*. 2: 1139–1158.

Bielo, James.

2011. *Emerging Evangelicals: Faith, Modernity, and the Desire for Authenticy*. New York: New York University Press.

Biernacki, Loriliai, and Philip Clayton.

2014. *Panentheism across the World's Traditions*. Oxford: Oxford University Press.

Blum, David.

1986. *The Art of Quartet Playing: The Guarneri Quartet in Conversation*. New York: Knopf.

Bobko, Jane, Matthew Fox, and Barbara Newman.

1995. *Vision: The Life and Music of Hildegard von Bingen*. New York: Penguin Studio.

Bolden, Tony.

2013. "Groove Theory: A Vamp on the Epistemology of Funk." *American Studies*. 52(4): 9–34.

Boros, Ladislaus.

1965. *The Mystery of Death*. New York: Herder and Herder.

Bourdieu, Pierre.

1977. *Outline of a Theory of Practice*. Cambridge: Cambridge University Press.

1991. *Language and Symbolic Power*. Cambridge: Polity.

Bourgeault, Cynthia.

nd. "FAQ's about Wisdom and Wisdom School." Victoria: The Contemplative Society. [www.contempative.org/pdfs/Wisdom_School_FAQ.pdf, accessed September 15, 2013].

2003. *The Wisdom Way of Knowing: Reclaiming an Ancient Tradition to Awaken the Heart*. San Francisco: Jossey-Bass.

2004. *Centering Prayer and Inner Awakening*. Cambridge, MA: Cowley.

2006. *Chanting the Psalms*. Boston: New Seeds.

2008. *The Wisdom Jesus: Transforming Heart and Mind—A New Perspective on Christ and His Message*. Boston: Shambhala.

2010a. "Centering Prayer and Witnessing Presence." *Sewanee Theological Review*. 53(3): 261–273.

2010b. *The Meaning of Mary Magdalene: Discovering the Woman at the Heart of Christianity*. Boston: Shambhala.

2011. "Introduction." In *Holy Week Liturgies from the Episcopal House of Prayer*, pp. 5–15. Collegeville, MN: Episcopal House of Prayer.

2013. *The Holy Trinity and the Law of Three: Discovering the Radical Truth at the Heart of Christianity*. Boston: Shambhala.

2016. *The Heart of Centering Prayer: Christian Nonduality in Theory and Practice*. Boston: Shambhala.

Bourgeault, Cynthia, Ward Bauman, and Darlene Franz.

2011. *Holy Week Liturgies from the Episcopal House of Prayer*. Collegeville, MN: Episcopal House of Prayer.

Bouyer, Louis.

1980. "Mysticism: An Essay on the History of the Word." In *Understanding Mysticism*, Richard Woods, ed., pp. 42–55. Garden City, NJ: Image Books.

Brittain, Christopher Craig, and Andrew McKinnon.

2011. "Homosexuality and the Construction of 'Anglican Orthodoxy': The Symbolic Politics of the Anglican Communion." *Sociology of Religion*. 72(3): 351–373.

Brock, Ann Graham.

2003. *Mary Magdalene, the First Apostle: The Struggle for Authority*. Cambridge, MA: Harvard University Press.

Brook, Peter.

1968. *The Empty Space*. New York: Atheneum.

Bruce, Scott G.

2007. *Silence and Sign Languages in Medieval Monasticism, the Cluniac Tradition c. 900–1200*. Cambridge: Cambridge University Press.

Bucko, Raymond A.

1998. *The Lakota Ritual of the Sweat Lodge: History and Contemporary Practice*. Lincoln: University of Nebraska Press.

Buckser, Andrew, and Stephen D. Glazier.

2003. *The Anthropology of Religious Conversion*. Lanham, MD: Rowman and Littlefield.

Cage, John.

1961. *Silence*. Middletown, CT: Wesleyan University Press.

Cannell, Fenella.

2005. "The Christianity of Anthropology." *Journal of the Royal Anthropological Institute*. 11(2): 335–356.

Cannell, Fenella, ed.

2006. *The Anthropology of Christianity.* Durham, NC: Duke University Press.

Carey, A.

1967. "The Hawthorne Studies: A Radical Criticism." *American Sociological Review.* 32: 403–416.

Casanova, José.

1994. *Public Religions in the Modern World.* Chicago: University of Chicago Press.

Casey, Michael.

2014. *Seventy-four Tools for Good Living: Reflections on the Fourth Chapter of Benedict's Rule.* Collegeville, MN: Liturgical Press.

Caussade, Jean-Pierre de.

1975 [ca. 1740]. *Abandonment to Divine Providence.* New York: Doubleday Image.

Celano, Thomas of.

1953 [1257]. *The Legend and Writings of Saint Clare of Assisi.* St. Bonaventure, NY: Franciscan Institute.

1963 [1228/ca.1244]. *St. Francis of Assisi: First and Second Life of St. Francis, with Selections from Treatise on the Miracles of Blessed Francis.* Chicago: Franciscan Herald Press.

Chadwick, Henry.

1993. *The Early Church.* Penguin History of the Church. Volume 1. London: Penguin.

Chadwick, Owen.

1972. *The Reformation.* Penguin History of the Church. Volume 3. Hammondsworth, UK: Penguin.

Cheetham, David, Douglas Pratt, and David Thomas, eds.

2013. *Understanding Interreligious Relations.* Oxford: Oxford University Press.

Chiesa, Mecca, and Sandy Hobbs.

2008. "Making Sense of Social Research: How Useful Is the Hawthorne Effect?" *European Journal of Social Psychology.* 38(1): 67–74.

Chilton, Bruce.

2005. *Mary Magdalene: A Biography.* New York: Doubleday.

Chittister, Joan, OSB.

1991. *Wisdom Distilled from the Daily: Living the Rule of St. Benedict Today.* San Francisco: Harper Collins.

2009. *The Liturgical Year: The Spiraling Adventure of the Spiritual Life.* Nashville, TN: Thomas Nelson.

2010. *The Rule of St. Benedict: A Spirituality for the 21st Century.* New York: Crossroad.

Classen, Constance.

1997. "Foundations for an Anthropology of the Senses." *International Social Science Journal.* 49(153): 401–412.

Claussen, Heather L.

2001. *Unconventional Sisterhood: Feminist Catholic Nuns in the Philippines.* Ann Arbor: University of Michigan Press.

Clifford, James.

1986. "On Ethnographic Allegory." In *Writing Culture: The Poetics and Politics of Ethnography*, James Clifford and George E. Marcus, eds., pp. 98–121. Berkeley: University of California Press.

Clifford, James, and George E. Marcus, eds.

1986. *Writing Culture: The Poetics and Politics of Ethnography*. Berkeley: University of California Press.

Coakley, Sarah.

2004. "Jail Break: Meditation as Subversive Activity." *Christian Century*. 121(13): 18–21.

2007. "Palliative or Intensification? Pain and Christian Contemplation in the Spirituality of the Sixteenth-Century Carmelites." In *Pain and Its Transformations: The Interface of Biology and Culture*, Sarah Coakley and Kay Kaufman Shelemay, eds., pp 77–100. Cambridge, MA: Harvard University Press.

Coakley, Sarah, and Kay Kaufman Shelemay, eds.

2007. *Pain and Its Transformations: The Interface of Biology and Culture*. Cambridge, MA: Harvard University Press.

Coats, Jamie.

2014. "A Daily Word—Using the Internet to Help People Pray Every Day." *Trinity News*. 61(2): 21–22.

Coleman, Simon.

2000. *The Globalisation of Charismatic Christianity: Spreading the Gospel of Prosperity*. Cambridge: Cambridge University Press.

2002. "Do You Believe in Pilgrimage? Communitas, Contestation, and Beyond." *Anthropological Theory*. 2(3): 355–368.

Coleman, Simon, and John Eade, eds.

2004. *Reframing Pilgrimage: Cultures in Motion*. London: Routledge.

Coleman, Simon, and John Elsner.

2003. *Pilgrim Voices: Narrative and Authorship in Christian Pilgrimage*. New York: Berghahn Books.

Coleman, Simon, and Rosalind I. J. Hackett, eds.

2015. *The Anthropology of Global Pentecostalism and Evangelicalism*. New York: New York University Press.

Collins, Fletcher, Jr.

1980. "The Home of the Fleury Playbook." *Comparative Drama*. 14(4): 312–320.

Comaroff, John.

2010. "The End of Anthropology, Again: On the Furture of the In/discipline." *American Anthropologist*. 112(4): 524–538.

Comaroff, John, and Jean Comaroff.

1991. *Of Revelation and Revolution: Christianity, Colonialism, and Consciousness in South Africa*. Chicago: University of Cahicago Press.

Connerton, Paul.

1989. *How Societies Remember*. Cambridge: Cambridge University Press.

Contemplative Outreach.

2009. *The Welcoming Prayer.* Pamphlet. Butler, NJ: Contemplative Outreach.

Corwin, Anna I.

2012. "Changing God, Changing Bodies: The Impact of New Prayer Practices on Elderly Catholic Nuns' Embodied Experience." *Ethos.* 40(4): 390–410.

Coulston, Rob.

2012. "We Meet God in Many Ways: Praying the Daily Office." *Cowley.* 39(1): 24–26.

Csikszentmihalyi, Mihaly.

1975. "Play and Intrinsic Rewards." *Journal of Humanistic Psychology.* 15: 41–63.

1997. *Creativity: Flow and the Psychology of Discovery and Invention.* New York: Harper Perennial.

Csordas, Thomas.

1990. "Embodiment as a Paradigm for Anthropology." *Ethos.* 18: 5–47.

2011. "Embodiment: Agency, Sexual Difference, and Illness." In *Companion to Anthropology of the Body and Embodiment*, Frances E. Mascia-Lees, ed., pp. 137–156. Chichester, UK: Wiley-Blackwell.

Dailey, Patricia.

2012. "The Body and Its Senses." In *The Cambridge Companion to Christian Mysticism*, Amy Hollywood and Patricia Z. Beckman, eds., pp. 264–276. Cambridge: Cambridge University Press.

Deleuze, Gilles.

1994. *Difference and Repetition.* New York: Columbia University Press.

Delio, Ilia, ed.

2014. *From Teilhard to Omega: Co-creating an Unfinished Universe.* Maryknoll, NY: Orbis.

de Mello, Anthony, SJ.

1990. *Awareness: The Perils and Opportunities of Reality.* New York: Crown.

Desjarlais, Robert.

2011. *Counterplay: An Anthropologist at the Chessboard.* Berkeley: University of California Press.

Desjarlais, Robert, and C. Jason Throop.

2011. "Phenomenological Approaches in Anthropology." *Annual Review of Anthropology.* 40: 87–102.

Donahue, Thomas.

2005. *A Guide to Musical Temperament.* Lanham, MD: Scarecrow Press.

Dreher, John D.

1997. "The Danger of Centering Prayer." *This Rock.* 8(11): 13–16.

Dubisch, Jill.

1995. *In a Different Place: Pilgrimage, Gender, and Politics at a Greek Island Shrine.* Princeton, NJ: Princeton University Press.

Dubisch, Jill, and Michael Winkelman, eds.

2005. *Pilgrimage and Healing.* Tucson: University of Arizona Press.

Duranti, Alessandro.

2011. "Ethnopragmatics and Beyond: Intentionality and Agency across Languages and Cultures." In *Hybrids, Differences, Visions: On the Study of Culture*, C. Baraldi, A. Borsari, and Augusto Carli, eds., pp. 151–168. Aurora, CO: Davies.

Durkheim, Emile.

2001 [1912]. *Elementary Forms of Religious Life*. Oxford: Oxford University Press.

Eade, John, Mario Katić, and Marijana Belaj, eds.

2014. *Pilgrimage, Politics, and Place-Making in Eastern Europe: Crossing the Borders*. Burlington, VT: Ashgate.

Eade, John, and Michael Sallnow, eds.

1991. *Contesting the Sacred: the Anthropology of Christian Pilgrimage*. London: Routledge.

Ebaugh, Helen Rose Fuchs.

1993. *Women in the Vanishing Cloister: Organizational Decline in Catholic Religious Orders in the United States*. New Brunswick, NJ: Rutgers University Press.

Ehrman, Bart D.

2003. *Lost Christianities: The Battles for Scripture and the Faiths We Never Knew*. Oxford: Oxford University Press.

Elisha, Omri.

2011. *Moral Ambition: Mobilization and Social Outreach in Evangelical Megachurches*. Berkeley: University of California Press.

Elliot, Alice.

2016. "The Makeup of Destiny: Predestination and the Labor of Hope in a Moroccan Emigrant Town." *American Ethnologist*. 43(3): 488–499.

Elliott, Dyan.

2012. "*Raptus*/Rapture." In *The Cambridge Companion to Christian Mysticism*, Amy Hollywood and Patricia Z. Beckman, eds., pp. 189–199. Cambridge: Cambridge University Press.

Engelke, Matthew.

2007. *A Problem of Presence: Beyond Scripture in an African Church*. Berkeley: University of California Press.

2012. "Angels in Swindon: Public Religion and Ambient Faith in England." *American Ethnologist*. 39(1): 155–170.

2013. *God's Agents: Biblical Publicity in Contemporary England*. Berkeley: University of California Press.

Engelke, Matthew, and Joel Robbins, eds.

2010. *Global Christianity, Global Critique*. Special Issue. South Atlantic Quarterly. 81(2).

Episcopal Church.

1979. *The Book of Common Prayer*. New York: Church Hymnal.

1982. *The Hymnal*. New York: Church Publishing.

2004. *The Book of Occasional Services*. New York: Church Hymnal.

Evans, G. R.

2003. *A Brief History of Heresy*. Oxford: Blackwell.

Fabian, Johannes.

2012. "Cultural Anthropology and the Question of Knowledge." *Journal of the Royal Anthropological Institute*. 18: 439–453.

Fanning, Steven.

2001. *Mystics of the Christian Tradition*. London: Routledge.

Faught, C. Brad.

2003. *The Oxford Movement: A Thematic History of the Tractarians and their Times*. University Park: Pennsylvania State University Press.

Feld, Steven.

1982. *Sound and Sentiment: Birds, Weeping, Poetics, and Song in Kaluli Expression*. Durham, NC: Duke University Press.

Finke, Roger, and Rodney Stark.

2005. *The Churching of America, 1776–2005: Winners and Losers in our Religious Economy*. New Brunswick, NJ: Rutgers University Press.

Fischer-Lichte, Erika.

2008. *The Transformative Power of Performance: A New Aesthetics*. London: Routledge.

Fitzpatrick-Hopler, Gail.

2006. "Contemplative Service." *The Contemplative Life Program Forty-Day Practice*. Butler, NJ: Contemplative Outreach.

Flannigan, C. Clifford.

1984. "The Fleury 'Playbook' and the Traditions of Medieval Latin Drama." *Comparative Drama*. 18(4): 348–372.

Flood, Gavin.

2004. *The Ascetic Self: Subjectivity, Memory, and Tradition*. Cambridge: Cambridge University Press.

Forbess, Alice.

2010. "The Spirit and the Letter: Monastic Education in a Romanian Orthodox Convent." In *Eastern Christianities in Anthropological Perspective*, Chris Hann and Hermann Goltz, eds., pp. 131–154. Berkeley: University of California Press.

Foucault, Michel.

1978. *The History of Sexuality*. New York: Pantheon.

1979. *Discipline and Punish: The Birth of the Prison*. New York: Vintage.

Fox, Matthew.

1985. *Illuminations of Hildegard of Bingen*. Santa Fe: Bear.

Frank, Karl Suso, and Joseph T. Lienhard.

1993. *With Greater Liberty: A Short History of Christian Monasticism and Religious Orders*. Kalamazoo, MI: Cistercian Publications.

Funk, Mary Margaret.

2001. *Tools Matter for Practicing the Spiritual Life*. New York: Continuum.

Garriott, William, and K. L. O'Neill.

2008. "Who Is a Christian? Toward a Dialogic Approach in the Anthropology of Christianity." *Anthropological Theory*. 8(4): 381–398.

Gavrilyuk, Paul L., and Sarah Coakley, eds.

2013. *The Spiritual Senses: Perceiving God in Western Christianity*. Cambridge: Cambridge University Press.

Geurts, K. L.

2002. *Culture and the Senses: Embodiment, Identity, and Well-Being in an African Community*. Berkeley: University of California Press.

Ghosh, Peter.

2008. *A Historian Reads Max Weber: Essays on the Protestant Ethic*. Wiesbaden: Harrassowitz Verlag.

Goffman, Erving.

1959. *The Presentation of the Self in Everyday Life*. Woodstock, NY: Overlook.

1961. "On the Characteristics of Total Institutions." In *Asylums: Essays on the Social Situation of Mental Patients and Other Inmates*. pp. 1–124. Garden City, NY: Anchor Books.

Griswold, Frank T.

2014. "Celebration of the Ministry of M. Thomas Shaw." Sermon. June 21, 2014. [http://ssje.org/ssje/2014/06/21/celebration-of-the-ministry-of-m-thomas-shaw-the-rt-rev-frank-t-griswold-25th-presiding-bishop/, accessed September 21, 2014].

Grundmann, Herbert.

1995. *Religious Movements of the Middle Ages: The Historical Links between Heresy, the Mendicant Orders, and the Women's Religious Movement in the Twelfth and Thirteenth Century, with the Historical Foundations of German Mysticism*. Notre Dame, IN: University of Notre Dame Press.

Guadeloupe, Francio.

2009. *Chanting Down the New Jerusalem: Calypso, Christianity, and Capitalism in the Caribbean*. Berkeley: University of California Press.

Guenther, Margaret.

1992. *On Holy Listening: The Art of Spiritual Direction*. Lanham, MD: Cowley.

Gurdjieff, G. I.

2002. *Meetings with Remarkable Men*. New York: Penguin.

Gursoy, Pamela, Gail Fitzpatrick-Hopler, and Timothy Koock.

2005. "Welcoming Prayer." *The Contemplative Life Program Forty-Day Practice*. Butler, NJ: Contemplative Outreach.

Guthrie, Suzanne.

2000. *Praying the Hours*. Cambridge, MA: Cowley.

Habermas, Jürgen, and Joseph Ratzinger.

2005. *The Dialectics of Secularization: On Reason and Religion*. San Francisco: Ignatius Press.

Hackett, Kevin.

2009. "Thanksgiving: Giving Thanks to the Giver Good." Sermon. October 14, 2009. Cambridge: Society of Saint John the Evangelist.

2013. "Psalms: Singing Our Lives." *Monastic Wisdom for Everyday Life* series. Supplement to *Cowley*. 39(2).

Haisten, Cherry.

2005. "The Practice of Welcoming Prayer." Unpublished document commissioned by Contemplative Outreach. [http://www.contemplativeoutreach.org/category/category/welcoming-prayer, accessed May 6, 2014.]

Halafoff, Anna.

2013. *The Multifaith Movement: Global Risks and Cosmopolitan Solutions.* Dordrecht: Springer Netherlands.

Hall, John A., and Charles Lindholm.

1999. *Is America Breaking Apart?* Princeton, NJ: Princeton University Press.

Hamans, P., and Ralph McInerny.

2010. *Edith Stein and Companions: On the Way to Auschwitz.* San Francisco: Ignatius Press.

Hamburger, Jeffrey F.

1998. *The Visual and the Visionary: Art and Female Spirituality in Late Medieval Germany.* New York: Zone Books.

2012. "Mysticism and Visuality." In *The Cambridge Companion to Christian Mysticism*, Amy Hollywood and Patricia Z. Beckman, eds., pp. 277–293. Cambridge: Cambridge University Press.

Handman, Courtenay.

2014. "Becoming the Body of Christ: Sacrificing the Speaking Subject in the Making of the Colonial Lutheran Church in New Guinea." *Current Anthropology.* 55(S10): S205–S215.

Hanganu, Gabriel.

2010. "Eastern Christians and Religious Objects: Personal and Material Biographies Entangled." In *Eastern Christianities in Anthropological Perspective*, Chris Hann and Hermann Goltz, eds., pp. 33–55. Berkeley: University of California Press.

Hann, Chris.

2007. "The Anthropology of Christianity Per Se." *European Journal of Sociology.* 48(3): 383–410.

Hann, Chris, and Hermann Goltz, eds.

2010. "Introduction: The Other Christianity?" In *Eastern Christianities in Anthropological Perspective*, pp. 1–29. Berkeley: University of California Press.

Harré, Rom, and Robert Finlay-Jones.

1986. "Emotion Talk across Times." In *The Social Construction of Emotions*, Rom Harré, ed., pp. 220–233. Oxford: Basil Blackwell.

Harris, Olivia.

2006. "The Eternal Return of Conversion: Christianity as Contested Domain in Highland Bolivia." In *The Anthropology of Christianity*, Fenella Cannell, ed., pp. 51–76. Durham, NC: Duke University Press.

Hefner, Robert, ed.

1993. *Christian Conversion: Historical and Anthropological Perspectives on a Great Transformation.* Berkeley: University of California Press.

Heider, Anne, and R. Stephen Warner.

2010. "Bodies in Sync: Interaction Ritual Theory Applied to Harp Singing." *Sociology of Religion.* 71(1): 76–97.

Herzfeld, Michael.

1990. "Icons and Identity: Religious Orthodoxy and Social Practice in Rural Crete." *Anthropological Quarterly.* 63(3): 109–121.

1997. *Cultural Intimacy: Social Poetics in the Nation-State.* New York: Routledge.

2004. *The Body Impolitic: Artisans and Artifice in the Global Hierarchy of Value.* Chicago: University of Chicago Press.

Hildegard von Bingen.

1994. *Sacred Music of the Middle Ages: Hildegard von Bingen (1098–1179) and Others.* CD. Performed by Anima. Cabot: Anima.

1996. *Symphony of the Harmony of Celestial Revelations.* CD. Performed by Sinfonye. Tucson: Celestial Harmonies.

Hiley, David.

2009. *Gregorian Chant.* Cambridge: Cambridge University Press.

Hill, Robert C.

1996. *Wisdom's Many Faces.* Collegeville, MN: Liturgical Press.

Hirota, Dennis.

1995. *Wind in the Pines: Classic Writings on the Way of Tea as a Buddhist Path.* Fremont, CA: Asian Humanities Press.

Hobsbawm, Eric, and Terence Ranger.

1983. *The Invention of Tradition.* Cambridge: Cambridge University Press.

Hollywood, Amy M.

2002. *Sensible Ecstasy: Mysticism, Sexual Difference, and the Demands of History.* Chicago: University of Chicago Press.

Hoskins, Janet.

2014. "An Unjealous God? Christian Elements in a Vietnamese Syncretistic Religion." *Current Anthropology.* 55(S10): S302–S311.

Howes, David.

2003. *Sensual Relations: Engaging the Senses in Culture and Social Theory.* Ann Arbor: University of Michigan Press.

Howes, David, and Sarah Pink.

2010. "The Future of Sensory Anthropology/the Anthropology of the Senses." Social Anthropology. 18(3): 331–340.

Hubbard, Barbara Marx.

2014. "Evolutionary Spirituality: An Emerging Meta-Religion." *World Future Review.* 6(3): 336–341.

Humphrey, Caroline.

2014. "Schism, Event, and Revolution: The Old Believers of Trans-Baikalia." *Current Anthropology.* 55(S10): S216–S225.

Husserl, Edmund.

1962. *Ideas: General Introduction to Pure Phenomenology.* New York: Collier.

Ignatius of Loyola.

1991. *Spiritual Exercises and Selected Works*. Mahwah, NJ: Paulist Press.

Ingold, Tim.

2010. *The Perception of Environment: Essays on Livelihood, Dwelling, and Skill*. London: Routledge.

2011a. *Being Alive: Essays on Movement, Knowledge, and Description*. London: Routledge.

2011b. "Worlds of Sense and Sensing the World: A Response to Sarah Pink and David Howes." *Social Anthropology*. 19(3): 313–317.

Iona Abbey.

nd. *Iona Abbey Music Book: Songs from the Iona Abbey Worship Book*. Glasgow: Wild Goose Publications.

Irvine, Richard D. G.

2010a. "The Experience of Ethnographic Fieldwork in an English Benedictine Monastery: Or, Not Playing at Being a Monk." *Fieldwork in Religion*. 5(2): 289–306.

2010b. "How to Read: *Lectio Divina* in an English Benedictine Monastery." *Culture and Religion*. 11(4): 395–411.

2013. "Stability, Continuity, Place: An English Benedictine Monastery as a Case Study in Counterfactual Architecture." In *Religious Architecture: Anthropological Perspectives*, Oskar Verkaaik, ed., pp. 25–45. Amsterdam: Amsterdam University Press.

Jackson, Michael.

1996. "Phenomenology, Radical Empiricism, and Anthropological Critique." In *Things as They Are: New Directions in Phenomenological Anthropology*, Michael Jackson, ed. pp. 1–50. Bloomington: Indiana University Press.

2002. *The Politics of Storytelling*. Copenhagen: Museum Tusculanum Press.

2005. *Existential Anthropology: Events, Exigencies, and Effects*. New York: Berghahn Books.

2012. *Between One and Another*. Berkeley: University of California Press.

2013. *Lifeworlds: Essays in Existential Anthropology*. Chicago: University of Chicago Press.

2015. "Afterword." In *Phenomenology in Anthropology: A Sense of Perpective*, K. Raan and C. Houston, eds., pp. 293–303. Bloomington: Indiana University Press.

Jacobsen, Douglas G.

2011. *The World's Christians: Who They Are, Where They Are, and How They Got There*. Chichester, UK: Wiley-Blackwell.

James, William.

2004 [1902]. *Varieties of Religious Experience: A Study in Human Nature*. New York: Barnes and Noble Classics.

Jaworski, Adam.

1993. *The Power of Silence: Social and Pragmatic Perspectives*. Newbury Park, CA: Sage.

Jaworski, Adam, ed.

1997. *Silence: Interdisciplinary Perspectives*. Berlin: Mouton de Gruyter.

Jenkins, Philip.

2002. *The Next Christendom: The Coming of Global Christianity*. Oxford: Oxford University Press.

2008. *The Lost History of Christianity: The Thousand-Year Golden Age of the Church in the Middle East, Africa, and Asia—and How It Died*. New York: Harper Collins.

Jenkins, Timothy.

2012. "The Anthropology of Christianity: Situation and Critique." *Ethnos.* 77(4): 459–476.

Jones, Alan.

2014. "Thank God the Archbishop Has Doubts." *Huffington Post.* September 30, 2014. [www.huffingtonpost.com/alan-jones/thank-god-the-archbishop-_b_5903214.htlml, accessed October 1, 2014].

Kanter, R. M.

1968. "Commitment and Social Organization: A Study of Commitment Mechanisms in Utopian Communities." *American Sociological Review.* 33(4): 499–517.

1972. *Commitment and Community: Communes and Utopias in Sociological Perspective.* Cambridge, MA: Harvard University Press.

Katz, Jack.

1999. *How Emotions Work.* Chicago: Chicago University Press.

Kearney, Richard.

2010. *Anatheism: Returning to God after God.* New York: Columbia University Press.

Keating, Thomas, OCSO.

1999. *The Human Condition: Contemplation and Transformation.* Harold M. Wit Lectures on Living a Spiritual Life in the Contemporary Age, Harvard Divinity School. Mahwah, NJ: Paulist Press.

2002a [1994]. *Intimacy with God: An Introduction to Centering Prayer.* New York: Crossroad.

2002b [1986]. *Open Mind, Open Heart: The Contemplative Dimension of the Gospel.* New York: Continuum.

2006. "Introduction: 'The Points of Agreement.'" In *The Common Heart*, N. Miles-Yepez, ed., pp. xvii–xix. New York: Lantern Books.

2008 [1987]. *The Mystery of Christ: The Liturgy as Spiritual Experience.* New York: Continuum.

2014. *Reflections on the Unknowable.* New York: Lantern Books.

Keenan, William.

2002. "Twenty-First Century Monasticism and Religious Life: Just Another New Millennium." *Religion.* 32(1): 13–26.

Keil, Charles, and Steven Feld.

1994. *Music Grooves.* Chicago: University of Chicago Press.

King, Karen L.

2003. *What Is Gnosticism?* Cambridge, MA: Harvard University Press.

Klassen, Pamela E.

2011. *Spirits of Protestantism: Medicine, Healing, and Liberal Christianity.* Berkeley: University of California Press.

Kleinman, Arthur.

1988. *The Illness Narratives: Suffering, Healing, and the Human Condition.* New York: Basic Books.

Koester, James, SSJE.

2010. "And It Was Night." Sermon. March 30, 2010. Cambridge: Society of Saint John the Evangelist. [http://ssje.org/ssje/2010/03/30/and-it-was-night-br-james-koester/, accessed April 14 2012].

2011. "The Scandal of Service." Sermon. April 21, 2011. Cambridge: Society of Saint John the Evangelist. [http://ssje.org/ssje/2011/04/21/the-scandal-of-service-br-james-koester/, accessed October 7, 2012].

2013. "Praying with Icons." Sermon. February 26, 2013. Cambridge: Society of Saint John the Evangelist. [http://ssje.org/2013/02/26/praying-with-icons-br-james-koester/, accessed November 4, 2013].

2014. Quoted on Facebook posting by *Friends of SSJE*. April 18, 2014.

Kroll, Norma.

2005. "Power and Conflict in Medieval Ritual and Plays: The Re-Invention of Drama." *Studies in Philology.* 102(4): 452–483.

Lampe, Frederick.

2010. "The Anthropology of Christianity: Context, Contestation, Rupture, and Continuity." *Reviews in Anthropology.* 39(1): 66–88.

Landers, David S.

1983. *Revolution in Time: Clocks and the Making of the Modern World.* Cambridge, MA: Harvard University Press.

Lantzer, Jason S.

2012. *Mainline Christianity: The Past and Future of American's Majority.* New York: New York University Press.

L'Esperance, Robert, SSJE.

2013a. "Belonging to Jesus." Sermon. September 24, 2013. Cambridge: Society of Saint John the Evangelist. [http://ssje.org/ ssje/2013/09/24/belonging-to-jesus-br-robert-lesperance/, accessed May 10, 2014].

2013b. "Prayer Shock Therapy: Praying the Psalms." *Cowley.* 39(2): 7–9.

2014. "Forgive." *Love Life* video series. April 3, 2014. Cambridge: Society of Saint John the Evangelist. [http://ssje.org/ssje/2014/04/03/love-life-forgive, accessed May 10, 2014].

Lester, Rebecca J.

2003. "The Immediacy of Eternity: Time and Transformation in a Roman Catholic Convent." *Religion.* 33(3): 201–219.

2005. *Jesus in Our Wombs: Embodying Modernity in a Mexican Convent.* Berkeley: University of California Press.

Levine, Steve.

1987. *Healing into Life and Death.* New York: Anchor.

Lindholm, Charles.

2008. *Culture and Authenticity.* Oxford: Blackwell.

2013. "Introduction: Charisma in Theory and Practice." In *The Anthropology of Religious Charisma: Ecstasies and Institutions.* Charles Lindholm, ed., pp. 1–30. New York: Palgrave Macmillan.

Lindholm, Charles, and José Zúquete.

2010. *The Struggle for the World: Liberation Movements for the 21st Century.* Stanford, CA: Stanford University Press.

Lindley, Mark.

1980a. "Equal Temperament." In *The New Grove Dictionary of Music and Musicians,* Stanley Sadie, ed., Volume 6, p. 218. London: Macmillan.

1980b. "Just (Pure) Intonation." In *The New Grove Dictionary of Music and Musicians,* Stanley Sadie, ed., Volume 9, pp. 756–758. London: Macmillan.

Linklater, Kristin.

2006. *Freeing the Natural Voice: Imagery and Art in the Practice of Voice and Language.* Hollywood, CA: Drama Publishers.

Little, Lester K.

1978. *Religious Poverty and the Profit Economy in Medieval Europe.* Ithaca, NY: Cornell University Press.

Louth, Andrew.

2012. "Apophatic and Cataphatic Theology." In *The Cambridge Companion to Christian Mysticism,* Amy Hollywood and Patricia Z. Beckman, eds., pp. 137–146. Cambridge: Cambridge University Press.

Luehrmann, Sonja.

2010. "A Dual Quarrel of Images on the Middle Volga: Icon Veneration in the Face of Protestant and Pagan Critique." In *Eastern Christianities in Anthropological Perspective,* Chris Hann and Hermann Goltz, eds., pp. 56–78. Berkeley: University of California Press.

Luhrmann, T. M.

2012. *When God Talks Back: Understanding the American Evangelical Relationship with God.* New York: Alfred A. Knopf.

Luhrmann, T. M., and Rachel Morgain.

2012. "Prayer as Inner Sense Cultivation: An Attentional Learning Theory of Spiritual Experience." *Ethos.* 40(4): 359–389.

Lynch, Owen M., ed.

1990. *Divine Passion: The Social Construction of Emotion in India.* Berkeley: University of California Press.

MacCulloch, Diarmaid.

2005. *The Reformation.* New York: Penguin.

2013. *Silence: A Christian History.* London: Penguin.

McDannell, Colleen.

1995. *Material Christianity: Religion and Popular Culture in America*. Boston: McGraw Hill.

McDougall, Debra.

2009. "Rethinking Christianity and Anthropology: A Review Article." *Anthropological Forum*. 19: 185–194.

McGinn, Bernard.

1994. *Meister Eckhart and the Beguine Mystics: Hadewijch of Brabant, Mechthild of Magdeburg, and Marguerite Porete*. New York: Continuum.

2012a. "Late Medieval Mystics." In *The Spiritual Senses: Perceiving God in Western Christianity*, Paul L. Gavrilyuk and Sarah Coakley, eds., pp. 190–209. Cambridge: Cambridge University Press.

2012b. "*Unio Mystica*/Mystical Union." In *The Cambridge Companion to Christian Mysticism*, Amy Hollywood and Patricia Z. Beckman, eds., pp. 200–210. Cambridge: Cambridge University Press.

McGuire, Meredith.

2008. *Lived Religion: Faith and Practice in Everyday Life*. Oxford: Oxford University Press.

Maguire, Nancy Klein.

2006. *An Infinity of Little Hours: Five Young Men and Their Trial of Faith in the Western World's Most Austere Monastic Order*. New York: Public Affairs.

Mahieu, Stéphanie.

2010. "Icons and/or Statues? The Greek Catholic Divine Liturgy in Hungary and Romania, between Renewal and Purification." In *Eastern Christianities in Anthropological Perspective*, Chris Hann and Hermann Goltz, eds., pp. 79–100. Berkeley: University of California Press.

Mahmood, Saba.

2005. *Politics of Piety: The Islamic Revival and the Feminist Subject*. Princeton, NJ: Princeton University Press.

Main, John, OSB.

2002. *Essential Writings*. Maryknoll, NY: Orbis Books.

Malara, Diego Maria.

2016. "The Alimentary Forms of Religious Life: Moral Imperfection, Relational Fasting, and Lenience in the Ethiopian Orthodox Church." Paper presented in Beyond Discipline: Discipline and Lenience in Religious Practice panel. American Anthropological Association annual meetings. Minneapolis.

Mankoff, Robert. 2014. "What Cartoons Can Do." *The New Yorker*. August 7, 2014. [www.newyorker.com/cartoons/bob-mankoff/cartoons-can, accessed September 8, 2014].

Margry, P. J., ed.

2008. *Shrines and Pilgrimage in the Modern World: New Itineraries into the Sacred*. Amsterdam: Amsterdam University Press.

Marshall, Melanie.

2011. "The Sound of Whiteness: Early Music Vocal Performance Practice in Britain." Unpublished paper. American Musicological Society Annual Meetings. San Francisco.

Marti, Gerardo, and Gladys Ganiel.

2014. *The Deconstructed Church: Understanding Emerging Christianity.* New York: Oxford University Press.

Mauss, Marcel.

2007. "Techniques of the Body." In *Beyond the Body Proper: Reading the Anthropology of Material Life*, Margaret Lock and Judith Farquhar, eds., pp. 50–68. Durham, NC: Duke University Press.

2008 [1909]. *On Prayer.* New York: Berghahn Books.

Meninger, William A., OCSO.

1997. *The Loving Search for God: Contemplative Prayer and the Cloud of Unknowing.* New York: Continuum.

1998. *Bringing the Imitation of Christ into the Twenty-First Century.* New York: Continuum.

Merton, Thomas, OCSO.

1948. *Seven Storey Mountain.* New York: Harcourt Brace.

1965. *The Way of Chuang-Tzu.* New York: New Directions.

1966. *Conjectures of a Guilty By-Stander.* Garden City, NY: Doubleday.

1968. *Zen and the Birds of Appetite.* New York: New Directions.

1969. *Contemplative Prayer.* New York: Doubleday.

Miles-Yepez, Netanel, ed.

2006. *The Common Heart: An Experience of Interreligious Dialogue.* New York: Lantern Books.

Mitchell, Claire, and Gladys Ganiel.

2011. *Evangelical Journeys: Choice and Change in a Northern Irish Religious Subculture.* Dublin: University College Dublin Press.

Mitchell, Donald William, and William Skudlarek, eds.

2010. *Green Monasticism: A Buddhist-Catholic Response to an Environmental Calamity.* New York: Lantern.

Moore, Peter Clement.

1970. *Tomorrow Is Too Late: Taizé: An Experiment in Christian Community.* London: Mowbray.

Morgan, D.

2005. *The Sacred Gaze: Religious Visual Culture in Theory and Practice.* Berkeley: University of California Press.

Morinis, E. Alan, ed.

1992. *Sacred Journeys: The Anthropology of Pilgrimage.* Westport, CT: Greenwood Press.

Muir, Anne.

2012. *Outside the Safe Place: An Oral History of the Early Years of the Iona Community.* Glasgow: Wild Goose Publications.

Murphy, Keith M., and C. Jason Throop, eds.
2010. *Toward an Anthropology of Will.* Palo Alto, CA: Stanford University Press.
Murphy, Robert.
1987. *The Body Silent: The Different World of the Disabled.* New York: Holt.
Naletova, Inna.
2010. "Pilgrimages as Kenotic Communities beyond the Walls of the Church." In *Eastern Christians in Anthropological Perspective,* Chris Hann and Hermann Goltz, eds., pp. 240–266. Berkeley: University of California Press.
Nasr, Seyyed Hossein.
1989. *Knowledge and the Sacred.* Albany: State University of New York Press.
Naumescu, Vlad.
2010. "Exorcising Demons in Post-Soviet Ukraine: A Monastic Community and Its Imagistic Practice." In *Eastern Christians in Anthropological Perspective,* Chris Hann and Hermann Goltz, eds., pp. 155–176. Berkeley: University of California Press.
Neitz, Mary Jo.
1987. *Charisma and Community: A Study of Religious Commitment within the Charismatic Renewal.* New Brunswick, NJ: Transaction Books.
Neitz, Mary Jo, and James V. Spickard.
1990. "Steps toward a Sociology of Religious Experience." *Sociological Analysis.* 51: 15–33.
Neville, Gwen.
1987. *Kinship and Pilgrimage: Rituals of Reunion in American Protestant Culture.* Oxford: Oxford University Press.
Nicoll, Maurice.
1996. *Psychological Commentaries on the Teaching of Gurdjieff and Ouspensky.* Boston: Shambhala.
Norris, Rebecca Sachs.
2003. "From Jehovah's Witness to Benedictine Nun: The Roles of Experience and Context in a Double Conversion." In *The Anthropology of Religious Conversion,* Andrew Buckser and Stephen D. Glazier, eds., pp. 171–182. Lanham, MD: Rowman and Littlefield.
2009. "The Paradox of Healing Pain." *Religion.* 39(1): 22–33.
Obeysekere, Gananath.
2012. *The Awakened Ones: Phenomenology of Visionary Experience.* New York: Columbia University Press.
Ogden, Dunbar H.
2002. *The Staging of Drama in the Medieval Church.* Newark: University of Delaware Press.
O'Leary, Brian.
2007. "The Mysticism of Ignatius of Loyola." *Review of Ignatian Spirituality.* 116: 77–97.

Oliphant, Elayne.

2016. "Contemporary Medievalism: The Temporal Architecture of Ambient Catholicism in France." Paper presented at The Power of Ambient Faith session. American Anthropological Association annual meeting. Minneapolis.

Oliver, Mary.

1992. "Sunrise." *New and Selected Poems*. Boston: Beacon Press.

2010. "Stone and Light." In *Stone and Light*, p. 53. Cambridge: Society of Saint John the Evangelist.

Ollard, S. L.

1932. *A Short History of the Oxford Movement*. London: Mowbray.

Ortega, Oliver.

2014. "Thousands Watch as New Episcopal Bishop Is Consecrated: Episcopal Diocese of Mass. Honors Work of Outgoing M. Thomas Shaw." September 13, 2014. *Boston Globe*. [http://www.bostonglobe.com/metro/2014/09/13/thousands-gather-watch-new-episcopal-bishop-consecrated/0SMByWX3swqF3mkyNOp3NM/story.html, accessed September 21, 2014].

Ostling, Richard N.

1984. "Religion: Merton's Mountainous Legacy." December 31, 1984. *Time*. 124: 65.

Ouspensky, P. D.

1949. *In Search of the Miraculous: Fragments of an Unknown Teaching*. London: Harcourt.

Pagels, Elaine.

1989. *The Gnostic Gospels*. New York: Vintage.

2004. *Beyond Belief: The Secret Gospel of Thomas*. New York: Vintage.

Panikkar, Raimón.

2004. *Christophany: the Fullness of Man*. Maryknoll, NY: Orbis.

Parkin, Robert.

2005. *One Discipline, Four Ways: British, German, French, and American Anthropology*. Chicago: University of Chicago Press.

Parsons, Talcott, and Edward A. Shils, eds.

1962. *Toward a General Theory of Action*. New York: Harper and Row.

Peña, Elaine A.

2011. *Performing Piety: Making Space Sacred with the Virgin of Guadelupe*. Berkeley: University of California Press.

Pendleton, Eldridge, SSJE.

2010. "Praying Your Way through Holy Week." Sermon. March 29, 2010. Cambridge: Society of Saint John the Evangelist. [http://ssje.org/ssje/2010/03/29/praying-your-way-through-holy-week-a-meditation-by-br-eldridge-pendleton/#more-1828, accessed July 12, 2017].

Pennington, M. Basil, OCSO.

1983. *A Place Apart: Monastic Prayer and Practice for Everyone*. Garden City, NY: Doubleday.

1987. *Thomas Merton, Brother Monk: The Quest for True Freedom*. San Francisco: Harper and Row.

2000. *Listening: God's Word for Today*. New York: Continuum.

Peth, Howard.

2012. *The Dangers of Contemplative Prayer*. Nampa, ID: Pacific Publishing.

Petroff, Elizabeth Avilda.

1986. *Medieval Women's Visionary Literature*. Oxford: Oxford University Press.

1994. "A New Feminine Spirituality: The Beguines and Their Writings in Medieval Europe." In *Body and Soul: Essays on Medieval Women and Mysticism*, pp. 51–65. Oxford: Oxford University Press.

Pfatteicher, Philip H.

1990. *Commentary on the Lutheran Book of Worship: Lutheran Liturgy in Its Ecumenical Context*. Minneapolis: Augsburg Fortress.

Pink, Sarah.

2009. *Doing Sensory Ethnography*. Los Angeles: Sage.

Poujeau, Anna.

2010. "Monasteries, Politics, and Social Memory: The Revival of the Greek Orthodox Church of Antioch in Syria during the Twentieth Century." In *Eastern Christians in Anthropological Perspective*, Chris Hann and Hermann Goltz, eds., pp. 177–192. Berkeley: University of California Press.

Pramuk, Christopher.

2011. "Wisdom, Our Sister: Thomas Merton's Reception of Russian Sophiology." *Spiritus: A Journal of Christian Spirituality*. 11(2): 176–199.

Pryce, Paula.

1999. *"Keeping the Lakes' Way": Reburial and the Re-creation of a Moral World among an Invisible People*. Toronto: University of Toronto Press.

2015. *The Porous Cell: Monastic Ritual, Intentional Living, and Varieties of Knowledge in American Contemplative Christianity*. Ph.D. dissertation. Boston University.

Quigley, Edward J.

1920. *The Divine Office: A Study of the Roman Breviary*. Dublin: Gill and Son.

Radler, Charlotte.

2012. "*Actio et Contemplatio*/Action and Contemplation." In *The Cambridge Companion to Christian Mysticism*, Amy Hollywood and Patricia Z. Beckman, eds., pp. 211–224. Cambridge: Cambridge University Press.

Ram, Kalpana, and Christopher Houston.

2015. "Introduction: Phenomenology's Methodological Invitation." In *Phenomenology in Anthropology: A Sense of Perspective*, K. Ram and C. Houston, eds., pp.1–28. Bloomington: Indiana University Press.

Rambo, Lewis R., and Charles E. Farhadian, eds.

2014. *The Oxford Handbook of Religious Conversion*. New York: Oxford University Press.

Rappaport, Roy A.

1999. *Ritual and Religion in the Making of Humanity*. Cambridge: Cambridge University Press.

Ratzinger, Cardinal Joseph.

1989. "Letter to the Bishops of the Catholic Church on Some Aspects of Christian Meditation." October 15, 1989. Congregation for the Doctrine of Faith. Rome: Vatican.

Reznikoff, Iegor.

2001. "Le chant d'Orphée: chamanisme, orphisme, sacrifice et puissance du son." *Sorgue*. 3: 85–103.

2003. "Transmission orale, transmission écrite: le chant chrétien antique." *Vivre et Transmettre la Tradition dans Connaissance des Religions*. 69–70: 191–210.

2005. *The Evidence of the Use of Sound Resonance from Palaeolithic to Medieval Times, Acoustics, Space and Intentionality: Identifying Intention in the Ancient use of Acoustic Space and Structure*, G. Lawson and C. Scarre, eds. Cambridge: McDonald Institute for Archaeological Research.

Rice, David Talbot.

1972. *Icons and Their History*. Woodstock, NY: Overlook.

Rich, Grant Jewell.

2001. "Anthropology, Consciousness, and Spirituality: A Conversation with Ken Wilber." *Anthropology of Consciousness*. 12(2): 43–60.

Ricoeur, Paul.

1976. *Interpretation Theory: Discourse and the Surplus of Meaning*. Fort Worth: Texas Christian University Press.

2005. *The Course of Recognition*. Cambridge, MA: Harvard University Press.

Robbins, Joel.

2003. "What Is a Christian? Notes toward an Anthropology of Christianity." *Religion*. 33(3): 191–199.

2004. *Becoming Sinners: Christianity and Moral Torment in a Papua New Guinea Society*. Berkeley: University of California Press.

2007. "Continuity Thinking and the Problem of Christian Culture: Belief, Time, and the Anthropology of Christianity." *Current Anthropology*. 48(7): 5–38.

2014. "The Anthropology of Christianity: Unity, Diversity, New Directions." *Current Anthropology*. 55(S10): S157–S171.

Rohr, Richard, OFM.

1991. *Simplicity: The Art of Living*. New York: Crossroad.

2003. *Everything Belongs: The Gift of Contemplative Prayer*. New York: Crossroad.

2009. *The Naked Now: Learning to See as the Mystics See*. New York: Crossroad.

2014. *Silent Compassion: Finding God in Contemplation*. Cincinnati: Franciscan Media.

Roof, Wade Clark.

2001. *Spiritual Marketplace: Baby Boomers and the Remaking of American Religion*. Princeton, NJ: Princeton University Press.

Ryan, Camille L., and Julie Siebens.

2012. "Educational Attainment in the United States: 2009, Populations Characteristics." [www.census.gov/prod/2012pubs/p20-566.pdf, accessed October 22, 2014.]

Sahlins, Marshall.

1993. "Goodbye to *Tristes Tropes*: Ethnography in the Context of Modern World History." *Journal of Modern History*. 65(1): 1–25.

Said, Edward.

1978. *Orientalism*. New York: Pantheon.

Saint-Benoît-sur-Loire Abbey.

nd. "Fleury Abbey." Pamphlet. Saint-Benoît-sur-Loire Abbey, France.

Sajavaara, Kari, and Jaakko Lehtonen.

1997. "The Silent Finn Revisited." In *Silence: Interdisciplinary Perspectives*, Adam Jaworski, ed., pp. 263–280. Berlin: Mouton de Gruyter.

Sallnow, Michael.

1981. "Communitas Reconsidered: The Sociology of Andean Pilgrimage." *Man*. 16(2): 163–182.

Sampson, Steven.

2003. "From Reconciliation to Coexistence." *Public Culture*. 15(1): 181–186.

Samudra, Jaida Kim.

2008. "Memory in Our Body: Thick Participation and the Translation of Kinesthetic Experience." *American Ethnologist*. 35(4): 665–681.

Saville-Troike, Muriel.

1985. "The Place of Silence in an Integrated Theory of Communication." In *Perspectives on Silence*, Deborah Tannen and Muriel Saville-Troike, eds., pp. 3–20. Norwood, NJ: Ablex.

Schechner, Richard.

1985. *Between Theater and Anthropology*. Philadelphia: University of Pennsylvania Press.

1993. *The Future of Ritual: Writings on Culture and Performance*. London: Routledge.

Schmidt, Leigh Eric.

2002. "The Making of Modern 'Mysticism.'" *Journal of the American Academy of Religion*. 71(2): 273–302.

Schultz, Thomas.

2003. *The Rosary for Episcopalians/Anglicans*. Berkeley, CA: Regent Press.

Schutz, Alfred.

1964. "Making Music Together: A Study in Social Relationship." In *Collected Papers II: Studies in Social Theory*, A. Brodersen, ed., pp. 135–158. The Hague: Martinus Nijhoff.

1967. *The Phenomenology of the Social World*. Evanston, IL: Northwestern University Press.

1970. *On Phenomenology and Social Relations*. Chicago: Chicago University Press.

Segal, William.

1987. *The Structure of Man*. Brattleboro, VT: Green River Press.

Seligman, Adam B., and Robert P. Weller.

2012. *Rethinking Pluralism: Ritual, Experience, and Ambiguity*. Oxford: Oxford University Press.

Seligman, Adam B., Robert P. Weller, Michael J. Puett, and Bennett Simon.

2008. *Ritual and Its Consequences*. Oxford: Oxford University Press.

Shapiro, Rami.

2013. *Perennial Wisdom for the Spiritually Independent*. Woodstock, VT: Skylight Illuminations.

Shaw, M. Thomas, SSJE.

2013. "Called to Reconciliation." Sermon. September 11, 2013. Cambridge: Society of Saint John the Evangelist. [http://ssje.org/ssje/author/br-tom-shaw, accessed November 26, 2013].

Sibley, Bryce Andrew.

2006. "The Fr. Richard Rohr Phenomenon." *New Oxford Review*. LXXIII (3). [http://www.catholicculture.org/culture/library/view.cfm?recnum=6819, accessed January 24, 2013].

Siegel, Daniel.

2008. *The Neurobiology of We: How Relationships, the Mind, and the Brain Interact to Shape Who We Are*. Audio recording. Louisville, CO: Sounds True.

Simon, Walter.

2012. "New Forms of Religious Life in Medieval Western Europe." In *The Cambridge Companion to Christian Mysticism*, Amy Hollywood and Patricia Z. Beckman, eds., pp. 80–113. Cambridge: Cambridge University Press.

Smith, Christian.

1998. *American Evangelism: Embattled and Thriving*. Chicago: University of Chicago Press.

Smith, Martin L.

1989. *The Word Is Very Near You: A Guide to Praying with Scripture*. Cambridge: Cowley Publications.

Society of Saint John the Evangelist (SSJE).

nd. "The Monastery Chapel of Saint Mary and Saint John." Pamphlet. Cambridge, MA: Society of Saint John the Evangelist.

1997. *The Rule of the Society of Saint John the Evangelist*. Lanham, MD: Cowley.

2009. *Rule of Life*. Monastic Wisdom for Everyday Living. Lenten Teaching Series. [http://ssje.org/ssje/monasticwisdom, accessed June 12, 2012].

2010. *Stone and Light: A Celebration of a Holy Place*. Cambridge, MA: Society of Saint John the Evangelist. 2011. *A Living Tradition*. Monastic Wisdom for Everyday Living. Lenten Teaching Series. [http://ssje.org/ssje/monasticwisdom, accessed March 20, 2012].

2013. *A Framework for Freedom*. Monastic Wisdom for Everyday Living. Lenten Teaching Series. [http://ssje.org/ssje/monasticwisdom, accessed February 10, 2014].

Southern, R. W.

1970. *Western Society and the Church in the Middle Ages*. Penguin History of the Church. Volume 2. London: Penguin.

Spencer, Herbert

1891. "The Social Organism." In Spencer, *Essays: Scientific, Political and Speculative*. London: Williams and Norgate.

Stoller, Paul.

1989. *The Taste of Ethnographic Things: The Senses in Anthropology.* University of Pennsylvania.

Svatos, W. H., Jr., and Peter Kvisto, eds.

1998. "Max Weber." In *Encyclopedia of Religion and Society,* pp. 547–552. Walnut Creek, CA: Altamira Press.

Symeon the New Theologian (attrib.).

1951 [10th c.]. "Three Methods of Attention and Prayer." In *Writings from the Philokalia on Prayer of the Heart,* E. Kadloubovsky and G. E. H. Palmer, trans., pp. 158–159. London: Faber and Faber.

Taizé Community.

1998. *Songs for Prayer: Assembly Edition.* Chicago: GIA Publications.

Targoff, Ramie.

1997. "The Performance of Prayer: Sincerity and Theatricality in Early Modern England." *Representations.* 60: 49–69.

2001. *Common Prayer: The Language of Public Devotion in Early Modern England.* Chicago: Chicago University Press.

Tarr, Jen.

2008. "Habit and Conscious Control: Ethnography and Embodiment in the Alexander Technique." *Ethnography.* 9(4): 477–497.

Taylor, Charles.

1989. *Sources of the Self: The Making of the Modern Identity.* Cambridge, MA: Harvard University Press.

2007. *A Secular Age.* Cambridge, MA: Harvard University Press.

Teresa of Ávila.

1979 [1588]. *The Interior Castle.* New York: Paulist Press.

Theophane the Monk [Theophane Boyd, OCSO].

1981. *Tales of a Magic Monastery.* New York: Crossroad.

Throop, C. Jason.

2009. "Intermediary Varieties of Experience." *Ethnos.* 74(4): 535–538.

2010. *Suffering and Sentiment: Exploring the Vicissitudes of Experience and Pain in Yap.* Berkeley: University of California Press.

Thurston, Herbert.

1907. "Angelus." *The Catholic Encyclopedia.* New York: Robert Appleton.

Tickle, Phyllis.

2008. *The Great Emergence: How Christianity Is Changing and Why.* Grand Rapids, MI: Baker Books.

2012. *Emergence Christianity: What It Is, Where It Is Going, and Why It Matters.* Grand Rapids, MI: Baker Books.

Tipton, Steven M.

1982. *Getting Saved from the Sixties: Moral Meaning in Conversion and Cultural Change.* Berkeley: University of California Press.

Tomaine, Jane.

2005. *St. Benedict's Toolbox: The Nuts and Bolts of Everyday Benedictine Living.* Harrisburg, PA: Morehouse.

Tristam, Geoffrey, SSJE.

2013. "Praying in the Present Moment." March 5, 2013. *Living Prayer* sermon series. [http://ssje.org/ssje/2013/03/05/praying-in-th-present-moment-br-geoffrey-tristam/, accessed June 10, 2013].

Trix, Frances.

1993. *Spiritual Discourse.* Philadelphia: University of Pennsylvania Press.

Turner, Edith.

2012. *Communitas: The Anthropology of Collective Joy.* New York: Palgrave MacMillan.

Turner, Victor.

1969. *The Ritual Process: Structure and Anti-Structure.* Ithaca, NY: Cornell University Press.

1974. *Dramas, Fields, and Metaphors: Symbolic Action in Human Society.* Ithaca, NY: Cornell University Press.

van de Port, Mattijs.

2011. *Ecstatic Encounters: Bahian Candomblé and the Quest for the Really Real.* Amsterdam: Amsterdam University Press.

Varty, Alexander. 2016.

"Chor Leoni Men's Choir Channels Leonard Cohen's Spirit." *The Georgia Straight.* November 9, 2016. [www.straight.com/arts/824091/chor-leoni-mens-choir-channels-leonard-cohens-spirit, accessed November 28, 2016].

Vatican.

2003. *Jesus Christ, the Bearer of the Water of Life: A Christian Reflection on the "New Age."* Report of the Pontifical Council for Culture and the Pontifical Council for Interreligious Dialogue. Rome: Vatican.

Verter, Bradford.

2003. "Spiritual Capital: Theorizing Religion with Bourdieu against Bourdieu." *Sociological Theory.* 21(2): 150- 174.

Virtue, David W.

2009. "Episcopal Presiding Bishop: Individual Salvation Is 'Heresy, Idolatry.'" *Catholic Online.* [www.catholic.org/news/national/story.php?id=34091, accessed September 21, 2014].

Vizenor, Gerald Robert.

1999. *Postindian Conversations.* Lincoln: University of Nebraska Press.

2012. *The White Earth Nation: Ratification of a Native Democratic Constitution.* Lincoln: University of Nebraska Press.

Vryhof, David, SSJE.

nd-a. *Living Intentionally: A Workbook for Creating a Personal Rule of Life.* Cambridge, MA: Society of Saint John the Evangelist.

nd-b. "Why We Choose This Life." Cambridge, MA: Society of Saint John the
    Evangelist. [http://www.ssje.org/whywechoose.html, accessed April 10, 2013].
2007. "Blessings and Woes." Sermon. February 11, 2007. Cambridge, MA: Society of
    Saint John the Evangelist. [http://ssje.org/ssje/2007/02/11/blessings-and-woes/,
    accessed September 27, 2014].
2010. "Called to Serve." Sermon. April 1, 2010. Cambridge, MA: Society of Saint John
    the Evangelist. [http://ssje.org/ssje/2010/04/01/called-to-serve-br-dav9d-vryhof/,
    accessed May 5, 2013].
2013. "Let Nothing Trouble You." Sermon. October 15, 201. Cambridge, MA: Society
    of Saint John the Evangelist. [http://ssje.org/ssje/2013/10/15/let-nothing-
    trouble-you-br-david-vryhof/, accessed January 15, 2014].
2014. "A Mysterious Way of Seeing." Sermon. March 2, 2014. Cambridge, MA: Society
    of Saint John the Evangelist. [http://ssje.org/ssje/2014/03/02/a-mysterious-way-
    of-seeing-br-david-vryhof/, accessed June 4, 2014].
Wacquant, Loïc.
2004. *Body and Soul: Notebooks of an Apprentice Boxer*. Oxford: Oxford University Press.
Wallace, Anthony F. C.
1956. "Revitalization Movements." *American Anthropologist.* 58(2): 264–281.
Ward, Benedicta, OSB, ed.
2003. *The Desert Fathers: Sayings of the Early Christian Monks.* London: Penguin
    Classics.
Warner, R. Stephen.
1993. "Work in Progress toward a New Paradigm for the Sociological Study of
    Religion in the United States." *American Journal of Sociology.* 98(5): 1044–1093.
2007. "2007 Presidential Address: Singing and Solidarity." *Journal for the Scientific
    Study of Religion.* 47(2): 175–190.
Webb, James.
1980. *The Harmonious Circle: The Lives and Work of G. I. Gurdjieff, P. D. Ouspensky,
    and Their Followers.* New York: Putnam.
Weber, Max.
1930. *The Protestant Ethic and the Spirit of Capitalism.* Los Angeles: Roxbury.
1946. "The Social Psychology of the World Religions." In *From Max Weber: Essays in
    Sociology*, H. H. Gerth and C. Wright Mills, eds., pp. 267–301. Oxford: Oxford
    University Press.
1978. *Economy and Society*, I. Roth and C. Wittich, eds. Berkeley: University of
    California Press.
Weiss, G.
1999. *Body Images: Embodiment as Intercorporeality.* New York: Routledge.
Weitzmann, Kurt.
1982. *The Icon.* New York: Knopf.

Whitehouse, Harvey.

2000. *Arguments and Icons: Divergent Modes of Religiosity.* Oxford: Oxford University Press.

Wichroski, Mary Anne.

1997. "Breaking Silence: Some Fieldwork Strategies in Cloistered and Non-Cloistered Communities." In *Reflexivity and Voice*, R. Hertz, ed., pp. 265–282. Thousand Oaks, CA: Sage.

Wikan, Unni.

1991. "Toward an Experience-Near Anthropology." *Cultural Anthropology.* 6(3): 285–305.

2012. *Resonance: Beyond Words.* Chicago: Chicago University Press.

Wilber, Ken.

1977. *The Spectrum of Consciousness.* Wheaton, IL: Quest.

1986. *Transformations of Consciousness: Conventional and Contemplative Perspectives on Development.* Boston: New Science Library.

2005. "Toward a Comprehensive Theory of Subtle Energies." *Explore: The Journal of Science and Healing.* 1(4): 252–270.

Wilde, Melissa.

2007. *Vatican II: A Sociological Analysis of Religious Change.* Princeton, NJ: Princeton University Press.

Wilken, Robert Louis.

1975. *Aspects of Wisdom in Judaism and Early Christianity.* Notre Dame, IN: University of Notre Dame Press.

Wittberg, Patricia.

1994. *The Rise and Fall of Catholic Religious Orders: A Social Movement Perspective.* Albany: State University of New York Press.

Wolpert, L.

1995. "Evolution of the Cell Theory." *Philosophical Transactions: Biological Sciences.* 349(1329): 227–233.

Wright, Matthew.

2014. "Second Axial Awakening." *Contemplative Journal.* Posted April 7, 2014. [http://www.contemplativejournal.com/index.php?option=com_k2&view=item&id+146, accessed April 25, 2014]

Wynn, L. L.

2015. "Writing Affect, Love, and Desire into Ethnography." In *Phenomenology in Anthropology: A Sense of Perspective*, K. Ram and C. Houston, eds., pp. 224–247. Bloomington: Indiana University Press.

Index

achievement and acquisition
  as American cultural norms, 37,
    41, 43, 65, 79, 102, 156 (*see also*
    habitus: of choice)
  spiritual, 82–83, 85
adab. *See* etiquette
aesthetics, ritual, 42–43, 104, 109–110,
    119, 133–135
agency, 6, 38–39, 46, 103–104, 137–138,
    183, 205–207, 320n17. *See also*
    attention; intention; will
  and habitus, 161–162, 188
  perceptual, 51–52, 135, 187, 188, 212,
    222, 245, 250, 302n18
Almquist, Br. Curtis, SSJE, 42–43,
    86–87, 137, 163, 164–165,
    301n7
ambiguity, 14–17, 138, 171. *See also*
    apophasis; unknowing
  in monastic architecture, 42–43, 164
  pluralism and, 14, 37, 70–71, 181
  transformative qualities of, 42,
    137, 181–183, 207–208,
    302n18
American contemplative Christians,
    demographic characteristics of,
    9, 11–12, 13–16, 18

American cultural norms. *See*
    achievement and acquisition;
    habitus: of choice
Ammerman, Nancy T., 295n2,
    298n22, 303n21
anatheism, 15, 70–71
Anglican rosary, 126, 312n36, 322n2
Anglicanism, 71, 105, 108, 138,
    308n24, 309n9, 311n17. *See also*
    Episcopal Church
anointing, 123–124, 127–128, 130, 234,
    235–236, 242
anthropology. *See also* ethnographic
    fieldwork
  of Christianity, 16, 28, 298n21
  of knowledge, 9, 103, 187, 206
  of the senses, 156, 212–215
apophasis, 7, 137, 182–183, 188, 197,
    206–208, 245. *See also* flow;
    kenosis; unknowing
architecture, symbolism of, 42–43, 106,
    109, 119–120, 164, 301n10. *See also*
    monastic enclosure
Arico, Fr. Carl, 44, 60–61
asceticism, 14, 44–45, 55, 70,
    79, 165
atonement, 113–115, 117, 122–123, 178